W9-AVY-386

A timely and impressive compilation of state-of-the-art approaches for teaching acceptance and mindfulness to younger populations.

—Zindel V. Segal, Ph.D., C.Psych., Morgan Firestone Chair in Psychotherapy and professor of psychiatry and psychology at the University of Toronto and author of *The Mindful Way Through Depression*

This is an absolutely outstanding book on applications of acceptance and mindfulness treatments to physical and mental health problems of children and adolescents. Impressive in its scope and the quality of the contributors, the book provides a broad, comprehensive, and cutting-edge examination of acceptance and mindfulness treatments with children and adolescents. The material in the book is presented in a clear, comprehensive manner, with excellent references and follow-up sources provided. Especially of interest are the applications of acceptance and mindfulness treatments to specific populations (e.g., children with anxiety, externalizing disorders, chronic pain, etc.), as well as to broad social contexts (e.g., parents, schools, primary care settings). Overall, this unique book provides excellent coverage of key issues and will be an important and valuable resource for today's child health professionals. This book is a "must read" for professionals in child health and mental heath who wish to understand and use mindfulness treatments in clinical research or practice.

—Annette M. La Greca, PhD, ABPP Cooper Fellow and professor of psychology and Pediatrics at the University of Miami and editor of the *Journal of Consulting and Clinical Psychology*

For the reader interested in acceptance and mindfulness in children and adolescents, this book is the definitive work on what is happening now and what is on the horizon.

—Bruce F. Chorpita, Ph.D., professor of clinical psychology in the Department of Psychology at the University of California, Los Angeles, and author of *Modular Cognitive-Behavioral Therapy for Childhood Anxiety Disorders*

Greco and Hayes' innovative book on acceptance and mindfulness treatments for children and adolescents is an invaluable new resource for students and faculty. Readers will appreciate the broad coverage and creative applications of acceptance and mindfulness treatments in specialized populations (e.g., anxiety disorders, chronic pain, etc.), and settings (e.g., primary care and schools). This book provides a foundation for practice and research in an important new area.

—Dennis Drotar, Ph.D., professor of pediatrics and director of the Center for the Promotion of Adherence and Self-Management in the Division of Behavioral Medicine and Clinical Psychology at Cincinnati Children's Hospital Medical Center

This groundbreaking volume is an important step to developing acceptance and mindfulness treatments for children and adolescents. The book highlights the many conceptual and practical challenges in extending this approach from adults to children and families. Chapters present leading-edge coverage of a range of child problems and contexts and include many rich examples of how these approaches can be developed and tested. This book will be of high interest to practitioners and students from a wide range of disciplines who wish to expand their work in new and creative ways. By grounding the development and testing of acceptance and mindfulness treatments in empirical science, there is great potential to improve on current approaches to child and family treatments and more broadly to influence cultural change.

—Eric J. Mash, Ph.D., professor of psychology at the University of Calgary

Acceptance & Mindfulness Treatments *for* Children & Adolescents

A Practitioner's Guide

Edited by LAURIE A. GRECO, PH.D.,
& STEVEN C. HAYES, PH.D.

Context Press
New Harbinger Publications, Inc.

Publisher's Note

This publication is designed to provide accurate and authoritative information in regard to the subject matter covered. It is sold with the understanding that the publisher is not engaged in rendering psychological, financial, legal, or other professional services. If expert assistance or counseling is needed, the services of a competent professional should be sought.

A copublication of New Harbinger and Context Press.

Distributed in Canada by Raincoast Books

New Harbinger Publications, Inc.
5674 Shattuck Avenue
Oakland, CA 94609
www.newharbinger.com

Cover design by Amy Shoup
Text design by Tracy Carlson
Acquired by Catharine Sutker
Edited by Jean Blomquist

Printed in the United States of America

Library of Congress Cataloging-in-Publication Data

Acceptance and mindfulness treatments for children and adolescents : a practitioner's guide / [edited by] Laurie A. Greco and Steven C. Hayes.
p. ; cm.
Includes bibliographical references and index.
ISBN-13: 978-1-57224-541-9 (hardcover : alk. paper)
ISBN-10: 1-57224-541-7 (hardcover : alk. paper) 1. Cognitive therapy for children. 2. Cognitive therapy for teenagers. 3. Acceptance and commitment therapy. I. Greco, Laurie A. II. Hayes, Steven C.
[DNLM: 1. Cognitive Therapy--methods. 2. Adolescent. 3. Awareness. 4. Child. 5. Patient Acceptance of Health Care--psychology. 6. Psychotherapy--methods. WS 350.6 A169 2008]
RJ505.C63A33 2008
618.92'891425--dc22

2008016261

12 11 10

10 9 8 7 6 5 4 3 2

To the children in my life: Cameron Michael, Madison Lily, and Tyler George

~ L.A.G.

To Steven Joseph Pistorello-Hayes: my precious son who will one day learn mindfulness skills but now teaches them

~ S.C.H.

Contents

PART 2
Applications to Specific Populations

Dear Reader:

Welcome to New Harbinger Publications. New Harbinger is dedicated to publishing books based on acceptance and commitment therapy (ACT) and its application to specific areas. New Harbinger has a long-standing reputation as a publisher of quality, well-researched books for general and professional audiences.

Most existing books in the Acceptance and Commitment Therapy Series focus on acceptance and mindfulness interventions for adults. This long-awaited book is the first that shows how to apply these methods to children and adolescents. Research on the effectiveness and ideal age-appropriate methodology for balancing acceptance and change in child and adolescent behavior therapy is still in its early stages. Yet throughout this exciting book, there are many examples of meeting the challenge of scaling acceptance and mindfulness methods to an age-appropriate level.

This book is very accessible and easy-to-read, and it avoids unnecessary jargon. It focuses on applications of acceptance and mindfulness interventions to child and adolescent populations across individual, family, school, and medical settings. At the same time, it does not attempt to be exhaustive. Instead it focuses on major problem areas such as anxiety, depression, and chronic pain in children. An extremely valuable contribution of the book is that it shows how to integrate acceptance and mindfulness methods with existing empirically supported treatments for children and adolescents such as parent training, contingency management, and skills training. All chapters provide lots of clinical examples, practical suggestions, and enough content and detail, so that readers may readily adapt these methods to their own area of practice and research.

One of the most formidable challenges is how to actually describe acceptance and mindfulness techniques to kids and adolescents. It is intriguing to read in this book how adult terms such as "one-mindfully" and "workability" are translated into simpler, more accessible terms such as "stay focused" and "do what works." In fact, after reading this book, readers who work with adults may actually find themselves using those "kid terms" for some of their adult clients who have difficulty relating to the somewhat elusive terms and concepts used in adult acceptance and mindfulness approaches. And it is the translation of "values" to "the important and cool stuff that really matters in life" that describes perfectly what this book is all about: How to teach kids in a fun way to relate differently to their critical minds and learn to focus on the important and cool stuff that really matters in life.

As part of New Harbinger's commitment to publishing sound, scientific, clinically based research, Steven C. Hayes, Ph.D., Georg H. Eifert, Ph.D., and John P. Forsyth, Ph.D., oversee all prospective ACT books for the Acceptance and Commitment Therapy Series. As ACT Series editors, we review all ACT books published by New Harbinger, comment on proposals and offer guidance as needed, and use a gentle hand in making suggestions regarding content, depth, and scope of each book. We strive to ensure that any unsubstantiated claims that are clearly ACT inconsistent are flagged for the authors so they can revise these sections to ensure that the work meets our criteria (see below) and that all of the material presented is true to ACT's roots (not passing off other models and methods as ACT).

Books in the Acceptance and Commitment Therapy Series:

- Have an adequate database, appropriate to the strength of the claims being made
- Are theoretically coherent—they fit with the ACT model and underlying behavioral principles as they have evolved at the time of writing
- Orient the reader toward unresolved empirical issues
- Do not overlap needlessly with existing volumes
- Avoid jargon and unnecessary entanglement with proprietary methods, leaving ACT work open and available
- Keep the focus always on what is good for the reader
- Support the further development of the field
- Provide information in a way that is of practical use

These guidelines reflect the values of the broader ACT community. You'll see all of them packed into this book. They are meant to ensure that professionals get information that can truly be helpful, and that can further our ability to alleviate human suffering by inviting creative practitioners into the process of developing, applying, and refining a more adequate approach. Consider this book such an invitation.

Sincerely,

Georg H. Eifert, Ph.D., John P. Forsyth, Ph.D., and Steven C. Hayes, Ph.D.

Part 1

General Issues in Assessment and Treatment

Chapter 1

Acceptance and Mindfulness for Youth: It's Time

Steven C. Hayes, Ph.D., University of Nevada, Reno;
and Laurie A. Greco, Ph.D., University of Missouri, St. Louis

It is an exciting time when a new area is born. We have seen that happen over the last fifteen years as the so-called third-generation behavioral and cognitive therapies (Hayes, 2004) such as acceptance and commitment therapy (ACT; Hayes, Strosahl, & Wilson, 1999), dialectical behavior therapy (DBT; Linehan, Armstrong, Suarez, Allmon, & Heard, 1991; Linehan, Heard, & Armstrong, 1993), mindfulness-based cognitive therapy (MBCT; Segal, Williams, & Teasdale, 2002), and mindfulness-based stress reduction (MBSR; Kabat-Zinn, 1994) caught hold. These methods differed from traditional cognitive behavior therapy models in their treatment of private events (e.g., internal experiences such as thoughts, feelings, and physical-bodily sensations). Rather than targeting and attempting to change the content, frequency, and form of thoughts and feelings directly, acceptance-based therapies such as those described in this book seek to alter the function of internal phenomena so as to diminish their behavioral impact.

Now we are seeing this trend take another step forward, in the application of these methods to children, adolescents, and families. Broadly based books on acceptance and mindfulness interventions for adults have existed for several years (e.g., Germer, Siegel, & Fulton, 2005; Hayes, Follette, & Linehan, 2004), but this book is the first to take a broad look at the application of these methods to children. Work on acceptance and mindfulness in children is still in its infancy. The efficacy of third-wave approaches has been demonstrated empirically across a broad range of adult clinical disorders (Baer, 2003; Grossman, Neimann, Schmidt, & Walach, 2004; Hayes, Luoma, Bond, Masuda, &

Lillis, 2006; Hayes, Masuda, Bissett, Luoma, & Guerrero, 2004). The effectiveness and ideal methodology for balancing acceptance and change in child and adolescent behavior therapy has only recently begun to be explored. It is not only that the research studies are just now arriving. It is that the field is preparing itself to address the many practical, scientific, conceptual, strategic, and philosophical challenges it will need to solve.

Shared Challenges

Some of these challenges are shared with clinicians and scientists focused on mindfulness and acceptance in adults. With the emergence and rapid development of third-generation cognitive behavioral therapies (CBT), empirical clinical science is walking into domains historically viewed as "less empirical" or even off-limits to practitioners and scientists committed to a naturalistic approach. Issues of acceptance, mindfulness, values, spirituality, compassion, and forgiveness are coming to the fore. Therapeutic process is assuming a significant role over content, and the client-therapist relationship is once again an essential element of treatment. Broadening our focus to include prescientific concepts, therapeutic process, and renewed emphasis on the therapeutic relationship may present empirical and clinical challenges that will take years for the field to overcome.

Science and Prescientific Concepts

Acceptance and mindfulness work emerged in the spiritual and religious traditions. That was true of all major religions in their mystical wings, but it was most obvious and emphasized in Eastern traditions. Bringing Western science into the center of these traditions is difficult. Buddhism, Taoism, and the like are prescientific systems, and their concepts are not scientific concepts when left on their own terms. It feels almost sacrilegious to pull them at their joints to create theories and methods that can pass scientific muster, but that is the task that must be done. Some think it can be avoided merely by defining Buddhism as scientific, but that only works if science itself is redefined and that is too high a price to pay.

You can see the issue clearly in the very definition of mindfulness. Mindfulness-based stress reduction was among the first programs to integrate Eastern practices such as meditation and yoga into treatments for chronic pain and illness. Offered at clinics around the world, MBSR appears to be useful with a wide range of problems, including stress and psychosomatic complaints (Grossman et al., 2004). Jon Kabat-Zinn, originator of MBSR, defines mindfulness as "paying attention in a particular way: on purpose, in the present moment, and nonjudgmentally" (Kabat-Zinn, 1994, p. 4). The DBT conceptualization of mindfulness includes a set of skills that are "the intentional process of observing, describing, and participating in reality nonjudgmentally, in the moment, and with effectiveness" (Dimidjian & Linehan, 2003, p. 230). Alan Marlatt defines it as "bringing one's complete attention to the present experience on a moment-to-moment basis" (Marlatt & Kristeller, 1999, p. 68). Langer describes mindfulness as "a flexible state of mind in which we are actively engaged in the present, noticing new things and sensitive to context," which she distinguishes from mindlessness, when we "act according to the sense our behavior made in the past, rather than the present … we are stuck in a single, rigid perspective and we are oblivious to alternative ways of knowing" (Langer, 2000, p. 220). Bishop et al. (2004, p. 232) define mindfulness in two parts: (1) "the self-regulation of attention so that it is maintained on immediate experience, thereby allowing for increased recognition of mental events in the present moment," and (2) "a particular orientation toward one's experiences in the present moment, an orientation that is characterized by curiosity, openness, and acceptance."

The various conceptualizations of mindfulness differ in their level of analysis. They variously focus on psychological processes, outcomes, techniques, or general methods (Hayes & Wilson, 2003). The terms included in these definitions are very often not themselves technical scientific terms or, if they are, they are controversial and have no agreed-upon meaning. The list is daunting and includes terms such as attention, purpose, intention, present moment, experience, state of mind, mental events, thoughts, emotions, nonjudgmental, and openness. Each of these can be the focus of years of debate. A modern scientific definition of mindfulness that is grounded in a testable theory in which all of the terms are well defined and researched is needed (Hayes, 2002). Some have been offered (Fletcher & Hayes, 2005) but, as the present volume will show, no consensus has yet been reached.

Focus on Process

The focus on processes of change is superficially more amenable to empirical clinical science, but there too the road ahead is not easy. Driven by the federal Food and Drug Administration standards for pharmacotherapy, over the last thirty years there has been an enormous emphasis on randomized controlled trials of well-defined packages in psychosocial treatment. This approach left processes of change behind. As they began to be examined, the sobering realization set in that the putatively important processes of change in our most established traditional CBT methods were largely unsupported by mediational (Longmore & Worrell, 2007) and component (Dimidjian et al., 2006) analyses. Fortunately this does not appear to be the case in third-generation CBT (e.g., see Hayes et al., 2006), but the field of empirical clinical science is not yet fully comfortable with a more bottom-up, processes orientation.

The Therapeutic Relationship

The therapeutic relationship shows the same issue described above. It has been known for some time that the therapeutic alliance correlates with clinical outcome (see

Horvath, 2001), but that is not the same as understanding how to improve the therapeutic relationship (Pierson & Hayes, 2007). Experimental work on the client-therapist relationship has been slow to arrive for a reason: the therapeutic relationship is difficult to define, measure, conceptualize, and modify. This problem does not go away merely by declaring that the relationship is important.

Unique Challenges

Many of the challenges faced by clinicians and researchers attempting to bring acceptance and mindfulness into clinical work with children are uniquely emphasized by the target population. One obvious challenge is learning how to scale these acceptance and mindfulness methods in an age-appropriate fashion. Several chapters will deal directly with that issue. But there are more subtle challenges that you can detect in these chapters as well. Although not exhaustive, let's point to some of these conceptual and practical challenges and issues relevant to working with children and adolescents.

Undermining What You Need to Establish

Mindfulness and acceptance undermines the dominance of certain kinds of verbal rules or modes of thinking. Normal human problem solving is based on a discrepancy-based, future-focused, judgmental state of mind. Yet those are some of the very features of thinking that mindfulness work seeks to rein in. Normal thinking processes lead to judgment and avoidance of difficult thoughts and feelings, yet that very process is what acceptance work is designed to counteract.

As children become more verbal, they begin to derive rules either implicitly or explicitly from their experiences and from interactions in and with the social-verbal community (e.g., parents, teachers, peers, siblings). They need to learn to think about the future, to consider possible outcomes for their own actions, and to compare and contrast the features of events analytically and judgmentally. Many rules and types of rule following are adaptive and necessary for school-age youth. As such, there is a certain tension that arises when acceptance and mindfulness work is designed for children. For example, when and how do we teach children to respond flexibly to verbal rules, given the developmental importance of problem-solving skills, rule formulation, and rule governance, which are critical to children's successful adaptation across a number of settings? What are possible implications of teaching children to "hold language lightly," especially during periods of early development when language and other verbal abilities are being acquired?

We do not yet know the answers to these questions, and it would be unwise to ignore them as we implement acceptance- and mindfulness-based methods. These questions may provide an opportunity for deeper understanding of processes and the construction of useful theories. In order to know how to balance methods that both build and rein in verbal control, we need to have a deeper understanding of how thinking itself works. As the Zen koan "Does a dog have Buddha nature?" asks us to ponder, the purpose of mindfulness is not to eliminate cognitive control—as if a nonverbal organism is the highest example of awareness and mindfulness. Instead it may be useful to teach new forms of thinking that share some features with the awareness of nonhuman animals or infants. It will then be essential to bring this practice and quality of awareness into balance with more typical forms of analytic thinking. Toward creating this balance, we will need to develop child-friendly methods for bringing the state of mind (or modes of thinking) under better contextual control. Done well, acceptance and mindfulness training should broaden children's repertoires without creating conflicts between different styles of interacting verbally with their world. To find that balance, however, more needs to be understood about mindfulness itself. Thus, work with children seems likely to take a leading role in the mindfulness area theoretically, even if so far it is following the path first blazed by adult clinicians and researchers.

Do as I Say, Not as I Do

We live in a society that teaches either explicitly or implicitly that it is not okay to hurt deeply. In Western culture, expression of emotion is often admonished. Indeed adults often demand that children do what they themselves do not know how to do. A parent saying "stop crying or I will give you something to cry about" is functionally saying to the child "because I cannot control my upset from seeing you upset, you control yours so I don't have mine." Children in such circumstances learn to be quiet, to suppress, and to internalize messages surrounding the need for emotional avoidance and control. Unfortunately, children will be no better off as adults than their parents were in actually avoiding or eliminating emotion on demand. Indeed, as we reach back into our personal histories, we wish that we had learned as children (both directly and by adult example) that it is okay to be vulnerable and to hurt; that there is no need to hide from our experiences, no matter how painful or unbearable they might seem; and that we are in fact not alone in our sufferings.

When acceptance and mindfulness are introduced into cultural contexts that support emotional control agendas, children essentially learn how to do something healthy that many of the adults in their environment do not know how to do. If this is not handled properly, children may receive conflicting messages as some adults in their lives demand emotional suppression while others counsel emotional openness. This is one reason why child and adolescent work cannot be separated from adult work or from the therapeutic relationship. When working with youth, it is essential to consider and ideally to intervene with broader social contexts such as families, schools, neighborhoods, and communities. A great deal remains to be learned about how to do this. We believe, however, that this process can begin within the therapeutic relationship. It is crucial for us as therapists to acknowledge that we too know what it is like to suffer deeply and to model acceptance and mindfulness of our own psychological pain. Without doing so, we are providing yet another sad example of "do as I say, not as I do."

Asking What One Does Not Know

The assessment of acceptance and mindfulness is a growing area of research, and a wide variety of measures are now available for adults (e.g., Baer, Smith, & Allen, 2004; Hayes, Strosahl, et al., 2004) and school-age children (e.g., Greco, Lambert, & Baer, in press; see chapter 3 in this volume). There are many challenges in assessing facets of mindfulness using self-report (Baer, Smith, Hopkins, Krietemeyer, & Toney, 2006), and these are multiplied many times when dealing with children who do not read or are otherwise unable to provide accurate reports of their own internal experiences. At the same time, it is unclear how we begin to measure acceptance and mindfulness processes in young children in the absence of self-report.

As with other such challenges, this problem presents an important opportunity for the entire area. Work with children will encourage the field to expand its view of the proper assessment of mindfulness processes. It will push the area to go beyond self-report alone, since it is so obvious that demanding self-reports of very young children about their states of mind will be of limited utility. The field does not know how to assess mindfulness behaviorally, but it needs to learn. It needs to know whether neurobiological methods are reliable and useful in the assessment of mindfulness in young children. Such questions can only deepen our understanding of the biological substrates of these processes.

Assessment issues with children will also move us to different levels of analysis. For example, we need to learn how to assess mindfulness within the context of parent-child and teacher-student relationships. We need to learn what mindful parenting or mindful teaching actually looks like behaviorally. If we intend to integrate acceptance and mindfulness into classrooms and larger communities, we will need to define what these processes look like and determine how to best measure them across broader social contexts. These issues will be repeatedly contacted as related constructs such as self-compassion, forgiveness, vitality, and values-consistent action are measured among youth.

Creating a More Mindful Culture

The empirical work in acceptance and mindfulness with adults began with a focus on clinical problems, but like the spiritual and religious traditions that launched this work, it has spread far beyond that. The work on acceptance and mindfulness in children shows the same process. If acceptance and mindfulness are applied to pain, anxiety, or depression in children, it will not be long before one wonders if these same methods could prevent problems in children. And no sooner do those studies begin, than we start wondering how to bring these methods into the schools (chapters 9 and 12) and homes (chapter 10). It is not long before the role of the media comes into focus. What happens, in other words, is no matter where one begins, what ends up on the table is how best to create a more mindful culture. This seems to be such an organic process that it is hard to see how the methods and issues raised in acceptance and mindfulness work can possibly be limited to the clinic. In the abstract, this is no less true in work with adults, but somehow it seems that the cultural issues are often put to one side with adults in a way that one simply cannot do with children.

This is but one exciting aspect of acceptance and mindfulness work with children. Cultural change is difficult to engineer and manage, but it has an impact that no set of psychotherapy practices (no matter how vastly used) can match. The issue here is not about what is new. Rather, it is about bringing into focus the undeniable potential for empirical clinical science to influence cultural change. It is one thing for a Buddhist teacher to recommend meditation in the schools—the public schools of Western culture can hardly be expected to respond to such a call without complaints of all kinds. It is quite another for major science panels to recommend meditation in the schools—the possibility for change and implementation suddenly becomes much larger. Clinical science has an important role and voice in the culture. Adding this voice to the conversation expands the dialogue from issues of spirituality to issues of health, wellness, and education. Standing atop those issues, the horizon of vast cultural change is visible even if it is not yet here.

Technical Issues

Treatment integration. Many of the treatments with adults that use acceptance and mindfulness methods can seemingly stand alone (e.g., Kabat-Zinn, 1994), although other such methods are specifically linked to traditional behavioral methods as part of the overall model (e.g., Hayes et al., 1999). In clinical work with children, it is immediately obvious that we need to learn how to integrate acceptance and mindfulness methods with existing child treatments. We are already seeing movement in this direction with child and adolescent programs combining acceptance, mindfulness, and parent training; or acceptance, mindfulness, and contingency management; or acceptance, mindfulness, and skills training. This is true in adult acceptance and mindfulness work as well, and together it calls for the development of more integrated theories and technologies.

New modes of intervention. Work with children will push therapists and researchers into new modes of intervention. Acceptance and mindfulness methods are already using child-friendly methods such as play or stories. As a result of these clinical innovations with children, it is not beyond imagination to see empirical clinical scientists working perhaps for the first time with video games, drawings, song, drama, and the like. This can only expand our field, if science values are not checked at the door.

Populations and methods. Acceptance and mindfulness methods appear to have broad applicability and impact. As such, researchers and clinicians have generally steered away from the critical issue of whether there are particular populations that are well suited for or not suited for these methods. The work we do with children may force this question into the empirical clinical spotlight. Clinically, some issues are perhaps more obvious and difficult to ignore with children. For example, a conduct-disordered child may differ dramatically from a socially withdrawn child in terms of how he or she carries out the struggle with psychological pain. The conduct-disordered youth may lash out at authority figures, evade personal responsibility, and break important social conventions and rules at every turn. The socially withdrawn child, in contrast, modifies important personal values in the name of fitting in and gaining approval from important adults in his or her life. Even if mindfulness and acceptance methods apply in much the same way to both children, it seems unlikely that we can avoid collateral issues such as how best to establish verbal regulation while also undermining it. These challenges, as they are overcome, will in turn enrich our understanding of mindfulness and acceptance itself.

Purposes and Structure of This Book

This book will focus on applications to child and adolescent populations across individual, family, school, and medical settings. The first part of this book is general in focus: chapter 2 provides a more detailed look at some of the acceptance and mindfulness technologies that are being developed and tested with children, and chapter 3 considers issues germane to the assessment of relevant processes in youth. These opening chapters provide a technological and intellectual context for the applications in the rest of the book.

Part 2 examines applications of acceptance and mindfulness methods to various populations: MBCT for anxiety; ACT for pediatric pain; DBT for adolescents with borderline features; MBSR for children in grades 4 through 6 and their parents; ACT for childhood externalizing disorders; and acceptance as it applies to body image and health in adolescence. This is hardly the full range of problems that can be treated successfully using an acceptance and mindfulness approach. This book is not meant to be exhaustive. Rather, our intention is to provide a sufficient range of examples so that students, practitioners, and researchers will be emboldened to try these methods with an awareness of possible challenges and the range of adjustments that have been worked out so far to meet these challenges.

Part 3 of the book examines how to expand acceptance and mindfulness work into new settings and contexts, including parent training programs, primary care, and the schools. As with the second part of this volume, the goal is to provide enough content and examples so that readers may readily adapt these methods to fit within their own research and practice. In focusing on broader sociocultural contexts, we hope to encourage researchers and practitioners who are already applying these methods to move toward larger-scale change.

In closing, this book is meant to be a collection of works in progress. We expect that the chapters will generate more questions than answers. We hope that readers will be as much inspired as they are informed. This is part of why it is an exciting time when a new area is born. This book will provide a sense of that excitement, as this discipline is learning how to adapt acceptance and mindfulness methods creatively to meet the needs of children, the adults who care for them, and the adults that they will one day become.

References

Baer, R. A. (2003). Mindfulness training as a clinical intervention: A conceptual and empirical review. *Clinical Psychology: Science and Practice, 10,* 125–143.

Baer, R. A., Smith, G. T., & Allen, K. B. (2004). Assessment of mindfulness by self-report: The Kentucky Inventory of Mindfulness Skills. *Assessment, 11,* 191–206.

Baer, R. A., Smith, G. T., Hopkins, J., Krietemeyer, J., & Toney, L. (2006). Using self-report assessment methods to explore facets of mindfulness. *Assessment, 13,* 27–45.

Bishop, S. R., Lau, M., Shapiro, S., Carlson, L., Anderson, N. D., Carmody, J., et al. (2004). Mindfulness: A proposed operational definition. *Clinical Psychology: Science and Practice, 11*(3), 230–241.

Dimidjian, S. D., Hollon, S. D., Dobson, K. S., Schmaling, K. B., Kohlenberg, R. J., Addis, M. E., et al. (2006). Randomized trial of behavioral activation, cognitive therapy, and antidepressant medication in the acute treatment of adults with major depression. *Journal of Consulting and Clinical Psychology, 74*(4), 658–670.

Dimidjian, S. D., & Linehan, M. M. (2003). Mindfulness practice. In W. O'Donohue, J. Fisher, & S. Hayes (Eds.), *Cognitive behavior therapy: Applying empirically supported techniques in your practice* (pp. 229–237). New York: Wiley.

Fletcher, L., & Hayes, S. C. (2005). Relational frame theory, acceptance and commitment therapy, and a functional analytic definition of mindfulness. *Journal of Rational Emotive and Cognitive Behavioral Therapy, 23,* 315–336.

Germer, C. K., Siegel, R. D., & Fulton, P. R. (Eds.). (2005). *Mindfulness and psychotherapy.* New York: Guilford.

Greco, L. A., Lambert, W., & Baer, R. A. (in press). Psychological inflexibility in childhood and adolescence: Development and evaluation of the Avoidance and Fusion Questionnaire for Youth. *Psychological Assessment.*

Grossman, P., Neimann, L., Schmidt, S., & Walach, H. (2004). Mindfulness-based stress reduction and health benefits: A meta-analysis. *Journal of Psychosomatic Research, 57,* 35–43.

Hayes, S. C. (2002). Buddhism and acceptance and commitment therapy. *Cognitive and Behavioral Practice, 9,* 58–66.

Hayes, S. C. (2004). Acceptance and commitment therapy, relational frame theory, and the third wave of behavioral and cognitive therapies. *Behavior Therapy, 35,* 639–665.

Hayes, S. C., Follette, V. M., & Linehan, M. M. (Eds.). (2004). *Mindfulness and acceptance: Expanding the cognitive behavioral tradition.* New York: Guilford.

Hayes, S. C., Luoma, J., Bond, F., Masuda, A., & Lillis, J. (2006). Acceptance and commitment therapy: Model, processes, and outcomes. *Behaviour Research and Therapy, 44,* 1–25.

Hayes, S. C., Masuda, A., Bissett, R., Luoma, J., & Guerrero, L. F. (2004). DBT, FAP, and ACT: How empirically oriented are the new behavior therapy technologies? *Behavior Therapy, 35,* 35–54.

Hayes, S. C., Strosahl, K. D., & Wilson, K. G. (1999). *Acceptance and commitment therapy: An experiential approach to behavior change.* New York: Guilford.

Hayes, S. C., Strosahl, K. D., Wilson, K. G., Bissett, R. T., Pistorello, J., Toarmino, D., et al. (2004). Measuring experiential avoidance: A preliminary test of a working model. *The Psychological Record, 54,* 553–578.

Hayes, S. C., & Wilson, K. G. (2003). Mindfulness: Method and process. *Clinical Psychology: Science and Practice, 10,* 161–165.

Horvath, A. O. (2001). The alliance. *Psychotherapy: Theory, Research, Practice, Training, 38,* 365–372.

Kabat-Zinn, J. (1994). *Wherever you go, there you are: Mindfulness meditation in everyday life.* New York: Hyperion.

Langer, E. J. (2000). Mindful learning. *Current Directions in Psychological Science, 9,* 220–223.

Linehan, M. M., Armstrong, H. E., Suarez, A., Allmon, D., & Heard, H. L. (1991). Cognitive-behavioral treatment of chronically parasuicidal borderline patients. *Archives of General Psychiatry, 48,* 1060–1064.

Linehan, M. M., Heard, H. L., & Armstrong, H. E. (1993). Naturalistic follow-up of a behavioral treatment for chronically parasuicidal borderline patients. *Archives of General Psychiatry, 50,* 971–974.

Longmore, R. J., & Worrell, M. (2007). Do we need to challenge thoughts in cognitive behavior therapy? *Clinical Psychology Review, 27,* 173–187.

Marlatt, G. A., & Kristeller, J. L. (1999). Mindfulness and meditation. In W. R. Miller (Ed.), *Integrating spirituality into treatment* (pp. 67–84). Washington, DC: American Psychological Association.

Pierson, H., & Hayes, S. C. (2007). Using acceptance and commitment therapy to empower the therapeutic relationship. In P. Gilbert & R. Leahy (Eds.), *The therapeutic relationship in cognitive behavior therapy* (pp. 205–228). London: Routledge.

Segal, Z. V., Williams, J. M. G., & Teasdale, J. D. (2002). *Mindfulness-based cognitive therapy for depression: A new approach to preventing relapse.* New York: Guilford.

Chapter 2

Third-Wave Behavior Therapies for Children and Adolescents: Progress, Challenges, and Future Directions

Karen M. O'Brien, BA, Christina M. Larson, BA,
and Amy R. Murrell, Ph.D., University of North Texas

According to Jon Kabat-Zinn, whose mindfulness-based stress reduction program has been credited with introducing mindfulness practice into Western medicine and health care, mindfulness is "paying attention in a particular way: on purpose, in the present moment, and nonjudgmentally" (Kabat-Zinn, 1994, p. 4). Mindfulness thus defined entails being present and nonjudgmental even in the most unpleasant and painful moments. Many recent psychotherapeutic approaches have embraced this concept of mindfulness as well as a range of similar methods of coping with that which is unpleasant and painful. Ruth Baer's (2006) recent volume on mindfulness-based treatment approaches includes discussions not only of Kabat-Zinn's mindfulness-based stress reduction (MBSR; Kabat-Zinn, 1982, 1990), but also of acceptance and commitment therapy (ACT; Hayes, Strosahl, & Wilson, 1999), dialectical behavior therapy (DBT; Linehan, 1993), and mindfulness-based cognitive therapy (MBCT; Segal, Williams, & Teasdale, 2002). Hayes, Follette, and Linehan's (2004) volume on mindfulness and acceptance adds functional analytic psychotherapy (FAP; Kohlenberg & Tsai, 1991) and integrative behavioral couples therapy (IBCT; Christensen, Jacobson, & Babcock, 1995) to that list. With the exception of Kabat-Zinn's MBSR, all of these treatments have been categorized as third-wave behavior therapies (Hayes, 2004).

The first wave of behavior therapy emphasized the application of basic behavioral principles to clinical problems. The second wave brought cognition into the picture and sought behavioral change via the elimination or replacement of problematic thoughts (Hayes, Follette, et al., 2004). The third wave of behavior therapy reemphasizes basic behavioral techniques, including functional analysis, skills building, and direct shaping (Hayes, Masuda, Bissett, Luoma, & Guererro, 2004) and focuses on effecting behavior change by changing the context, rather than the content, of thoughts and feelings. Though difficult to characterize as a group, Hayes and colleagues note that most of these third-wave behavior therapies incorporate not only mindfulness techniques, but also techniques involving acceptance, cognitive defusion, dialectics, and values (Hayes, Masuda, et al., 2004). The goal of these techniques is not to change problematic thoughts or emotions, but rather to accept them for what they are—just private experiences, not literal truth. In this view, acceptance is accompanied by change, but the change is of a different sort than that seen in traditional cognitive behavioral therapies: rather than changing the content of their thoughts, clients are changing their relationship to their thoughts. The careful balance of acceptance and change, referred to as the central dialectic in DBT (Linehan, 1993), characterizes a dialectic common to all third-wave therapies. When clients are able to balance acceptance and change, accepting their thoughts as thoughts and thereby changing their relationship to their thoughts, they gain the flexibility to move in valued directions.

Though third-wave behavior therapies represent some of the most recent therapeutic approaches, concepts of mindfulness and acceptance are not recent. Before being introduced into the Western medical and health care community by Jon Kabat-Zinn, mindfulness and acceptance fell under the domain of spiritual practice; indeed, mindfulness meditation has been practiced by Buddhists for over twenty-five hundred years (Kabat-Zinn, 2003). It is the empirical study of mindfulness, then, that began relatively recently. In response to the criticism that third-wave behavior therapies were abandoning empiricism (Corrigan, 2001), Hayes and colleagues reviewed the existing empirical literature for FAP, DBT, and ACT, citing forty-two outcome studies that had been conducted in the past five years (Hayes, Masuda, et al., 2004). Since that time, substantial empirical support for mindfulness-based interventions with adults has accumulated.

As evident in this book, there is growing support for the use of third-wave behavior therapies for children and adolescents. In this chapter, we describe some of the third-wave approaches and how they are being modified to fit child and adolescent populations. We briefly review some of the evidence supportive of specific methods and present some of the challenges and future directions third-wave therapies have in becoming mainstream approaches to treatment with children.

Acceptance and Mindfulness Interventions with Youth: An Overview

From one point of view, mindfulness and youth seem especially closely linked. In Buddhism, the concept of "beginner's mind" refers to certain qualities of mindfulness, including openness, receptiveness, and readiness to learn (Goodman, 2005; Kabat-Zinn, 1990). Beginners are more enthusiastic and less cynical about learning; they possess a curiosity that adults seem to have lost and are more receptive to new ideas and experiences (Goodman, 2005). Compared to adults, youth are beginners in life's journey, and the therapist who adopts a beginner's mind gains a window into the mind of the child as beginner and can better enter into the child's world (Goodman, 2005). As such, acceptance and mindfulness practices seem particularly suited to working with youth.

Whether or not they overtly address the concept of beginner's mind, adherents to the various mindfulness-based treatment approaches have begun to realize the applicability of their methods to children and adolescents. For example, the use of experiential exercises and metaphors in ACT and other third-wave approaches render it a particularly appropriate treatment for children (Greco, Blackledge, Coyne, & Ehrenreich, 2005; Murrell, Coyne, & Wilson, 2004); concepts that would normally be too abstract for children to understand become accessible through experience, and children's ability to think in less literal terms supports the use of metaphorical language. Indeed children may have an advantage over adults in that they have not lived as long—consequently they have had less opportunity to develop unworkable behavioral repertoires and related psychopathologies (Greco et al., 2005).

Acceptance and Commitment Therapy (ACT)

ACT (Hayes et al., 1999) is based on a philosophy of science known as functional contextualism, which requires practitioners to analyze behaviors in terms of their function in a particular context. The social-verbal context is of special interest to ACT practitioners, as ACT is based on a theory of language and cognition: relational frame theory (RFT; Hayes, Barnes-Holmes, & Roche, 2001). ACT goes beyond a focus on perceived "abnormalities" and syndromes, and instead focuses on ordinary psychological processes, especially those involving human language. From its philosophical and theoretical roots, ACT proposes that psychological suffering stems from language processes that foster psychological inflexibility. The ACT goal of greater psychological flexibility is acquired through the use of metaphors, paradox, and experiential exercises to help clients develop the ability to contact the present moment in a way in which they can decide whether a behavior is values consistent (Hayes et al., 1999).

Mindfulness, Acceptance, and ACT

As a third-wave behavior therapy, ACT integrates mindfulness and acceptance training with behavior-change processes (Baer & Krietemeyer, 2006). Mindfulness and acceptance interventions are used to promote behavior change and, in turn, clients' movement toward valued living. One of the key components in investigating problematic behavior from an ACT perspective is examining what might be viewed as the opposite of acceptance—experiential avoidance. Experiential avoidance is the "phenomenon that occurs when a person is unwilling to remain in contact with particular experiences (e.g., bodily sensations, emotions, thoughts, memories, behavioral predispositions) and takes steps to alter the form or frequency of these events and the contexts that occasion them" (Hayes, Wilson, Gifford, Follette, & Strosahl, 1996, p. 1154). Experiential avoidance, then, implies a lack of acceptance of private events as they occur, uncontrolled and unregulated. Of note, experiential avoidance correlates with a range of adjustment problems in both adults (Hayes et al., 1996) and children (Greco, Lambert, & Baer, in press).

Accordingly, ACT emphasizes the need to undermine the avoidance of unwanted private experiences. The goal of treatment is psychological flexibility, which requires willingness to experience and accept thoughts and feelings in the present moment, as they are. This, in turn, requires mindfulness, which involves noticing thoughts, feelings, and sensations without attempting to change or avoid them. In this sense, then, mindfulness is a means of fostering acceptance (Hayes, Follette, et al., 2004). Mindfulness techniques are often used in ACT as tools to help clients take note of and experience their world directly. In broad terms, mindfulness can be considered the summation of four of the six processes of ACT: acceptance, defusion, self as context, and contact with the present moment (Hayes, Masuda, et al., 2004). Together, acceptance and mindfulness foster psychological flexibility and the shift toward values-based living. Therapeutically, acceptance and mindfulness are promoted through the use of client-specific exercises, metaphors, and behavioral tasks.

From Adults to Children

Conceptual and empirical research suggests that ACT can be adapted for children in developmentally appropriate and effective ways (e.g., Greco et al., 2005; Murrell et al., 2004; Murrell & Scherbarth, 2006). In recent years, ACT with children has expanded for use with a variety of populations and settings (see chapters 5, 8, 9, 11, and 12 for more detailed accounts of some of these applications). ACT with children, like ACT with adults, focuses on behavioral inflexibility resulting from language processes and how this resultant rigidity hinders valued living.

Children's suffering and distress is not hugely different than that experienced by adults; yet, special considerations of the form and context of children's suffering and distress is necessary. Given that ACT is heavily grounded in functional contextualism, the first step of therapy with both adults and children is a functional analysis of the problem behavior(s). However, with children there is the additional consideration that parents may be inadvertently reinforcing negative behavior. Attention must be given to the family and the potential role it may play as a context for the problematic behavior. This part of functional analysis is unique to working with children and can serve to shed light on discrepancies between what the child and parents consider to be the problem at hand. Additionally, parents need to be aware of and understand the need for their child to experience something negative to have positive behavior changes.

As a treatment where active participation is required, ACT may initially be thought to be too complex or beyond the intellectual understanding of children. In part, this impression seems to come because ACT can be counterintuitive for adults. In its actual methods, however, ACT appears to be especially suited to use with children since it relies so heavily on experiential exercises and metaphors, much like teaching methods already used in educational settings. However, ACT interventions may be less directive than some of the environments in which children live and function on a daily basis (e.g., school settings), and therapists encourage children to take an active role in treatment decisions. To foster involvement and resultant "ownership" of the treatment process, clinicians must be attentive to children's need for more developmentally appropriate explanations and interactive exercises to help them grasp concepts.

Children have the ability to apply knowledge of language and are adept at using symbols to represent objects by the age of eight (Devany, Hayes, & Nelson, 1986; Lipkens, Hayes, & Hayes, 1993). Between the ages of nine and fifteen years, thinking becomes more abstract, and by sixteen to eighteen years of age, thought incorporates hypothesizing and deductive reasoning. Throughout these early years, the ability for youth to comprehend complex ideas related to mindfulness emerges. Even relatively complex concepts such as a sense of self that is separate from thoughts and feelings can be addressed using age-appropriate methods. Two common techniques used with children that specifically target acceptance and mindfulness include the Mule in the Well Metaphor and the Leaves on a Stream Exercise (see Hayes et al., 1999, for complete descriptions).

ACT has been applied successfully across a variety of child and adolescent populations (Murrell & Scherbarth, 2006). Empirical support for ACT interventions with youth includes the successful treatment of adolescents at risk for dropping out of school (Moore et al., 2003), pediatric pain patients (Greco, Blomquist, Acra, & Mouton, 2008; Wicksell, Dahl, Magnusson, & Olsson, 2005), adolescent girls engaging in high-risk sexual behavior (Metzler, Biglan, Noell, Ary, & Ochs, 2000), and adolescent girls struggling with anorexia (Heffner, Sperry, Eifert, & Detweiler, 2002). For adolescents at risk for dropping out of school, ACT interventions resulted in a decrease in discipline referrals and improved attendance records (Moore et al., 2003). For pediatric pain patients, ACT interventions have resulted in improved quality of life and increased school attendance (Greco et al., 2008; Wicksell et al., 2005). A small, randomized trial found that adolescent girls could be taught better decision-making skills regarding safe sex behaviors using ACT methods as a component of intervention (Metzler et al., 2000). Finally, a case study by Heffner and colleagues (2002) illustrated that the ACT focus on unworkable control strategies was especially appropriate for the treatment of anorexia nervosa.

Some studies have not directly examined ACT treatment outcomes but have instead considered issues that pertain to ACT methods. For example, there is some empirical support for the use of metaphorical versus literal instructions with children, as is common in ACT (Heffner, Greco, & Eifert, 2003). Future studies examining the effectiveness of ACT treatment components will reveal the unique role and incremental contribution of various exercises and techniques. As is the case with many of the newly emerging treatments for children and adolescents, much progress remains to be made in empirically evaluating the effectiveness of ACT with youth. However, results appear promising and suggest that ACT may serve to be an engaging, developmentally appropriate treatment model suitable for use with a variety of disorders.

Dialectical Behavior Therapy (DBT)

DBT (Linehan, 1993) is based on a dialectical worldview whose therapeutic aim is to balance the dialectic of acceptance and change—that is, clients will accept themselves while simultaneously working toward change. DBT was developed for the treatment of adult suicidal females with a diagnosis of borderline personality disorder (BPD) and has a solid body of empirical support (e.g., Robins & Chapman, 2004). For the DBT practitioner, the borderline personality can be explained by biosocial theory, whose tenet is that both biological and social factors inform personality.

Acceptance, Mindfulness, and DBT

As noted, the core dialectic in standard DBT for adults is the careful balance of acceptance and change (Linehan, 1993). Since according to biosocial theory the borderline personality results from the combination of a biological predisposition toward emotional dysregulation and an invalidating social environment, DBT therapists attempt to provide validation through acceptance. Acceptance under this framework refers to the ability to view previously unacceptable thoughts, emotions, and behaviors as valid given a particular context.

Mindfulness is one of the core skills taught to individuals struggling with polarities such as those described above. Though not the only skill taught in DBT for adolescents, mindfulness practice provides a stable base from which to develop distress tolerance skills, emotion regulation skills, and interpersonal effectiveness skills (Wagner, Rathus, & Miller, 2006). By cultivating a nonjudgmental awareness of the present moment, individuals with BPD can better observe and label their emotions without impulsively acting on them; their tolerance for distressing feelings thereby increases, their ability to regulate emotions improves, and they can thus more effectively relate to others, whose emotions are also observed and labeled nonjudgmentally (Wagner et al., 2006).

In DBT, mindfulness has been stripped of any religious or spiritual connotation and instead attempts to focus clients on what is true in the present moment (Wagner et al., 2006). Three states of mind are introduced to the client in the mindfulness module: reasonable mind, emotion mind, and wise mind. Wise mind integrates both reason and emotion, and it is wise mind that is able to be mindful of the present moment. Mindfulness skills are further broken down into more concrete "what" skills and "how" skills, which are easily defined and targeted for improvement (see chapter 6 for a more detailed account of these skills).

The "what" skills provide a working definition of mindfulness that includes observing, describing, and participating. The "how" skills provide guidance in the methods of mindfulness and include nonjudgmentally, one-mindfully, and effectively. Regarding the "what" skills, observing entails watching one's own thoughts, feelings, and behaviors without trying to change them; describing refers to the labeling of thoughts, feelings, and behaviors without judgment; and participating requires complete involvement in the present moment, without self-consciousness.

From Adults to Children: Dialectical Behavior Therapy for Adolescents (DBT-A)

The dialectics identified by Rathus and Miller (2000) as central to adolescents and families include the balance between leniency and authoritarianism in the family; the balance between normalizing pathological behaviors and pathologizing normal behaviors; and the balance between forcing autonomy and fostering dependence. In families of suicidal adolescents, these dialectical dilemmas are in need of synthesis and resolution (Rathus & Miller, 2002). Accordingly, DBT-A (Miller, Rathus, Linehan, Wetzler, & Leigh, 1997) has been adapted and tested with suicidal adolescents and their families.

The adaptation of DBT for adolescents and their families involves diagnostic, developmental, and contextual issues (see chapter 6 in this volume). Briefly, diagnostic issues refer to the debate around the appropriateness of the borderline personality disorder diagnosis for adolescents. Developmental issues have resulted in several structural modifications, including reduced treatment length, reduced number of skills taught, simplification of the language used in skills training, the inclusion of family members in skills training groups, the addition of family sessions, and handouts as needed, and the addition of an optional follow-up group (the "graduate group") that allows adolescents who have completed the first phase of treatment to share their experiences with each other in a group setting (Miller et al., 1997). Contextual issues require clinicians and researchers to consider the family and school contexts within which adolescents are situated.

More specific adaptations regarding the teaching of dialectics, acceptance, and mindfulness require the clinician to use stories, metaphors, and examples that are relevant to the lives of adolescents when introducing these concepts. Adolescents may learn certain mindfulness skills more easily than others; for example, though adolescents may have difficulty with the somewhat abstract task of observing thoughts and feelings, their everyday experience with describing their thoughts and feelings to others renders the latter skill more familiar (see chapter 6 in this volume). Still, both the "what" and "how" skills remain identical to those skills taught to adults, except that the "how" skills have been renamed for adolescents (Miller, Rathus, & Linehan, in press). Regarding the "how" skills, "don't judge" corresponds to the "nonjudgmentally" component of "how" skills for adult DBT. Adolescents are taught to notice their experiences without evaluating them as either good or bad. "Stay focused" corresponds to the "one-mindfully" component of "how" skills for adult DBT. This skill enables adolescents to focus their attention on one experience at a time. "Do what works" corresponds to the "effectively" component of "how" skills for adult DBT. Doing what works involves behaving appropriately and practically in the context of the reality of the current situation.

Empirical support for the effectiveness of DBT-A is promising. Studies have been conducted with suicidal adolescents in a variety of settings, including inpatient (Katz, Cox, Gunasekara, & Miller, 2004), residential care (Sunseri, 2004), and outpatient clinics (Miller, Wyman, Huppert, Glassman, & Rathus, 2000; Rathus & Miller, 2002; Woodberry & Popenoe, in press). DBT-A has also been applied successfully with adolescents diagnosed with oppositional defiant disorder (Nelson-Gray et al., 2006); both parent and child reports indicated a reduction in externalizing and internalizing symptoms as well as an increase in positive behaviors. In sum, DBT-A appears to be a promising approach for a range of adolescent populations, including those struggling with externalizing behavior problems and suicidal ideation. Treatment component studies will be useful in determining the mechanisms by which DBT-A produces change, and of particular relevance to this volume will be a more precise understanding of the effects of teaching acceptance and mindfulness on treatment outcome.

Mindfulness-Based Stress Reduction (MBSR)

As noted in the introduction to this chapter, Jon Kabat-Zinn's MBSR program has been credited with the introduction of mindfulness practice into Western medicine and health care. Since the founding of his stress reduction clinic at the University of Massachusetts Medical School in 1979, more than seventeen thousand people have completed the eight-week MBSR program (see Center for Mindfulness in Medicine, Health Care, and Society, www.umassmed.edu/cfm/mbsr/). A summary of major research findings indicates that MBSR has proven effective in reducing both medical and psychological symptoms not only in individuals experiencing stress and anxiety, but also in those suffering from chronic pain and chronic illness.

Acceptance, Mindfulness, and MBSR

Unlike ACT and DBT, for which mindfulness is just one of many treatment components, MBSR conceptualizes mindfulness practice as the primary mode of treatment. The role of acceptance as such is not specifically addressed. MBSR sessions focus almost singularly on the practice and refinement of mindfulness meditation, and home practice is also encouraged. Notably, practitioners of MBSR are expected to be dedicated and experienced practitioners of mindfulness mediation themselves. Kabat-Zinn (2003) believes that therapists cannot effectively teach mindfulness skills to their clients unless they themselves develop and regularly practice these skills.

From Adults to Children

In adapting MBSR for children in a school setting, Saltzman and Goldin emphasize the use of age-appropriate language and the importance of making mindfulness exercises fun and engaging (see chapter 7 in this volume). Saltzman's Still Quiet Place achieves both of these ends by providing children with a developmentally appropriate means of guided practice. Other exercises used include Mindful Eating, which is a particularly useful exercise for children given the concreteness of food, as well as the Thought Parade, which has been modified from the adult version by the use of more visual imagery and personal examples. Seaweed Practice offers children (who become restless more quickly than adults) the opportunity to integrate movement with mindful attention to physical sensations. For a more complete description of Saltzman and Goldin's MBSR program for school-age children, refer to chapter 7 of this volume.

Though the use of MBSR with adults predates the development and refinement of the other mindfulness-based interventions discussed in this chapter, its adaptation for a youth population is in an early stage of research. Currently Saltzman and Goldin are conducting two studies for relatively well-adjusted children in grades 4 through 6 and their parents. Preliminary findings indicate improvements in attention, mood, compassion, and mindfulness (see Saltzman & Goldin, chapter 7 in this volume). MBSR has also been effective in the treatment of more at-risk youth populations, including a nine-year-old girl with gastroesophageal reflux disease (Ott, 2002) and adolescents with insomnia and substance-abuse problems (Bootzin & Stevens, 2005). Finally, Wall (2005) combined tai chi and MBSR in a Boston public middle school; subjective reports of student participants indicated an increase in calmness and relaxation as well as improved sleep and self-care. Given the established success of MBSR with adults (Kabat-Zinn, 2003), the adaptation of MBSR for a youth population seems especially warranted. Future research will outline specific treatment protocols adapted for children and adolescents and also further elucidate the effectiveness of MBSR with the youth population.

Mindfulness-Based Cognitive Therapy (MBCT)

Developed for prevention of depressive relapse in adults, MBCT is based on an integration of cognitive behavior therapy (CBT) for depression and components of MBSR (Kabat-Zinn, 1990). In contrast to the more general applicability of MBSR, however, MBCT was initially developed to prevent relapse of major depression among adult clinical populations.

Acceptance, Mindfulness, and MBCT

Similar to other acceptance-based approaches, MBCT does not focus on changing the content of thoughts; instead MBCT integrates select aspects of CBT and MBSR that facilitate altering the awareness of and relationship to thoughts (Segal, Teasdale, & Williams, 2004). Though not labeled as such, this shift in emphasis is similar to acceptance as defined by ACT—that is, thoughts are observed and accepted rather than changed. Mindfulness in MBCT is conceptualized as an appropriate way to prevent relapse and recurrence of major depressive episodes (Segal et al., 2004). The automatic, ruminative processing associated with depression is disrupted by the mindful awareness of negative thoughts, feelings, and bodily sensations. Mindfulness techniques thus serve as a tool to help individuals break the automatic, dysfunctional thought processes that are likely to result in relapse and recurrence of depressive episodes.

From Adults to Children

Mindfulness-based cognitive therapy for children (MBCT-C) was adapted from the adult group program (see chapter 4 for further discussion). As it appears that both depressive and anxiety disorders share a common ruminative component, MBCT-C described in this volume focuses on integrating the mindfulness components of MBCT for treatment of anxiety in children (see also Semple, 2006). Keeping in mind that children are not merely "little adults," MBCT-C has been tailored to suit the developmental abilities of children. Specifically, MBCT-C differs from the structured adult MBCT used in the treatment of depression in three ways (Semple & Miller, 2006).

The first consideration in treatment of children is that children have less developed memory and attentional capacities. To counter potential inattention brought about by lengthy sessions, the MBCT-C program described in chapter 4 consists of weekly ninety-minute sessions over the course of twelve weeks as compared to the two-hour weekly sessions of the eight-week MBCT program. During the ninety-minute sessions, children engage in frequent meditations in three- to five-minute blocks of time rather than the longer twenty- to forty-minute adult meditations of MBCT.

Second, in working with adults, psychotherapies draw on verbal abilities such as abstract and logical thinking. Cognitively, children have limited verbal fluency, abstract reasoning, and conceptualization. Thus it is necessary to integrate experiential learning exercises that teach mindfulness by focusing on specific body sensations (e.g., sight, sound, touch, taste, smell) and perceptions (Semple & Miller, 2006). In keeping with the activity level and attention span of children, several exercises including sensory activities, sitting meditations, body scans, visualization practices, and drawing or writing are performed over the course of a session.

Third, as with any treatment involving children, attention must be paid to the fact that children are part of a larger system involving their family. MBCT-C includes parents as a vital part of the treatment process. In addition to assisting with home practice exercises, parents are given the opportunity to attend an orientation session before the beginning of the program as well as a review session at the end of the program. Thus the program is designed to keep parents actively involved from start to finish.

While still in its earliest stages of investigation, research with children suggests that MBCT-C appears to be useful in the treatment of children with anxiety. Children seven to twelve years old identified as having clinically significant anxiety symptoms have shown reductions in internalizing and externalizing problems as well as improved academic functioning (Semple, 2006; Semple, Lee, & Miller, 2004; Semple, Reid, & Miller, 2005). Overall the results support the feasibility of a mindfulness-based training program for children with anxiety. Further research is warranted to focus on the relationship between mindfulness and anxiety in children. Additionally, future research may also help to shed light on the feasibility of a more general application of MBCT-C and its mindfulness techniques to other childhood disorders.

Similarities and Differences Among Models

Rarely do any two psychotherapies, particularly of different theoretical orientations, match up in terms of intervention procedures. Even among the various acceptance- and mindfulness-based interventions reviewed in this chapter, considerable variation exists among session format as well as the duration, length, and intensity of treatment sessions The techniques of ACT, DBT-A, MBCT-C, and MBSR for parents, adolescents, and children, though they share a focus on acceptance and mindfulness, differ in important ways.

Though both ACT and DBT-A are theory-driven approaches, they are based on two widely different theories. ACT is based on relational frame theory (Hayes et al., 2001), a theory of language and cognition. For example, ACT techniques generally target experiential avoidance, a construct theorized to be a natural by-product of language and cognition. Without language and cognition, we would not be able to say to ourselves, "I am anxious all the time," or "My parents were horrible," or "I will never be happy." Neither would we be able to remember our past nor worry about the future. As such, it is a theoretical stance that supports the use of acceptance- and mindfulness-based interventions; acceptance and mindfulness are meant to be present focused and to separate individuals from their thoughts. DBT, in contrast, is based on a biosocial theory of personality wherein personality is conceptualized as a product of biology and the social world. The borderline personality, under this framework, is seen as a product of a biologically based difficulty with emotion regulation and of an invalidating social environment.

Despite their theoretical differences, ACT and DBT share a common ground: acceptance and mindfulness. Chapman, Gratz, and Brown (2005), for example, have proposed that experiential avoidance is the primary mechanism underlying adolescent self-injury. Though experiential avoidance is theoretically tied to ACT, Chapman and colleagues (2005) propose both ACT and DBT as appropriate forms of treatment, given their focus on acceptance and mindfulness. If both ACT and DBT prove to be effective treatments for adolescent self-injury, then researchers will need not only to compare them to therapies outside of the acceptance and mindfulness tradition, but also to each other. As repeated throughout this chapter, careful component studies are needed to determine what role acceptance and mindfulness play in therapeutic change.

Mindfulness techniques, though important, are not the sole components of ACT and DBT, whose broad theories provide rationale for the use of other techniques and skills. In contrast, mindfulness is the primary component for both MBSR and MBCT. The establishment of these interventions as efficacious would lend even greater support to the proposal that acceptance and mindfulness play a pivotal role in treatment success. As previously noted, providers of both of MBSR and MBCT are expected to be dedicated and experienced practitioners of mindfulness. In contrast, practitioners of ACT and DBT are not always expected to have extensive personal experience with mindfulness meditation practice.

Mindfulness, Acceptance, and Parenting

If acceptance and mindfulness interventions with youth are to be successful, parents need to be involved as well. The mindful parenting literature consists of both descriptive and theoretical pieces (Coyne & Wilson, 2004; Dumas, 2005; Greco & Eifert, 2004; Kabat-Zinn & Kabat-Zinn, 1997) as well as several published empirical studies (Singh et al., 2006; Singh et al., in press; Blackledge & Hayes, 2006). Perhaps the earliest work on mindful parenting is that of Kabat-Zinn and Kabat-Zinn (1997), which lays the groundwork for empirical studies through an exploration of the definition and practice of mindfulness in the context of parenting. For Kabat-Zinn and Kabat-Zinn, mindful parenting is not about conflict-free parent-child relationships, but rather about a "moment-to-moment awareness" of children's overt behavior and subjective experience. These authors identify three foundations of mindful parenting: sovereignty, empathy, and acceptance.

First, parents must honor the sovereignty of their children. This does not mean that children are allowed free rein to behave as they please. Rather, it means that parents respect the dignity of their children's "true selves." Kabat-Zinn and Kabat-Zinn (1997) liken sovereignty to the Buddhist concept of Buddha nature, which is the true nature of the self. Instead of attempting to change their children, parents are called upon to recognize who their children really are and to honor that—to honor their sovereignty. This is accomplished by remaining mindful of children's true selves in difficult moments. For example, instead of responding to their own need to silence the rebellion of an adolescent, parents should take the opportunity to appreciate the forces that adolescents struggle with and remain mindful of the adolescent's experiences and struggles.

To honor sovereignty in difficult moments requires that parents cultivate empathy; that is, they must attempt to see the world from their children's perspectives. When a child falls down and scrapes his or her knee, empathy seems to come naturally. When a child is yelling, screaming, or throwing things, empathy can be difficult to muster

(Kabat-Zinn & Kabat-Zinn, 1997). Similarly, when a child's desires or opinions are at odds with the desires and opinions of grown-ups, parents may have difficulty responding with empathy. Empathy therefore requires a deliberate attention to the present moment; parents must be able to separate what they are thinking and feeling from what their child is currently experiencing (Kabat-Zinn & Kabat-Zinn, 1997).

Acceptance is closely related to both sovereignty and empathy. When parents can honor their children's sovereignty and provide them with empathy, they are demonstrating an acceptance of their children's true selves, their unique desires, thoughts, feelings, and perspectives. Together, then, sovereignty, empathy, and acceptance form the foundation for mindful parenting.

Other Theoretical Models

Dumas (2005) has proposed a model of mindfulness-based parent training influenced, in part, by the work of Kabat-Zinn and Kabat-Zinn (1997) and by the observation that traditional behavioral parent training programs have often proved inadequate in their efforts to change highly resistant behaviors. Dumas's model is based on the idea that behavior that is highly resistant to change is behavior that has become automatized. He believes that this automaticity, or mindlessness, is the cause of most disruptive and problematic patterns of behavior within families (Dumas, 2005). Though no empirical investigations into the effectiveness of this model have been published at the time of this writing, Dumas provides an overview of his model and introduces three strategies that therapists can implement to decrease automaticity in the family context: facilitative listening, distancing, and motivated action plans.

Facilitative listening requires a nonjudgmental stance, not only toward the client but also toward the therapist's own reactions to what the client is saying and feeling (Dumas, 2005). The two aims of facilitative listening are (1) to listen to parents' presenting concerns without criticizing, judging, or giving advice, and (2) to help parents themselves (by example) refrain from self-criticism and judgment. Therapists may also encourage distancing—that is, therapists may help parents to separate their thoughts and feelings at any given moment from the behaviors they choose to enact in that moment. Parents are thus taught not to let their thoughts and feelings control their overt behavior and interactions with their children.

Motivated action plans (MAPs) are behavioral strategies intended to bridge the gap between motivation and action (Dumas, 2005). Parents' motivation to improve their relationship with their children does not always directly result in actions consistent with that goal. To increase the likelihood that parents attain their goals, they need to be able to specify, in advance, the behavioral strategies that they will employ in a given situation (Dumas, 2005). Having such a specific plan, or MAP, facilitates parents' ability to respond mindfully to challenging situations because they have planned in advance how they will react (Dumas, 2005). This is an intentional, deliberate attempt to remain mindful in a situation that would normally elicit automatized, or mindless, behavior. For example, a parent might develop a MAP to walk away calmly and sit on the couch for a specified duration during the next temper tantrum rather than lose his or her own temper (Dumas, 2005).

Coyne and Wilson (2004) provide a different theoretical rationale for the use of mindfulness in impaired parenting. Specifically, they discuss how cognitive fusion can lead to maladaptive parenting patterns and how mindfulness and acceptance may be helpful in breaking those patterns. Cognitive fusion occurs when thoughts are responded to in terms of their literal content (Hayes et al., 1999). If a parent has the thought "I am a bad parent," then he or she will tend to respond to that thought as if it were literally true and engage in behaviors to eliminate that thought. These behaviors, similar to those identified by Patterson (1982) as indicative of coercive family processes, are likely to include acquiescence to child noncompliance or escalating the intensity of efforts to ensure compliance (Coyne & Wilson, 2004). Rather than attending to and being mindful of what the child is experiencing in the present moment then, parents are attending to and responding to their own thoughts of failure.

Only when parents are able to be mindful and accepting of their children's experience and defuse (separate) from their own thoughts can they begin to respond in more adaptive ways to their children's distress. ACT provides the framework to accomplish this cognitive defusion; experiential exercises and metaphors help parents to see that their thoughts are just thoughts—they are not literal truth. Additionally, ACT provides parents with the motivation to do the difficult work of cognitive defusion by encouraging them to determine their values (Coyne & Wilson, 2004). If parents are in contact with why mindful parenting is important to them, they are more likely to practice mindful parenting.

Greco and Eifert (2004) propose the incorporation of ACT into existing behavioral interventions for parent-adolescent conflict. They first propose that experiential avoidance plays a role in interpersonal family conflict. Both parents and adolescents, in their attempts to avoid distressing experiences, often behave in ways that provide short-term relief but are inconsistent with their long-term values as family members. Regular mindfulness practice and defusion promote acceptance of such painful thoughts and feelings, and can be useful during times of great conflict. As parents and adolescents learn to hold their thoughts and judgments lightly and become mindful of the present moment, they are better able to respond adaptively to each other and to choose actions that are more congruent with their values.

Finally, in their parenting clinic at the University of Tennessee, Wahler and colleagues integrate mindfulness with behavioral parent training (BPT) and narrative restructuring therapy (NRT); their preliminary findings are promising, indicating increased mindfulness in parents and decreased behavioral problems in children (see chapter 10 in this volume). The treatment procedures at Wahler's parenting clinic have been informed by the mindfulness practices outlined by Baer (2003), Bishop and colleagues (2004), and Kabat-Zinn (1994), as well as by the theoretical work of Dumas (2005) and empirical studies by Singh and colleagues (2004, in press).

Following their successes with training mindfulness in nonparental caregivers of individuals with profound, multiple disabilities, Singh and colleagues conducted two empirical studies on mindfulness training for parents of autistic children. In both the original (2004) and the follow-up (in press) studies, mothers who attended a series of mindfulness trainings reported increases in satisfaction with parenting skills and parent-child interaction as well as increased use of mindfulness skills and decreased perceptions of stress. Their children experienced a decrease in aggressive behavior and an increase in social skills. Similarly, support for the use of both ACT and MBSR with parents of children with chronic conditions or disabilities can also be found in two recent studies (Blackledge & Hayes, 2006; Minor, Carlson, Mackenzie, Zernicke, & Jones, 2006).

In summary, theory, experience, and empirical results all indicate the usefulness and effectiveness of mindfulness training for parents. This support is especially promising given that the successful treatment of youth depends on the procurement of parental support. If mindfulness-based interventions prove successful for both youth and their parents, then we are better prepared to face the challenges inherent to psychotherapeutic interventions with children and adolescents.

Other Challenges

In addition to the challenge of successfully integrating parents into acceptance- and mindfulness-based treatments for youth, other challenges remain. Measurement issues in particular will need to be addressed, as will the question of how to reconcile the relationship between acceptance- and mindfulness-based treatments and existing interventions for children and adolescents.

Measuring Outcome

Conclusions about treatment efficacy become clouded when the outcome measures differ among interventions. The heterogeneity among acceptance- and mindfulness-based interventions for children will naturally result in a heterogeneous set of treatment outcome measures. This is further complicated by the fact that clinicians working with children and adolescents face unique challenges in measuring treatment efficacy. For example, measurement is limited by a lack of self-report measures available for early childhood use. This deficit is due in part to the variance in the ability of children to reliably report functioning and symptoms. Coupled with this apparent unreliability in self-report is the belief that others (e.g., parents, teachers) may serve as better informants. Parents are often viewed as an important source of information as they have knowledge of a child's behavior across time and situations. Parents are also most likely to be making the referral in the first place. However, parent reports are not without error, especially in the presence of parent psychopathology, marital discord, stress, and social support outside the home (Kazdin, 1994). Gathering information from multiple sources (e.g, children, parents, teachers, peers) is one way to improve data.

A related measurement problem revolves around the difficulty in assessing acceptance, mindfulness, and related constructs. For example, in ACT the goal of treatment is to increase psychological flexibility and values-consistent behavior, not the removal of symptoms. Assessing therapeutic gains in ACT will therefore not involve the measurement of psychopathology (e.g., a reduction in symptoms of depression and anxiety); instead researchers are faced with the challenge of measuring psychological flexibility (for review, see chapter 3 in this volume).

Integrating Acceptance and Mindfulness into Existing Therapies

Acceptance- and mindfulness-based treatments have their roots in more established, empirically validated cognitive and behavioral therapies and as such are not wholly inconsistent with existing interventions for youth. However, because acceptance- and mindfulness-based treatments attempt to change the context rather than the content of thoughts, and because the rationale for this shift is grounded in theory and supported by research, we believe that the addition of acceptance and mindfulness components to existing therapies can only serve to enhance them. To test this assertion, studies that examine the relative contributions of acceptance and mindfulness techniques and exercises are needed, so we return again to the call for component research.

Conclusion: Future Directions

As mentioned throughout this chapter and as will be detailed in several chapters later in this text, acceptance and mindfulness techniques have been creatively applied in a number of youth-relevant contexts. For example, recent child treatments use metaphor and story to focus on acceptance of distressing thoughts and feelings rather than on changing them. Mindfulness exercises have also recently been introduced in classroom settings and assigned as homework on teen-friendly CDs. While acceptance and mindfulness have long been practiced as part of spiritual and religious traditions, these concepts are relatively novel in mainstream contexts such as education and treatment. As acceptance and mindfulness are brought into these settings, several noteworthy issues and questions about future directions arise.

Another issue to address in the future is whether there are populations for whom acceptance and mindfulness procedures work better than others. The only way to answer this question is through a series of carefully designed studies that identify important clinical processes and outcome variables. As an example of the importance of empirical examination, consider the following: It is reasonable to see both sides of a debate about the utility of acceptance in early adolescence. For example, one clinician might say that a self-absorbed girl in early adolescence could not step back from her imagined audience long enough to recognize that her distress about her appearance may be a large part of the foundation of many of her strongest friendships. A second clinician may view the same client as being able to accept the distress entirely because she is so aware of it and her relation to others paying attention to her. Theoretically, neither clinician is more correct than the other—the data would be the judge of whether this teen could or could not accept her distress; and over time, in similar situations, the data would prove whether an acceptance-based approach would work in this population.

Although it is important to be guided by data, it is equally important to remember that acceptance- and mindfulness-based approaches require creativity, especially when used with youth. Many of the chapters in this volume are the result of clinician creativity and novel thinking. Many of these authors were told that such work could not be done with youth. Fortunately we were able to stay in the present moment, experience fully, and move our work in a valued direction. We hope as you read, and as acceptance- and mindfulness-based treatments move forward, that an extraordinary difference can be made.

References

Baer, R. A. (2003). Mindfulness training as a clinical intervention: A conceptual and empirical review. *Clinical Psychology: Science and Practice, 10*(2), 125–143.

Baer, R. A. (Ed.). (2006). *Mindfulness-based treatment approaches: A clinician's guide*. San Diego, CA: Elsevier.

Baer, R. A., & Krietemeyer, J. (2006). Overview of mindfulness- and acceptance-based treatment approaches. In R. A. Baer (Ed.), *Mindfulness-based treatment approaches: A clinician's guide* (pp. 3–27). San Diego, CA: Elsevier.

Bishop, S. R., Lau, M., Shapiro, S., Carlson, L., Anderson, N. D., Carmody, J., et al. (2004). Mindfulness: A proposed operational definition. *Clinical Psychology: Science and Practice, 11*(3), 230–241.

Blackledge, J. T., & Hayes, S. C. (2006). Using acceptance and commitment training in the support of parents of children diagnosed with autism. *Child and Family Behavior Therapy, 28*, 1–18.

Bootzin, R. R., & Stevens, S. J. (2005). Adolescents, substance abuse, and the treatment of insomnia and daytime sleepiness. *Clinical Psychology Review, 25*, 629–644.

Center for Mindfulness in Medicine, Health Care, and Society. Retrieved June 26, 2007, from www.umassmed.edu/cfm/mbsr/.

Chapman, A. L., Gratz, K. L., & Brown, M. Z. (2005). Solving the puzzle of deliberate self-harm: The experiential avoidance model. *Behaviour Research and Therapy, 44*, 371–394.

Christensen, A., Jacobson, N. S., & Babcock, J. C. (1995). Integrative behavioral couple therapy. In N. S. Jacobson & A. S. Gurman (Eds.), *Clinical handbook of couples therapy* (pp. 31–64). New York: Guilford.

Corrigan, P. W. (2001). Getting ahead of the data: A threat to some behavior therapies. *Behavior Therapist, 24,* 189–193.

Coyne, L. W., & Wilson, K. G. (2004). The role of cognitive fusion in impaired parenting: An RFT analysis. *International Journal of Psychology and Psychological Therapy, 4,* 469–486.

Devany, J. M., Hayes, S. C., & Nelson, E. O. (1986). Equivalence class formation in language-able and language-disabled children. *Journal of the Experimental Analysis of Behavior, 56,* 243–257.

Dumas, J. E. (2005). Mindfulness-based parent training: Strategies to lessen the grip of automaticity in families with disruptive children. *Journal of Clinical Child and Adolescent Psychology, 34,* 779–791.

Goodman, T. A. (2005). Working with children: Beginner's mind. In C. K. Germer, R. D. Siegel, & P. R. Fulton (Eds.), *Mindfulness and psychotherapy* (pp. 197–219). New York: Guilford.

Greco, L. A., Blackledge, J. T., Coyne, L. W., & Ehrenreich, J. (2005). Integrating acceptance and mindfulness into treatments for child and adolescent anxiety disorders: Acceptance and commitment therapy as an example. In S. M. Orsillo & L. Roemer (Eds.), *Acceptance and mindfulness-based approaches to anxiety: Conceptualization and treatment* (pp. 301–322). New York: Springer Science.

Greco, L. A., Blomquist, K. K., Acra, S., & Mouton, D. (2008). *Acceptance and commitment therapy for adolescents with functional abdominal pain: Results of a pilot investigation.* Manuscript submitted for publication.

Greco, L. A., & Eifert, G. H. (2004). Treating parent-adolescent conflict: Is acceptance the missing link for an integrative family therapy? *Cognitive and Behavioral Practice, 11,* 305–314.

Greco, L. A., Lambert, W., & Baer, R. A. (in press). Psychological inflexibility in childhood and adolescence: Development and evaluation of the Avoidance and Fusion Questionnaire for Youth. *Psychological Assessment.*

Hayes, S. C. (2004). Acceptance and commitment therapy, relational frame theory, and the third wave of behavior therapy. *Behavior Therapy, 35,* 639–665.

Hayes, S. C., Barnes-Holmes, D., & Roche, B. (2001). *Relational frame theory: A post-Skinnerian account of human language and cognition.* New York: Kluwer/Plenum.

Hayes, S. C., Follette, V. M., & Linehan, M. M. (2004). *Mindfulness and acceptance: Expanding the cognitive behavioral tradition.* New York: Guilford.

Hayes, S. C., Masuda, A., Bissett, R., Luoma, J., & Guererro, L. F. (2004). DBT, FAP, and ACT: How empirically oriented are the new behavior therapy technologies. *Behavior Therapy, 35,* 35–54.

Hayes, S. C., Strosahl, K. D., & Wilson, K. G. (1999). *Acceptance and commitment therapy: An experiential approach to behavior change*. New York: Guilford.

Hayes, S. C., Wilson, K. G., Gifford, E. V., Follette, V. M., & Strosahl, K. D. (1996). Experiential avoidance and behavioral disorders: A functional dimensional approach to diagnosis and treatment. *Journal of Consulting and Clinical Psychology, 64*, 1152–1168.

Heffner, M., Greco, L. A., & Eifert, G. H. (2003). Pretend you are a turtle: Children's responses to metaphorical versus literal relaxation instructions. *Child and Family Behavior Therapy, 25*, 19–33.

Heffner, M., Sperry, J., Eifert, G. H., & Detweiler, M. (2002). Acceptance and commitment therapy in the treatment of an adolescent female with anorexia nervosa: A case example. *Cognitive and Behavioral Practice, 9*, 232–236.

Kabat-Zinn, J. (1982). An outpatient program in behavioral medicine for chronic pain patients based on the practice of mindfulness meditation: Theoretical considerations and preliminary results. *General Hospital Psychiatry, 4*, 33–47.

Kabat-Zinn, J. (1990). *Full catastrophe living: Using the wisdom of your body and mind to face stress, pain, and illness*. New York: Delacorte.

Kabat-Zinn, J. (1994). *Wherever you go, there you are: Mindfulness meditation in everyday life*. New York: Hyperion.

Kabat-Zinn, J. (2003). Mindfulness-based interventions in context: Past, present, and future. *Clinical Psychology: Science and Practice, 10*, 144–156.

Kabat-Zinn, J., & Kabat-Zinn, M. (1997). *Everyday blessings: The inner work of mindful parenting*. New York: Hyperion.

Katz, L. Y., Cox, B. J., Gunasekara, S., & Miller, A. L. (2004). Feasibility of applying dialectical behavior therapy to suicidal adolescent inpatients. *Journal of the American Academy of Child and Adolescent Psychiatry, 43*, 276–282.

Kazdin, A. E. (1994). Informant variability in the assessment of childhood depression. In W. M. Reynolds & H. Johnston (Eds.), *Handbook of depression in children and adolescents* (pp. 249–271). New York: Plenum.

Kohlenberg, R. J., & Tsai, M. (1991). *Functional analytic psychotherapy: Creative intense and curative therapeutic relationships*. New York: Plenum.

Linehan, M. M. (1993). *Cognitive-behavioral treatment of borderline personality disorder*. New York: Guilford.

Lipkens, G., Hayes, S. C., & Hayes, L. J. (1993). Longitudinal study of derived stimulus relations in an infant. *Journal of Experimental Child Psychology, 56*, 201–239.

Metzler, C. W., Biglan, A., Noell, J., Ary, D. V., & Ochs, L. (2000). A randomized controlled trial of a behavioral intervention to reduce high-risk sexual behavior among adolescents in STD clinics. *Behavior Therapy, 31*, 27–54.

Miller, A. L., Rathus, J. H., Linehan, M. M., Wetzler, S., & Leigh, E. (1997). Dialectic behavior therapy adapted for suicidal adolescents. *Journal of Practical Psychiatry and Behavioral Health, 3*, 78–86.

Miller, A. L., Wyman, S. E., Huppert, J. D., Glassman, S. L., & Rathus, J. H. (2000). Analysis of behavioral skills utilized by suicidal adolescents receiving dialectical behavioral therapy. *Cognitive and Behavioral Practice, 7*, 183–187.

Minor, H. G., Carlson, L. E., Mackenzie, M. J., Zernicke, K., & Jones, L. (2006). Evaluation of a mindfulness-based stress reduction (MBSR) program for caregivers of children with chronic conditions. *Social Work in Health Care, 43*, 91–109.

Moore, D., Wilson, K. G., Wilson, D. M., Murrell, A. R., Roberts, M., Merwin, R., et al. (2003, May). *Treating at-risk youth with an in-school acceptance and commitment training program.* Paper presented at the meeting of the Association for Behavior Analysis, San Francisco, CA.

Murrell, A. R., Coyne, L. W., & Wilson, K. G. (2004). ACT with children, adolescents, and their parents. In S. C. Hayes & K. D. Strosahl (Eds.), *A practical guide to acceptance and commitment therapy* (pp. 249–273). New York: Springer.

Murrell, A. R., & Scherbarth, A. J. (2006). State of the research and literature address: ACT with children, adolescents, and parents. *International Journal of Behavioral Consultation and Therapy, 2*, 531–543.

Nelson-Gray, R. O., Keane, S. P., Hurst, R. M., Mitchell, J. T., Warburton, J. B., Chok, J. T., et al. (2006). A modified DBT skills training program for oppositional defiant adolescents: Promising preliminary findings. *Behaviour Research and Therapy, 44*, 1811–1820.

Ott, M. J. (2002). Mindfulness meditation in pediatric clinical practice. *Pediatric Nursing, 28*, 487–490.

Patterson, G. R. (1982). *A social learning approach. Vol. 3: Coercive family process*. Eugene, OR: Castalia.

Rathus, J. H., & Miller, A. L. (2000). DBT for adolescents: Dialectical dilemmas and secondary treatment targets. *Cognitive and Behavioral Practice, 7*, 425–434.

Rathus, J. H., & Miller, A. L. (2002). Dialectical behavior therapy adapted for suicidal adolescents. *Suicidal and Life-Threatening Behavior, 32*, 146–157.

Robins, C. J., & Chapman, A. L. (2004). Dialectical behavior therapy: Current status, recent developments, and future directions. *Journal of Personality Disorders, 18*, 73–89.

Segal, Z. V., Teasdale, J. D., & Williams, M. G. (2004). Mindfulness-based cognitive therapy: Theoretical rationale and empirical status. In S. C. Hayes, V. M. Follette, & M. M. Linehan (Eds.), *Mindfulness and acceptance: Expanding the cognitive-behavioral tradition* (pp. 45–65). New York: Guilford.

Segal, Z. V., Williams, J. M. G., & Teasdale, J. D. (2002). *Mindfulness-based cognitive therapy for depression.* New York: Guilford.

Semple, R. J. (2006). Mindfulness-based cognitive therapy for children: A randomized group psychotherapy trial developed to enhance attention and reduce anxiety (Doctoral dissertation, Columbia University, 2005). *Dissertation Abstracts International, 66*, 5105.

Semple, R. J., Lee, J., & Miller, L. F. (2004). *Mindfulness-based cognitive therapy for children: A treatment model for childhood anxiety and depression.* Manuscript in preparation.

Semple, R. J., & Miller, L. F. (2006). Mindfulness-based cognitive therapy for children. In R. A. Baer (Ed.), *Mindfulness-based treatment approaches: Clinician's guide to evidence base and applications* (pp. 143–166). San Diego, CA: Elsevier.

Semple, R. J., Reid, E. F. G., & Miller, L. F. (2005). Treating anxiety with mindfulness: An open trial of mindfulness training for anxious children. *Journal of Cognitive Psychotherapy: An International Quarterly, 19*, 379–392.

Singh, N. N., Lancioni, G. E., Winton, A. S. W., Fisher, B. C., Wahler, R. G., McAleavey, K., et al. (2006). Mindful parenting decreases aggression, noncompliance, and self-injury in children with autism. *Journal of Emotional and Behavioral Disorders, 14*, 169–177.

Singh, N. N., Lancioni, G. E., Winton, A. S. W., Singh, J., Curtis, W. J., Wahler, R. G., et al. (in press). Mindful parenting decreases aggression and increases social behavior in children with developmental disabilities. *Behavior Modification.*

Singh, N. N., Lancioni, G. E., Winton, A. S. W., Wahler, R. G., Singh, J., & Sage, M. (2004). Mindful caregiving increases happiness among individuals with profound multiple disabilities. *Research in Developmental Disabilities, 25*, 207–218.

Sunseri, P. A. (2004). Preliminary outcomes on the use of dialectical behavior therapy to reduce hospitalization among adolescents in residential care. *Residential Treatment for Children and Youth, 21*, 59–76.

Wagner, E. E., Rathus, J. H., & Miller, A. L. (2006). Mindfulness in dialectical behavior therapy (DBT) for adolescents. In R. A. Baer (Ed.), *Mindfulness-based treatment approaches: Clinician's guide to evidence base and applications* (pp. 167–189). San Diego, CA: Elsevier.

Wall, R. B. (2005). Tai chi and mindfulness-based stress reduction in a Boston public middle school. *Journal of Pediatric Health Care, 19*, 230–237.

Wicksell, R. K., Dahl, J., Magnusson, B., & Olsson, G. L. (2005). Using acceptance and commitment therapy in the rehabilitation of an adolescent female with chronic pain: A case example. *Cognitive and Behavioral Practice, 12*, 415–423.

Woodberry, K. A., & Popenoe, E. J. (in press). Implementing dialectical behavior therapy with adolescents and their families in a community outpatient clinic. *Cognitive and Behavioral Practice.*

Chapter 3

Assessment of Acceptance and Mindfulness Processes in Youth

Lisa W. Coyne, Ph.D., Psychology Department, Suffolk University;
Daniel Cheron, MA, and Jill T. Ehrenreich, Ph.D.,
Center for Anxiety and Related Disorders, Boston University

The ability to accurately describe and assess constructs such as experiential avoidance, mindfulness, and acceptance is central to the pursuit of improving models of developmental psychopathology and developing more effective psychosocial treatments for children and teens. Formal assessment of these constructs is essential to provide a description of baseline functioning, therapy process, and treatment outcome. Thus, in this chapter, we will make a case for why mindfulness and acceptance are important processes as well as outcomes, provide a description of these constructs, review measures from the adult and child literature commonly used to assess them, and discuss limitations and new opportunities for research and clinical practice.

Why Study Mindfulness and Acceptance in Children?

Cognitive behavioral approaches have dominated the adult treatment literature and, in the past twenty years or so, have informed assessment and intervention with children and adolescents. A wealth of empirical studies highlight their utility with a broad variety of childhood disorders, including anxiety, depression, disruptive behavior problems, and numerous others (Lonigan, Elbert, & Johnson, 1998). However, there is room for continued growth. Recent work has underscored the need to comprehensively evaluate why and for whom treatment works (Kazdin & Nock, 2003). Notably, the child treatment literature is less developed than that of adults in this regard. This knowledge gap highlights the need to develop more effective, theoretically coherent, and empirically based assessment and treatment approaches.

Of late, empirical inquiry has turned toward mindfulness and acceptance. Some examples of approaches that rely on acceptance and mindfulness–based techniques include acceptance and commitment therapy (ACT; Hayes, Strosahl, & Wilson, 1999), mindfulness-based cognitive therapy (MBCT; Segal, Williams, & Teasdale, 2002), and dialectical behavior therapy (DBT; Linehan, 1987, 1993), among others. The recent incursion of mindfulness and acceptance–based approaches into the empirical literature reflects efforts to better understand the role of cognitive processes in psychopathology. It also provides us with an opportunity to further develop our knowledge of effective psychosocial treatments for children.

The Road Less Traveled: Cognition as Process vs. Cognition as Content

The idea that cognition is important in the production of overt behavior is not new. However, recent "third-wave" behavioral approaches are more interested in the process, or the "how," of cognition rather than its content, or what people think about. Some researchers have suggested that cognitive therapy may work through changing one's relationship to one's thoughts rather than changing cognitive content (Segal, Teasdale, & Williams, 2004). Contemporary behavioral theory has begun to address these issues through focusing on cognitive processes rather than merely on cognitive content (e.g., Bouton, Mineka, & Barlow, 2001; Hayes, Wilson, Gifford, Follette, & Strosahl, 1996; Segal et al., 2004; Orsillo, Roemer, Block-Lerner, & Tull, 2004).

Recent work has focused on the concept of experiential avoidance, or deliberate attempts to modify, suppress, escape, or avoid unwanted internal psychological experiences (Hayes et al. 1999; Hayes et al. 1996). Although the concept of experiential avoidance is not linked uniquely with one particular theoretical paradigm, this chapter will rely on a behavioral definition of experiential avoidance derived from the work of Hayes and colleagues in their description of ACT (Hayes et al., 1999). From this perspective, experiential avoidance is defined functionally and may refer to thought suppression, emotion avoidance, or distraction from unpleasant interoceptive or physiological cues, as well as avoidance of all contexts associated with these unwanted experiences. Such avoidant coping strategies, used pervasively, inflexibly, and over a period of time, may not only be ineffective but may also lead to increased intensity of feared events (e.g., Wegner, 1994; Wenzlaff, Wegner, & Klein, 1991). Across a breadth of literatures, experiential avoidance has been identified as a maladaptive process characterized by inflexible and narrow responding, and has been linked with poor mental health outcomes and low quality of life.

When does experiential avoidance become problematic? Consider the following description: Bethany is a seven-year-old separation-anxious child. Upon her parents' departure, Bethany feels frightened and sad and makes desperate attempts to prevent their leaving. Human children are verbal creatures and, as such, can contemplate past and future events. When Bethany and her parents discuss the situation later, some of the psychological properties of the actual separation—fear, perhaps muscle tension, visions of her parents never coming back, and so on—will inevitably show up for her. This may occur regardless of whether a parent is with Bethany sitting at the kitchen table helping with homework, reading a story, or snuggled on the living room couch. Reasons for this are that the original separation and the discussed separation are verbally represented and bidirectionally related in Bethany's mind. Certainly some contexts are more evocative than others, yet Bethany may strive to avoid all situations in which thoughts, feelings, or physiological sensations linked with real or imagined parent separation occur—or are even simply discussed. Separation is seen as catastrophic.

Following this example, situations that Bethany "must" avoid rapidly multiply, as do behaviors to prevent parental separation, such as tantrums at school, resistance at bedtime, continual reassurance seeking, clinginess, and refusal to go on play dates or to attend birthday parties. In this sense, Bethany's experiential avoidance is pervasive and leads to significant impairment across a number of domains. Unfortunately, her attempts at avoidance are always yoked to separation, whether the separation is imagined or real. Thus efforts to suppress or escape the private event "separation" are doomed to failure.

Conceptualizations of Mindfulness

Mindfulness and acceptance are processes that constitute viable alternatives to experiential avoidance. Hayes and colleagues (Hayes & Wilson, 2003; Hayes & Shenk, 2004) note that mindfulness is not, as of yet, well defined, as it developed centuries ago within Eastern contemplative traditions. Although definitions of mindfulness vary somewhat across different literatures, it generally refers to a state of consciousness in which individuals attend to their experiences in the present moment in a nonevaluative, nondefensive way (Baer, 2003; Hayes & Wilson, 2003; Hayes & Shenk, 2004; Shapiro, Carlson, Astin, & Freedman, 2006). Although investigators continue to develop precise, lab-based operational definitions of mindfulness, the notions of awareness and attention serve as critical aspects. Thus mindfulness can be conceptualized as allowing distancing from one's private experiences (Hayes et al., 1999; Segal et al., 2004). It is thought of as purposeful or characterized by intention, and being mindful engenders an openness and willingness to experience one's internal experience (Shapiro et al., 2006). Acceptance of emotional content is of vital importance, as are the concepts of self-awareness and self-compassion. Some approaches posit that mindfulness is important as an end goal in itself, while others hold that mindful awareness of one's experience allows one to pursue valued activities and goals.

One of the most theoretically sophisticated conceptualizations of mindfulness and acceptance processes comes from acceptance and commitment therapy (ACT; Hayes et al., 1999; Hayes, Luoma, Bond, Masuda, & Lillis, 2006). Hayes and colleagues (2006) describe ACT as composed of eight core components, broadly divided into two domains: (1) mindfulness and acceptance processes, and (2) commitment and behavior change processes (see figure 1 for a graphic depiction).

Figure 1. Mindfulness, Acceptance, and Behavior Change Processes in Acceptance and Commitment Therapy (ACT)

The ACT Therapeutic Model

Contact with the Present Moment

Acceptance

Values

Defusion

Committed Action

Self as Context

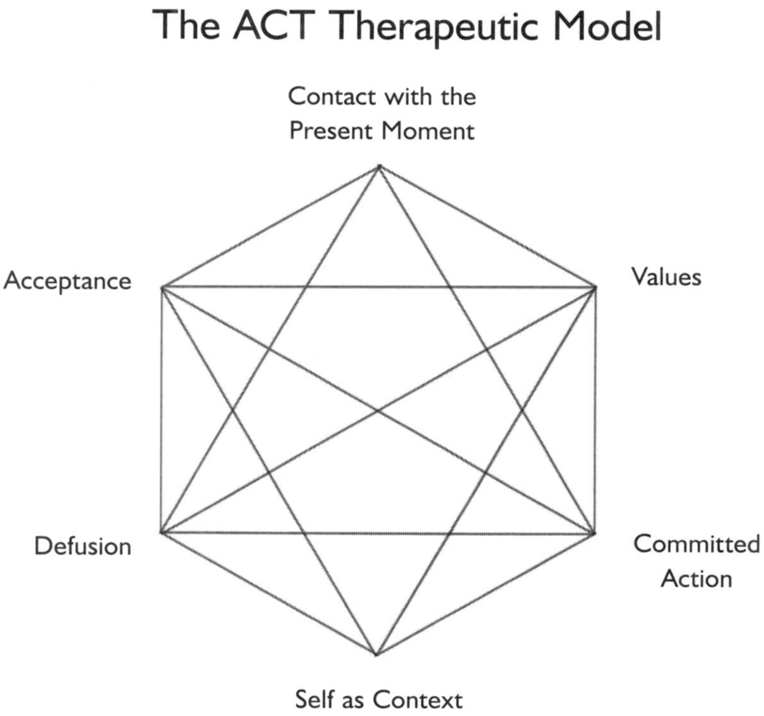

Acceptance and mindfulness processes, which include acceptance, defusion, contact with the present moment, and self as context, directly target experiential avoidance. For example, *acceptance* is described as active awareness of private events without attempts to change them. In the ACT paradigm, acceptance is not an end in itself but a vehicle for values-consistent action. *Defusion*, or *mindfulness*, refers to exposure to unwanted private events toward the end of altering their function rather than their content. Examples of defusion techniques include nonjudgmental self-monitoring of thoughts and recognizing thoughts as simply thoughts rather than taking them to be literal truths. *Contact with the present moment* is described as nonevaluative contact with contingencies. *Self as context* describes a set of therapeutic techniques that help clients experience the self as a stable perspective or a context, rather than overidentifying with or attaching to the content of their experience. The goal of these processes is psychological flexibility in the context of avoided private events—thus measurement of psychological flexibility is also important.

All mindfulness and acceptance–based processes are for a purpose—to promote valued action. Thus, although valuing is conceptualized as a behavior change strategy, it is also important to consider what is meant by values. *Valuing* refers to purposeful action consistent with meaningful, desired outcomes. Values do not refer to goals or end points, in the sense that they can never be reached. To engage in an activity consistent with one's values is inherently reinforcing (Wilson & Murrell, 2004). Thus there is need to assess individual values in a broad variety of domains. Additionally, individuals can pursue valued directions with more or less integrity and efficacy. As such, it is important to assess the degree to which one pursues values in the context of extant or emerging skill sets as well as how valuing may be derailed by attempts to avoid private events.

Measuring Mindfulness and Acceptance Processes

Given the inherent complexity of concepts such as mindfulness and acceptance, it is no wonder that quantitative assessment of these constructs has also been challenging. In a compilation of assessment measures of adults as well as children, Ciarrochi has divided measurement of the construct of experiential avoidance into three broad categories. These are self-report measures, behavioral measures (e.g., latency to looking away from a noxious stimulus), and what he refers to as "indirect self-report measures" (Ciarrochi & Blackledge, 2006; Ciarrochi, personal communication). This last category involves adaptation in broadly used attributional measures in which scores are intended to reflect psychological flexibility (e.g., Fresco, Williams, & Nugent, 2006).

The state of the literature regarding assessment of acceptance and mindfulness in children and adolescents is much like the population it is trying to assess: young and developing. Currently several researchers are examining ways to ascertain levels of mindfulness in youth. In this next section, we will discuss several measures that have been proposed to measure acceptance, mindfulness, and related constructs in youth. We begin by briefly reviewing existent tools for the measurement of mindfulness and acceptance in adults across the following constructs: awareness, avoidance, fusion, and action orientation. These constructs map onto underlying theories of mindfulness (see Baer, 2003; Brown & Ryan, 2003), and all have at least some supporting psychometric data. Next, we discuss recent developments in the assessment of mindfulness and acceptance in children and adolescents. In an effort to better understand mindfulness across child-rearing environments, we also discuss methods researchers have developed to better understand mindfulness and acceptance capacities in the parenting context. Finally, we present recent literature assessing mindfulness in pediatric populations, including adolescents with diabetes and those with chronic pain. A summary of all the measures discussed in this section and their psychometric status is provided in table 1.

Adult Measures

The development of empirical measures for adults has helped guide the field of mindfulness and its applications with children and adolescents. Therefore a brief review of selected adult measures is presented here. However, the descriptions below are in no way an exhaustive representation of knowledge regarding adult measures available to date.

Mindful Awareness

Mindfulness typically refers to awareness of the present moment, without judgment or attempts to alter the experience in any way (e.g., Baer, Smith, & Allen, 2004; Brown & Ryan, 2003; Hayes & Wilson, 2003). The concept and practice of mindfulness originated in Eastern thought and have been adapted for use in Western psychological and health-related interventions. Mindfulness skills have been most commonly assessed with self-report measures such as those described below.

Mindfulness Attention Awareness Scale (MAAS; Brown & Ryan, 2003). Developed through critical review of the mindfulness literature and the experience of mindfulness experts, the MAAS is a fifteen-item measure in which adults provide self-reported ratings of various experiences on a six-point Likert scale (e.g., "I tend not to notice feelings of physical tension or discomfort until they really grab my attention"). The MAAS is scored by calculating a mean of all the responses on the one-to-six scale. Respondents with higher scores purportedly demonstrate greater mindfulness, or "individual differences in the frequency of mindful states over time" (Brown & Ryan, 2003, p. __). Scale items include a variety of mindful experiences and the extent to which they are true for each respondent. Psychometric analysis of the MAAS was conducted on seven separate samples totaling 1,492 subjects. The age range of subjects was eighteen to seventy-seven years (M = 25.5 years). Participants were predominantly Caucasian. Results indicate good internal consistency, with alpha levels ranging from .82 to .87. Furthermore, in correlational analyses, the MAAS demonstrated good convergent and divergent validity with a variety of psychometrically supported measures.

Kentucky Inventory of Mindfulness Skills (KIMS; Baer et al., 2004). The KIMS is a thirty-nine-item self-report inventory designed to assess four mindfulness components (observing, describing, acting with awareness, and allowing without judgment) in adults. Respondents to the KIMS use a five-point Likert-type scale to indicate the extent to which an item represents themselves. Higher scores indicate that the statement is very often true about the respondent (e.g., "I pay attention to how my emotions affect my thoughts and behavior"; "I make judgments about how worthwhile or worthless my experiences are"). High scores on the KIMS purportedly denote higher levels of mindfulness skill. Psychometric analysis suggests that internal consistency across components was good (alpha = .79 to .91). Test-retest reliability correlations ranged between .65 and

Table 1. Summary of Mindfulness and Acceptance Measures (in alphabetical order)

Measure Name	Authors	Population	Length	Temporal Stability (r =)	Internal Consistency (α =)	Validity
Acceptance and Action Questionnaire	Hayes et al., 2004	A	9 items	.64	.70	Good
Affective Control Scale	Williams, Chambless, & Ahrens, 1997	A	42 items	.78	.93 to .94	Good
Avoidance and Fusion Questionnaire for Youth	Greco, Murrell, & Coyne, 2005	C, Ad	17 items	*	.90 to .93	Good
Child Acceptance and Mindfulness Measure	Greco & Baer, 2006	C, Ad	25 items	*	.84	Good
Diabetes Acceptance and Action Scale for Children and Adolescents	Greco & Hart, 2005	C, Ad	42 items	*	*	Good
Difficulties in Emotion Regulation Scale	Gratz & Roemer, 2004	A	36 items	.88	.93	Good
Kentucky Inventory of Mindfulness Skills	Baer, Smith, & Allen, 2004	A	39 items	.65 to .86	.79 to .91	Good
Mindfulness Attention Awareness Scale	Brown & Ryan, 2003	A	15 items	*	.82 to .87	Good
Mindful Thinking and Action Scale for Adolescents	West, Sbraga, and Poole, 2007	Ad	32 items	*	.63 to .85	*
Parental Acceptance and Action Questionnaire	Ehrenreich & Cheron, 2005	C, Ad	15 items	.68 and .74	.64 to .65	Good
Personal Striving Assessment	Emmons, 1986	A	15 items in 8 domains	*	.73 to .77	*
Personal Values Questionnaire	Blackledge & Ciarrochi, 2006a	Ad, A	9 items in 9 domains	*	*	*
Psychological Inflexibility in Pain Scale	Wicksell, Renöfält, Olsson, Bond, & Melin, 2007	A	16 items	*	.75 and .90	Good
Social Values Survey	Blackledge & Ciarrochi, 2006b	Ad, A	9 items in 3 domains	*	*	*
Valued Living Questionnaire	Wilson & Groom, 2002	Ad, A	2 items in 10 domains	.75 to .90	.75	*

Note: A = Adult, C = Child, Ad = Adolescent. * = Data Unavailable.

.86. When compared with the MAAS, the KIMS act with awareness subscale correlated highly with the MAAS. The KIMS's convergent validity was further demonstrated by significant positive correlations with measures of emotional intelligence (Trait Meta-Mood Scale; Salovey, Mayer, Goldman, Turvey, & Palfai, 1995) and significant negative correlations with measures of experiential avoidance and psychological symptoms.

Experiential Avoidance

Individuals may over-rely on experiential avoidance, or attempts to alter, control, or minimize unwanted psychological experiences (Hayes et al., 1999). Psychological acceptance can be conceptualized as the opposite of experiential avoidance and refers to willingness to accept one's thoughts, emotions, and physiological sensations without evaluation. When individuals hold a compassionate and nonjudgmental stance toward their own psychological experience, they are generally more able to effectively pursue valued goals (see Hayes et al., 2006). As is the case with mindfulness, experiential avoidance and action are often assessed via self-report.

Acceptance and Action Questionnaire (AAQ; Hayes et al., 2004). Having undergone several revisions, the AAQ and the subsequent AAQ-2 were constructed to measure experiential avoidance, immobility (e.g., inability to engage in valued action), acceptance, and action. All versions of the AAQ are scored on a seven-point Likert scale. Originally consisting of forty-nine items, the AAQ was subject to rigorous psychometric analysis (Hayes et al., 2004) resulting in a nine-item version consisting of a single factor measuring experiential avoidance in which high scores indicate more experiential avoidance and low scores indicate greater levels of acceptance and action.

Validation of the AAQ was conducted on 1,349 participants with a mean age of 20.2 years. Internal consistency of the nine-item version was reported at .70. The test-retest reliability of the nine-item AAQ is approximately .64 over a four-month time period. To assess the convergent validity of the AAQ, it was compared with measures of a similar nature, such as the White Bear Suppression Inventory (WBSI; Wegner & Zanakos, 1994), as well as measures likely to be correlated with AAQ responses, including the Beck Depression Inventory (BDI; Beck, Rush, Shaw, & Emory, 1979), the Beck Anxiety Inventory (BAI; Beck, Epstein, Brown, & Steer, 1988), and the Quality of Life Inventory (QoL; Frisch, 1992). The AAQ displayed the highest correlations with measures of thought suppression (WBSI; r = .44 to .50; Hayes et al., 2004; Bond & Bunce, 2003) suggesting acceptable validity. The AAQ also demonstrated correlations with additional measures of thought suppression (Thought Control Questionnaire, TCQ; Wells & Davies, 1994), avoidance coping (e.g., Ways of Coping Questionnaire, WOC; Folkman & Lazarus, 1988), depression and anxiety (e.g., BDI, BAI), traumatic stress (e.g., Trauma Symptom Inventory, TSI; Briere, 1995), quality of life (e.g., QoL), and health behavior (General Health Questionnaire-12, GHQ-12; Goldberg, 1978). This suggests that the common core processes of experiential avoidance may cut across a broad range of constructs, thereby providing a unique view of avoidance behavior (see Hayes et al., 2004, for more discussion).

Action Orientation

Action orientation refers to awareness of, and movement toward, one's personal goals. Although not precisely a mindfulness-related construct, personal striving is certainly related to and may be useful in assessing personal efficacy in the pursuit of valued ends.

Personal Striving Assessment (PSA; Emmons, 1986). The PSA assesses motives for personal goals (e.g., extrinsic versus intrinsic), and the results represent respondents' personal striving in relation to extrinsic versus intrinsic motivations (see Sheldon & Kasser, 1995, 1998, 2001). This measure may be useful in the mindfulness literature to empirically assess the relationship between personal goals and components of subjective well-being (Ciarrochi & Bilich, 2006). Respondents are asked to rate how much they are pursuing these goals on an eight-point Likert scale. Limited psychometric data are available for the PSA, which demonstrated adequate internal consistency, with alphas ranging from .73 to .77 (see Sheldon & Kasser, 2001).

Emotion Regulation

Emotion regulation is related to psychological acceptance as it refers one's awareness of emotions and ability to act effectively when difficult emotions are experienced (see Gratz & Roemer, 2004). In contrast, *emotion dysregulation* involves ineffective attempts to manage difficult emotions and in some traditions is conceptualized as a core component of psychopathology (e.g., Linehan, 1993).

Difficulties in Emotion Regulation Scale (DERS; Gratz & Roemer, 2004). The DERS is a thirty-six-item self-report of clinically relevant difficulties in regulating emotions in adults. The content of items on the DERS was structured to assess four dimensions of emotion regulation: (1) awareness and understanding of emotions (e.g., "I am attentive to my feelings" [reverse scored]; "I have difficulty making sense of my feelings"); (2) acceptance of emotions (e.g., "When I am upset, I feel ashamed of myself for feeling that way"); (3) ability to engage in goal-directed behavior and refrain from impulsive behavior when experiencing negative emotions (e.g., "When I am upset, I believe that there is nothing I can do to make myself feel better"); and (4) access to emotion regulation strategies perceived to be effective (e.g., "When I am upset, I have difficulty thinking about anything else"; "When I'm upset, I become out of control"). Respondents are asked to indicate the extent to which items apply to themselves on a five-point Likert scale, with high scores reflecting greater difficulties with emotion regulation.

When subject to factor analysis (Gratz & Roemer, 2004), data indicate that the DERS has a six-factor structure, yielding six subscales: nonacceptance of emotional responses, goal-directed behavior, impulse control difficulties, lack of emotional awareness, limited access to emotion regulation strategies, and lack of emotional clarity. The DERS has demonstrated high internal consistency ($\alpha = .93$) based on research with 357 undergraduate psychology participants with a mean age of 23.10 years (Gratz & Roemer, 2004). Additionally, temporal stability calculated from a sample of 21 participants was good over a four- to eight-week period ($r_I = .88$, $p < .01$). The DERS also accounted for additional clinical constructs and behavioral outcomes when compared to other measures of mood regulation, indicating adequate validity for this measure (Gratz & Roemer, 2004).

Affective Control Scale (ACS; Williams, Chambless, & Ahrens, 1997). The ACS is a forty-two-item measure that was designed to assess fear of losing control over one's emotions as well as behavioral reactions to these emotions. Items are rated on a seven-point Likert scale, with higher scores signaling a greater fear of emotional responding. The measure is composed of four scales: (1) fear of anger (e.g., "I am concerned that I will say things I'll regret when I am angry"); (2) fear of depression (e.g., "Depression is scary to me—I'm afraid that I could get depressed and never recover"); (3) fear of anxiety (e.g., "I am afraid that I will babble or talk funny when I am nervous"); and (4) fear of positive emotion (e.g., "I can get too carried away when I am really happy"). The ACS has good overall internal consistency (α = ,93 to .94; Williams et al., 1997); however, alphas have been variable across subscale items (alpha = .45 to .91; Shapiro, 1995; Roemer, Salters, Raffa, & Orsillo, 2005). Test-retest reliability was also demonstrated to be acceptable ($r = .78$) for the total score (Williams et al., 1997). The ACS displayed good validity through significant positive correlations with measures of neuroticism (Williams et al., 1997), as well as the finding that the three nonanxiety subscales predict fear of laboratory-induced panic sensations above and beyond that accounted for by the anxiety subscale alone (see Roemer et al., 2005; Williams et al., 1997).

Psychological Flexibility

Psychological inflexibility, or the unwillingness or inability to engage in a broad repertoire of behaviors informed by situational contingencies, is at the heart of many psychological disorders (Hayes et al., 2006). *Psychological flexibility*, on the other hand, is conceptualized as a primary treatment goal in ACT and refers to one's ability to engage in values-consistent action even in the presence of great psychological pain.

Psychological Inflexibility in Pain Scale (PIPS; Wicksell, Renöfält, Olsson, Bond, & Melin, 2007). The PIPS is a sixteen-item measure currently under development that assesses avoidance of pain as well as fusion with pain in adults with chronic pain.

Although current research on the PIPS is limited to adult populations, the measure does not seemingly preclude adolescent or even child respondents on the basis of complexity. Recent psychometric analysis has been conducted on 203 patients with pain duration of between three and six hundred months (M = 132 months). Patients were nineteen to seventy years old (M = 45.5 years). Results of factor analysis yielded a two-factor solution that included an avoidance factor (e.g., "I postpone things on account of my pain") and a fusion factor (e.g., "It is important to understand what causes my pain"). Data indicate acceptable internal consistency, with alpha levels between .75 and .90. Furthermore, regression analyses indicate that the PIPS contributed significantly to the prediction of pain severity, interference, life control, and affective distress, as well as physical and mental well-being and quality of life (Wicksell et al., 2007).

Valued Action

Concepts of mindfulness, emotion regulation, and psychological flexibility are important insofar as they help individuals effectively pursue the things that they most care about. Valuing refers to pursuits that are inspiring and meaningful in an individuals' life. Effective pursuit of what one holds as most important is another important therapeutic goal in ACT. Several questionnaires have been developed to assess the extent to which individuals engage in values-consistent behavior.

Valued Living Questionnaire (VLQ; Wilson & Groom, 2002). The VLQ is a clinical tool used to assess ten domains of living and the values associated with each of those domains in adults. Respondents are asked to first assign a level of importance to each of the domains: family, marriage/couples/intimate relations, parenting, friendship, work, education, recreation, spirituality, citizenship, and physical self-care. The measure indicates that respondents are not expected to hold personally important values across all domains. Following these initial ratings, respondents are then asked to rate how consistent their actions have been with each of these value domains over the past week (e.g., "Rate the importance of each area by circling a number on a scale of 1–10. Now, rate how much energy or effort you have put into each of these areas within the past two weeks"). Adequate test-retest reliability with college-age students has been demonstrated (r = .75 to .90) and available data indicate acceptable internal consistency of items (α = .75). The authors believe that assessing and examining values of individuals helps address adversity. Adversity is considered an important part of life, and the reaction to adversity, namely acceptance, is important to mindful actions. Understanding an adolescent's values in these domains may help address the tendency to avoid situations when personal values conflict or when adolescents fail to take action congruent with their values (Greco & Eifert, 2004; Wilson & Murrell, 2004).

Child and Adolescent Measures

Although significant theoretical and psychometric research has been conducted to determine reliable and valid measures of adult mindfulness and acceptance, efforts directed at examining how to best capture these constructs in the assessment of children and adolescents are much more recent. While the measurement of adult mindfulness is complicated by the fact that items are "too darned complex," the measurement of child mindfulness and acceptance might be considered even more daunting, given the developmental and neurological changes that occur during childhood and adolescence (Dahl, 2004; Segalowitz & Davies, 2004). Nonetheless, the majority of existent assessment measures available for children and adolescents follow similar theoretical lines to those associated with mindfulness in adults, namely awareness, avoidance, fusion, and action orientation.

Acceptance and Mindfulness

Mindfulness is conceptualized as an important and useful skill in children and adolescents. Recent efforts have focused on carefully tailoring the measure of mindfulness in developmentally sensitive ways for youth.

Child Acceptance and Mindfulness Measure (CAMM; Greco & Baer, 2006). The CAMM is a twenty-five-item measure designed to assess the extent to which children and adolescents observe internal experiences (e.g., "I pay close attention to my thoughts"), act with awareness (e.g., "I walk from class to class without noticing what I'm doing" [reverse scored]), and accept internal experiences without judgment (e.g., "I get upset with myself for having certain thoughts" [reverse scored]). Respondents use a five-point Likert scale to indicate the degree to which the items on the measure reflect their experiences. After reverse scoring negatively worded items, scores are obtained by summing the item total, yielding a possible range of scores from 0 to 100. The CAMM addresses the core aspects of attention, awareness, and acceptance that complement the current trends in defining mindfulness.

Much like the MAAS and KIMS, the CAMM provides an overall measure of mindfulness where higher scores indicate greater levels of mindfulness and acceptance. However, the construction and wording of the CAMM make it far more appropriate for younger respondents, and it has been used with children and adolescents between the ages of nine and eighteen years. The CAMM was evaluated with a sample of 606 public middle school students with a mean age of 12.8 years; 62 percent were girls, and 81 percent were Caucasian. Empirical analysis indicates that the CAMM has good internal consistency ($\alpha = .84$). Concurrent validity has also been supported for the CAMM. The CAMM correlates negatively with the Avoidance and Fusion Questionnaire for Youth ($r = -.47$; AFQ-Y; Greco, Murrell, & Coyne, 2005) and measures of cognitive suppression ($r = -.36$, WBSI; Greco et al., 2007).

Mindful Thinking and Action Scale for Adolescents (MTASA; West, Sbraga, and Poole, 2007). Developed through consultation with experts in the mindfulness field as well as critical review of the mindfulness literature, the MTASA is a thirty-two-item measure designed to assess mindful thinking and actions in children and adolescents ages eleven to nineteen years. Results of exploratory factor analysis yielded four factors: (1) healthy self-regulation (e.g., "Others could describe me as patient with myself"), (2) active attention (e.g., "I plan before I act on my ideas"), (3) awareness and observation (e.g., "I feel my moods in my body"), and (4) accepting experience (e.g., "It is interesting to sit quietly"). These subscales are indicative of the notion that the MTASA provides a theoretically driven sampling of mindfulness across several domains. The authors of the measure exerted significant effort to construct a measure that was comprehensible to younger populations and indicate that it may also be useful for other populations who have fewer opportunities for autonomy, such as those in residential facilities or incarcerated individuals. In a sample of 163 children and adolescents ages eleven to nineteen years (M = 15.7 years), internal consistency ranged from .63 to .85 across subscales, and reading level for the MTASA was determined to be at the fourth-grade level.

Psychological Inflexibility

Adult measures of psychological flexibility such as the AAQ may be useful for older adolescents; however, it may be difficult for younger children to understand its item content. Thus, recent efforts have been made to develop child-friendly measures of psychological inflexibility characterized by high levels of experiential avoidance and cognitive fusion ("getting stuck" on one's thoughts).

Avoidance and Fusion Questionnaire for Youth (AFQ-Y; Greco, Murrell, & Coyne, 2005). The AFQ-Y is a seventeen-item self-report measure designed to assess child and adolescent psychological inflexibility characterized by high levels of experiential avoidance (e.g., "I push away thoughts and feelings that I don't like"), cognitive fusion (e.g., "The bad things I think about myself must be true"), and behavioral ineffectiveness in the presence of unpleasant emotions (e.g., "I do worse in school when I have thoughts that make me feel sad"). Items were modeled on the AAQ (Hayes et al., 2004) and constructed to contain appropriate content and structure for a youth population. Independent expert raters assisted in the creation and modification of these items. Items are rated on a five-point Likert scale with high scores indicating greater psychological inflexibility. In a subsequent psychometric analysis, a one-factor solution reflecting psychological inflexibility was supported.

Greco, Lambert, and Baer (in press) administered the AFQ-Y to 1,369 children and adolescents across five samples, ranging in age from nine to seventeen. Approximately 55 percent of participants were girls, and 80 percent were Caucasian. The authors reported good internal consistency (Cronbach's α = .90 to .93) and convergent validity. Scores on the AFQ-Y correlated positively with measures of child internalizing symptoms and externalizing behavior problems and negatively with quality of life. Construct validity of the AFQ-Y was also supported through negative correlations with measures of mindfulness and acceptance (*r* = −.44 to −.53, CAMM) and positive correlations with measures of thought suppression (*r* = .55, WBSI; see Greco et al., in press).

Action Orientation

An alternative measure to the VLQ is the Personal Values Questionnaire (PVQ), which may be more useful with children and adolescents. Assessing effectiveness in pursuing personal goals may be an important process and outcome measure in ACT-based treatment models.

Personal Values Questionnaire (PVQ; Blackledge & Ciarrochi, 2006a) and Social Values Survey (SVS; Blackledge & Ciarrochi, 2006b). The PVQ and SVS are adaptations of the Personal Striving Assessment, and both assess value origins, importance, and commitment. The PVQ assesses the values of adolescents and adults across nine separate domains: family relationships, friendships/social relationships, couples/romantic relationships, work/career, education/schooling, recreation/leisure/sport, spirituality/religion, community/citizenship, and health/physical well-being. Respondents are asked to list values they hold in each of these domains. Children and adolescents then rate items on a five-point Likert scale to indicate how the value relates to them (e.g., "I value this because I would feel ashamed, guilty, or anxious if I didn't"; "I value this because doing these things makes my life better, more meaningful, and/or more vital"), how successful and committed they have been to their value, how personally important the value is, and how much they desire to improve their adherence to these values. After scoring, determinations can also be made as to whether respondents have intrinsic or extrinsic motives for their values.

The SVS is similar in its construction but directs youth and adults to respond to values held in social and interpersonal relations, including friendship/social relationships, family relationships, and couples relationships. Item responses are organized in the same manner as the PVQ, and the resulting information yields indications of a respondent's extrinsic or intrinsic motivations for interpersonal interactions. Although formal psychometric data are not yet available for the PVQ or SVS, data soon to be published indicate that youth who score high on intrinsic items may experience more joy and less sadness, and those with more extrinsic motives may experience more hostility (Ciarrochi & Bilich, 2006; Blackledge, personal communication, May 9, 2007).

Mindfulness and Assessment in the Parenting Context

The degree to which parents are able to be mindful and accepting of their own—or their children's—difficult emotions may have a positive impact on children's emotional development and behavior. Thus examining parental mindfulness constructs through formal assessment may help guide case conceptualization and treatment efforts.

Parental Acceptance and Action Questionnaire (PAAQ; Ehrenreich & Cheron, 2005). The PAAQ was developed with the expressed intent of administering such a measure to parents of children, requiring them to reflect on their emotional and behavioral experiences with their child and their own reactions to those experiences. The PAAQ is a fifteen-item measure composed of modified items from the AAQ (Hayes et al., 2004; Bond & Bunce, 2003) and is purported to measure the degree of experiential avoidance in the parenting context. The items were changed to reflect parenting experiences (e.g., "I am able to take action about my fears, worries, and feelings even if I am uncertain what is the right thing to do" was changed to "I am able to take action about my child's fears, worries, and feelings even if I am uncertain what is the right thing to do"). Parents respond to the fifteen items on a seven-point Likert scale indicating how true the item is for them. After reverse scoring negatively worded items, scores are obtained by summing the item total. Results of exploratory factor analysis revealed a two-factor structure consisting of a parental action subscale (e.g., "When I feel depressed or anxious, I am unable to help my child manage their fears, worries, or feelings") and a parental willingness subscale (e.g., "It's OK for my child to feel depressed or anxious").

High scores on the parental action factor indicate parental hesitancy to engage in child emotion management. High scores on the parental willingness factor indicate parental avoidance or inability to tolerate heightened emotional experiences in themselves or their child (Cheron, 2006). While currently still undergoing psychometric testing and modification, the PAAQ has been administered to the parents of 154 children and adolescents ranging in ages from six to eighteen and a half years old (M = 11.9 years). Participants were 59 percent female and 80 percent Caucasian. The PAAQ has evidenced moderate levels of internal consistency (alpha = .64 to .65 across scales) and temporal stability (correlations between .68 and .74 across scales). Furthermore, convergent validity of the PAAQ is supported by positive correlations with measures of child psychopathology and behavior problems (Child Behavior Checklist, CBCL; Achenbach, 1991) as well as measures of parental control (Parental Locus of Control, PLOC; Campis, Lyman, & Prentice-Dunn, 1986). Additionally, regression analyses indicate that, when holding parents' psychopathology symptom report and parents' own experiential avoidance constant, the PAAQ predicts a significant amount of variance in child psychopathology (Cheron, 2006).

Mindfulness and Acceptance in Pediatric Populations

Mindfulness-based assessments are being incorporated into new and varied clinical settings at a very fast pace. This incorporation has resulted in the development of additional mindfulness measures to suit the individual needs of different populations, such as children and adolescents seen in pediatric settings. New applications for mindfulness and acceptance measures continue to be developed, and the pediatric measure described below is only one of several currently and soon to be available measures.

Diabetes Acceptance and Action Scale for Children and Adolescents (DAAS; Greco & Hart, 2005). The DAAS is a forty-two-item measure currently utilized in pediatric settings to investigate the degree of psychological flexibility in children who have been diagnosed with type 1 diabetes. Responses are given on a five-point Likert scale reflecting the degree to which the item is perceived to be true about the respondent. After reverse scoring negatively worded items, scores are obtained by summing the item total. High scores indicate greater levels of acceptance and action. Items on the DAAS assess constructs such as acceptance (e.g., "It's OK to feel sad or afraid about having diabetes"), experiential avoidance (e.g., "I play video games or use the internet to take my mind off of my health"), and cognitive fusion (e.g., "Thoughts about diabetes can really hurt me"). Preliminary data indicate significant positive correlations between the DAAS and diabetes-related quality of life ($r = .36$) as well as adherence to medical regimes ($r = .30$) and significant negative correlations with diabetes-related worry ($r = -.41$) and social anxiety ($r = -.36$; Ciarrochi and Bilich, 2006).

Ongoing Studies: Emerging Measures and Methodologies

Emerging research in the assessment of acceptance and mindfulness processes has also involved the development of observational coding systems. Observational assessment of experiential avoidance and experiential acceptance is a complex undertaking, as both of these constructs are functionally defined. To date, there are two relevant ongoing studies involving behavioral assessment of experiential avoidance as well as acceptance and mindfulness. Coyne, Burke, and Davis (2006) have developed a coding system to assess experiential avoidance and acceptance, as well as willingness in the context of a family-based cognitive behavioral treatment for young children with OCD. Specifically, this coding system measures parent, child, and therapist experiential avoidance/acceptance, as well as motivational variables such as parent and child engagement in treatment and homework compliance. Initial reliability analyses suggest the promise of this coding system, although this work is still in its infancy (Coyne et al., 2006).

Similarly, Silvia and Coyne (2008) are currently investigating the role of mindfulness in parent-child interaction. Recent work has linked experiential avoidance with parents' negative emotional experiences and ineffective parenting (Berlin, Sato,

Jastrowski, Woods, & Davies, 2006; Greco, Heffner, and Poe, 2005; Coyne, Burke, et al., 2006), and mindfulness processes with improved outcomes for parents (Blackledge & Hayes, 2006) and children (Singh et al., 2006). However, to date, no studies have linked these processes to parenting sequences that are behaviorally observed in parent-child interactions. Thus the goals of the Silvia and Coyne study are threefold: (1) to investigate whether experiential avoidance is related to behaviorally observed parenting behaviors during a parent-child interaction task, (2) to explore the relationship between parental risk status and experiential avoidance, and (3) to compare parenting behaviors of mothers who have been randomly assigned to a brief mindfulness exercise to those in an attentional control condition. Data collection is ongoing; however, use of this methodology may prove fruitful in elucidating whether and how mindfulness may be used to help parents use effective parenting skills in difficult or challenging situations with their children.

Other directions in which to explore assessment of experiential avoidance and mindfulness involve the use of narrative technologies. For example, Schwartzman and Wahler (2006) have studied increasing coherence in parent narratives about their children and parenting difficulties as a means of improving adherence to parent training protocols. Restructuring narratives involves elements of mindfulness, including purposeful attention and self-monitoring, and thus evaluating degree of coherence may constitute a useful methodology for assessment. In a similar vein, Coyne, Low, Miller, Seifer, and Dickstein (2006) have assessed mothers' mindful awareness of their children using indices of attunement and representation of their children. Generally, these indices described mothers' empathic understanding of their children and their ability to describe their motives, predict their behaviors, and integrate new and unexpected information into their existing perspectives of their child. The investigators found that mothers who demonstrated greater attunement to and representation of their children reported less depression, fewer child behaviors problems, and higher levels of observed sensitive parenting behaviors (Coyne, Low, et al., 2006).

Conclusion

Assessment of mindfulness and acceptance, as well as related processes such as experiential avoidance, is in its beginning stages. However, establishing objective, reliable, and valid measures is a critical step in ascertaining the importance of acceptance-related processes in overt behavioral outcomes. Perhaps the most important direction in which to expand this small but steadily growing literature involves more precise specification of constructs being measured, and their relationship to therapeutic processes and outcomes.

Most emerging measures of acceptance, mindfulness, and related processes are self-report. Ideally these measures would exhibit adequate specificity and sensitivity to change over time and over the course of treatment. This is especially true in treatment focused on increasing acceptance and committed action. The use of interview techniques is embedded in a number of different treatment approaches; however, as with all clinician-administered or -interpreted interview tools, these may have low reliability in terms of decision-making value. More objective measures of these processes would also be sufficiently flexible and correspond with functional definitions of mindfulness and acceptance. For these reasons, the development of observational coding systems that can be translated to the context of therapy may be a promising supplemental approach. Assessment of physiological reactivity may also be useful in evaluating the degree of mindful awareness/acceptance, as well as experiential avoidance of noxious internal stimuli.

In sum, measurement of assessment and mindfulness processes has proven a difficult and yet extremely worthwhile task. Assessing these processes in children also stands to advance our knowledge of developmental psychopathology as well as socioemotional and cognitive processes throughout childhood and adolescence. The development and empirical validation of developmentally sensitive measures are also critical in informing acceptance- and mindfulness-based treatment approaches for youth.

References

Achenbach, T. M. (1991). *Integrative Guide to the 1991 CBCL/4-18, YSR, and TRF Profiles.* Unpublished manuscript, University of Vermont, Burlington, Department of Psychology.

Baer, R. A. (2003). Mindfulness training as a clinical intervention: A conceptual and empirical review. *Clinical Psychology: Science and Practice, 10*, 125–143.

Baer, R. A., Smith, G. T., & Allen, K. B. (2004). Assessment of mindfulness by self-report: The Kentucky Inventory of Mindfulness Skills. *Assessment, 11*(3), 191–206.

Barlow, D. H., Craske, M. G., Cerny, J. A., & Klosko, J. S. (1989). Behavioral treatment of panic disorder. *Behavior Therapy, 20,* 261–282.

Beck, A. T., Epstein, N., Brown, G. K., & Steer, R. A. (1988). An inventory for measuring clinical anxiety: Psychometric properties. *Journal of Consulting and Clinical Psychology, 56,* 893–897.

Beck, A. T., Rush, A. J., Shaw, B. R., & Emery, G. (1979). *Cognitive therapy of depression.* New York: Guilford.

Berlin, K. S., Sato, A. F., Jastrowski, K. E., Woods, D. W., & Davies, W. H. (2006, November). Effects of experiential avoidance on parenting practices and adolescent outcomes. Paper presented at the Association for Behavioral and Cognitive Therapies Annual Convention, Chicago.

Blackledge, J. T., & Ciarrochi, J. (2006a). *Personal Values Questionnaire.* Available from the first author at University of Wollongong, New South Wales, Australia.

Blackledge, J. T., & Ciarrochi, J. (2006b). *Social Values Survey*. Available from the first author at University of Wollongong, New South Wales, Australia.

Blackledge, J. T., & Hayes, S. C. (2006). Using acceptance and commitment training in the support of parents with children diagnosed with autism. *Child and Family Behavior Therapy, 28*, 1–18.

Bond, F. W., & Bunce, D. (2003). The role of acceptance and job control in mental health, job satisfaction, and work performance. *Journal of Applied Psychology, 88*, 1057–1067.

Bouton, M. E., Mineka, S., & Barlow, D. H. (2001). A modern learning theory perspective on the etiology of panic disorder. *Psychological Review, 108*, 2–32.

Briere, J. (1995). *Trauma symptom inventory professional manual.* Odessa, FL: Psychological Assessment Resources.

Brown, K., & Ryan, R. (2003). The benefits of being present: Mindfulness and its role in psychological well-being. *Journal of Personality and Social Psychology, 84*, 822–848.

Campis, L. K., Lyman, R. D., & Prentice-Dunn, S. (1986). The Parental Locus of Control Scale: Development and validation. *Journal of Clinical Child Psychology, 15*(3), 260–267.

Cheron, D. M. (2006, November). Assessing parental experiential avoidance: Preliminary psychometric data from the Parental Acceptance and Action Questionnaire (PAAQ). In panel discussion, "Experiential Avoidance and Mindfulness in Parenting," D. M. Cheron & J. T. Ehrenreich (Moderators). Presented at the 40th Annual Convention of the Association for Cognitive and Behavioral Therapies, Chicago.

Ciarrochi, J., & Bilich, L. (2006). Acceptance and commitment measures packet: Process measures of potential relevance to ACT. Retrieved February 11, 2007, from University of Wollongong website, www.uow.edu.au/health/iimh/act_researchgroup/resources.html.

Ciarrochi, J., & Blackledge, J. (2006). Mindfulness-based emotional intelligence training: A new approach to reducing human suffering and promoting effectiveness. In J. Ciarrochi, J. Forgas, & J. Mayer. (Eds.), *Emotional intelligence in everyday life: A scientific inquiry* (2nd ed., pp. 206-228). New York: Psychology Press/Taylor & Francis.

Coyne, L. W., Burke, A., & Davis, E. (2006). *Observational coding manual: Assessing therapist, parent, and child behavioral and emotional avoidance in the context of exposure-based treatment.* Available from the first author at the Psychology Department, Suffolk University, Boston, MA.

Coyne, L. W., Burke, A., & Davis, E. (2008). *Emotion avoidance in families of young children with OCD.* Manuscript in preparation.

Coyne, L. W., Low, C. L., Miller, A. M., Seifer, R., & Dickstein, S. (2006). Mothers' empathic understanding of their toddlers: Associations with maternal depression and sensitivity. *Journal of Child and Family Studies, 16*, 483–497.

Dahl, R. (2004). Adolescent brain development: A period of vulnerabilities and opportunities. *Annals of the New York Academy of Sciences, 1021*, 1–22.

Ehrenreich, J. T., & Cheron, D. M. (2005). Parental Acceptance and Action Questionnaire. Available from Daniel M. Cheron, Department of Psychology, Boston University.

Emmons, R. A. (1986). Personal strivings: An approach to personality and subjective well-being. *Journal of Personality and Social Psychology, 51*, 1058–1068.

Folkman, S., & Lazarus, R. S. (1988). *Ways of Coping Questionnaire Manual.* Palo Alto, CA: Mind Garden/Consulting Psychologists Press.

Fresco, D., Williams, N. L., & Nugent, N. R. (2006). Flexibility and negative affect: Examining the associations of explanatory flexibility and coping flexibility to each other and to depression and anxiety. *Cognitive Therapy and Research, 30*, 201–210.

Frisch, M. B. (1992). Use of the Quality of Life Inventory in problem assessment and treatment planning for cognitive therapy of depression. In A. Freeman & F. M. Dattilio (Eds.), *Comprehensive casebook of cognitive therapy* (pp. 27–52). New York: Plenum.

Goldberg, D. (1978). *Manual of the General Health Questionnaire.* Windsor, England: National Foundation for Educational Research.

Gratz, K. L., & Roemer, L. (2004). Multidimensional assessment of emotion regulation and dysregulation: Development, factor structure, and initial validation of the Difficulties in Emotion Regulation Scale. *Journal of Psychopathology and Behavioral Assessment, 26*(1), 41–54.

Greco, L. A., & Baer, R. A. (2006). Child Acceptance and Mindfulness Measure (CAMM). Available from the first author at Department of Psychology, University of Missouri, St. Louis.

Greco, L. A., & Eifert, G. H. (2004). Treating parent-adolescent conflict: Is acceptance the missing link for an integrative family therapy? *Cognitive and Behavioral Practice, 11*, 305–314.

Greco, L., A., & Hart, T. A. (2005). Diabetes Acceptance and Action Scale for Children and Adolescents. Available from the first author at Department of Psychology, University of Missouri, St. Louis.

Greco, L. A., Heffner, M., & Poe, S. (2005). Maternal adjustment following preterm birth: Contributions of experiential avoidance. *Behavior Therapy, 36*, 177–184.

Greco, L. A., Lambert, W., & Baer, R. A. (in press). Psychological inflexibility in childhood and adolescence: Development and evaluation of the Avoidance and Fusion Questionnaire for Youth. *Psychological Assessment.*

Greco, L. A., Murrell, A. R., & Coyne, L. W. (2005). Avoidance and Fusion Questionnaire for Youth. Available from the first author at Department of Psychology, University of Missouri, St. Louis, and online at www.contextualpsychology.org.

Hayes, S. C., Luoma, J. B., Bond, F. W., Masuda, A., & Lillis, J. (2006). Acceptance and Commitment Therapy: Model processes and outcomes. *Behaviour Research and Therapy, 44,* 1–25.

Hayes, S. C., & Shenk, C. (2004). Operationalizing mindfulness without unnecessary attachments. *Clinical Psychology: Science and Practice, 11,* 249–254.

Hayes, S. C., Strosahl, K., & Wilson, K. G. (1999). *Acceptance and commitment therapy: An experiential approach to behavior change.* New York: Guilford.

Hayes, S. C., Strosahl, K. D., Wilson, K. G., Bissett, R. T., Pistorello, J., Toarmino, D., et al. (2004). Measuring experiential avoidance: A preliminary test of a working model. *The Psychological Record,* 54, 553–578.

Hayes, S. C., & Wilson, K. G. (2003). Mindfulness: Method and process. *Clinical Psychology: Science and Practice, 10,* 161–165.

Hayes, S. C., Wilson, K. G., Gifford, E. V., Follette, V. M., & Strosahl, K. (1996). Experiential avoidance and behavioral disorders: A functional dimensional approach to diagnosis and treatment. *Journal of Consulting and Clinical Psychology, 64,* 1152–1168.

Kazdin, A. E., & Nock, M. K. (2003). Delineating mechanisms of change in child and adolescent therapy: Methodological issues and research recommendations. *Journal of Child Psychology and Psychiatry, 44,* 1116–1129.

Linehan, M. M. (1987). Dialectical behavioral therapy: A cognitive-behavioral approach to parasuicide. *Journal of Personality Disorders, 1,* 328–333.

Linehan, M. M. (1993). *Cognitive-behavioral treatment of borderline personality disorder.* New York: Guilford.

Lonigan, C. J., Elbert, J. C., & Johnson, S. B. (1998). Empirically supported psychosocial interventions for children: An overview. *Journal of Clinical Child Psychology, 27,* 138–145.

Orsillo, S. M., Roemer, L., Block-Lerner, J., & Tull, M. T. (2004). Acceptance, mindfulness, and cognitive-behavioral therapy: Comparisons, contrasts, and application to anxiety. In S. C. Hayes, V. M. Follette, & M. M. Linehan (Eds.), *Mindfulness and acceptance: Expanding the cognitive-behavioral tradition* (pp. 66–95). New York: Guilford.

Roemer, L., Salters, K., Raffa, S. D., & Orsillo, S. M. (2005). Fear and avoidance of internal experiences in GAD: Preliminary tests of a conceptual model. *Cognitive Therapy and Research, 29*(1), 71–88.

Salovey, P., Mayer, J. D., Goldman, S. L., Turvey, C., & Palfai, T. P. (1995). Emotional attention, clarity, and repair: Exploring emotional intelligence using the Trait Meta-Mood Scale. In J. W. Pennebaker (Ed.), *Emotion Disclosure and Health* (pp. 125–154). Washington, DC: APA.

Schwartzman, M. P., & Wahler, R. (2006). Enhancing the impact of parent training through narrative restructuring. *Child and Family Behavior Therapy, 28,* 49–65.

Segal, Z. V., Teasdale, J. D., & Williams, M. G. (2004). Mindfulness-based cognitive therapy: Theoretical rationale and empirical status. In S. C. Hayes, V. M. Follette, & M. M. Linehan (Eds.), *Mindfulness and acceptance: Expanding the cognitive-behavioral tradition* (pp. 45–65). New York: Guilford.

Segal, Z. V., Williams, M. G., & Teasdale, J. D. (2002). *Mindfulness-based cognitive therapy for depression: A new approach to preventing relapse.* New York: Guilford.

Segalowitz, S. J., & Davies, P. L. (2004). Charting the maturation of the frontal lobe: An electrophysiological strategy. *Brain and Cognition,* 55, 116–133.

Shapiro, N. (1995). *An analogue of agoraphobic avoidance as attachment-related symptomatology.* Unpublished master's thesis, Department of Psychology, the American University, Washington, DC.

Shapiro, S. L., Carlson, L. E., Astin, J. A., & Freedman, B. (2006). Mechanisms of mindfulness. *Journal of Clinical Psychology, 62,* 373–386.

Sheldon, K. M., & Kasser, T. (1995). Coherence and congruence: Two aspects of personality integration. *Journal of Personality and Social Psychology,* 68, 531–543.

Sheldon, K. M., & Kasser, T. (1998). Pursuing personal goals: Skills enable progress but not all progress is beneficial. *Personality and Social Psychology Bulletin, 24,* 1319–1331.

Sheldon, K. M., & Kasser, T. (2001). Getting older, getting better? Personal strivings and psychological maturity across the life span. *Developmental Psychology, 37*(4), 491–501.

Silvia, K. A., & Coyne, L. C. (2008). *Experiential avoidance and mindfulness in parenting: Preliminary data from an experimental study.* Manuscript in preparation.

Singh, N. N., Lancioni, G. E., Winton, A. S. W., Fisher, B. C., Wahler, R. G., McAleavey, K., et al. (2006). Mindful parenting decreases aggression, noncompliance, and self-injury in children with autism. *Journal of Emotional and Behavioral Disorders, 14,* 169–177.

Wegner, D. M. (1994). Ironic processes of mental control. *Psychological Review, 101,* 34–52.

Wegner, D. M., & Zanakos, S. (1994). Chronic thought suppression. *Journal of Personality, 62,* 615–640.

Wells, A., & Davies, M. I. (1994). The Thought Control Questionnaire: A measure of individual differences in the control of unwanted thoughts. *Behaviour Research and Therapy, 32,* 871–878.

Wenzlaff, R. M., Wegner, D. M., & Klein, S. B. (1991). The role of thought suppression in the bonding of thought and mood. *Journal of Personality and Social Psychology, 60,* 500–508.

West, A. M., Sbraga, T. P., & Poole, D. A. (2007). *Measuring mindfulness in youth: Development of the Mindful Thinking and Action Scale for Adolescents.* Unpublished manuscript, Central Michigan University.

Wicksell, R. K., Renöfält, J., Olsson, G. L., Bond, F. W., & Melin, L. (2007). *Avoidance and fusion: Central components in pain related disability? Development and preliminary validation of the Psychological Inflexibility in Pain Scale.* Manuscript in preparation, Astrid Lindgren Children's Hospital, Karolinska University Hospital, Stockholm, Sweden.

Williams, K. E., Chambless, D. L., & Ahrens, A. (1997). Are emotions frightening? An extension of the fear of fear construct. *Behaviour Research and Therapy, 35,* 239–248.

Wilson, K. G., & Groom, J. (2002). The Valued Living Questionnaire. Available from the first author at the University of Mississippi.

Wilson, K. G., & Murrell, A. R. (2004). Values work in acceptance and commitment therapy: Setting a course for behavioral treatment. In S. C. Hayes, V. M. Follette, & M. M. Linehan (Eds.), *Mindfulness and acceptance: Expanding the cognitive-behavioral tradition* (pp. 120–151). New York: Guilford.

Part 2

Applications to Specific Populations

Chapter 4

Treating Anxiety with Mindfulness: Mindfulness-Based Cognitive Therapy for Children

Randye J. Semple, Ph.D., College of Physicians and Surgeons, Columbia University; and Jennifer Lee, Ph.D., Teachers College, Columbia University

Anxiety disorders are the most common mental health problems of childhood. The one-year prevalence rate of childhood anxiety disorders is between 10 percent (Chavira, Stein, Bailey, & Stein, 2004) and 20 percent (Shaffer, Fisher, Dulcan, & Davies, 1996), with girls being more affected than boys. While children can develop any of the anxiety spectrum disorders at different stages of development, some are more common than others. Specific phobias appear frequently in young children, whereas generalized anxiety disorder, social anxiety disorder, and panic disorder are more common in middle childhood and adolescence (Barlow, 2002). About half of all children and adolescents with anxiety disorders have a secondary anxiety disorder or another diagnosis, such as depression (U.S. Department of Health and Human Services, 1999). In addition, these children are at increased risk to develop other problems in the future. Data from the National Comorbidity Survey suggest that anxiety disorders are the most common precursors to major depression (Kessler et al., 1996). Left untreated, children with anxiety disorders are also at higher risk for academic difficulties, social skills problems, and substance abuse.

Mindfulness with Children

Mindfulness-based group interventions for adults with anxiety disorders have gained popularity in recent years. However, as is typical in the early years of psychotherapy research, there has been little development or evaluation of mindfulness therapies for children. Although there are few clinical trials of mindfulness-based treatment approaches with children, these approaches do seem to be effective in reducing core anxiety symptoms in adults (see review by Baer, 2003). Clinical reports suggest that mindfulness techniques can be useful in treating anxiety symptoms in school-age children (Goodman, 2005; Greco, Blackledge, Coyne, & Ehrenreich, 2005; Semple, Reid, & Miller, 2005), so it seems reasonable to develop and evaluate mindfulness-based interventions for this population. In this chapter, we will describe the development, structure, and components of mindfulness-based cognitive therapy for children (MBCT-C), a twelve-session group therapy for anxious children ages nine to twelve years. We begin this chapter by defining mindfulness and then describe the theoretical basis of MBCT and research support for the effectiveness of this type of intervention in the treatment of childhood anxiety.

Mindfulness Defined

Consensus on an operational definition of mindfulness has not yet emerged. Most mindfulness practices can be conceptualized as techniques for training attention. Beyond that, idiosyncratic definitions abound (see discussion by Bishop et al., 2004). As we use it here, mindfulness means "paying attention in a particular way: on purpose, in the present moment, and nonjudgmentally" (Kabat-Zinn, 1994, p. 4). Mindfulness is a very specific type of attention that includes the qualities of intentionality, present focus, and nonjudgmental acceptance. In mindfulness, one's attention is consciously directed toward something specific, be it internal (thoughts, emotions, or body sensations) or external (via sense perceptions). Consequently, mindful attention also creates a particular relationship between the observer and the object of attention. In addition, mindfulness is frequently associated with conscious awareness, exploratory interest, nonattachment, and liberation.

Mindfulness and Mental Health

Buddhist psychology and cognitive theories inform our approach to treating anxiety with mindfulness. Buddhist psychology suggests that the root cause of suffering is not seeing clearly. It is our own thoughts, inaccurate beliefs, unrealistic expectations, and insatiable desires that obscure and distort our direct perceptions. Thinking is actually the problem, not (as we often assume) the solution. As human beings, we prefer familiarity and meaningfulness to uncertainty. To accomplish this, we create "connect-the-dot" pictures of experiences. In each moment, we modify the perceived event by adding inaccurate beliefs about the past, unrealistic expectations about the present, and unattainable desires about the future. When we connect all of these "moment-dots," a familiar picture appears that satisfies the need to make sense of our experiences. However, the dot-picture is not an accurate representation of the reality.

We do not see clearly; therefore, we suffer. Through the distorted dot-picture, we experience emotional distress, create inappropriate cognitive interpretations, and make unwise behavioral choices. For example, many of us believe that to be happy, we must avoid unpleasant experiences. Holding that belief, unhappiness arises each time we fall ill, we miss a flight, our car breaks down, or it rains on our picnic. When one of these events occurs, we vehemently want it to go away so that we can be happy again. From the Buddhist perspective, the development of pathological anxiety is in constructing a personal dot-picture that includes all the imaginary dots and then unhappily living in the delusion that the dot-picture accurately represents reality. However, we can learn to see which dots are imaginary and which are real by giving mindful attention to our present-moment experiences.

Attention and Anxiety

Attention is a multifaceted process and is a core component of consciousness. Attention can be diffuse or concentrated, vigilant or relaxed, inwardly or outwardly focused, shifting or still. Attentional problems are characteristic of most anxiety disorders. For example, difficulties shifting attention away is one quality of the ruminations associated with obsessive-compulsive disorder, while difficulty attending (i.e., poor concentration) is a symptom of generalized anxiety disorder. Specific phobias are associated with attentional bias toward the feared stimuli (Teasdale, 2004), while attentional avoidance is common in those showing post-traumatic stress symptoms. Self-focused attention is characteristic of children with social anxiety. In the extreme, the anxious self-observer has minimal awareness of external events.

Attention that is overly focused on past and future events is also characteristic of most childhood anxiety disorders. Mindfulness training offers practice in keeping one's attention in the present. Left unattended, normal anxiety can spiral out of control and produce significant impairments in functioning. Perhaps children can stop living with chronic, "automatic pilot" anxiety by giving mindful attention to this moment. Living in the present, they may find that this moment is manageable, even when it is not the most wonderful moment of all.

Only a few studies have investigated the direct relationship between mindfulness practices and the quality of attention, but there is some support for this relationship in adults (Semple, 1999; Valentine & Sweet, 1999) and in children (Rani & Rao, 1996; Semple, 2005). However, much more research is needed before we can definitively say that mindfulness-based interventions have a direct influence on attentional impairments.

Cognitive Theory and Mindfulness-Based Cognitive Therapy

The primary intent of cognitive therapy (CT) is to change patients' beliefs in their automatic thoughts and dysfunctional attitudes (Beck, 1976). For many years, it was generally accepted that CT effects changes by changing the content of maladaptive thinking. Segal, Williams, and Teasdale (2002) suggested that the effectiveness of CT may instead be the result of changing patients' relationships to their thoughts and feelings. Mindfulness-based cognitive therapy (MBCT; Teasdale et al., 2000) experientially validates this metacognitive perspective, which is referred to as *decentering*. Decentering describes one's ability to observe thoughts as just thoughts (rather than evidence of reality) and is considered the core component of therapeutic change. Decentering may sound relatively simple. It is not. Seeing clearly what is actually happening in the present moment is a demanding practice.

MBCT was developed as a treatment for the prevention of depressive relapse in adults and is largely based on mindfulness-based stress reduction (MBSR; Kabat-Zinn, 1994). MBSR and MBCT are structured eight-week group mindfulness training programs for adults. These programs emphasize direct experience with mindfulness techniques, and the integration of mindful practices into everyday life. Both programs call for instructors and therapists to develop an understanding of mindfulness that is based on sustained personal mindfulness practice. MBCT uses many of the same mindfulness training exercises as MBSR but also integrates elements of CT, which helps patients recognize the influence of depressogenic cognitions on mood and behaviors. Both MBSR and CT maintain an observing and accepting stance toward thoughts, emotions, and behaviors. Mindfulness-based cognitive therapy for children (MBCT-C) is a downward adaptation of MBCT.

Initial Evaluations of MBCT-C

Semple, Reid, and Miller (2005) conducted a six-week pilot study to examine the feasibility and acceptability of a mindfulness-based intervention for children. The authors concluded that mindfulness training is acceptable and teachable to children, and holds promise as an intervention for childhood anxiety.

The first randomized clinical trial of MBCT-C followed (Lee, 2006; Semple, 2005). Twenty-five clinic-referred children between the ages of nine and thirteen participated. There were fifteen girls and ten boys. All were from low-income, inner-city families, and mostly from minority ethnic/cultural backgrounds (fifteen Hispanic, seven African American, three Caucasian). Seventeen children (68 percent) completed the program. Completion was defined as attending ten of twelve sessions ($M_{sessions} = 11.3$, $SD = .77$). Five other children attended more sporadically ($M_{sessions} = 7.6$, $SD = 1.14$; Lee, Semple, Rosa, & Miller, in press). Significant reductions in attention problems were found as measured by the attention problems scale of the Child Behavior Checklist (CBCL; Achenbach, 1991). We found indications of clinical effectiveness for six children who initially reported clinically elevated levels of anxiety (Semple, 2005). The high recruitment (74 percent), retention (84 percent), and attendance rates (94 percent for those who completed the program; 78 percent for the intent-to-treat sample) provided initial support for the acceptability and feasibility of MBCT-C.

Getting from MBCT to MBCT-C

MBCT-C is a twelve-session group psychotherapy that was developed for children with anxiety and depression. Table 1 presents a summary of each session. As a downward extension of the adult MBCT protocol (Segal et al., 2002), MBCT-C required a number of age-appropriate changes.

Table 1. Overview of the Twelve-Session Program

Session 1	Developing community; defining expectations; emphasizing the importance of homework; orientation to mindfulness; mindful smiling while waking up exercise.
Session 2	Dealing with barriers to practice; introduction to mindfulness of the breath; eating a raisin exercise.
Session 3	Practice differentiating thoughts, feelings, and body sensations; introduction to mindful body movements (yoga postures).
Session 4	Mindful hearing; receptive listening exercise to identify thoughts, feelings, and body sensations; introduction to body scan exercise.
Session 5	Mindful hearing (continued); creating expressive sounds exercise; introduction to three-minute breathing space exercise.
Session 6	Mindful seeing; learning what we don't see; practice differentiation of judging from describing; guided imagery exercise.
Session 7	Mindful seeing (continued); practice directing attention; seeing optical illusions exercise; mindful movement exercise: be a flower opening, a tall tree, and a butterfly.
Session 8	Mindful touch; learning how to stay present with what is here right now; body scan exercise.
Session 9	Mindful smell; continue practice of differentiating between judging and describing; mindful body movements (yoga postures).
Session 10	Mindful taste; thoughts are not facts exercise; mindful body movements (yoga postures).

Session 11	Mindfulness in everyday life; review of previous sessions; integrating acceptance of experiences through mindfulness.
Session 12	Generalizing mindfulness to everyday life; exploring and sharing personal experiences of the program; brief graduation ceremony.

Developmental Adaptations

Developmental modifications addressed differences in children's attentional capacities, abstract reasoning, and family involvement.

Attentional capacity. Children have less refined attentional capacities than adults (Siegler, 1991). Consequently, children may benefit from shorter and more frequent sessions. MBCT-C thus consists of twelve ninety-minute sessions, instead of eight two-hour sessions as with MBCT for adults. Similarly, longer mindful breath and body exercises were replaced with shorter, more frequently repeated exercises.

Multisensory learning. Children demonstrate less capacity for abstract reasoning and verbal fluency than adults (Noshpitz & King, 1991). As a result, stories, games, and activities are commonly included in child protocols to increase engagement in treatment (Gaines, 1997). MBCT-C uses a variety of multisensory exercises that give children practice in mindfully experiencing the world via sight, sound, touch, taste, smell, and kinesthetics. Examples include drawing pictures, listening to or creating music, touching a variety of objects, tasting different foods, and smelling various scents. These exercises require active participation and focus on mindfulness in a single sensory mode, with attention to the moment-by-moment experiences, both internal and external.

Family involvement. Since children are more embedded within their families than are adults, family involvement is expected to enhance treatment outcomes (Kaslow & Racusin, 1994). During our initial studies, we found that children's engagement in the program was related to parental interest and involvement. Parents are invited to attend an orientation session, during which they experience a few mindfulness exercises that their children will learn in the coming weeks. Therapists emphasize the importance of supporting the child by participating in home-based exercises and encouraging mindful intentions, speech, and behaviors. Parents are encouraged to ask questions and maintain a dialogue with the therapists throughout the program. To facilitate parental involvement, children bring home written materials after each session. These include session summaries, instructions for home practice exercises, and forms to record mindfulness activities. At the end of the program, parents participate in a review session with the therapists to practice mindfulness, to share their vicarious experiences of MBCT-C, and to discuss ways to continue supporting their child's mindfulness practice.

Structural and Logistical Adaptations

In addition to developmental adaptations, MBCT-C needed both structural and logistical modifications to address practical concerns inherent in working with children.

Creating safety. Mindfulness interventions require the creation of a safe and confidential therapeutic milieu. For children, this includes responding to their need for guidance and structure. During the first session, five written rules for mindful behavior are reviewed:

1. Act and speak to group members with care and kindness.
2. Stay quiet when another person is talking.
3. Raise your hand to share ideas with the group.
4. Refrain from talking during mindfulness exercises.
5. Sit in "My Quiet Space" if you do not wish to participate in an activity.

My Quiet Space is a designated chair in one corner of the room where a child can choose to sit quietly until he or she wishes to rejoin the group. If a child is acting out or being disruptive to the group, he or she may be invited to sit in My Quiet Space to gather himself or herself before reengaging with the group activities. This space is not intended to be used as a time-out technique but instead offers each child more freedom to choose how he or she participates in the program.

Class size, age range, and format. Children require more individualized attention than adults. For that reason, MBCT-C groups consist of seven to eight children and two cotherapists instead of one therapist for eight to twelve participants as in MBCT. Within the age range thus far evaluated (seven to thirteen years), the group seems more cohesive when the children are no more than two years apart. Similar to MBSR or MBCT, group discussions are a significant component of MBCT-C. Primarily by sharing experiences with each other, the children learn that their past memories; present beliefs, judgments, and affective states; and future expectations influence their personal interpretations of present-moment experiences.

Environment and therapists' role. A number of steps are taken to differentiate MBCT-C from a standard classroom environment. A sign on the outside door announces "Mindfulness in Progress," and children remove their shoes upon entering. Children and therapists sit on floor cushions in an inward-facing circle. This milieu informs the children that the therapists will be equal players—participating in and facilitating the process of self-discovery. Therapists' names are included on the attendance board along with the children's, and they also earn stickers for "being present" each week. Therapists actively participate in all program activities, complete the weekly home practice exercises, and share personal experiences with the group.

MBCT-C Goals and Strategies

By becoming more mindful of normal anxiety and what contributes to its exacerbation or improvement, children may be better equipped to befriend the anxiety without being overwhelmed. In part, pathological anxiety arises from living in an imaginary dot-picture rather than being present and seeing clearly what is actually happening in the moment. Attending to thoughts, feelings, and body sensations (particularly mindfulness of the breath) facilitates staying present long enough to see clearly. Judgments about experiences become seen as the root of suffering and unnecessary to the experience itself. The goals of the first few sessions are to provide children with an orientation to mindfulness, review the parameters of the program, and establish a safe and secure group environment. Core themes include identifying thoughts, feelings, and body sensations; differentiating judging from describing; and enhancing awareness of the present moment using all five senses. Therapists repeat these themes in subsequent sessions through the use of multisensory attention-training exercises. As mindfulness skills develop, session goals focus on the application and integration of mindfulness into everyday life.

Identifying Thoughts, Feelings, and Body Sensations

A primary goal of MBCT-C is to help children develop an increased awareness of their thoughts, feelings, and body sensations. Through repeated experiences, they develop a personal understanding of how these separate but interrelated phenomena interact to influence their interpretations of present-moment events. For example, during one in-class exercise adopted from MBCT, children listen to the following passage:

> *You are walking down the street, and on the other side of the street, you see somebody you know. You smile and wave. The person just doesn't seem to notice and walks by.*

Therapists invite children to imagine this scenario as vividly as possible, observe their own thoughts, feelings, and body sensations, record them in their notebooks, and then share their experiences with the group. One child expressed the thought that the other person did not want to say hello, identified feelings of embarrassment, and noticed the body sensation of her face getting warm. Another had the thought that his friend was mad and was trying to ignore him. This boy experienced feelings of anger, felt his heart rate increase, and had a tight feeling in his chest. While offering group members opportunities to share their experiences, therapists look for opportunities to guide children's understanding of why different experiences were elicited even when each child heard the same passage. Through these discussions, children become aware of the idiosyncratic thoughts, feelings, and body sensations that color their perceptions of everyday events. The primary goal of this exercise is to show that what we experience consists of an actual event plus our own interpretations. These judgmental interpretations then influence subsequent cognitive, affective, physiological, and behavioral responses to the event.

Judging and describing are *not* the same. Another goal of MBCT-C is to help children develop the capacity to be in the moment without falling into automatic habits of evaluating and judging their experiences. We typically want more of an experience that we judge as "good" or "positive," and wish to move away from an experience that we judge as "bad" or "negative." When children experience distressing thoughts, feelings, or body sensations, they are encouraged to simply observe them, without labeling or judging the experience as being "bad." Children discover that thoughts, feelings, and body sensations are not facts about reality or fundamental aspects of the self, but rather conditioned algorithms with which they have learned to interpret internal and external events. Children discover that thoughts are merely passing events in the mind. Thoughts can be accepted as just thoughts. Learning to decenter, they cultivate an attitude of acceptance and nonidentification with their experiences.

Becoming aware of this moment. MBCT-C helps children recognize times spent absorbed in past or future thinking. Past-oriented thoughts are often associated with regret, remorse, guilt, and shame. Future-oriented thoughts trigger anticipatory anxiety, worries, and fear. Children who have developed depressive or anxious schemas learn to redirect their attention from past- or future-oriented thinking and be more present in this moment. Sensory-focused exercises challenge the tendency to avoid anxiety by becoming lost in thought. We use several mindfulness training exercises adapted from MBSR and MBCT, such as mindful breathing, mindful walking, the body scan, and simple yoga postures, to cultivate present-focused attention. Children first learn to see clearly and then find the "choice points" at which conscious choices can be made. This gives them the ability to respond mindfully (rather than react) to events, which tends to improve outcomes. For example, the child who consciously chooses to obey her mother's reasonable request is likely to experience a more pleasant outcome than the child who thoughtlessly makes the decision to rebel.

The Importance of Homework

As in CBT and MBCT, homework is a vital component of MBCT-C. Segal and his colleagues (2002) underscore the importance of the "everydayness" of practice. Daily mindfulness practice sustains children's motivation, helps develop a consistent habit (discipline) of mindfulness, and enhances the generalization of mindfulness across settings. Fortunately children love repetition. The forty-seventh game of tic-tac-toe is as engaging to a child as the first, whereas an adult is most likely to become bored or disinterested. Schoolchildren are accustomed to homework assignments, so the daily home practice assignments used in MBCT-C are a familiar and expectable activity. Two to four short experiential home practice exercises, which take five to fifteen minutes to complete, are assigned after each session. Children practice the exercises nearly every day and record them on written handouts. Each session begins with a review of the home practice exercises from the previous week, and ends with a discussion of the exercises for the coming week. The everyday routine of learning and practicing new skills, along with the child's tolerance for repetition, work to our advantage as we help them replace automatic habits with mindful habits.

Obstacles to Mindfulness

In our clinical work with children, we have identified common obstacles to regular mindfulness practice (described below). In MBCT-C, we discuss many of these obstacles with child participants in sessions two and three and as needed thereafter.

Remembering. The children generally find that practicing short mindfulness exercises is not particularly difficult. The key obstacle is simply remembering to do so. We create strategies to support the discipline of remembering to be mindful each day. For example, children are given several paper smiley faces that they color and strategically place in their homes or at school. One child positions a smiley face on the ceiling over his bed to remember to practice mindful breathing while waking up. Another child places a smiley face on the bathroom mirror as a reminder to brush her teeth mindfully. She places one on her knapsack as a reminder to practice mindfulness during her school day. The smiley faces are positioned wherever a child finds it helpful in remembering.

Patience. With children, it is usually necessary to discuss the importance of patience. Therapists discuss how gains in mindfulness may manifest in small increments, and how alterations of old, maladaptive habits are directly related to daily practice between sessions. We describe this process as akin to gardening. After the ground is prepared, the seeds are planted, and the sprouts are watered and fed. We then wait patiently for the results. Likewise, children are encouraged to participate in the exercises with patience, being mindful of each moment. Through direct experience, children learn that products of their efforts may not be immediately apparent, but with continued practice, the inherent benefits of mindfulness are likely to manifest over time.

Incentives. Unlike most adults in psychotherapy, children do not typically attend the sessions voluntarily, so small incentives can increase their interest in participating.

Children earn colorful stickers for attending sessions and completing their home practice exercises. They also create and decorate their own book, called My Book of Mindfulness, over the course of the twelve-week program. Children keep session notes, weekly session summaries, home practice worksheets, poems, stories, and drawings in their personalized mindfulness books. We often use inexpensive three-ring binders to create these books so that children can take them home at the end of the program.

The importance of practice … yours! We cannot learn to swim without actually getting in the water. No one has ever learned to play a violin by reading everything there is to know about violins. The experience of mindfulness cannot be learned through books or in classrooms, and adopting a theoretical approach to MBCT-C will not be sufficient to attain positive outcomes for your patients. In fact, therapists who are not themselves practicing mindfulness are likely to be limited in how much they can help distressed patients using this program. The therapist's own ability to remain mindful facilitates the patients' efforts to integrate acceptance and change strategies (Lau & McMain, 2005; Segal et al., 2002). In the next section, we provide an example of how mindfulness may be used with children who experience elevated levels of anxiety during group sessions.

Practicing Mindfulness in the Moment

Nine-year-old Tracy was usually a cheerful child, although somewhat shy and retiring. One morning, she arrived looking agitated and upset. Tracy reported feeling worried and scared. Her upset was palpable in the room. Not yet knowing what the problem was, the other children offered their support and tried to comfort her. Initially held back, Tracy's tears spilled over as she explained her distress. The previous evening, Tracy and her father had watched a movie together in which a man had murdered his own child. During the movie, Tracy's father had made an offhand comment implying that this is what happens to bad children. Tracy had always enjoyed a close and loving relationship with her father. This did not protect her from suffering a night filled with vivid nightmares about being killed by her own father.

The residue of the nightmares spilled into the next morning. Tracy told the group about waking up, getting dressed, trying to eat breakfast—all while feeling intense fear. She described having heart palpitations, nausea, shortness of breath, and hot flashes. The child was ruminating over every "bad" thing she had ever done. Her busy mind created vivid images of how much it would hurt to be killed and what it might feel like after she was dead. It was obvious that Tracy had created a terrifying dot-picture that bore no resemblance to her actual experiences. The fear was real, but Tracy was afraid of an event that existed only in her own mind.

Tracy's description of her fears was so graphic that some of the other children also began to show signs of upset. Their fears were not precipitated by any reality or any lived experience either. In reality, the room was the same familiar and comfortable clinic group therapy room that it seemed to be the previous week. Seven children and two adults sat in a circle on floor cushions. Outside the sun was shining; adults were running errands; children were playing. In fact, there was not a single real threat in sight.

One of the older children then stood up and walked over to the "bell of mindfulness." Children could ring this bell anytime they felt a desire to practice mindful breathing. The children straightened their postures, crossed their legs, and settled onto their cushions. Tracy's hands unclenched as she shifted her attention to her posture. Her face showed extreme concentration and she seemed to struggle with the effort of observing her thoughts, feelings, and body sensations without pushing them away. Her breathing slowed as she brought her attention to her breath at her belly. She placed her hand on her belly to better focus, being mindful of its smooth rising on the in-breath and the slower fall during the out-breath. Little by little, she relaxed.

Afterward Tracy seemed to be a different child. She remembered that the movie was just a movie, not reality. She may have remembered that it was only attachment to anxiety-provoking thoughts and images that had created her suffering. Tracy may have decentered, experiencing her thoughts as just thoughts, her emotions as just emotions, and her body sensations as just body sensations. Even a brief moment of decentering—of finding a different way to relate to our own thoughts, feelings, and body sensations—can be a profound experience. During moments of decentering, we remember … and then we see clearly. During her moments of mindfulness, Tracy remembered. Being mindful of her breathing (such a simple act) returned her to the present. She then participated in the activities along with the rest of the children. Throughout the MBCT-C program, children learn to relate to anxiety and other difficult emotions in a different way. This is done through regular mindfulness practice, including exercises used to promote mindfulness through the senses (described below).

Learning Mindfulness Through the Senses

By the end of the first session, children have been exposed to many new ideas. In order to develop and sustain the practice of being mindful, each child must discover personal reasons to do so. These reasons will be found in their own day-to-day lives. Ordinary experiences are transformed when memories, expectations, and judgments are not added to the dot-picture. It is important for therapists to exemplify mindfulness in the way each exercise is presented and in the inquiries that follow. Therapists should attend to the level of restlessness in the room and not exceed the children's current attentional abilities. This applies to all the activities. Controlled for too long, any mindfulness practice can become drudgery. To act overly controlling also undermines our clear emphasis on freedom of choice. Other basic guidelines are these:

- Keep instructions and explanations brief—it is better to say too little than too much.

- Elicit focused descriptions of the actual experience and discourage analytical commentary about the experience.
- Seek opportunities to remark on the distinction between describing an actual experience versus evaluating, judging, ruminating about, analyzing, or comparing it to other experiences.
- Convey an attitude of curiosity, inquiry, and acceptance rather than providing detailed explanations.
- Facilitate acceptance by avoiding criticism or making judgments.
- Invite participation rather than calling on a specific child to respond.
- Ask open-ended questions. Example questions include the following:
    - Does anyone have any comments about this exercise?
    - Did anyone observe anything different from the way you usually walk?
    - Would anyone like to describe his or her experiences of mindful listening?
    - It is really interesting that your mind kept wandering to other times you have eaten raisins. What happened after you found yourself doing this?
    - Did these kind of thoughts change the experience for anyone else?

Mindfulness of the Breath

Mindful breathing is the initial and most basic mindfulness practice. The breath is a wonderful thing to be mindful of—and we can't leave home without it. Mindfulness of the breath is practiced at least twice each session and is integrated in other exercises. We begin with a simple exercise that we call "taking three mindful breaths." At each successive session, this exercise is gradually lengthened (in blocks of three breaths with a moment of "rest" in between each block). A longer exercise, the "three-minute breathing space," is introduced during session five.

Therapists help the children find comfortable sitting positions that can be maintained for at least five minutes. Individuals can chose where and how to sit. Most of the children in our groups choose to sit in a circle on the floor. We generally sit cross-legged on firm cushions, although some children prefer to sit on low chairs or lie down on a floor mat. Children who are disinclined to close their eyes during the mindfulness exercises are not required to do so. Instead we invite children to have "soft eyes" (looking downward with an unfocused gaze).

Taking three mindful breaths. Initially, verbal instruction is used to guide this exercise. The verbal support is minimized in subsequent sessions. It is often easier for children to focus on their breath at the belly rather than at the nostrils; however, they can choose either option. After making a choice, they are encouraged to stay with it throughout the exercise. We describe mindful breathing as an exercise in "belly breathing." Children may naturally engage in diaphragmatic breathing more frequently than do adults and appear to understand the concept easily. They will sometimes place one hand on their abdomen as an aid to help focus their attention. Introduce mindful breathing by saying something like this:

> *I invite you to bring your attention to the breath. You can focus on the breath at your nostrils—watching how the air feels cool coming in and may be slightly warmer as it leaves your body. Or you can focus on the breath at your belly—feeling it rise and fall as air enters and leaves your body. Stay focused, as best you can, on your breath. Just watch the air as it enters and as it leaves, entering and leaving. If your mind wanders, that's okay. Simply bring your attention back to the in-breath and the out-breath. Breathing in and breathing out. Your mind will naturally wander off and get lost in thoughts. That's okay—it's just what minds do. Your job is to gently bring your attention back to the breath every time you notice it has wandered. Tell yourself "great job" for noticing, and then continue to watch your breath*

The three-minute breathing space. After a recent controlled trial of MBCT-C (Lee, 2006), many children rated the "three-minute breathing space" as their most preferred mindfulness activity. The three-minute breathing space is a three-step exercise adopted from MBCT (see Segal et al., 2002, p. 184). As children learn the three steps—awareness, gathering, and expanding—the exercise becomes silent and self-paced. The acronym AGE can help younger children remember each step.

Awareness begins with grounding oneself in the present moment by consciously assuming an attentive posture. In this first step, children learn to focus awareness on the present moment by observing thoughts, feelings, and body sensations, each as separate entities. We sometimes call this step "taking inventory." There is no attempt to encourage relaxation or to change the experience in any way, merely to acknowledge the thoughts, feelings, and body sensations just as they are. Gathering begins by redirecting attention to the breath and shifting into a traditional concentrative breath meditation. Initially this is maintained for only one to two minutes. Finally, expanding involves widening one's attention to become aware of the entire body, sensations, posture, and facial expressions. Children can also be guided to expand their attention so that they become aware of others in the room and their location in the room relative to the others present.

We recommend initially keeping this activity to the advertised three minutes. Thereafter, the time can be increased up to approximately ten minutes. In our experience, ten minutes seems to be the longest time that nine- to twelve-year-old children can usually maintain their concentration. Of course each child will show individual differences. Generally, older children can sit quietly longer than younger ones. Some children may arrive early and can be invited to join the therapists' own preparatory presession mindfulness practice. A few may be able to sit quietly with the therapists for fifteen to twenty minutes.

Mindfulness of the Body

We each live our entire lives in one body. While our thoughts are often in the past or future, our bodies live in the present. Becoming more mindful of the body is one way to ground ourselves in the present. We practice a shortened version of the body scan exercise and yoga postures similar to those used in MBSR and MBCT. Several other movement exercises were added to MBCT-C specifically for use with children. In these exercises, attention is focused inward to practice observing body sensations rather than judging them. For example, we might ask a child who reported feeling itchy during one body scan exercise to describe the thoughts, feelings, and body sensations that she observed as she refrained from scratching.

- Where was the itchy body sensation?
- What did it feel like?
- How big was it?
- Did thoughts arise with the itchy sensation?
- Did you observe if the thoughts changed the sensation in any way?
- Were there feelings (emotional reactions) stuck to the thoughts about feeling itchy?
- Did those feelings affect the itchy sensation?
- Was there an urge to move or scratch?
- Can you describe the experience of sitting through the itch?
- Did the itch go away without you scratching it?

Early in the program, we suggest that it is possible to increase mindful attention. Seated in a circle, we start by mindfully passing a half-full paper cup of water from child to child. At this point, the goal of not spilling the water is not much of an attentional challenge. For the second circuit, we fill the cup nearly to the brim so that passing to the next child without spilling water now demands more attention. Before we begin passing the almost-full cup around the circle for the third time, we turn out the lights. The children then experience what it is like to bring maximum attention to an act that requires highly coordinated movements. And if they do spill? Well, a few giggles and a little water never hurt anyone.

After sitting for twenty or thirty minutes, many children become restless. Mindful movement exercises offer opportunities for children to be active. During simple yoga exercises, we encourage the natural playfulness of children to emerge. In the posture called "the cat and the cow," we augment the mindful body movements with verbal "meows" and "moos." Other exercises provide an outlet for accumulated energy while developing strength of attention. Children pair off for one exercise. One child becomes the "leader" and the other child matches the leader's body movements as closely as possible. Movements may be fast or slow, smooth or jerky, rhythmic or random. The task is for the two children to mirror each other as closely as possible. The atmosphere in the room becomes more playful as the leaders invent increasingly wild movements. This produces giggles from both children as the second child frantically tries to keep up with the impossible pace demanded of him or her. The "invisible ball" exercise is another playful exercise done in pairs. Two children select an invisible ball of any size, weight, and color. They toss and catch this invisible ball to each other as quickly or slowly as they wish. Each child attends to his or her own and the other child's movements as they throw the ball back and forth. They strive to see the ball clearly, as if it were actually there. Of course, the mindfulness challenge in this exercise is to not drop the ball.

Mindful Eating

Eating is a particularly valuable activity to increase awareness of how we often function on automatic pilot. The Mindfully Eating a Raisin Exercise (adapted from Semple, 2005) offers children a new way to relate to everyday experiences when actions are performed slowly and with conscious attention. Mindful eating demonstrates how paying attention in a particular way (that is, intentionally, in the present moment, and without judgment) actually changes the quality of the experience. The aim is to enhance experiential understanding of mindfulness. Clinicians can begin this exercise by asking children to assume mindful postures, passing out a few raisins to each child, and saying like this:

> *Hold this object in your hand. Look at it very carefully, as if you must describe it to a Martian who has never seen one before. As best you can, be aware of thoughts or old images that may sneak in as you look at this object. Just note that they are just thoughts and return your attention to this object. Note the colors of the object. What does the surface look like? Is it bumpy or smooth? Does the object feel dry or moist? Explore the object with your eyes and fingers. Is it soft or hard? Do the ridges form patterns? Is the texture the same all over*

the object? How heavy is it? Does this object have any smells? Explore it with your eyes, your fingers, and your nose. Is your attention on this object in your hand? Then, whenever you're ready, place it in your mouth. Explore the object with your tongue. Does it taste or feel different in different parts of your mouth when you roll it around? Is your mouth watering in anticipation of eating the object? What do you taste before you bite it? Smell? Any sounds? Does the texture change the longer it's in your mouth? As best you can, keep attending to this object and also watch your thoughts. Are the thoughts looking forward to swallowing this object and eating another, or are they attending to the sensations of the one that is in your mouth? Gently bite the object. Taste the flavor. Are the textures on the inside different from the outside? Is there a different moistness or flavor? Slowly chew the object while noting every sensation. As you swallow the object, feel it slide down your throat. Follow it all the way down to your tummy. Bring your attention back to the sensations in your mouth. Are there different tastes or flavors in your mouth now? Are you still noticing your thoughts and sensations as you eat this object? Can you feel that your body is now exactly one raisin heavier than it was a few minutes ago?

Mindful Listening

Sounds hold idiosyncratic meanings for each of us, and each sound is present only in this moment. Sounds elicit different emotional responses, which are associated with prior experiences, schemas, and cognitive interpretations. If one child has a puppy and hears the sound of a dog barking, she may smile and have happy thoughts about her pet. If another child hears the same sound but his puppy has recently died, he may cry and feel sad that his beloved pet is gone. Using mindful listening exercises, children develop an awareness of their personal "filters" and better understand how emotions are related to the meanings that they give to particular sounds. Exploring both receptive and expressive sounds, children further develop their skills at differentiating thoughts, feelings, and body sensations.

Receptive Sounds

Music is an easily accessible way to teach mindful hearing. In one in-class exercise, the children lie down on yoga mats and listen to short segments of music (30–60 seconds) from a variety of musical genres (pop, rock, classical, new age, country-western, etc.). Including music from different parts of the world that children are less likely to have heard can facilitate the process of disengaging from automatic pilot. We dim the lights to better focus attention on the sounds and lessen distraction from things seen in the room. We invite children to bring their attention to their sense of hearing and to mindfully hear the sounds. When one listens mindfully, sounds are experienced as patterns of pitch, tone, and volume. They note any thoughts or images, feelings, and body sensations that arise as they listen to the music. Every time the mind wanders, they simply note it and gently redirect their attention to just hearing the sounds.

After listening to each segment, the children record the images, thoughts, feelings, and body sensations in their notebooks. These are shared in the group discussion that follows. One child observes that a ballad reminded her of a wedding (thought or image). She felt joyful (feeling) and noticed that her toes were slowly tapping to the rhythm (body sensation). Another child reported that the same song evoked images of a funeral. He felt somewhat sad and noticed a heavy feeling throughout his body. By sharing their differing experiences of the same music, children learn that their own judgments and interpretations have a profound influence on how they experience the events that fashion their lives. Mindful listening helps increase awareness of the "mind chatter" and of the thoughts that govern how they make sense of what they hear.

Expressive Sounds

In the following session, children have the opportunity to become creators and conductors of their own music. Children take turns being the "orchestra conductor," while the other children select an instrument to play. Instruments may include a triangle, tambourine, drum, horn, and maracas. It is not necessary to purchase expensive musical instruments for this exercise. We can learn to hear any sound as music. For example, a pair of wooden blocks provides a light percussion background. A partially filled water bottle creates the soothing sound of moving water. A pillow-drum sounds as interesting as bongo drums. The conductors are invited to explore other sounds (e.g., singing or clapping hands) to enhance their personal concerts.

The designated conductor instructs each musician (each of the other children) to play a specific instrument, in a particular order, with the intention of creating their own song. The only instruction is to create a one- to two-minute song that expresses how he or she feels at that moment. After each song, each child creates a title for that song and writes down the thoughts, feelings, and body sensations they associated with the music. Children rotate into the role of conductor, and all have opportunities to play the various musical instruments. During the group discussion, experiences and the song titles are shared. For example, one child felt angry and created a cacophonous song by instructing the musicians to play their instruments simultaneously and as loudly as they could. Another child felt happy, so she selected instruments with higher, softer tones to create her song. As in the receptive sounds exercise, the expression of sounds evokes unique thoughts or images, feelings, and body sensations. The child conductor who felt angry titled her song "The Fight." Another child creating and listening to that song reported a completely different experience—he felt upbeat and energetic. His song title was "The Festival." Afterward the children discuss having different associations to the same song. Using focused inquiry, therapists have the opportunity to reinforce one main theme: emotions emerge from an objective stimuli (sound) coupled with one's own interpretation of its meaning.

In the related home practice exercise, children are invited to become more aware of sounds in their environment. For example, they are asked to describe a self-identified "pleasant sound" event, such as walking home from school and stopping to hear a bird sing. They identify thoughts (e.g., "Spring is coming; it will be so nice to play outside"), feelings (e.g., joy, happiness), and body responses (e.g., smiling and feeling light and energetic) that arose while listening. Mindfulness only "works" when we are willing to pay attention to all our experiences. Accordingly, the children also describe a self-identified "unpleasant sound" event, such as being awakened by the sound of a garbage truck. This sound evokes different thoughts (e.g., "I wish that truck would go away so I can go back to sleep"), different feelings (e.g., irritability or anger), and different body sensations (e.g., teeth grinding, fists clenching). Practicing these exercises, children become more aware of the thoughts they have learned to associate with ordinary sounds and how the thoughts influence their experience. Instead of judging sounds as either pleasant or unpleasant, children practice listening mindfully to the sounds of that garbage truck—the grinding of the compactor and the squealing brakes—without adding their belief-dots, expectation-dots, and desire-dots to the experience. As they become less invested in defining the sounds as "pleasant" or "unpleasant," the experiences change.

Mindful Seeing

Over time we habituate to seeing things in certain ways. We like seeing a beautiful bed of roses, a magnificent sunset, a stunning view of the mountains, or a cute little kitten. We dislike seeing an ugly industrial plant, a vile snake, or a disgusting pile of garbage. We associate certain images with specific adjectives and, with little awareness, make nearly instantaneous judgments that are based on a cursory visual inspection. In this ever-changing, lightning-paced, technology-driven world, there is barely a moment to slow down to see what surrounds us. How often do we look at any object as a unique collection of shapes, forms, colors, sizes, and features without also judging what we are looking at? When we practice looking with mindful awareness, we replace distorted and myopic lenses with ones that can see clearly. Mindful seeing is simply observing with attention and accepting what we see—just as it is.

Many wonderful and meaningful details in our environment are missed altogether, simply because we do not pay attention to them. Some children begin the program with the belief that they see "everything," missing nothing at all. If you then ask them to describe a familiar, personal object that they use every day, most will say that they can, accurately and in detail, describe the object. In one mindful seeing exercise, the children are asked to draw from memory any object that they use on a daily basis. The chosen object may be a television, telephone, game cube, favorite pen, book bag, bed, or alarm clock. They take the drawing home, look at the actual object, and then correct all the misplaced, distorted, or missed details on the original drawing. At the next group discussion, we invite the children to present their "new and improved" drawings and explore what they learned from the exercise. Most are surprised at how many details they miss altogether or how some parts appear in a different location or are actually a different shape or color than what was remembered. In their own drawings, children can see how they function on automatic pilot when they are not practicing mindful seeing.

For a home practice exercise, children are invited to be more mindful of their various environments—at home, in school, in the park, on the school bus—and write down their observations. When a child says, "I never noticed before that ..." he or she is choosing to see with conscious awareness and increased mindfulness. He never noticed the shape of a chair he sits on every day. She was unaware of the pattern on the rug in her own bedroom. Another never saw a map of the world hanging at the back of the classroom. Through the repeated practice of looking, we learn to see. In seeing, we rediscover the amazing world around us.

Another mindful seeing exercise makes use of a dozen different optical illusions. The pictures are presented one at a time, and the children record what they saw in their notebooks. Looking at the "young lady and old hag" illusion, some children report seeing the profile of a young girl while others see the face of an old woman. After the series is complete, each picture is presented again and discussed. Most can't see the second image until it is pointed out to them. The children are invited to stare at a picture and consciously shift their attention between images. In doing this, they also discover that it is not possible to see both images simultaneously. The image seen is the image to which they choose to direct their attention. The children quite literally see that they have choices in how they relate to their experiences. They experience the freedom of disengaging from automatic pilot by practicing being mindful of this moment.

Mindful Touching

The sense of touch is essential for survival. Newborn infants bond with their mothers partially through physical contact. As children grow, they explore and learn much about their world through tactile sensations. From repeated associations, they categorize and learn to make assumptions about the multitude of sensations experienced every day. We learn to avoid objects that appear hot or slimy, like stoves and snails. We learn to feel attracted to objects that are soft or supple, like furry kittens and silk scarves. As soon as we judge an object as being pleasant or unpleasant, we attend less to it, thus losing an opportunity to bring greater awareness and mindfulness into our lives. How often are we mindfully aware of our clothing—the feelings of different fabrics and textures touching our bodies? How often do we pay attention to the feel of the sun or the wind on our bare skin?

To learn mindful touching, children practice identifying tactile sensations without labeling or judging them. In one exercise, we collect a variety of objects—a pinecone, a smooth stone, sandpaper, a hairbrush, a piece of velvet, and a rubber toy. The more unusual the object, the better. The weight of a piece of pumice is much different than it appears to be. When we focus only on the sense of touch, the striking discrepancy between this rock's weight and its appearance helps clarify the distinction between describing and judging.

We blindfold one child and place an object in his or her hands. The blindfolded child explores the object using only his or her sense of touch. We encourage the child to describe the object and avoid naming it or judging it. The other children are "observers" who can see the object but not touch it. The observers help identify when descriptions become judgments. If the blindfolded child responds, "It feels gross" or "I don't like the touch of it" or "It feels nice," the observers provide feedback that those statements are not descriptions but rather personal judgments. If a child has problems describing the object without judging, the observers can help by asking questions: is the object soft or hard, rough or smooth, hot or cold, wet or dry, heavy or light, fuzzy or prickly? The observers can also contribute their visual knowledge of the object, such as the color, to the collective understanding. Each child rotates positions until everyone practices mindfully touching a different object. In addition to helping children distinguish between describing and judging, this exercise reinforces the fact that no single sensory mode ever provides complete information about an object or an event.

For the related home practice exercise, we encourage children to become more mindful of different household objects. Although they have presumably touched these things many times before, they can mindfully explore the texture, shape, size, temperature, and weight of an object as if touching it for the first time. For example, a child mindfully touches a white cotton ball and describes the object as light, round, soft, nice, and fluffy. She categorizes each thought as being a description or a judgment. This gives the child more practice in differentiating between descriptions and judgments. While touching the cotton ball, the child continues to observe her thoughts, feelings, and body sensations. She identifies associated thoughts of her soft and fluffy white dog and is aware of feeling relaxed and happy. Given that cotton balls are not known for helping people feel relaxed and happy, the child learns the power of thoughts and how they influence experiences. Overall, mindful touching exercises provide opportunities to be fully attentive to tactile sensations, to observe the thoughts that are elicited by the sensations, and to do so without making judgments. This is how we learn to see clearly.

Mindful Smelling

The sense of smell may be our earliest developed sense perception. This sense is essential to our survival as it helps us to distinguish between wholesome and noxious foods. Babies are born with a well-developed sense of smell, and the ability to identify odors generally decreases with age. Perhaps because the sense of smell is associated with areas of the brain related to emotions (amygdala and hypothalamus), scents often trigger emotionally laden memories. The smell of warm bread reminds us of our family kitchen. A certain perfume reminds us of someone we know. Rather than being experienced as it is, the perfume elicits thoughts and feelings about that person. Engrossed in memories, we are less mindful in this moment. Mindful smelling exercises present a challenge for children because scents are very difficult to describe. We often describe one scent by comparing it to other scents. "It smells like fresh-cut grass" or "It smells like chocolate." The essential message of mindful smelling exercises is that the act of smelling and the process of judging what we smell are two different activities. As with other activities that are not done on automatic pilot, mindful smelling is likely to change the actual experience.

Before the session, therapists select a number of scent samples, such as ground coffee beans, cotton balls soaked in vinegar, perfumes, flowers, cinnamon bark, gingerroot, dill, cloves, camphor, and aromatic soaps or lotions. If a smell is particularly strong, children usually offer their judgment of the smell first and may need some assistance in finding descriptive words. A quantity of each item is placed in an odor-proof container, such as a plastic film canister. Resealable plastic bags can be used for a short time but need to be newly prepared before each session.

One scent at a time is passed around the group. Each child smells the scent, offers a single word to describe it, and records scent-related thoughts, feelings, and body sensations in his or her notebook. The distinction between just smelling bubble gum and judging its appeal can be challenging for young children. In discussion, we presume that the judgment of the experience is separate from the experience itself.

Home practice exercises for mindful smelling are easily implemented at the dinner table. Children do these exercises at home and are asked to record their observations. In preparation for this, we may give instructions like these:

> *Continue to apply mindful smelling to meals at home. Before eating your dinner, take a moment to mindfully smell the different foods on your plate. What smells do you notice that you might have overlooked in the past? How are you describing them in your head? What body sensations do you experience when mindfully smelling the various foods in front of you? As you begin to eat, continue to focus your attention on the smells. Attend to how, with each food, the smells and the tastes are different, but linked together. Write down your observations in your mindfulness notebook.*

Conclusion

Life always includes some suffering. Events conspire to create challenging situations. Difficult moments will occur—moments that are stressful and moments that are filled with anxiety. Efforts to avoid this reality are futile and only serve to produce additional anxiety. Mindfully accepting the full range of our experiences is an alternative strategy to cope with the inevitable vicissitudes of life. Potentially, mindfulness offers an opportunity to be happy even in the midst of life's challenges.

During the MBCT-C program, children learn that the invention of catastrophic scenarios in one's mind can exacerbate anxiety. They learn that judging an experience is not the same as the experience itself. They learn that judgmental thinking increases the discomfort of a challenging experience. They develop greater awareness of how often they transform their present-moment experiences by adding beliefs, expectations, and desires to their personal dot-pictures. We lay the groundwork for children to experience thoughts as just thoughts, feelings as just feelings, and body sensations as just body sensations. Through mindfulness practice, children learn that choice points occur in each moment of their lives. Being mindful helps them recognize which choice points can be most helpful to themselves and to others around them. Seeing clearly grants them the freedom to choose their own life paths.

One handout each child receives at the last session is called "Things We Can Learn from a Dog." Dogs are present focused, let go of disappointments easily, do not worry about the future, engage with others with gusto and enthusiasm, and experience life as joyful. Mindfulness gives children a means by which they can engage in their own lives with the same awareness, enthusiasm, and empathic joy. The challenge for each child (and adults too) is that mindfulness can never be taught but rather must be learned through personal experience and discipline.

As mental health professionals, it is important to remember that mindfulness is not a panacea for all mental health problems. Although there is growing evidence of the effectiveness of clinical interventions that use mindfulness-based approaches (Baer, 2003), there is little consistency across studies regarding what mindfulness is, what techniques and practices might help develop mindfulness, or even what outcomes can be expected from practicing mindfulness techniques. There are also no published studies that compare the effectiveness of mindfulness-based therapies with pharmacotherapy or combined treatments. However, there are no obvious contraindications to concurrent treatment with anxiolytic medications while participating in mindfulness-based psychotherapies.

Attention is the mechanism that brings our world into conscious experience and is the conduit through which we create our individual realities. At its simplest, mindfulness practices are attention-training practices. We limit ourselves so much by simply not paying attention. Mindlessly we hold ourselves captive in a prison of false beliefs, built on dubious expectations of reality, and populated with unattainable desires. Mindfulness offers a way to cleanse those doors of perception, enriching the lives of our clients—as well as our own lives. We must not be surprised, however, if the experience of seeing infinity results in a mind state that includes benefits reaching far beyond what is conventionally regarded as psychological well-being.

References

Achenbach, T. M. (1991). *Manual for the Child Behavior Checklist: Ages 4–18 and 1991 profile.* University of Vermont, Department of Psychiatry, Burlington, VT.

Baer, R. A. (2003). Mindfulness training as a clinical intervention: A conceptual and empirical review. *Clinical Psychology: Science and Practice, 10,* 125–143.

Barlow, D. H. (2002). *Anxiety and its disorders: The nature and treatment of anxiety and panic* (2nd ed.). New York: Guilford.

Beck, A. T. (1976). *Cognitive therapy and the emotional disorders*. New York: International Universities Press.

Bishop, S. R., Lau, M., Shapiro, S., Carlson, L., Anderson, N. D., Carmody, J., et al. (2004). Mindfulness: A proposed operational definition. *Clinical Psychology: Science and Practice, 11*, 230–241.

Chavira, D. A., Stein, M. B., Bailey, K., & Stein, M. T. (2004). Child anxiety in primary care: Prevalent but untreated. *Depression and Anxiety, 20*, 155–164.

Gaines, R. (1997). Key issues in the interpersonal treatment of children. *The Review of Interpersonal Psychoanalysis, 2*, 1–5.

Goodman, T. A. (2005). Working with children: Beginner's mind. In C. K. Germer, R. D. Siegel, & Paul R. Fulton (Eds.), *Mindfulness and psychotherapy* (pp. 197–219). New York: Guilford.

Greco, L. A., Blackledge, J. T., Coyne, L. W., & Ehrenreich, J. (2005). Integrating acceptance and mindfulness into treatments for child and adolescent anxiety disorders: Acceptance and commitment therapy as an example. In S. M. Orsillo & L. Roemer (Eds.), *Acceptance and mindfulness-based approaches to anxiety: Conceptualization and treatment* (pp. 301–322). New York: Springer Science.

Kabat-Zinn, J. (1994). *Wherever you go, there you are: Mindfulness meditation for everyday life*. New York: Hyperion.

Kaslow, N. J., & Racusin, G. R. (1994). Family therapy for depression in young people. In W. M. Reynolds & H. F. Johnston (Eds.), *Handbook of depression in children and adolescents: Issues in clinical child psychology* (pp. 345–363). New York: Plenum.

Kessler, R. C., Nelson, C. B., McGonagle, K. A., Liu, J., Swart, M., & Blazer, D. G. (1996). Comorbidity of *DSM-III-R* major depressive disorder in the general population: Results from the US National Comorbidity Survey. *British Journal of Psychiatry, 168*, 17–30.

Lau, M. A., & McMain, S. F. (2005). Integrating mindfulness meditation with cognitive and behavioural therapies: The challenge of combining acceptance- and change-based strategies. *Canadian Journal of Psychiatry. Revue Canadienne de Psychiatrie*, 50(13), 863–869.

Lee, J. (2006). *Mindfulness-based cognitive therapy for children: Feasibility, acceptability, and effectiveness of a controlled clinical trial.* Unpublished doctoral dissertation, Columbia University, Teachers College, New York.

Lee, J., Semple, R. J., Rosa, D., & Miller, L. (in press). Mindfulness-based cognitive therapy for children: Results of a pilot study. *Journal of Cognitive Psychotherapy*.

Noshpitz, J. D., & King, R. A. (1991). *Pathways of growth: Essentials of child psychiatry: Vol. 1. Normal development; Vol. 2. Psychopathology*. New York: John Wiley.

Rani, N. J., & Rao, P. V. K. (1996). Meditation and attention regulation. *Journal of Indian Psychology, 14,* 26–30.

Segal, Z. V., Williams, J. M. G., & Teasdale, J. D. (2002). *Mindfulness-based cognitive therapy for depression: A new approach to preventing relapse.* New York: Guilford.

Semple, R. J. (1999). *Enhancing the quality of attention: A comparative assessment of concentrative meditation and progressive relaxation.* Unpublished master's thesis, University of Auckland, New Zealand.

Semple, R. J. (2005). *Mindfulness-based cognitive therapy for children: A randomized group psychotherapy trial developed to enhance attention and reduce anxiety.* Unpublished doctoral dissertation, Columbia University, New York.

Semple, R. J., Reid, E. F. G., & Miller, L. F. (2005). Treating anxiety with mindfulness: An open trial of mindfulness training for anxious children. *Journal of Cognitive Psychotherapy: An International Quarterly, 19,* 387–400.

Shaffer, D., Fisher, P., Dulcan, M. K., & Davies, M. (1996). The NIMH diagnostic interview schedule for children version 2.3 (DISC-2.3): Description, acceptability, prevalence rates, and performance in the MECA study. *Journal of the American Academy of Child and Adolescent Psychiatry, 35,* 865–877.

Siegler, R. S. (1991). *Children's thinking* (2nd ed.). Upper Saddle River, NJ: Prentice-Hall.

Teasdale, J. D. (2004). Mindfulness-based cognitive therapy. In J. Yiend (Ed.), *Cognition, emotion and psychopathology: Theoretical, empirical and clinical directions* (pp. 270–289). New York: Cambridge University Press.

Teasdale, J. D., Segal, Z. V., Williams, J. M. G., Ridgeway, V. A., Soulsby, J. M., & Lau, M. A. (2000). Prevention of relapse/recurrence in major depression by mindfulness-based cognitive therapy. *Journal of Consulting and Clinical Psychology, 68,* 615–623.

U.S. Department of Health and Human Services. (1999). *Mental health: A report of the Surgeon General.* Rockville, MD: U.S. Department of Health and Human Services, Substance Abuse, and Mental Health Services Administration, National Institutes of Health, National Institute of Mental Health.

Valentine, E. R., & Sweet, P. L. G. (1999). Meditation and attention: A comparison of the effects of concentrative and mindfulness meditation on sustained attention. *Mental Health, Religion and Culture, 2,* 59–70.

Chapter 5

Acceptance and Commitment Therapy for Pediatric Chronic Pain

Rikard K. Wicksell, MS, Astrid Lindgren Children's Hospital, Department of Clinical Neuroscience, Karolinska Institute, Stockholm, Sweden; and Laurie A. Greco, Ph.D., University of Missouri, St. Louis

In this chapter, we will present acceptance and commitment therapy (ACT; Hayes, Strosahl, & Wilson, 1999) as a treatment approach for youth struggling with chronic or recurrent pain conditions and associated disabilities. Beginning with a brief overview of chronic pain syndromes and existing evidence-based treatments for pediatric chronic pain, we situate ACT as part of a behavioral medicine approach to pediatric care, and present recommendations for conducting an ACT-consistent behavioral assessment and adapting ACT methods to meet the unique psychosocial challenges of pediatric pain patients and their families. We will conclude by suggesting future directions for integrating ACT into clinical practice and empirical research focused on pediatric pain.

Pediatric Chronic Pain

Pain has been defined by the International Association for the Study of Pain (IASP) as "an unpleasant sensory and emotional experience associated with actual or potential tissue damage" (Merskey & ISAP, 1979). Chronic or recurrent (i.e., that persists or recurs for three months or longer) pain syndromes such as headache, abdominal pain, and musculoskeletal pain are common in children and adolescents, with prevalence rates between 15 percent and 32 percent (El-Metwally, Salminen, Auvinen, Kautiainen, & Mikkelsson, 2004). The mean cost per adolescent experiencing chronic pain is approximately £8,000 ($13,800 U.S.) a year (Sleed, Eccleston, Beecham, Knapp, & Jordan, 2005). Pediatric chronic pain is highly comorbid with emotional disorders (anxiety and depression), and is associated with activity restriction, school absence, academic difficulties, and peer relationship problems (Greco, Freeman, & Dufton, 2006; Palermo, 2000). Moreover, a subset of pediatric pain patients exhibit marked disability and functional impairment for months or even years following their initial evaluation (Brattberg, 2004; Palermo, 2000).

Although significant advances have been made in our understanding of chronic pain syndromes, a substantial proportion of patients continue to suffer from detrimental effects due to long-standing pain of unclear origin. Thus a large proportion of youth with chronic pain experience persistent or recurrent episodes of pain in the absence of demonstrable disease and without evidence of metabolic, biochemical, or structural abnormalities underlying the reported symptoms (often referred to as "pain syndrome," "idiopathic pain," or "medically unexplained pain"). Discrepant with medical findings, the child experiences his or her pain as resulting from tissue damage (i.e., nociceptive input) and may feel invalidated when receiving physician feedback that "nothing is wrong," medically speaking at least. Idiopathic pain is often unresponsive to analgesics and other pharmacological treatments. The continuation of symptoms and concomitant disability may in turn elicit fear, frustration, and hopelessness in children and their families.

Child and family distress, coupled with unwillingness to tolerate uncertainty, may become the impetus for excessive treatment seeking and costly medical visits. Despite recommendations from health care providers to resume normal activities, a subgroup of youth continue to exhibit marked impairment in daily functioning. The child's subjective experience of pain and the family's search for an answer continues and, as a result, these youth may undergo excessive medical procedures to answer questions such as "What's wrong with me [or my child]?" "Why can't the doctors figure this out?" Children and adolescents may attach to the belief that "I cannot live a normal life until my pain goes away." Parents may reinforce this notion and steadfastly cling to their own belief that "We must find a diagnosis for my child. Our lives are on hold until my child is well."

All too often, family distress and possible distrust of the medical system are exacerbated when medical tests fail to produce either an improved understanding of the organic cause of pain or any clear recommendations regarding long-term symptom alleviation. Medical providers may similarly experience feelings of helplessness and frustration in working with a patient population whose clinical presentation tends to be elusive and unresponsive to standard medical care. Thus behavioral health consultants and clinicians are often integral to the effective treatment of youth with idiopathic pain.

Evidence-Based Treatment

Given the high prevalence rates, economic burden, and intensive personal suffering associated with chronic pain syndromes, it is essential to develop effective treatment approaches that improve functioning and reduce disability among young patients and their families. In contrast to treatments for acute pain, pharmacological strategies are often insufficient in alleviating chronic pain and do little to increase patient functioning and quality of life. Thus an interdisciplinary approach involving a physician and a mental health professional, as well as a nurse practitioner and/or physical therapist (when needed), is normally the treatment of choice.

Research suggests that cognitive behavior therapy (CBT) may be particularly promising in chronic pain management for youth presenting with a wide range of conditions, including headache (e.g., Holden, Deichmann, & Levy, 1999), recurrent abdominal pain (e.g., Janicke & Finney, 1999), idiopathic musculoskeletal pain (e.g., Eccleston, Malleson, Clinch, Connell, & Sourbut, 2003), and disease-related pain (e.g., Walco, Sterling, Conte, & Engel, 1999). CBT for chronic pain is a broad-spectrum treatment that encompasses a variety of interventions, including education, relaxation and biofeedback, operant approaches, skills training, and goal setting (Turk, Meichenbaum, & Genest, 1983). Traditionally, the primary goal of chronic pain management in CBT has been to reduce pain and distress in order to increase overall functioning and to facilitate physical and social activities.

Within the behavior and cognitive traditions, there is growing evidence that acceptance of pain leads to enhanced physical and emotional functioning, whereas attempts to control pain may paradoxically lead to increased pain and disability (e.g., Hayes, Bissett, et al., 1999; McCracken & Eccleston, 2003). Acceptance-based approaches such as ACT have garnered increasing empirical support in the treatment of chronic pain patients in both adult populations (e.g., Dahl, Wilson, & Nilsson, 2004; McCracken, Mackichan, & Eccleston, 2007; McCracken, Vowles, & Eccleston, 2004; Wicksell, Ahlqvist, Bring, Melin, & Olsson, 2008) and child and adolescent populations (e.g., Greco, Blomquist, Acra, & Moulton, 2008; Wicksell, Melin, Ahlqvist, Lekander, & Olsson, 2008; Wicksell, Melin, & Olsson, 2007). Of note, ACT and other acceptance-based therapies differ from traditional CBT in their emphasis on willingness to experience pain (i.e., acceptance of pain) and other negatively evaluated private events such as thoughts, feelings, and physical sensations. In ACT, acceptance involves abandoning unworkable and potentially destructive efforts to control physical and emotional pain, focusing instead on taking responsibility in meaningful areas of life that are amenable to change. Symptom alleviation is not explicitly sought within an ACT approach and, if it does occur, is viewed as a transient by-product of treatment that need not influence one's ability to create a meaningful life.

ACT uses acceptance and mindfulness interventions to promote psychological flexibility, or "the ability to contact the present moment more fully as a conscious human being and to change or persist in behavior when doing so serves valued ends" (Hayes, Luoma, Bond, Masuda, & Lillis, 2006, p. 7). ACT methods are also used to weaken cognitive fusion and experiential avoidance, clinically relevant processes that often interfere with our ability to engage in values-consistent behavior. According to Hayes and colleagues, "cognitive fusion" refers to the tendency for human beings to attach to the content of private events and subsequently respond to these experiences as if they were literally true. In some contexts, cognitive fusion produces unworkable levels of experiential avoidance, or attempts to avoid, manage, and control certain private experiences (Hayes et al., 2006). By definition, pain management strategies such as progressive muscle relaxation, imagery, and cognitive restructuring represent attempts to manage or control internal experiences and are therefore examples of experiential avoidance.

Adopting a Behavioral Medicine Approach

A behavioral medicine approach is particularly important when pain sensations are neither fully understood nor effectively treated. In such cases, it is essential to shift focus from symptoms to adaptive functioning and life quality, both of which are emphasized in ACT (Robinson, Wicksell, & Olsson, 2004). Standard medical care does not effectively address psychosocial factors that play a prominent role in the subjective experience of idiopathic pain and related disability. Moreover, medical interventions alone are generally inadequate, due in part to the absence of an identifiable disease or organic cause that can be linked to a specific medical regimen. A behavioral medicine approach takes organic factors into account; however, interactions among triggering stimuli, pain behavior, and reinforcing consequences are emphasized and used to guide assessment, case conceptualization, and treatment planning.

A "true" behavior medicine approach implies a fully integrated treatment team which, depending on the type of pain syndrome (e.g., abdominal pain, headache, musculoskeletal pain), may consist of a physician, nurse practitioner, mental health professional, and physiologist (if needed). Ideally, members of the treatment team share the same philosophies regarding the genesis of pain and disability, the final goals of treatment, and the interventions that are most likely to succeed with each patient. Strategies discussed by Robinson (see chapter 11 in this volume) may be particularly useful in educating the treatment team about ACT and gaining support for an interdisciplinary approach.

Our experience suggests that an integrated behavioral medicine approach guided by ACT principles may be an effective treatment to restore functioning in pediatric patients who experience chronic or recurrent pain. Three core assumptions underlie this approach: (1) experiential avoidance, or attempts to avoid chronic or recurrent physical and emotional pain, greatly increases the potential for long-term disability and suffering; (2) exposure is central to working with chronic pain populations; and (3) acceptance and adaptive functioning are given priority over pain management and symptom reduction, as it may be difficult to obtain lasting positive effects on symptoms. Moreover, pain reduction does not appear to have a clear causal relationship with functioning.

As each of us began working with pediatric pain patients, a potential dilemma emerged. Exposure treatment with pediatric patients is often met with resistance when symptom alleviation does not occur. ACT appeared to be a good match for our patients due to its emphasis on personal values, which can be used to enhance motivation and to facilitate difficult exposure exercises. The clinical model described in this chapter was guided both by ACT principles and by a set of assumptions related to idiopathic pain and the effective treatment of pain-related disability:

- Chronic pain of unclear origin (idiopathic pain) is very unpleasant but is not dangerous. The perception of pain is not due to peripheral pathophysiological processes that necessitate treatment; rather, pain perception may result from inadequate central processing (a false alarm).

- Avoidance of these unpleasant private events leads to avoidance of important activities that would elicit pain, which results in disability. Not engaging in valuable activities is, over time, harmful.

- Avoidance of activities that elicit these false alarms might, over time, decrease the pain threshold, creating hypervigilance to stimulation and increased pain sensation.

- Avoidance of pain and distress leads away from valued activities, and is central in the development of pain-related disabilities and the primary target in treatment.

- People with chronic pain and distress are capable of living a vital life in the presence or absence of negative private events (e.g., pain, anxiety, sadness, fear).

- An increase in psychological flexibility will result in broader and more flexible behavior repertoires. In ACT, the emphasis is on developing broader repertoires characterized by values-oriented action and life vitality.

We turn now to an overview of how one might conduct a behavioral assessment with pediatric pain patients and their families following physician referral for behavioral health services.

Behavioral Assessment of Pain Behavior

Prior to initiating ACT interventions, we use basic behavioral principles to identify the function(s) of pain-related disability, often manifested as frequent medical visits, school absence, academic difficulties, problems with peers, strained family relations, activity restriction, social withdrawal, and high levels of sedentary behavior. Behavior analysis provides a helpful framework for understanding the link between pain and disability (Fordyce, 1976). In accordance with learning theory, avoidance of painful experiences results in short-term relief. Although adaptive in acute pain, this reinforcing effect does not lead to any lasting comparable symptomatic improvements in chronic pain. For chronic pain patients, avoidance behavior is "functional" in the short run if the goal is to provide immediate relief from physical and emotional discomfort; however, in the long run, avoidance of aversive private events tends to have life-narrowing and disabling effects.

Although the clinician might inquire about the specific topography of the child's pain symptoms, the primary purpose of assessment is to identify how children and families respond to pain episodes and how these behavioral responses might interfere with values-based living and life vitality. Toward this end, goals of the initial assessment session(s) are to (1) validate and normalize the child's subjective experience of physical and emotional pain; (2) provide education regarding the child's pain condition; (3) identify the function(s) of pain-related behavior; (4) begin to conceptualize pain behavior in terms of ACT clinical processes (i.e., cognitive fusion and experiential avoidance); and (5) introduce the goals of an ACT approach, with emphasis on learning to create a life that works even when the "pain monster" rears its ugly head.

Validating the Family's Experience

Many families come to us feeling defensive and invalidated, reporting that nobody in the health care system seems to believe that their child is in tremendous pain. For this work to be effective, an essential first step is to join with the family, allowing them to be heard, possibly for the first time. In doing so, the clinician should validate and normalize the child's experience of pain, while at the same time emphasizing that there may not be a guaranteed way to eliminate or cure this discomfort altogether. The clinician might say something like this: "Yes, you're absolutely right. Your pain is very real, and it doesn't sound fun at all. In fact, it sounds horrible, like this big, ugly pain monster has completely taken over your life. And you've worked hard to get this pain monster under control. And what does your experience tell you in terms of how well this has worked? Is the pain monster still here?"

Without question, the child and family have worked hard to eliminate the child's pain and have used many of their financial and life resources searching for an answer or cure, but to no avail. Pain is still here, and the family's life has been turned upside down. During the initial assessment, the clinician might ask:

> *What if there really is no guarantee that your life will be pain free? Your experience suggests that, despite all your hard work, there may not be an immediate or obvious solution here, medical or otherwise. You've worked really*

hard, and pain is still here. So, what if you had to choose right here, right now, between living your life fully with pain (if and when pain is there), or putting your life on hold until pain goes away completely? Really let your experience be the guide here—what will your life look like five years from now if you continue to do what you've always done? Would you still have pain? Would you be living your life, or would you be searching for answers and trying to eliminate pain? Is that the kind of life you truly want—the life you would choose for yourself [or for your child] if anything were possible?

Providing Information

Pain education is an important part of recasting "the problem," as we move away from an underlying disease model that relies heavily on pain management to a model of acceptance, in which life vitality is given priority over symptom reduction. In keeping with an interdisciplinary behavioral medicine approach, it is important to work in concert with the child's medical team and referring physician to ensure that the family is receiving consistent messages. Some of the educational content will vary depending on the child's specific pain complaints; however, a few key points can be emphasized with most children:

Your pain is very real and very big. We don't deny that at all. But the "good news" (if there is any to be found) is that, based on the results of your medical tests, your symptoms do not appear to be dangerous or life threatening. Painful and yucky? Yes, absolutely. You have living proof of that. But not dangerous, and that's a good thing. For one, it means that there is no physical harm in your continuing to move about and do the things you really enjoy and want to do. Not that this will be easy by any means. Especially when the pain monster is there telling you to quit. But that's part of what our work together will be about: learning to create the life you truly want, even when the pain monster is there. Does this [e.g., your values, your dreams, your life] sound like something you'd be willing to work for?

Ongoing Functional Assessment

We suggest conducting a descriptive (as opposed to experimental) functional analysis at the initial assessment and over the course of treatment. In doing so, the clinician identifies (1) antecedents (A)—the situations, experiences, and events that trigger or give way to clinically relevant behavior; (2) clinically relevant behavior (B) that may be targeted over the course of treatment; and (3) consequences (C), or the consequent experiences and events that play a role in maintaining clinically relevant behavior.

Using an ACT approach, it is often useful to conceptualize aversive private experiences (including pain symptoms) and the situations that occasion them as antecedents. Child and parent responses to physical and emotional pain (rather than pain itself) are then conceptualized as clinically relevant behavior that leads to pain-related disability. Finally, the child's and parent's consequent private experience, level of functioning in valued domains, and reactions from others are viewed as the short- and long-term consequences of engaging in the clinically relevant behavior.

In conducting a functional analysis of pain behavior, there are many ways to identify the ABCs. The clinician might begin by identifying the topographical and contextual features of pain and pain-related behavior: In what situations does the pain typically occur (A)? What types of thoughts and feelings are experienced before and during the pain episodes (A)? The clinician might then identify the problem behavior, or ways in which the child seeks to control his or her pain: What does the child or parent actually do when pain comes up (B)? How does the child respond to the thought that "this pain is unbearable" (B)? Finally, the clinician might ask the child and parent to describe what happens after he or she exhibits clinically relevant behavior. In ACT, personal values represent the desired long-term consequences (C) that the child and parent wish to pursue. Thus, when exploring consequences of pain behavior, it is important to inquire about the child's values across a number of domains (e.g., family, friends, school, fun, dating). Have attempts to manage or control pain interfered with meaningful areas of life (C)? From an ACT perspective, the "problem" can often be conceptualized as this: when children experience physical or emotional pain (A), their attempts to manage or control these symptoms (B) have the paradoxical effect of perpetuating pain-related disability and moving them away from their valued life directions and goals (C).

Identifying Relevant ACT Processes

During the initial assessment and throughout treatment, we look for instances of cognitive fusion and experiential avoidance in the client's life and in the therapy room. We ask questions to identify private events that the child and caregiver are fused with and ways in which they seek to avoid, manage, or control these experiences. In conducting a functional analysis, the clinician might discover that the child is fused with thoughts such as "there must be something wrong with me; I can't live a good life as long as I have all this pain." The functional analysis will similarly point to instances of experiential avoidance. For example, the child may respond to his or her thoughts as if they were literally true by restricting daily activities, visiting the nurse's office most days of the school week, and declining social invitations in anticipation of future pain. An ACT approach to pediatric pain targets unworkable avoidance behavior that interferes with life quality and values-based living. Notably, most pain-related behavior can be conceptualized as such, even when other functions (e.g., attention from caregivers) are present. Table 2 presents common antecedents, behaviors, and consequences that might be used to facilitate an ACT case conceptualization.

Table 1. Sample Functional Analysis to Identify Variables Maintaining Pain Behavior

Antecedents (External and Internal)	**Clinically Relevant Behavior**	**Consequences**
Lower back pain; thought that "something must be wrong"; thought that "doctors don't know what they're doing"; feelings of frustration and anxiety.	Seek medical services; emergency room visit; undergo invasive medical procedures to find out what's wrong; child misses school and Dad misses work to attend appointments; child restricts activities.	**Short-term:** Less worry because at least something is being done; attention from Dad and medical staff. **Long-term:** Increased frustration and anxiety because back pain persists; distrust toward medical system; child falling behind in school; increase in depression due to isolation and lack of physical activity; Dad takes leave of absence to care for child.
Friend invites to a party; anticipation/fear of future pain; stomach upset; thought that "it will be embarrassing to have to leave early because of my pain."	Turn down invitation; stay home and watch television alone in bed.	**Short-term:** Anticipation and fear are alleviated; stomach feels better; avoids potential embarrassment. **Long-term:** Misses out on opportunity to spend time with friends; possibly reduces likelihood of future invitation.
Migraine (intense throbbing) and sensitivity to light and sound; thoughts that "this pain is unbearable and there's no way I can make it through the day"; feelings of sadness; fatigue due to lack of sleep.	Go to the nurse's office; take headache medicine; call Mom because symptoms continue; child comes home to rest.	**Short-term:** Mom leaves work and picks child up from school; throbbing sensations go down; unpleasant thoughts go away. **Long-term:** Mom misses more and more work to care for child; child falls behind in school due to repeated absences; child misses softball game and is unable to spend time with friends due to dropping grades and increasing amount of makeup work.

Providing Feedback and Clarifying Treatment Goals

When providing feedback and discussing treatment goals, we find it useful to begin by validating the family's experience. Many youth experience the pain itself as unmanageable. Thus it is important to communicate an understanding of how hard the pain experience has been and how attempts to manage this pain have resulted in a decrease of important activities. We also address the frustration and anxiety of not knowing what to do to make things better. When talking to children, caregivers, and other health care professionals, it's important to describe treatment objectives in a very straightforward, nontechnical way. After discussing the case history, we normally conclude that (1) attempts to manage pain have resulted in disability; (2) many different interventions have been tried without any lasting improvements; and (3) increased functioning is an important goal of treatment. We address our shift in focus from the pain experience to creating a meaningful life that works even when pain is there. We express our commitment to the family, describing ourselves as advocates whose primary role is to support the child in creating a meaningful and valued life.

At this point, we might ask children and caregivers if they feel as though they are stuck. If so, it can be important to validate both the experience of pain and the frustration of being (often increasingly) disabled without any plan for how to reduce pain and return to normal functioning. By acknowledging the child's and family's sense of not knowing what to do, the clinician opens the door for introducing a fundamentally different way of approaching physical and emotional pain. This is an entryway to discussing a shift in perspective from symptom reduction to radical acceptance in the service of creating a vital life.

ACT Interventions for Pediatric Pain

The ACT interventions described below have become central in our work with pediatric pain patients. For ease of reading and clarifying purposes, we present various core clinical methods separately. It is important to note, however, that these methods are typically implemented in conjunction with each other rather than in isolation. This is perhaps unsurprising, as most or all of ACT's clinical processes are targeted in any given session. As such, the sequencing of interventions proposed in this chapter should be viewed as one of many possible pathways to effective treatment delivery.

Values Work: Shifting the Focus

In the first treatment session, we revisit the goals of an ACT approach and distinguish between (1) working to control pain no matter the cost, and (2) living a meaningful life even when pain is there. Our goal as clinicians is to empower families in doing the latter. From an ACT perspective, values represent a chosen life direction that cannot be achieved in a static or absolute sense as can concrete goals (although concrete goals can be set in the service of moving in a valued direction). We introduce values work early in the program to enhance client motivation and to establish a course for treatment. Values work is also critical in facilitating difficult exposure tasks that may or may not result in symptom reduction. As noted earlier, ACT differs from some behavioral approaches in that symptom reduction is not an end goal. Yet we do not ask our clients to face pain for pain's sake. Instead clients are asked to make commitments that may involve facing pain when the costs of not doing so are high and in many ways life deadening. In this way, values work dignifies the patient's engagement in painful exposure exercises that offer no promise of symptom reduction (e.g., Dahl et al., 2004; Robinson et al., 2004).

We begin to identify valued domains at the start of treatment; however, values clarification is an ongoing process that continues throughout the course of therapy (and life). At the start of treatment, the clinician might dialogue with the child about what a valued life would look like in a world full of possibilities and without limitations. We keep it simple with children, perhaps starting out with an empty blackboard and asking the child what he or she would like to do more of. Oftentimes patients provide "reasons" and "stories" for why a valued life is not possible (e.g., "my pain keeps me from doing fun things"; I need to get rid of my pain"; "I can never have a normal life because of my pain").

We begin right away to use defusing language with the child (e.g., "so your mind is at it again, telling you 'the good life' isn't possible"; "you're having the thought that this is going to be really hard, if not impossible"). Rather than disagreeing or diving into content, the clinician might write down all of the reasons, stories, and rules that surface during the values-identification process and simply acknowledge that this is what our chattering minds do. We recommend staying connected with the child's values and asking the child to suspend reality for a moment: "Okay, just for this exercise, let's wipe pain off the table altogether. What would your life look like in a world with no pain? What would you choose to do in a world where you're in charge and pain doesn't stand in your way? What would you be doing, like with your hands and your feet?" The clinician might also introduce or revisit the pain monster at this point.

Therapist: Last time we met, I got the impression that life isn't really the way you want it to be right now.

Child/Teen: No, it sucks. Everything hurts.

Therapist: I also got the feeling that you have tried a bunch of different things to make your pain go away, but this hasn't worked all that well. You're still in pain.

Child/Teen: Yeah. It doesn't matter what I do. Acupuncture worked for a while but not anymore.

Therapist: It sounds like you're stuck. You've tried everything and nothing has worked.

Child/Teen: Yeah.

Therapist: And it's costing you big time. So much of your life has become about managing pain—not about living and doing those things you truly want to do.

Child/Teen: Pretty much. I wish it wasn't like this.

Therapist: Of course. This sounds really yucky. Like a big pain monster standing between you and what you really care about. And that's what I'd like to talk about today. I want to learn more about you and your values—what you really, really care about; what matters most in your life; you know, the important and cool stuff. I want to learn more about what you enjoy doing, the people you enjoy spending time with, and what you dream about doing now and in the future. How does that sound?

Child/Teen: Sounds okay, I guess. It'll be kind of hard though. There are a lot of things that I can't do right now—not because I don't want to but because I can't.

Therapist: I agree that this exercise is really hard at times. You might have thoughts like "I won't be able to do this" and "I don't want to talk about my values because I'll just be disappointed afterward when I can't do anything." If your mind gives you thoughts like these, simply notice them. You might even say to yourself, "There's another thought." And you can let me know what your mind is saying—what thoughts you're having and how you're feeling inside. If and when discomfort comes up for you, we can think of it as a little pain monster sitting on your shoulder, chatting away. [The clinician might enlist the child's/teen's help in drawing the pain monster on the board.] Does your mind ever bully you, boss you around, or put you down like this?

Child/Teen: Sometimes, like when I study for an exam. I think, "What if I fail?" and "I'm not as smart as the other kids." Is that what you mean?

Therapist: Yes, that's it exactly. That's your mind giving you a hard time. It's like a little pain monster that follows you wherever you go. My mind does that too; sometimes it kicks my butt, telling me all kinds of wacky or hurtful things. So here's my suggestion: When our minds start chattering away and giving us reasons why we can't do this exercise or why we can't have a good life, then we'll simply notice what our minds are saying. And we'll sit with the pain monster and listen without necessarily doing what it says. Instead we'll continue writing out your values, even if the pain monster interrupts, says this will never work, or whatever. We'll come up with things that you want to do, and we'll talk about your dreams and what you long for, even if the pain monster says you will never get there. Are you willing to do this?

Child/Teen: Sure. I can try.

At the beginning of treatment, youth often describe their "values" in terms of concrete goals. In this case, the clinician can help the child find the value by asking why various activities are meaningful—what makes it special to the child? During the initial values-identification process, children and adolescents may also state that they don't know what their values are or that there isn't anything they wish was different in their life. Almost always, such responses are instances of experiential avoidance. After all, it hurts to care deeply about something, especially when we're fused with the belief that we can never have or achieve it. Thus the youth's verbal reports may be functioning as avoidance of anxiety and sadness associated with caring ("valuing") about something that is seemingly unattainable. In such cases, the child might be asked what he or she would choose to do if pain went away. The clinician might also ask the patient to recall an earlier time in life when things were different, a time when he or she remembers having goals and dreams. The child can describe meaningful moments in his or her life—what he or she was doing, whether anyone else was there, and what made this moment special. It may also be useful to initiate defusion and mindfulness work at this point to promote acceptance of painful experiences that might otherwise interfere with the values-clarification process.

In our work with pediatric pain patients, the purpose of values work extends beyond goal setting to initiate treatment. Valuing in ACT is itself an ongoing process of exposure to painful private experiences (such as thoughts, emotions, and memories) that inevitably arise when we honestly evaluate our lives (e.g., thoughts about past failures, fear of future rejection, perceived injustices, feelings of hopelessness, and sadness over a "wasted life"). By revisiting valued domains and barriers to living a meaningful life, patients are exposed to unpleasant thoughts and feelings as well as to challenges in their physical environment (which may also elicit aversive private events). Repeated exposure to these aversive experiences combined with defusion and mindfulness practice promotes willingness to enter fully into values work in and out of the therapy room.

Creative Hopelessness: Getting "Unstuck"

Creative hopelessness refers to the process of altering the context from attempts to control pain (i.e., unwillingness) to one of radical acceptance, or willingness to experience pain in the service of creating a vital life (Hayes et al., 1999). The child's and caregiver's efforts to control pain are challenged by focusing on the three critical questions: What do you want? What have you tried? How well has this worked in the short and long term (both in terms of alleviating pain and in terms of creating a valued life)? The process of creative hopelessness brings patients into direct contact with the workability of their current efforts to make the problem better. Oftentimes children and parents connect wholeheartedly with the futility of their efforts to control pain and acknowledge that they are completely and utterly stuck. The situation is indeed hopeless and cannot be won, at least not within the current system based on the culturally reinforced rule that to have a good life, you've got to get rid of your pain (or at the very least get it down to tolerable levels). We're sure to highlight that the "control pain" agenda may be hopeless; however, the patient is quite the opposite. The child is "response-able" (Hayes et al., 1999), or able to respond however he or she chooses, no matter what the pain monster says.

We have found the following illustration to be a useful clinical tool, representing both the child's struggle to control pain (unwillingness) and the costs of carrying out this struggle (loss of valued life directions). By successively drawing this figure with the child, previous and future change agendas can be discussed concretely and collaboratively. As with most ACT interventions, the clinician should guard against making this an intellectual exercise and continually check in with the child's actual experience. The discussion itself provides an opportunity for emotional exposure and may be done in conjunction with mindfulness and defusion exercises as unpleasant internal experiences begin to show up.

Figure 1. The Patient's Dilemma

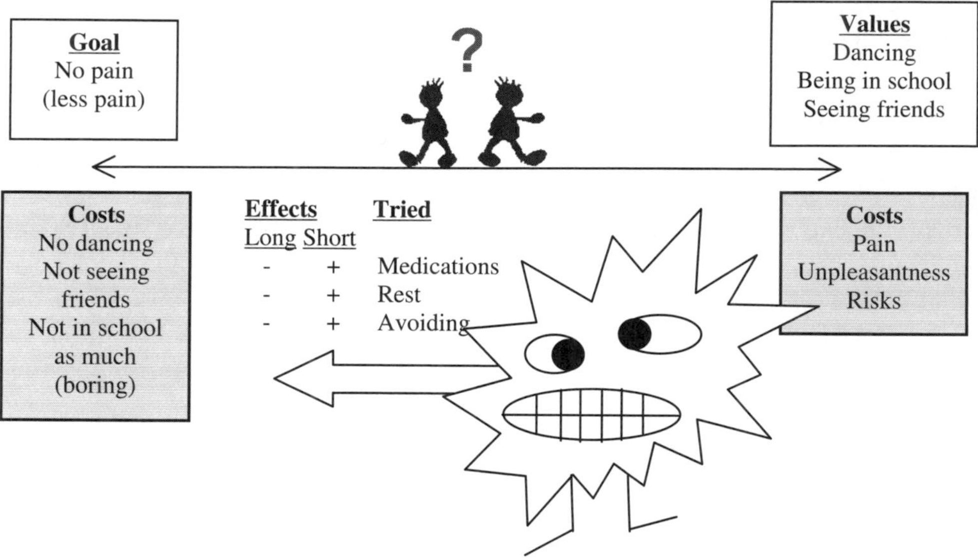

This illustration is used during creative hopelessness and throughout treatment to examine the workability of current and previous change strategies, as well as the short- and long-term consequences of the pain-avoidance agenda. The pain monster represents thoughts, emotions, and bodily sensations that children and families struggle with, often at the cost of living out their personal values.

Workability of Previous Strategies

We typically initiate the exercise in figure 1 after identifying several core values as well as associated control efforts that interfere with the child's pursuit of these values. The left side of the figure is essentially about the workability of previous strategies and goals. It is important to ask what the child has considered to be the ultimate goal of the strategies and treatments he or she has tried. Perhaps the most common answer is "it's impossible to have no pain, but my goal is to have as little pain as possible." Once we have established the purpose of current and past change efforts, we list what the child has done to achieve this goal of "as little pain as possible." Common examples include pain medication, acupuncture, heat, massage, and rest. We can also ask if there are things that the child has not done or has avoided in an effort to reduce pain (e.g., do you stay home from school, stay in bed instead of going out with friends, sit out during softball practice, or stop playing altogether?). No matter the content, it is important to validate the child's and caregiver's efforts, which have often been considerable: "It sounds as if you have been trying really hard. I get the impression that you've got a fighting spirit."

After identifying key change efforts, we move to the middle of the figure to evaluate the short- and long-term workability of the child's and caregiver's efforts to control pain. Most of the strategies work quite well in the short term, and this should be acknowledged: "Many of the things you've tried really seem to reduce your pain, at least in the short run. No wonder you keep working at it. This seems like the natural and reasonable thing to do." Based on the child's experience, however, efforts to control or reduce pain produce long-term effects that are neutral at the very least (pain is still here) and are quite often negative or harmful. If this isn't the case, there may be little reason for the family to continue in treatment given that symptom reduction is not an end goal in ACT. Most of the time, however, children and caregivers connect immediately with the long-term costs associated with their current and previous efforts to manage the child's pain.

Next we ask the child to restate some of his or her personal values—"the important and cool stuff" that really matters in life. We ask the child to mark any valued areas in life that involve some risks, including risks of physical and emotional pain. Inevitably nearly all of the child's valued areas are marked, illustrating that it may not be possible to achieve both "as little pain as possible" and "the important and cool stuff" at the same time. We spend a moment talking about where on this line the child's values seem to fit. Given that living a meaningful life entails some amount of risk and pain, we extend the line to the right so that it represents a direction counter to that of "no pain" or "as little pain as possible."

Using this exercise, we can discuss an important choice that needs to be made: "If the goal in life is as little pain as possible, and the important stuff hurts … in what direction will you choose to go?" Using the pain monster metaphor, we ask whether the child will choose a direction suggested by the pain monster or a direction suggested by his or her values and dreams. At times, patients react with sadness, anxiety, or frustration. These and any other emotional reactions should be noticed with compassion. Although the choice presented may sound easy, the child is faced with the tremendously difficult task of having to let go of what he or she has always done. Moreover, most trusted adults have suggested, modeled, and reinforced these efforts to control pain. Even medical experts have supported the symptom reduction agenda through ongoing efforts to assess and treat the pain. Thus this exercise represents another opportunity to practice acceptance in the presence of difficult thoughts and emotions, perhaps adding a little creativity to this apparently "hopeless" situation.

Acceptance and Defusion

At the start of treatment, we move away from a symptom reduction model and begin to conceptualize efforts to control pain as "the problem." With chronic pain patients, we emphasize that acceptance is not restricted to physical pain but extends to all private experiences, including painful thoughts, feelings, memories, and the like. It may be helpful to make this important point concretely, such as by drawing an "experience cake" (a simple circle will do). Different pieces of the cake represent different types of unpleasant private experiences, such as back pain, worry, sadness, disappointment, self-critical thoughts, fear of failure, headache, dizziness, and fatigue. As the child describes his or her struggles, the therapist can clearly label each type of experience. In this way, the "experience cake" can be used to facilitate discrimination training of experiences that occur inside versus outside the child's skin while helping youth to distinguish among various types of private events (e.g., "that's a thought"; "fear is an emotion"; "dizziness is like a bodily sensation"; "sadness, that's another feeling"). We then emphasize the general experience of pain or discomfort rather than trying to intervene with each separate piece of the cake. Working collaboratively with the child, we name the whole cake using a term that fits with the child's subjective experience. Most often, children agree that these private experiences, though different in content and form, all represent "pain," "discomfort," and "unpleasantness" to some degree. We use whatever terms the child agrees to as a way of talking about physical and emotional pain (the pain monsters) in the child's life. The very process of labeling private events without evaluation, and writing them "out there" as separate from the child, can be a defusing experience. Throughout this exercise, we are sure to use defusing language and ask the child to do the same ("My mind tells me this pain is unbearable," "I'm having the thought that I can't do this," etc.).

Early in treatment, we begin to conceptualize the pain monster as something that appears very scary, like an actual monster that can do serious harm. In reality, however, the pain monster is not dangerous nor can it literally harm us. Rather, the harm comes from our natural tendency to listen to and obey whatever the pain monster says. In this way, we personally bring our painful private experiences front and center, and our lives largely become about keeping the peace with these monsters. Our hopes and dreams become secondary or fall away altogether. We've found that talking about private experiences in this more concrete and externalized way can itself be defusing, as the child begins to experience his or her private events as separate from who he or she is. In our work with young children and adolescents, we also use the many acceptance and defusion strategies described elsewhere (e.g., see Hayes et al., 1999; and chapters 8, 9, and

11 of this volume). As with any child-focused approach, the clinician should be sure to adapt these exercises to meet the child's unique situational and historical context and developmental level.

Mindfulness and Values-Based Exposure

Exposure in ACT differs from most exposure procedures in its emphasis on values and life vitality and on the centrality of acceptance. In ACT, acceptance is promoted to facilitate values-based exposure aimed explicitly at increasing life vitality in the presence of pain and distress (Robinson et al., 2004). (Exposure does not imply increasing nociceptive stimulation, i.e., tissue damage. The pain sensation discussed in this chapter results from an exaggerated activity in a sensitized central nervous system. Thus the pain experience is not dangerous, i.e., it does not correspond with tissue damage, in itself.) Across situations, the child will experience reasonable doubts about whether exposure to physical and emotional pain is worth it or not. An important role of the clinician is to support the child in persisting with difficult exposure tasks by clearly situating these tasks within the context of the child's deepest values. Thus the child faces pain in the service of something that matters—the important and cool stuff that brings meaning to life.

Exposure can also be done in conjunction with mindfulness exercises, in which the child practices nonjudgmental awareness of the present moment. Mindfulness practice has a defusing effect; by noticing the transitory nature of painful thoughts and feelings, we begin to experience them for what they really are—thoughts and feelings that, no matter how painful, cannot do us any harm (the pain monster will, of course, suggest otherwise). Thoughts and feelings come and go, yet the person behind our eyes (the "observer self") continues to notice our monsters, all the while remaining completely unharmed and unchanged (Hayes et al., 1999).

Depending on the child's developmental level, the clinician might begin with relatively short mindfulness exercises (e.g., 1–3 minutes) using more concrete targets of awareness (e.g., tastes, sights, and sounds). We sometimes use a singing bowl or handmade musical instruments to practice mindfulness of sound and chewy fruit candies to facilitate mindfulness of taste. As children learn to observe and describe more benign experiences without judgment, we begin to lengthen the duration of mindfulness exercises and extend the targets of awareness to include private experiences and, eventually, the dreaded pain monsters (e.g., painful thoughts, feelings, and physical-bodily sensations).

After we help the child to build a regular mindfulness practice both in and out of session, we move to mindfulness-based exposure tasks set within the context of the child's personal values. As with other behavioral approaches, exposure in ACT may be done in vivo or as an eyes-closed imaginal exercise. When done as an eyes-closed exercise, the clinician describes the avoided or feared situation in vivid detail and instructs the child to notice any internal experiences that arise. The clinician might check in throughout the exercise, asking the child to describe a painful thought or feeling without evaluation (e.g., "My stomach is hurting" or "My mind says I can't do this"). The clinician leads a "mindfulness-of-experience" exercise using whatever content the child provides. The clinician works to deepen the child's emotional experience (exposure to painful content) by asking him to notice, describe, observe, and sit with whatever experiences come up. The child practices "making space" for the pain monsters by adopting an observer perspective. He might, for example, be asked to assume the posture of a curious scientist looking down through a microscope at his specimen (Greco, Blackledge, Coyne, & Ehrenreich, 2005). The scientist looks down through the microscope with great interest, yet does so without attachment and without judgment.

The purpose of combining mindfulness exercises with exposure is to facilitate open, nonjudgmental awareness of painful private experiences at critical moments. Using mindfulness, the child is brought into intimate contact with her physical and emotional pain. She learns to "sit with" her experience, whatever it may be. Rather than struggle to avoid the pain monsters, she becomes a curious, nonjudgmental observer who watches the monsters as they come and go. Through regular mindfulness practice, our child patients begin to experience physical and emotional pain monsters as less threatening and less real. As a result, they are more willing to face their monsters head-on during difficult exposure tasks without engaging in even subtle or covert forms of avoidance such as distraction, imagery, or cognitive restructuring.

There are several issues the therapist needs to consider when doing exposure with chronic pain patients. In essence, making a commitment to values-based exposure implies accepting pain and distress even if no obvious reinforcement is present. This illustrates the importance of ongoing values work, which psychologically brings the long-term contingencies and desired ends into the present. The clinician should also attend to important socialization agents and influences in the child's life. Even when our child patients make space for pain, at least some members of their immediate support system (e.g., family, friends, teachers, and other treatment providers) continue to embrace a symptom reduction model. This issue may be addressed in part by working directly with some of the most important people in the child's life—his or her parents.

Working with Parents

As noted above, it is common for adults in the child's life to model and reinforce a control agenda that steers the child off course in pursuing his or her valued directions. Although there are many important and influential people in a child's life (parents, peers, teachers, other relatives, health care providers), we focus here on ways in which the clinician might work with caregivers. Although children and adolescents are often the identified patients, our interventions almost always extend to the parenting and family context.

Individual Work with Parents

Many of the parents we work with report feeling guilty about "forcing" their children to engage in daily activities (e.g., chores, school, and sports) when they are in pain or not feeling well. These parents are frequently fused with thoughts such as these: "My child is injured or sick." "Only bad parents would make their injured or sick child go to school." "What if this is really serious?" "I must take care of my child." "My child's pain needs to go away before he can do what other kids do." Parents frequently engage in avoidance behavior to alleviate unpleasant thoughts and emotions surrounding both their child's pain and their role as parents. For example, to assuage his sadness and guilt, a father allows his daughter to stay home from school and excuses her from responsibilities such as household chores and homework. A substantial number of families we work with may even withdraw their children from school, with the belief that homeschooling is a more suitable option for their sick or injured children. Some parents take a leave of absence or quit their jobs so that they may better care for their child.

Every parent feels bad about seeing his or her child in pain. Some parents respond to this discomfort by engaging in what we refer to as "nursing," a pattern of caretaking behavior that serves to reduce both the child's pain and the parent's emotional distress. Although parents may believe that nursing will have beneficial effects, this form of experiential avoidance almost inevitably yields life-narrowing consequences for both the child and the parent. If at all possible, we suggest working individually with parents who exhibit elevated fusion and experiential avoidance, as the resulting parenting behavior (e.g., nursing) is likely to interfere with the child's treatment. Moreover, many of these parents are themselves suffering and may benefit from participating in an ACT-oriented therapy.

Most of the parents we work with agree to participate in at least several individual sessions. During these sessions, we focus on the parents' emotional experience as parents and as human beings more generally. We validate and normalize parents' experience of their child's pain and initiate values work that focuses largely on (1) family and parenting values, (2) the type of relationship parents want to have with their children, and (3) the parents' hopes and dreams, as well as the life they most want for themselves and their children. Similar to our work with youth, we use mindfulness and defusion strategies to promote psychological acceptance and to facilitate values work with parents. We support parents in living consistently with their parenting and family values, even when their child is hurting and when painful emotions such as fear, doubt, guilt, insecurity, and sadness arise for the child and parent.

Doing individual ACT work with parents has the benefit of getting everyone on the same page. Parents are now oriented to a context of acceptance and, through the process of creative hopelessness, they are connected with the long-term costs of trying to control both their own and their child's pain. We introduce parents and children to "valuing" as a lifelong process and teach them mindfulness skills that can be practiced in and out of session. By having this shared set of experiences, family members begin to approach their own and each other's pain with more openness and flexibility. This common perspective assists with joint therapy sessions and supports generalization and maintenance of skills outside of therapy.

Joint Sessions

Even when it is not possible to do a full or truncated course of ACT with parents, it is essential to include them in the treatment process. At the very least, the clinician should provide information regarding an ACT case conceptualization and corresponding treatment goals. Far too often, parents are told that their child's disability results primarily from "laziness" or "secondary gain." From an ACT perspective, it is more useful to explain the child's pain behavior in terms of cognitive fusion and experiential avoidance. Using the same exercise in figure 1, clinicians can help parents connect with the short- and long-term consequences of pursing the goal "as little pain as possible." If the child has already participated in creative hopelessness, he or she might colead this exercise with the therapist. It can be fun for children to teach parents and other important adults about their personal values, the big bad pain monsters, and what happens when we do what the pain monsters say (e.g., we lose sight of our values, the pain monsters get bigger as life gets smaller, we miss out on the cool and important stuff in life).

Parents as Coaches

It is important to provide guidance and alternatives for how parents might best support improvements in their child's functioning. It is much more common for the parents we work with to do too much than too little. "Not doing" for their child often results in feelings of guilt or unpleasant thoughts about their child's pain and about themselves as parents. Parents frequently respond by intervening at times and in situations that may represent important opportunities for problem solving and growth. In some situations, the growth-promoting action for children and parents alike is to allow the child to be "big enough" to have the problem, even when the problem is pain. Instead of stepping in to rescue or nurse, we might ask parents to leave their child to develop a self-generated plan for how to accomplish or do something important. In essence, we ask parents to give their child space to experience pain. In the short term, this can be equally difficult for parents and children. In the long term, however, making space for one's own and another's pain may have unexpected benefits that foster personal growth and enhance life vitality.

Many of the parents we work with describe being a good caregiver and supporting their child's growth and development as important parenting values. Parents also describe long-term wishes for their child such as wanting them to be happy and successful in social and academic arenas. Using the exercise in figure 1, we can help parents connect with the experienced workability of their current parenting strategies and responses to their child's pain behavior. Oftentimes parents are quick to identify the long-term costs of trying to manage their child's and their own pain such as through nursing, taking a leave of absence to care for their child, and encouraging their child to "take it easy" or "sit this one out."

It would be similarly unworkable for parents to abandon their involvement altogether; we therefore ask them to assume a different role of great importance throughout their child's treatment—that of a coach. By enlisting parents as coaches, we essentially provide an opportunity for them to enact some of their most important parenting values (e.g., being a good caregiver, supporting their child's healthy development, helping their child to persevere in difficult times). We invite parents to become involved in a way that will promote their child's and their own well-being and quality of life. As coaches, parents might facilitate difficult out-of-session exposure tasks, practice mindfulness with their child (or remind their child to do so on his or her own), and support their child in following through with values-consistent action steps and goals for the week. Parent coaches are also instrumental in their child's return to normal day-to-day functioning. For example, a mother coach reminds her son of his education and friendship values while driving him to school on a day that he wakes up with pain and asks to stay home from school. As discussed earlier, it is important to attend to the parents' emotional experience throughout treatment. Many of our parent coaches report feeling guilty or sad for "pushing" their child, which provides an ideal opportunity to do acceptance and values work within a parenting and family context.

Recruiting

Another way to involve parents is through the use of recruiting, in which the child and possibly the therapist have a serious talk with important adults who may be steering the child off course inadvertently by supporting a pain-avoidance agenda. As mentioned, it is natural for adults to point children in the direction of "as little pain as possible," such as by suggesting that the child sit out during gym class, rest instead of going to a friend's house, or stay home from school after a night of pain and poor sleep. We find that most significant others such as parents, teachers, and friends (1) have not considered the possible functions of child pain behavior (e.g., avoidance), (2) are unaware of how their own responses contribute to the child's pain behavior and associated disability, and/or (3) believe that this is the only supportive and compassionate way of behaving toward a child who is "sick" or in pain. Parent behavior is an important focus in the functional assessment and is directly or indirectly targeted throughout treatment (e.g., goal setting around parenting values; education on how parent responses may inadvertently reinforce child pain behavior). Still, it is often difficult for parents to give up this particular control strategy. As illustrated on the following page, recruiting may be used to encourage parental involvement that supports the child's efforts to create a meaningful life if and when pain is there.

Use of Recruiting to Enlist Parental Support in Treatment

A sixteen-year-old adolescent girl presented with diffuse neurological symptoms (e.g., jerks, numbness, and itches in lower extremities) resulting in severe difficulties with walking. She underwent extensive medical testing without any positive findings. Her mother was very concerned and called the hospital repeatedly to discuss her daughter's symptoms and to request additional assessment and intervention. The daughter was eventually referred to participate in outpatient ACT sessions. The mother agreed to participate in a single session, during which the goals of an ACT approach were described, with emphasis on shifting perspective from symptom reduction to increased functioning, life vitality, and personal values. Although the mother expressed support for the treatment plan, she continued to phone various members of the treatment team regarding her daughter's symptoms. Eight weeks into treatment, the adolescent girl was progressing extremely well but expressed concern that her mother continued to focus on pain management and was starting to interfere with her ability to engage in valued activities. At this point, a recruiting strategy was used to enlist the mother's support. Together the therapist and adolescent outlined what needed to be said:

1. Ask Mom if we can talk; schedule a day and time to do so.
2. Tell Mom that she's important to me and that I really need her support right now.
3. Explain that I've changed my goal from having as little pain as possible to doing all of the things I really want to do in life (my values).
4. Let her know that I think it's okay and normal to have pain (both physical and emotional).
5. Let her know that I understand it is hard for her to see me in pain and that I know it is hard for her to push me to do things when I'm really down or in pain.
6. Tell her that it would mean a lot to me if she did this anyway—just like a coach.
7. Share with Mom that I will love her no matter what (even when I feel angry or sad or am in pain). Let her know that I really want to do the "important and cool stuff," and she can really help me out with this.
8. Give an example, like the time she told me to skip swim practice because my leg hurt or the time she made me rest instead of going to the movies with my friends.
9. Ask her if she would be willing to support me in my values, even when it's hard for me and for her. Let her know that even though this will probably be really hard, this is what I want for my life.

Conclusion

Scientific advances in the understanding and treatment of pediatric chronic pain leave us with an impressive armamentarium of possible interventions to choose from. Nevertheless, a substantial number of pediatric patients continue to exhibit marked impairment and functional disability in response to chronic pain syndromes. Clinicians and researchers have long emphasized the usefulness of an integrated behavioral medicine approach to working with pediatric patients and their families, with emphasis on psychosocial functioning rather than focusing narrowly on symptoms. Despite widespread agreement on the insufficiency of disease models, there continues to be a strong focus in psychological research and practice on symptom reduction and cognitive-emotional regulation. Such an approach may reinforce beliefs that physical and emotional pain should be managed or controlled, and must be substantially reduced for functioning and life quality to improve. An ACT approach, emphasizing values-based exposure and acceptance of uncontrollable pain and distress, is clearly a decided departure from traditional pain management models.

We presented an ACT conceptualization of pediatric chronic pain and suggested ways of adapting ACT clinical methods for children and their families. Central to this model of chronic pain is a radical shift in perspective from managing symptoms to promoting acceptance and learning to live well in the presence of pain and distress. In medical settings, the successful implementation of ACT requires ongoing collaboration with physicians, other members of the treatment team, and important adults in the child's life. As described in this chapter, a contextual shift from symptom alleviation to valued living in the presence of pain involves other people in the child's life. The illustration of the patient's dilemma (figure 1), along with discussions regarding acceptance, defusion, and mindfulness, can be used with parents and health care professionals to conceptualize the problem and treatment objectives. Empirical research with children and adults (e.g., Dahl et al., 2004; Greco et al., 2008; McCracken et al., 2007; McCracken, Vowles, & Eccleston, 2005; Wicksell et al., 2007) and our clinical experience suggest that ACT may be a beneficial approach for chronic pain patients. In the coming years, it will be essential to conduct well-designed randomized controlled trials to identify long-term outcomes and mechanisms of change in pediatric populations.

References

Brattberg, G. (2004). Do pain problems in young school children persist into early adulthood? A 13-year follow-up. *European Journal of Pain*, 8, 187–199.

Dahl, J., Wilson, K. G., & Nilsson, A. (2004). Acceptance and commitment therapy and the treatment of persons at risk for long-term disability resulting from stress and pain symptoms: A preliminary randomized trial. *Behavior Therapy*, 35, 785–801.

Eccleston, C., Malleson, P. N., Clinch, J., Connell, H., & Sourbut, C. (2003). Chronic pain in adolescents: Evaluation of a programme of interdisciplinary cognitive behaviour therapy. *Archives of Disease in Childhood, 88*, 881–885.

El-Metwally, A., Salminen, J. J., Auvinen, A., Kautiainen, H., & Mikkelsson, M. (2004). Prognosis of non-specific musculoskeletal pain in preadolescents: A prospective 4-year follow-up study till adolescence. *Pain, 110*, 550–559.

Fordyce, W. E. (1976). *Behavioral methods for chronic pain and illness.* Saint Louis, MO: The C. V. Mosby Company.

Greco, L. A., Blackledge, J. T., Coyne, L. W., & Ehrenreich, J. (2005). Integrating acceptance and mindfulness into treatments for child and adolescent anxiety disorders: Acceptance and commitment therapy as an example. In S. M. Orsillo & L. Roemer (Eds.), *Acceptance and mindfulness-based approaches to anxiety: Conceptualization and treatment* (pp. 301–322). New York: Springer.

Greco, L. A., Blomquist, M. A., Acra, S., & Moulton, D. (2008). *Acceptance and commitment therapy for adolescents with functional abdominal pain: Results of a pilot investigation.* Manuscript submitted for publication.

Greco, L. A., Freeman, K. A., & Dufton, L. M. (2006). Peer victimization among children with frequent abdominal pain: Links with social skills, academic functioning, and health service use. *Journal of Pediatric Psychology, 32*, 319–329.

Hayes, S. C., Bissett, R. T., Korn, Z., Zettle, R. D., Rosenfarb, I., Cooper, L., et al. (1999). The impact of acceptance versus control rationales on pain tolerance. *The Psychological Record, 49*, 33–47.

Hayes, S. C., Luoma, J. B., Bond, F. W., Masuda, A., & Lillis, J. (2006). Acceptance and commitment therapy: Model processes and outcomes. *Behaviour Research and Therapy, 44*, 1–25.

Hayes, S. C., Strosahl, K. D., & Wilson, K. G. (1999). *Acceptance and commitment therapy: An experiential approach to behavior change.* New York: Guilford.

Holden, E. W., Deichmann, M. M., & Levy, J. D. (1999). Empirically supported treatments in pediatric psychology: Recurrent pediatric headache. *Journal of Pediatric Psychology, 24*, 91–109.

Janicke, D. M., & Finney, J. W. (1999). Empirically supported treatments in pediatric psychology: Recurrent abdominal pain. *Journal of Pediatric Psychology, 24*, 115–127.

McCracken, L. M., & Eccleston, C. (2003). Coping or acceptance: What to do about chronic pain? *Pain, 105*, 197–204.

McCracken, L. M., Mackichan, F., & Eccleston, C. (2007). Contextual cognitive-behavioral therapy for severely disabled chronic pain sufferers: Effectiveness and clinically significant change. *European Journal of Pain, 11*, 314–322.

McCracken, L. M., Vowles, K. E., & Eccleston, C. (2004). Acceptance of chronic pain: Component analysis and a revised assessment method. *Pain, 107*, 159–166.

McCracken, L. M., Vowles, K. E., & Eccleston, C. (2005). Acceptance-based treatment for persons with complex, long standing chronic pain: A preliminary analysis of treatment outcome in comparison to a waiting phase. *Behaviour Research and Therapy, 43*, 1335–1346.

Merskey, H. (chairman), & International Association for the Study of Pain (IASP). (1979). Subcommittee on taxonomy: pain terms. A list with definitions and notes on usage. *Pain, 6*, 249–252.

Palermo, T. M. (2000). Impact of recurrent and chronic pain on child and family daily functioning: A critical review of the literature. *Developmental and Behavioral Pediatrics, 21*, 58–69.

Robinson, P., Wicksell, R. K., & Olsson, G. L. (2004). ACT with chronic pain patients. In S. C. Hayes & K. D. Strosahl (Eds.), *A practical guide to acceptance and commitment therapy* (pp. 315–345). New York: Springer.

Sleed, M., Eccleston, C., Beecham, J., Knapp, M., & Jordan, A. (2005). The economic impact of chronic pain in adolescence: Methodological considerations and a preliminary costs-of-illness study. *Pain, 119*, 183–190.

Turk, D. C., Meichenbaum, D., & Genest, M. (1983). *Pain and behavioral medicine: A cognitive behavioral perspective*. New York: Guilford.

Walco, G. A., Sterling, C. M., Conte, P. M., & Engel, R. G. (1999). Empirically supported treatments in pediatric psychology: Disease-related pain. *Journal of Pediatric Psychology, 24*, 155–167; discussion 168–171.

Wicksell, R. K., Ahlqvist, J., Bring, A., Melin, L., & Olsson, G. L. (2008). *Can exposure and acceptance strategies improve functioning and quality of life in people suffering from chronic pain and whiplash associated disorders (WAD)? A randomized controlled trial.* Manuscript submitted for publication.

Wicksell R. K., Melin L., Ahlqvist J., Lekander M., & Olsson, G. L. (2008). *Exposure and acceptance vs. a multidisciplinary treatment in children and adolescents with chronic pain: A randomized controlled trial.* Manuscript submitted for publication.

Wicksell, R. K., Melin, L., & Olsson, G. L. (2007). Exposure and acceptance in the rehabilitation of adolescents with idiopathic chronic pain: A pilot study. *European Journal of Pain, 11*, 267–274.

Chapter 6

Dialectical Behavior Therapy for Adolescents with Borderline Features

Kristen A. Woodberry, MSW, MA, doctoral student in clinical psychology, Harvard University;
Rosemary Roy, MSW, manager, Adult and Adolescent Dialectical Behavior Therapy Programs, ServiceNet Inc., Northampton, Massachusetts;
and Jay Indik, MSW, program director, Cutchins Programs for Children and Families, Northampton, Massachusetts

Dialectical behavior therapy (DBT) is a well established, empirically supported treatment for adult women diagnosed with borderline personality disorder (BPD; Linehan, 1993a). Grounded in a dialectical framework, balancing opposing ideas within a larger whole, it synthesizes acceptance strategies from Eastern traditions and change strategies from cognitive behavioral therapies to effectively manage the complex clinical presentation of this population. Multiple randomized controlled trials have now demonstrated DBT's superiority to treatment as usual (see Robins & Chapman, 2004, for a review) and even to treatment by experts (Linehan et al., 2006) in reducing problems associated with BPD.

It is not surprising, given the evidence base and widespread popularity of DBT (Swenson, Torrey, & Koerner, 2002), that there has been great enthusiasm for adapting this approach for adolescents (Miller, Rathus, & Linehan, 2006). Preliminary controlled trials support the feasibility and potential promise of this endeavor (e.g., Katz, Cox, Gunasekara, & Miller, 2004; Rathus & Miller, 2002). In this chapter, we provide a short review of the basic theory, structure, and strategies of DBT with a particular focus on the concepts of acceptance and mindfulness. Next we review the major issues encountered in conducting DBT with adolescents and some common adaptations these have fostered. Finally, the majority of the chapter is devoted to specific strategies and exercises we have employed in conducting DBT with adolescents in both outpatient and residential care settings. In keeping with the focus of this book, we emphasize methods for teaching acceptance and mindfulness to adolescents and their families.

A Brief Overview of DBT

DBT is a comprehensive treatment for adults with borderline personality disorder (BPD). It is dialectical in its synthesis of opposing ideas, the most fundamental being that of acceptance and change. DBT is grounded in a biosocial theory, which posits that the behavioral patterns characterizing BPD develop out of a transactional process between an emotionally vulnerable individual (presumably due to largely biological factors) and an invalidating environment (one that communicates to the individual that her private experience is somehow wrong or inappropriate). The treatment is highly structured around a hierarchy of behavioral targets and stages of treatment. The overall goal is to increase dialectical behavior patterns, or the ability to effectively manage intense and conflicting emotions and truths. However, the primary behavioral targets of stage one are first, to decrease suicidal and suicide-related behaviors; second, to decrease behaviors interfering with effective therapy; and third, to decrease behaviors that interfere with the individual's quality of life. The final goal of this stage is to increase behavioral skills (Linehan, 1993a).

These targets are addressed within four typical modes of treatment: individual therapy, skills training (typically in group format), telephone consultation, and therapist consultation meetings. Ancillary modes, such as pharmacotherapy, are often included as well. The core methods of DBT consist of dialectical strategies, acceptance-oriented validation strategies, and change-oriented problem-solving strategies. These are supplemented by stylistic and case management strategies. As the name implies, dialectical strategies are at the center of DBT and synthesize its otherwise contradictory components. They facilitate the balance of acceptance and change within the therapeutic relationship and the treatment over time (Linehan, 1993a).

Validation strategies are the primary means for facilitating acceptance, as they communicate to a client that her experience makes sense. In recognizing the validity of emotions, cognitions, or behaviors within a given context, validation is placed in sharp contrast to the idea of change. Validation can occur both verbally (e.g., "of course you're mad") and functionally (e.g., bringing a thirsty person water). Finally, problem-solving strategies, drawn primarily from cognitive behavioral treatments, include behavioral and solution analyses, skills training, contingency management, exposure, and cognitive modification (Linehan, 1993a). Skills training, although only one component of this complex treatment, is manualized and given protected time separate from the individual treatment. This assures that skill acquisition and strengthening are not repeatedly set aside in the face of crises. Skills of mindfulness, emotion regulation, interpersonal effectiveness, and distress tolerance are taught to address deficits common in this population. While all skill areas encompass aspects of both acceptance and change, mindfulness and distress tolerance predominantly facilitate acceptance, while emotion regulation and interpersonal effectiveness skills focus more explicitly on change.

Distinctions from Other Acceptance-Based Treatments

DBT is distinct from other acceptance-based treatments in this book in three ways: the population for which it was designed, the overarching emphasis on dialectics, and the manner in which mindfulness is conceptualized and taught. Borderline personality disorder is a particularly challenging disorder to treat, as it is typically characterized by affective instability, intense anger, impulsivity, unstable interpersonal relationships, and recurrent suicidal threats and behavior. A dialectical frame facilitates the integration of contrasting perspectives and strategies necessary for clients and therapists to effectively solve complex problems. Acceptance and mindfulness are critical to facilitating the tolerance of lower priority problems so that the highest priority problems can be solved (Linehan, 1993a).

Acceptance is conceptualized in relation to understanding the world contextually and dialectically. "The practice of acceptance includes focusing on the current moment, seeing reality as it is without 'delusions,' and accepting reality without judgment" (Robins, Schmidt, & Linehan, 2004, p. 39). Mindfulness in DBT relates specifically to "the quality of both awareness and participation that a person brings to everyday living" (Robins et al., 2004, p. 37). At the most basic level, DBT mindfulness skills are taught as a method of attentional control. The better individuals are able to control what they attend to or notice, the better they are able to choose and employ emotion regulation or other strategies. Yet the ultimate goal of mindfulness in DBT is not to distance oneself from one's experience but to fully participate in it. Individuals with BPD are generally considered avoidant of emotional experiencing (Linehan, 1993a, 1993b). Mindfulness and acceptance are both tools for emotional exposure and the learning of new responses to emotional cues (Lynch, Chapman, Rosenthal, Kuo, & Linehan, 2006).

Given the severity of emotional avoidance in individuals with BPD, practice is typically brief, on the order of seconds at first, then minutes. And while the eventual goal is increased awareness of present experience, attention is focused on external events and observations as well as thoughts and body sensations, especially in the beginning. Individuals are directed to practice in concrete, simple ways to start, such as mindfully noticing sensations while petting a cat. Longer and more difficult mindfulness exercises are encouraged only after practicing with shorter time periods and easier foci.

Issues in Adapting DBT for Adolescents and Families

There are a number of important issues in adapting DBT for adolescents and families. We've divided these into three categories: diagnostic, developmental, and contextual.

Diagnostic Issues

Diagnostically there is ongoing debate about the appropriateness of diagnosing BPD in adolescents (Meijer, Goedhart, & Treffers, 1998; Miller et al., 2006), and thus the obvious question of whether or not DBT, a treatment designed specifically for BPD, is appropriate for this age group. Several arguments are typically made in favor of DBT with adolescents: (1) many adolescents demonstrate emotional and behavioral patterns consistent with this *DSM-IV-TR* diagnosis, including self-injury and suicidal behavior (e.g., Becker, Grilo, Edell, & McGlashan, 2002); (2) personality disorders often begin in adolescence (American Psychiatric Association, 2000); (3) suicidal and self-injuring adolescents presenting for treatment are similar to adults with BPD in their heterogeneity, multiproblem presentation, and high rates of comorbidity (Becker et al., 2002; D'Eramo, Prinstein, Freeman, Grapentine, & Spirito, 2004); (4) DBT is particularly well suited for multiproblem populations at risk for self-harm or suicide as it provides a clear hierarchy of treatment targets for behavioral shaping, along with skills training to address a number of common and relevant skill deficits (Miller et al., 2006); and (5) DBT appears to be beneficial for a number of multiproblem populations, even in the absence of a BPD diagnosis (Robins & Chapman, 2004). In the end, the emphasis in adolescent DBT is on behavioral targets (e.g., suicide attempts and ideation, self-injury, intense and inappropriate anger) and thus on features of BPD rather than on the diagnosis per se. This may ultimately be helpful to early intervention and even prevention of adult BPD (Miller et al., 2006).

Developmental Issues

The developmental stage of adolescence represents a dialectic, in that it involves aspects of both childhood and adulthood. It is a time of multiple and complex biological, social, and psychological changes. Although adolescents can be experienced as powerful to the adults responsible for them, the power they wield has practical and legal limits. The behaviors of adolescents with features of BPD typically evoke more rather than less adult control. In spite of a capacity for dialectical thinking, adolescents with BPD features are often poorly equipped for increased independence. In general, adolescents tend to have a different perspective on time (one year can seem like forever), and their behavior may be more transient because they have shorter, less ingrained learning histories.

A final developmental consideration in working with adolescents relates to the importance of reaching developmental milestones on time (e.g., transition to next grade).

Clinicians experience increased pull to intervene in hospitals, schools, families, and other environments to help teens stay on track. In fact, Linehan (1993a) specifically notes the need for more environmental intervention in the case of minors. Yet very active intervention in the environment is in dialectical tension with a basic principle of DBT: consulting with the patient. Rather than acting on behalf of the patient, the therapist consults with her on how to interact effectively with her own environment. For example, instead of calling the special education director to discuss appropriate classroom placement or adaptations, the clinician's job is to coach the young person in advocating for herself in her own special education meeting. Learning to identify and understand what one needs and advocate for oneself in a potentially intimidating context takes time. Unfortunately, delays in environmental change can increase risk for poor outcomes such as out-of-home placement. Our treatment teams have managed this dialectic by prioritizing consultation with the adolescent while simultaneously educating families, physicians, and school or residential treatment staff about DBT (see also Miller et al., 2006).

Contextual Issues

Families are perhaps the most important contextual variable to consider, even when adolescents are living away from their parents. They typically provide the most significant emotional triggers and reinforcers in the young person's life. One of the major differences in treating adolescents and adults is that the majority of adolescents live at home and under their parents' authority and care. Parents and other caregivers bear the major responsibility for the adolescents' safety and typically pay for their health care services. Clinicians are directly responsible to parents, and parents may have legal rights to inclusion in treatment. Most importantly, parents can be a tremendous resource.

And finally, you cannot treat adolescents without respecting the importance of peers. Clinicians conducting a behavioral treatment face heavy competition from peers in the reinforcement of behaviors. They must use whatever is at their disposal to be very juicy carrots if they have any hope of shaping skillful behaviors. Once the natural teen "leaders" in a group are invested in DBT, peers will shape skillful behaviors in each other. In our experience, taking time to connect with each adolescent, making sure that they know you recognize what's important to them and what they have to offer, and being radically genuine and vulnerable can be critical to this endeavor.

Specific Strategies for DBT with Adolescents and Families

The basic principles and strategies of standard DBT are appropriate for adolescents as well as adults. Adaptations relate primarily to format and style. With this in mind, we highlight four areas in which additional strategies or a shift in emphasis may be helpful: commitment strategies, strategies for working with families, stylistic strategies, and adaptations in skills training.

Commitment Strategies

In contrast to most adults, adolescents are often in treatment not by their own initiative or choice, but by the initiative of those for whom their behaviors are a problem. This creates an interesting dilemma, as DBT puts a great deal of emphasis on and devotes an entire stage of treatment to the process of commitment. For adolescents who identify themselves as neither in pain nor in need of treatment, DBT is essentially "sold" as a means for increasing their power to pursue their own goals. With youth who deny interest in treatment because they feel hopeless about being able to change anything, the task is to elicit evidence of a capacity to learn skills and make necessary changes. The therapist may need to help others identify goals or simply ask whether they are ready or willing to do what is needed to have more power. Having a treatment contract that holds therapists and family members equally accountable to the treatment can be empowering; ultimately, however, DBT must be directly related to achieving the adolescent's own goals (e.g., return home from a residential placement, feel more secure with friends, get adults off one's back, or create a life worth living). Explaining how DBT will address both short- and long-term goals within its hierarchy of treatment targets may help to prepare the adolescent for both the work involved and the process of change.

Some adolescent DBT treatment programs reward an active commitment, attendance, or skills practice with privileges or money, or coach families or schools to do this if clinically indicated and logistically feasible. In other programs, adolescents may be assigned to DBT treatment without being required to make a commitment ahead of time. This is essentially "DBT whether you like it or not." A stance of "we are stuck in this together" may be helpful as long as it is clear to the adolescent that the therapist wants a commitment in order to truly work together. External contingencies may continue to play a large role in securing the adolescent's engagement and eventual commitment until the relationship or benefits of change are sufficiently reinforcing on their own.

Strategies for Working with Families

Standard DBT is a cognitive behavioral treatment for individuals. At first glance, the inclusion of families may appear to conflict with this individual focus. However, DBT's dialectical worldview provides a natural framework for synthesizing the two (Linehan, 1993a; Woodberry, Miller, Glinski, Indik, & Mitchell, 2002). As Linehan explains, "[D]ialectics stresses interrelatedness and wholeness. It assumes a systems perspective on reality" (1993a, p. 31). It takes into account not only how the family shapes the adolescent but how the adolescent shapes the family. Dialectical strategies are obviously important as the therapist attends to tensions and balance; validation and problem-solving strategies are equally important. Let us provide an example.

A mother contacts her seventeen-year-old daughter's individual therapist, wanting to know whether her daughter is using drugs because she is scared for her daughter's safety when she doesn't come home on time. Indeed the adolescent is abusing a number of substances and has been in situations that put her at risk for sexual exploitation. The mother's fear is valid, as is the adolescent's right to confidentiality. If there is another clinician who can coach the mother, this is obviously ideal. However, when cotherapy is not an option, the individual therapist can engage a dialectical frame for managing these competing demands and rights. For instance, the therapist can reflect that the mother may not actually need to know what her daughter is doing to decide what she herself can or cannot do to protect her. Sometimes just validating a parent's concern can be sufficient to prompt effective problem solving. For example, the therapist might acknowledge the parent's difficult position of having to figure out how to allow the adolescent to be an adolescent while at the same time doing what needs to be done to keep her safe. Alternatively, the therapist might ask the mother what she thinks her daughter needs from her the most. This is both in keeping with the therapist's role with the girl and simultaneously reinforcing appropriate parenting.

While some parents may need much more directive and concrete help in this situation, and some at-risk behaviors may exceed the therapist's threshold for protecting adolescent confidentiality, these responses are consistent with DBT dialectical, validating, and problem-solving strategies. Both individual and family experiences can be honored simultaneously. Ideally both parents and adolescents learn to respect each other's experiences and take responsibility for effectively shaping each other's responses. While we often expect parents to initiate this change, it can be extremely empowering and can facilitate active acceptance to teach adolescents to take the lead.

Miller and colleagues (2006) have developed an extra module of skills training, "Walking the Middle Path," to help address some of the specific challenges of adolescents and their families in balancing acceptance and change strategies. While the standard dialectical dilemmas outlined by Linehan (1993a) remain very appropriate to work with adolescents, this module covers dialectical dilemmas specific to adolescents and their families (Rathus & Miller, 2000). These focus on the tendency for adolescents, their parents, and other adults, including therapists, to vacillate among (1) excessive leniency and authoritarian control; (2) normalizing pathological behaviors and pathologizing normative behaviors; and (3) forcing autonomy versus fostering dependence. Making these dilemmas explicit facilitates discussions of dialectical solutions to common adolescent-parent conflicts. It also provides an important framework for teaching validation and principles of behaviorism, the other two major emphases of this module.

Adolescent DBT programs have incorporated families in a number of ways. Parents may join the end of an adolescent's individual therapy sessions or participate in regular adjunctive family therapy. Some programs hold separate skills training groups for parents; others integrate parents into multifamily group skills training. Adolescents typically find it validating to not be the sole focus of treatment and to have their parents realize just how hard it is to learn new ways of behaving. Relationships can shift more readily when all family members are practicing skills, and parents are more likely to reinforce skillful behavior when they recognize it as such. Skills coaching to parents can be provided by skills training group leaders, a separate clinician assigned specifically for this role, or the individual therapist for the adolescent, especially if he or she is also conducting family therapy.

Stylistic Strategies

Stylistic strategies in DBT relate to the style and form of the therapist's communication. They include the use of warmth, edge, speed, and responsiveness. There is a role for both reciprocity and irreverence, and the therapist must be able to move rapidly between the two. Irreverence typically plays a larger role in work with adolescents than adults. When used judiciously, it can become one of the most validating and engaging skills a clinician has in working with this population. Relating to adolescents also involves constant attention to movement and timing. The term "jazz" has now come into use in DBT for incorporating movement, speed, and flow, a concept particularly important with younger populations.

A brief example of the role of timing with adolescents is illustrated by the story of Joey, a boy so impulsive and potentially violent that he was assigned to one-on-one staff at a residential school. He could not pass a pencil or fork on the edge of a table without flipping it. One day, however, he came to a pencil on the edge of a table. He raised his hand but paused before flipping it. The one-on-one staff with him in the school brought his attention to the fact that, in pausing, he showed awareness of the urge to flip the pencil before flipping it. Once mindful of the urge, he could take control of whether he flipped the pencil or chose an alternative behavior. Although Joey's application of this awareness to the urge to punch staff was even more greatly appreciated, the change in his behavioral control was facilitated by a simple, nicely timed observation and intervention.

Clinicians skilled in working with adolescents are dialectical masters. They take adolescents seriously and not seriously at the same time. They communicate deep respect for each adolescent, his experience, his strengths, his potential, his pain, and his fear. At the same time, they joke, answer the ridiculous in matter-of-fact tones, and get even distressed adolescents to laugh at themselves. They take challenges seriously and transform power struggles into opportunities for validation and learning. They learn when to hold firm or move in to push for change, and when to back off and let an adolescent come to new awareness in her own time. These skills have everything to do with the jazz of DBT. But they depend on clarity of purpose, which in DBT is to help adolescents build lives worth living. Perhaps most importantly, they rely on humility, which adolescents will be sure to return to any clinician who has lost hers.

Skills Training

Developmental considerations have spawned a number of common adaptations to skills training materials, such as age-appropriate, accessible language to accommodate different interests and vocabulary levels, and shorter text to engage young people with presumably shorter attention spans. These materials are then enhanced by visual images or examples from typical adolescent situations, often co-created with adolescents. Adolescent DBT programs often shorten the length of skills training sessions (e.g., 1–1.5 hours rather than 2.5 hours) as well as overall treatment duration or commitment (e.g., four months rather than six to twelve months). Similarly, skills training may be conducted in multifamily groups in which parents and adolescents have the opportunity to practice skills with parents or adolescents from other families, before trying to change the long-term interactional patterns within their own family. To the extent that the multifamily group context elicits more prosocial behavior than the individual family context, the multifamily group context may enhance learning. Families with very high tension or stormy relationships may better utilize individual family therapy after a round of skills training.

Teaching DBT skills to adolescents takes creativity, courage, and flexibility. Adolescents do not typically tolerate a lot of didactic time. In general, teens like to be involved in discussion, debate, activities, or role plays. Skills trainers need to be focused on the major points they want to convey and have clear and adolescent-relevant examples. Especially when leading multifamily groups, leaders need to be comfortable with potentially conflicting perspectives in the room and focus the group's energy toward learning skills. Although skills training groups are the primary mode for skill acquisition and strengthening, individual and family sessions or contacts play an important role in skill strengthening and generalization.

Teaching Dialectics

As with the entire treatment, skills training is conceptualized within a dialectical framework; we therefore begin by teaching the concept of dialectics. As with teaching other abstract concepts, our experience is that it is often best to start with examples or stories. With a judicious dose of humor, teens can relate to the experience of wanting someone's affection and approval and at the same time wanting to never talk to him or her again. In our experience, it's often the parents who have somehow come to believe that they cannot have contradictory views or feelings and be good parents. While many will welcome the "permission" to have conflicting ideas or feelings, they need help knowing how to maintain authority within the context of multiple truths.

Cognitive behavioral therapies have demonstrated success in teaching adolescents to recognize black-and-white or all-or-nothing thinking such as "things will never change" or "no one likes me." In DBT, dialectical themes are repeated across skills training lessons from mindfulness (integrating feelings and reason in "wise mind"), distress tolerance (for example, radical acceptance of injustices that can't be corrected), emotion regulation (for example, acting opposite to the action urge of an emotion), and interpersonal effectiveness (for example, validating someone even while disagreeing with him). In this way, adolescents and their families can be taught to look beyond the immediate, seemingly irresolvable conflict and recognize that what may initially look like giving in (not demanding something right away) will help them accomplish something they want (permission to stay out late).

Metaphors can validate a sense of letting go that is necessary for dialectical thinking. However, the clinician must choose a metaphor to which his or her particular adolescent or group is likely to relate. Here are two that we've used: (1) a dialectical perspective feels like Alice in Wonderland falling down the rabbit hole (it isn't without fear, but it feels curious and creative), and (2) like jazz, it incorporates both predictable themes and improvisations; it is fluid and powerful (think of how water made the Grand Canyon and contrast that to being stuck between a rock and a hard place). Adolescents themselves often have examples of times they have taken a dialectical stance; for instance, quickly shifting back and forth between offense and defense in a sporting event or driving well on a winding road, anticipating the next turn even while managing the pull of the one they are in. Miller et al. (2006) provide handouts for helping adolescents and families learn to think more dialectically. Once familiarity with the basics of dialectical thinking has been established, the following exercise can be fun for practicing with real-life problems.

Exercise 1. Dial "Ectical"

One person volunteers to be "Ectical," the provider of possible dialectical solutions.

Other people "call in" with a dialectical dilemma, a situation in which they feel stuck.

Alternatives:
1. Two group leaders can model this to start, or
2. The whole group can brainstorm dialectical solutions.

Call-In Examples	Possible Dialectical Solutions
"I want to get my nose pierced and my mother won't let me. She says it will make me look like a whore."	Do some research together in person or online to learn about different types of piercings and why people get them.
"If I don't get my son to school, he will be removed from my house, but he won't listen to me when I tell him that. He still refuses to go."	Make him his favorite dinner and ask him what would make school doable. Contact the guidance counselor or vice principal to explore what alternatives the school can offer.
"I want to be close to my daughter, and I am afraid she will hit me."	Once a week, go somewhere public together to talk or do something you know she will like.
"I want my mother to see how hard I am trying, but all she does is criticize me."	Ask your mother what she is proud of in being a mother. Thank her for trying so hard to make sure you make it.

Teaching Acceptance and Mindfulness to Adolescents

Acceptance strategies in DBT are explicitly taught to balance change strategies. In actuality, acceptance often implies or leads to change just as change depends on acceptance. We focus here on three strategies or skill areas for teaching acceptance: validation, distress tolerance, and mindfulness.

Validation

As previously discussed, validation is the primary strategy for facilitating acceptance and balancing an otherwise strong emphasis on change. It is expected to be a part of every therapeutic interaction within DBT and is essential for eliciting commitment and building a relationship with the power to reinforce new and skillful behaviors. In addition, our experience suggests that validation is one of the most transformative skills for adolescent-parent relationships.

A simple but poignant story is often useful to communicating the essence of validation. One we've found effective is the story of a young child and her mother. The young child came to her mother crying after accidentally breaking a glass item in a store. We ask what group members think the mother said. Invariably they suggest "Oh, it's okay" or "Don't cry" or "Don't worry, I'll pay for it." In reality, the mother said tenderly, "Oh, of course you're upset. You didn't mean to break that, did you?" We allow the quiet that inevitably follows. There is something so powerful about validating shame. It is typically a new experience for both adolescents and their parents to allow someone the experience of their painful emotions without trying to "make it better" (or worse, exacerbating and extending an otherwise temporary emotion). This story also sets the stage for recognizing that invalidation does not have to be intentional to have an invalidating effect, and for learning to validate themselves as well as others. Learning to validate in terms of current context and not just past history or learning is critical for youth and families with very painful histories and difficulty imagining going forward with their lives. A focus on the present can be very important to shifting from defending their experience and behaviors to taking an active role in building a life worth living.

As Linehan discovered in the development of DBT, an exclusive emphasis on change can be experienced as invalidating to individuals in intense pain. Similarly, overemphasis on acceptance minimizes how intolerable life is for the suicidal client and her very real need for something to change. Effective validation depends on an adept and dynamic balance of empathy and the nonjudgmental verification of someone's experience and sense of self with aggressive efforts toward establishing progress toward goals and a life worth living. With adolescents and their parents, this balancing act extends to validating both adolescents and parents even when the validation of one might be perceived as invalidating to the other. It is easy to feel like one has to choose sides. Validation by the therapist is important, especially for modeling; however, it is critical to teach adolescents to validate their parents and parents to validate their adolescents.

For example, in one family therapy session, eighteen-year-old Lisa was nearing the end of a stay in residential treatment. She had been planning to live independently, but with difficulty brought up the possibility of returning home if she could not find a job. Her mother, Ellen, asked if Lisa had called Aunt Sally, who had a possible job lead. Jeff, her stepfather, mentioned how he had made it on his own at that age and was concerned that Lisa was giving up too easily. Lisa quickly jumped in:

Lisa: You think I didn't try everything myself? You think I want to go home? I'm just saying—*as a last resort*!

Therapist: *(interrupting)* What do you hear Lisa saying?

Mother: Lisa, I want to make sure you know that you always have a place at our home.

Stepfather: Of course you do.

Therapist: *(to mother)* What did you hear Lisa saying that led you to want to say that?

Mother: I guess I realized that Lisa …

Therapist: *(breaking in)* Tell her directly so you can find out if your understanding is correct.

Mother: *(to Lisa now)* It sounded like you might think we don't want you home. I just want you to know that the issue is not whether we want you home.

Therapist: Can you find out if you've read her correctly?

Mother: *(to Lisa)* Is that what you were thinking?

Lisa: *(Nods)*

Mother: I'm just scared we'll go back to how things were before.

Therapist: Can you let your mom know what you hear her saying?

Lisa: You're scared. I'm scared too.

Therapist: *(to Lisa)* It seemed like there was something else that you were worried your dad didn't get.

Lisa: He thinks I haven't changed at all, like I haven't been trying to find a job.

Stepfather: I think she's made a lot of changes, but I'm afraid now she's giving up.

Therapist: Can you tell Lisa directly that you see she's changed?

Stepfather: I'm proud of the changes you have made—you've helped me change too.

Lisa: *(Lisa tears up)*

In early sessions or particularly emotional ones, one might spend the entire session on validation. Not only can validation facilitate readiness for problem solving, it can help clarify what problem needs to be solved. Lisa was better able to problem solve actively with her parents once she knew that they recognized her progress and weren't simply against her coming home. But, as with individual DBT, there is a careful balance in family sessions between acceptance and change. If this session stopped with validation and didn't problem solve the next step, the family's realistic concerns would be invalidated.

Family sessions can provide rich opportunities for practicing skills and helping family members generalize skill use to the very situations in which they are needed. Highly structured homework can help families learn new styles of interacting that more effectively balance validation and problem solving. They can also learn to recognize cues that balance needs to be reestablished. If someone is getting defensive or complaining that the other doesn't understand, the therapist might practice reflective listening and temporarily drop efforts for change. If someone is repeatedly anxious that nothing is going to change, it may be time to shift to problem solving. Saying "I understand that you feel nothing is changing" can be especially invalidating.

"Radical genuineness" is a particularly important level of validation when working with adolescents. An example of radical genuineness comes from a family session with a mother (Debra) and daughter (Eliza) who have weathered a turbulent course of treatment. The daughter is finally ready to leave the acute care setting when this exchange occurred:

Debra: I just want to have a good relationship with my daughter.

Therapist: *(ironically)* Good luck.

Eliza: *(laughing)* That's the last thing I expected you to say.

Debra: *(also laughing)* You're not kidding. You know how hard it is.

Had the therapeutic relationship not been so well established, Debra and Eliza might have taken offense and felt insulted. In this case, the therapist's radical genuineness acknowledged the desire for relationship and how difficult it had been to achieve and might be to maintain, and reflected the progress they'd made in being able to laugh at something previously so difficult.

Radical genuineness can also be a dialectical form of validation. "You goofball," spoken lovingly to someone who is complaining of being worthless can be far more validating of the person's self-worth than a more overtly supportive remark. When expressed within the context of trust and caring, carefully worded irony or extending (i.e., taking the person more seriously than they intend) can simultaneously validate feelings of insecurity or hopelessness and foster hope, competence, and connection. Like functional validation, this validates someone's experience by responding to it behaviorally. Speaking an adolescent's language (e.g., quick quips) or using nonverbal expressions can often be more validating than reflective listening. However, as its name implies, radical genuineness has to be genuine as well as radical. Adolescents have very little tolerance for halfhearted and overused comments or fake familiarity.

In skills training, role plays are essential for teaching and practicing validation. They provide an especially rich opportunity for having parents and teens to switch roles and consider each other's perspectives. Teaching points can be introduced or strengthened in context as increasingly more challenging role-play scenarios are introduced. By asking the person (in role) whom people expect should be validated to actually do the validating, we introduce the idea of using validation to alter otherwise predictable and negative interaction styles. This challenges both adolescents and parents to not wait to be validated before validating the other. Exercise 2 illustrates a range of possible role plays suitable for adolescents and their parents.

Exercise 2. Validation Role Plays

Instructions:

1. Leaders match roles to each participant's skill level. It is often fun and challenging to reverse typical roles (e.g., have the adolescent play the role of parent or teacher).
2. Participants may use relevant handouts or ask the group for suggestions.
3. Encourage both verbal and functional validation.
4. The person validated determines whether validation has occurred. Teach those doing the validating to look for nonverbal signs and ask if the recipient feels validated.

Validate This Person	Possible Responses
1. Child beaming after tying his shoes.	1. "Wow—you must be proud of yourself!"
2. Your mother is tired and not listening.	2. "Would it be better if I tell you this later?"
3. Teacher (sarcastically): "Finally, you did your homework. What a nice surprise!"	3. "Yup. You've waited a long time for this day."
4. Father: "When I need help, you cop an attitude. But as soon as you need something, you're all sugar sweet!"	4. "You're right, Dad. I don't blame you for being fed up. I've been pretty selfish lately."
5. Teen: "We're having spinach tonight? You know I've had a miserable week."	5. "Oh honey, it would have been a good night for pure chocolate, eh?"
6. Teen is watching TV; his homework is not done.	6. Sitting down next to the teen, "Hard to get started?"
7. Friend says she's ugly and fat. (Kids have been teasing her.) Can you validate her feelings without telling her she's *not* fat and ugly?	7. "Those kids were really mean. It's gotta be hard not to believe them."

Distress Tolerance

Distress tolerance skills are for surviving intense negative emotion without engaging in some type of problem behavior (self-harm, aggression, substance use, etc.). The primary task is learning to accept pain and the situations that cause pain when changing them is not an option. When teaching adolescents acceptance, we follow a progression from more concrete "survival skills" to deeper, longer-lasting acceptance. Adolescents grab onto crisis survival skills very quickly. They are eager for what might work in the moment, for instance, snapping a rubber band on the wrist to distract from the urge to cut. Table 1 provides a list of other activities adolescents find particularly useful.

Table 1. Sample Crisis Survival Skills for Adolescents

In class or group space	
Count the colors in the classroom	Squeeze a stress ball
Draw, doodle, or journal	Picture a calm or favorite place
Drum with hand quietly	Picture myself doing something fun
Focus on the class work	Breathe deeply; count on the exhale
Listen to how the teacher's voice changes as he talks	Sing a favorite song in my head
Think about a favorite pet or a little sister or brother	Look at a magazine
Ask to leave the room to talk with someone	
At home or in private	
Talk on the phone	Juggle
Read a favorite book or story	Smell perfume or cologne
Make jewelry	Take the dog for a walk
Paint my nails	Write a friend a nice note
Complete a word search	Help my sister with homework
Play computer games	Dance or exercise to music
Make brownies	Go running
Make something for a stuffed animal	Put on makeup; fix my hair in new do
Call my grandmother	Sort baseball cards
Go for a bike ride	Arrange pictures in a photo album
	Play the drums

In teaching the more challenging skill of acceptance, we have found stories to be especially effective. Reading aloud is typically soothing and quiets most groups, facilitating the openness necessary for acceptance. Effective stories for teaching acceptance paint the picture of a dire situation in which someone is able to "make lemonade out of lemons," give to others even when he has very little himself, or find beauty in an otherwise unhappy place. We then make a list of situations group members have learned to accept or are trying to accept: parents divorcing, having to live away from home, acne, getting cut from a sports team, or losing a boyfriend to a supposed best friend. Asking "How did you come to accept that?" or "When did you realize you'd accepted that?" can prevent this exercise from deteriorating into a competition for who has the worst events or issues to accept. Teens are usually eager to relay what they've learned to accept, and even when the clinician wonders if they really have accepted what they say they have, verbalizing the issue can be an important first step. Personal examples by the clinician of times she thought she'd accepted something only to have to let go and accept it again and again can be helpful in normalizing the process.

Groups also have fun highlighting signs of nonacceptance. Both teens and parents can provide examples of digging their heels in, spreading lies about the boyfriend and best friend who got together, or insisting that a son or daughter was wrong about something when, in fact, they were right. The leader can remind everyone that we often avoid acceptance because it opens us up to painful feelings. Laughter at what we all do to avoid pain is mixed with a quiet acknowledgment that pain hurts.

Physical images and activities seem to be particularly useful for adolescents. Members can make tightly closed fists and open them slowly, or feel the difference in stability (especially if pushed gently) between standing rigidly with feet close together and spreading them apart while bending the knees. Clinicians or other staff can then evoke this type of image to teach willingness simply by referring to having "willing hands" or taking on a "willing stance." Helping them observe how they hold tension in their bodies and then practice letting it go provides a concrete step toward acceptance. One of our programs teaches this as a "shrug and a sigh." Practicing "a shrug and a sigh" three times helps with acceptance even when one does not agree with the situation. Adolescents can usually provide examples from skiing, dancing, skateboarding, or other activities of performing better when they "let go," such as facing directly downhill and bending their knees or throwing themselves fully into a specific maneuver. The clinician might ask each person to identify at least one image from his own life of accepting or letting go to help in situations in which he feels stuck and unable to accept.

Mindfulness

Introducing mindfulness in terms adolescents can relate to and that are consistent with their goals is critical to enlisting their participation. Some groups are already familiar or immediately fascinated with the concept of mindfulness, and individuals will quickly offer to lead a group mindfulness exercise. Others will complain that mindfulness is "stupid" or "boring." Creativity and energy are needed to teach mindfulness exercises that lead to a sense of competency and success. Additional flexibility and commitment are sometimes needed to engage adolescents who are committed to making sure you feel as much the fool as they do.

Linehan introduces mindfulness with the concept of "wise mind," which is the synthesis of "emotion mind" and "reasonable mind." A simpler way of describing this is that knowing involves both feeling and thinking. Since adolescents are preoccupied with relationships, one can talk about being madly infatuated with someone as an example of emotion mind (it's exciting, inspirational, energizing, and terribly distracting). In contrast, carefully thinking through what values and interests you have in common or whether your backgrounds and goals are compatible uses reasonable mind (quieter, following a logical, step-by-step process). Wise mind is achieved when you can integrate the passion of emotion mind with the logic of reasonable mind. If you act on passion alone, you're headed for pain when the passion fades and there's nothing left. If you act just on reason, you risk getting into a passionless and uninspiring relationship. In wise mind, you take into consideration both your feelings and your reason. Metaphors help teens jump the gap from abstract concepts to real-life applications. Linehan (1993a, 1993b) offers rich metaphors, many of which work well with teens. Here are some of our favorite activities for teaching wise mind to this age group.

Exercises for Teaching Wise Mind

Red and blue make purple. Using a resealable plastic bag, place a quarter-cup of blue paint in one corner and a quarter-cup of red paint in the other. Ask the adolescents to think of blue as reasonable mind and red as emotion mind. Blend the two colors together to make wise mind (purple). See if they can see elements of red and blue within this new color.

Settling mud. Fill the bottom one-third of a bottle or jar with sand or dirt that will settle clearly when shaken. Add water and seal the top. Shake up into mud and then watch it settle. Talk about how time can help one get to wise mind. Keeping the bottle or jar in their rooms can remind adolescents to take the time to let feelings and thoughts settle before acting.

Dime and book. Request a volunteer by asking, "Who would like a dime?" Have the volunteer come to the front of the group, identify a real-life dilemma, and put her hands out. On one hand, put the dime. "If you were just listening to reason and could ignore your emotions, what would you do? (Reason can be quiet when you have strong emotions.)" In the other hand, put a large book like a dictionary. "If you were just listening to your emotions, what would you do? (Emotion mind is often loud and obvious like the heavy book you are holding.)" Then explain, "Wise mind is when you can feel both at the same time. It doesn't let the loud emotion drown out the quiet of reason. It keeps both short-term and long-term interests in mind. What can you do that respects both your emotion mind and your reasonable mind?" The answers are often surprisingly creative. Then give them a choice: "You can take the dime and spend it, or you can keep it in your pocket and use its wise-mind magic. When you have a dilemma, rub the dime and listen carefully to what your wise mind has to say."

Talking through real-life dilemmas provides one more step to prepare adolescents for practicing wise mind. For instance, "You have to remind your best friend that you really need the twenty dollars he borrowed two weeks ago. He probably doesn't have it. What do emotion mind and reasonable mind suggest? What might be a wise-mind way to manage this?"

Teaching mindfulness in DBT begins with teaching individuals to take control of their minds, particularly their attention. One exercise we found particularly useful has individuals look around the room and find (silently) everything in the room that is gray, then everything that is black. We then have them close their eyes and try to remember what they saw that was gray, then black. Without opening their eyes, they are then instructed to try to remember what was red or green or blue (pausing to give time for each color). Most people report noticing a lot that was gray or black but feel either tricked or embarrassed that they didn't notice other colors. The leader's job is to point out that if they noticed mostly what was gray and black, they were successful at taking control of their attention. They probably noticed a lot of objects or features that they never noticed before. We give lots of praise for this to make sure they understand this as success. But this exercise can also be used to illustrate a more abstract teaching point: how we focus our attention determines what we see. Clinicians can then elicit examples of interpersonal or other situations in which people only "saw" what they were looking for.

We have found some of Ellen Langer's (1997) strategies for mindful learning particularly helpful with adolescents, even if her overall conceptualization of mindfulness differs from that of DBT (Langer, 1997). These strategies include keeping the teens' attention moving (e.g., take a walk while looking for people wearing a certain color or for a specific type of plant), and teaching them to look for novelty, change, or difference (e.g., have someone leave the room, change one aspect of their appearance and then return; see how long it takes for others to notice what is different). Learning to ask themselves questions and to use multiple senses may awaken adolescents' natural curiosity. As another example, the clinician might give each person one flower of a particular type and color (e.g., everyone is given a purple tulip). Rather than simply labeling each flower as a "purple tulip," adolescents are instructed to see if they can notice what's unique about each of their tulips. For example, how would they describe their tulips to someone else? After engaging with the flower in this way, each adolescent returns his or her tulip to a vase and the clinician mixes them up. Later in the session, adolescents are asked to find their original flowers. They are typically eager to share how they did so.

The strategies adolescents have learned can then be transferred to focusing on body sensations, the breath, or even thoughts. Active, multimodal exercises are especially useful for teaching young people with high rates of learning disabilities or attentional dyscontrol. A particularly popular game is Snap, Crackle, Pop (exercise 3). The advantage of this game is that there is competition and social pressure to practice both focused attention and flexibility, but the best role is actually given to those who make a mistake. They become "distracters," trying to confuse those still working on the main task. The challenge to stay focused within a context of increasing chaos becomes a great metaphor for trying to be mindful in real life. Teens begin to recognize how their minds wander and the training needed to bring their attention back again and again.

Exercise 3. Snap, Crackle, Pop

This exercise is especially useful for teaching the DBT "how" skill "one-mindfully." You may want to discuss times participants have had difficulty being one-mindful before getting started.

1. Get everyone in a circle, and teach the three arm movements:

   SNAP: one arm bent across chest, fingers pointing at the person to the left or right

   CRACKLE: arm bent across the top of the head, fingers pointing to the left or right

   POP: arm out straight, fingers pointing at anyone in the circle

   Practice so everyone has the movements down, then practice the sequence slowly:

   One person starts with Snap and says "Snap!" at the same time.

   The person pointed to must then do and say Crackle!

   The new person pointed to must then do and say Pop!

   That person pointed to starts over again with Snap, etc.

2. Explain the role of DISTRACTERS. Elicit examples of distractions that interfere with being one-mindful: thoughts, people, senses, emotion, etc. Explain that when someone makes a mistake (e.g., hand across the top of the head for Snap, or saying Crackle after Pop, or taking a long time), they are not out of the game. However, they have a new role—that of a distracter.

   Encourage group members to be creative and take their jobs seriously in distracting other group members from being one-mindful. However, set whatever ground rules are necessary (e.g., no touching; no saying or doing anything that could cause harm to people or furniture—hurt feelings count along with risk for injury or material damage).

3. The leader must be clear about who will start. Be ready to judge when someone becomes a distracter, and direct the game if it needs help (e.g., if the pace needs to be picked up).

Start the game when everyone seems clear on the movements, sequence, and rules. The point is to stay one-mindful and keep the sequence going. When someone misses and becomes a distracter, the person to his or her left starts a new sequence. The game ends when one or two people are left making the Snap, Crackle, Pop movements or a set time is reached.

4. Debrief, using questions like these:

- What was most distracting? Why?
- What did you do to stay focused (e.g., look only within the circle, repeat Snap, Crackle, Pop in your head, stay relaxed and planted in a comfortable position)?
- What was successful?
- What can you use to become more one-mindful in real-life situations?

Linehan outlines six mindfulness skills for achieving wise mind (Linehan, 1993b). These are separated into "what" and "how" skills. "What skills" encompass skills for developing a life of awareness and include observing, describing, and participating. If you are "observing," you are noticing and sensing what is. "Describing" involves putting words on your experience. "Participating" is being fully present and throwing yourself into an experience.

Teaching adolescents simply to "observe" can be challenging because it is an abstract task to observe without labeling. One tactic is to have them sit absolutely still for forty-five seconds and notice all the urges they have to move. An added benefit of this exercise is that observing an impulse becomes an alternative to acting on it. We might also ask teens to think of times they've noticed something without having a label for it (e.g., a vague pain or discomfort). Teaching "describe" is often easier, since adolescents are accustomed to verbalizing what they know or think. The task in teaching describe has more to do with helping clients break down broad impressions into descriptive detail. For instance, parents and adolescents may be quick to determine when they think someone is "pissed off." Yet they need to be taught to observe and then describe the physical expressions associated with specific emotions. We've often used pictures of animals to introduce this, as teens take pride in recognizing a raised, thickened tail on a cat or flattened ears on a dog. Role-playing provides practice in describing the specific sensations and expressions associated with different emotions.

"Participate" is the goal of mindfulness training, and yet adolescents often have great examples of prior experience with this skill. Truly playing involves throwing oneself fully and non-self-consciously into a game or piece of music or other activity. To the extent that kids play more often and more freely than many adults, they may grasp the concept of this skill more readily. Adolescents may relate to this skill, as they participate fully in a range of activities such as dancing to music, playing a sport, and creating art.

In DBT, the "how skills" describe the manner in which one practices the what skills in approaching wise mind. The how skills include "nonjudgmentally," "one-mindfully," and "effectively." Practicing "nonjudgmentally" involves learning to observe, describe, or participate without judgment. Teaching this how skill can be challenging, as adolescents are often quick to judge and, like adults, have difficulty detaching judgment from fact. We put examples on the board, with one column for judgments and one for facts. Under judgments, we put phrases that categorize something as good/bad, right/wrong, or fair/not fair. Under facts, we see what's left when the judgment is removed. For instance, "My teacher is mean" is a judgment. "My teacher gave me an F on my last test" may be a fact. "I'm fat and ugly" is certainly a judgment. "I weigh 118 pounds and have curly brown hair" may be a fact. Next, we ask a couple participants to role-play a conflict. The job of the rest of the group is to clap whenever they hear a judgment rather than a fact.

Engaging in an activity "one-mindfully" requires coming back to the present moment or activity over and over. It can be fun to elicit stories of how doing multiple tasks at once has led to disaster. An exercise to promote one-mindful experiencing involves turning out the lights and giving one person a flashlight. This person is asked to slowly shine the light on areas and objects in the room. The task for other group members is to focus only on what is in the light. The group discusses how this experience is like (or not like) how we tend to focus our attention. Then it's important to discuss a specific plan for practicing one-mindfully. For example, an adolescent might plan to engage one-mindfully in simple, everyday tasks (e.g., talk on the phone without doing anything else—just be there and really listen; work on the computer without responding to instant messaging; or shut off the computer and phone while talking with a parent).

Finally, doing a task "effectively" involves doing just what is needed, no more and no less. It means knowing what is called for and playing by the rules. This can be particularly challenging for adolescents who want to argue about all that is unjust or unfair in their lives. The important point is to validate that a set of rules might be unfair, *and* one may still be most effective in reaching one's goals when one plays along. The therapist might tell stories of teens who carefully built up trust within relationships or achieved independence because they played by the rules rather than insisting on their own way.

Conclusion

Dialectical behavior therapy is an empirically supported treatment for adults with borderline personality disorder that has gained widespread popularity with mental health providers who work with adolescents. Although the evidence to support this application is preliminary, the DBT model offers structure, a clear hierarchy of targets, and flexible strategies for working with multiproblem and suicidal youth. Its dialectical framework provides conceptual guidance for including families and facilitating therapeutic change at both individual and systemic levels.

DBT differs from other acceptance- and mindfulness-based therapies in the population it targets and in its explicit emphasis on dialectics. The entire treatment is oriented around the dynamic interplay between acceptance and change in the pursuit of increasingly dialectical behavior. Mindfulness is a central component of this process, helping individuals become observers of internal and external aspects of their experience with the ultimate goal of full participation in this experience.

Adapting DBT for adolescents requires the appreciation of a number of developmental issues, the dialectical incorporation of families and larger systems into the treatment, and stylistic changes for effectively engaging this fun and challenging age group. While the strategies and examples covered in this chapter are just a sampling of what can be done to accomplish this, our hope is that we have communicated the feasibility of conducting this complex treatment with a younger population in a way that fosters greater curiosity and research into what adaptations work best and for whom.

References

American Psychiatric Association. (2000). *Diagnostic and statistical manual of mental disorders* (4th ed., text revision). Washington, DC: Author.

Becker, D. F., Grilo, C. M., Edell, W. S., & McGlashan, T. H. (2002). Diagnostic efficiency of borderline personality disorder criteria in hospitalized adolescents: Comparison with hospitalized adults. *American Journal of Psychiatry, 159*, 2042–2047.

D'Eramo, K. S., Prinstein, M. J., Freeman, J., Grapentine, W. L., & Spirito, A. (2004). Psychiatric diagnoses and comorbidity in relation to suicidal behavior among psychiatrically hospitalized adolescents. *Child Psychiatry and Human Development, 35*, 21–35.

Katz, L. Y., Cox, B. J., Gunasekara, S., & Miller, A. L. (2004). Feasibility of dialectical behavior therapy for suicidal adolescent inpatients. *Journal of the American Academy of Child and Adolescent Psychiatry, 43*, 276–282.

Langer, E. J. (1997). *The power of mindful learning.* Reading, MA: Addison-Wesley.

Linehan, M. M. (1993a). *Cognitive behavioral therapy of borderline personality disorder.* New York: Guilford.

Linehan, M. M. (1993b). *Skills training manual for treating borderline personality disorder.* New York: Guilford.

Linehan, M. M., Comptois, K. A., Murray, A. M., Brown, M. Z., Gallop, R. J., Heard, H. L., et al. (2006). Two-year randomized controlled trial and follow-up of dialectical behavior therapy vs therapy by experts for suicidal behaviors and borderline personality disorder. *Archives of General Psychiatry, 63*, 757–766.

Lynch, T. R., Chapman, A. L., Rosenthal, M. Z., Kuo, J. R., & Linehan, M. M. (2006). Mechanisms of change in dialectical behavior therapy: Theoretical and empirical observations. *Journal of Clinical Psychology, 62*, 459–480.

Meijer, M., Goedhart, A. W., & Treffers, P. D. A. (1998). The persistence of borderline personality disorder in adolescence. *Journal of Personality Disorders, 12*, 3–22.

Miller, A. L., Rathus, J. H., & Linehan, M. M. (2006). *Dialectical behavior therapy with suicidal adolescents*. New York: Guilford.

Rathus, J. H., & Miller, A. L. (2000). DBT for adolescents: Dialectical dilemmas and secondary treatment targets. *Cognitive and Behavioral Practice, 7*, 425–434.

Rathus, J. H., & Miller, A. L. (2002). Dialectical behavior therapy adapted for suicidal adolescents. *Suicide and Life-Threatening Behavior, 32*, 146–157.

Robins, C. J., & Chapman, A. L. (2004). Dialectical behavior therapy: Current status, recent developments, and future directions. *Journal of Personality Disorders, 18*, 73–89.

Robins, C. J., Schmidt, H. I., & Linehan, M. M. (2004). Dialectical behavior therapy: Synthesizing radical acceptance with skillful means. In S. C. Hayes, V. M. Follette, & M. M. Linehan (Eds.), *Mindfulness and acceptance: Expanding the cognitive-behavioral tradition* 30–44. New York: Guilford.

Swenson, C. R., Torrey, W. C., & Koerner, K. (2002). Implementing dialectical behavior therapy. *Psychiatric Services, 53*, 171–178.

Woodberry, K. A., Miller, A. L., Glinski, J., Indik, J., & Mitchell, A. G. (2002). Family therapy and dialectical behavior therapy with adolescents: Part II: A theoretical review. *American Journal of Psychotherapy, 54*(4), 585–602.

Chapter 7

Mindfulness-Based Stress Reduction for School-Age Children

Amy Saltzman, MD, Still Quiet Place, Menlo Park, California; and Philippe Goldin, Ph.D., Stanford University

During the past several decades, numerous studies have documented the benefits of teaching mindfulness skills to adults within the context of mindfulness-based stress reduction (MBSR; Kabat-Zinn, 1990) courses. These skills have proven to be reliably effective in reducing symptoms of anxiety and depression (Ramel, Goldin, Carmona, & McQuaid, 2004; Segal, Williams, & Teasdale, 2002) and increasing self-regulated behavior and positive emotional states (Brown & Ryan, 2003). However, little is known about modifying MBSR to make it applicable and effective for children. The goals of this chapter are to (1) provide an overview of an MBSR curriculum designed for children in grades 4 through 6 and their parents, and (2) report preliminary research findings based on the implementation of this curriculum. Specifically, the data address whether mindfulness training is feasible for children and whether such training enhances attention, self-regulation, social competence, and, perhaps most importantly, children's overall well-being.

Drs. Amy Saltzman and Philippe Goldin met and began collaborating to study the effects of mindfulness training for children and families. While Philippe brought his knowledge of research methodology, laboratory resources, and experience of offering mindfulness to adults with anxiety disorders, Amy brought her expertise in delivering mindfulness to children and families. Because the goal of this book is to provide a practical how-to description of mindfulness training for children, we have chosen to write this chapter in an informal style that reflects what works well with children.

First, we provide some background. When Amy's daughter was six months old, her three-year-old son asked if he could meditate with his sister. Based on this request, Amy began sharing the practice of mindfulness with her children. Over time, together they created and adapted the practices included in the current child MBSR course curriculum. After developing the practices with her children and reading repeatedly about childhood stress in both the professional and lay literature, Amy began to wonder what it would be like if children learned mindfulness skills early in their development. Do children who are able to experience thoughts, feelings, and bodily sensations without being overwhelmed become individuals who are more resilient in the face of stress? Can access to a natural sense of peace and trust in one's internal wisdom lead to decreased susceptibility to peer pressure and risky behaviors?

Initially Amy explored these possibilities in an informal way by sharing mindfulness practices in elementary schools and community settings. Teachers commented that their students were calmer and more focused when beginning their day with mindfulness. Teachers of older students reported that the students were more aware of, and thus better able to deal with, their increasingly complex thoughts and emotions. While these observations were encouraging, the scientist in Amy wanted to know if the children were really benefiting from mindfulness in measurable and meaningful ways.

Meanwhile Philippe had been documenting the benefits of teaching mindfulness to adults with anxiety disorders. Many of the adults in his mindfulness groups commented that they became aware of their anxiety around age ten and that they wished they had learned mindfulness skills decades earlier. This piqued Philippe's curiosity about offering the practices of mindfulness to children.

The following research questions arose from our combined experiences:

- Do children benefit from mindfulness training in measurable and meaningful ways?
- What are the most skillful ways to teach mindfulness to children?
- In what settings are children most likely to learn mindfulness skills?

Age-Appropriate Adaptations

When sharing mindfulness with children, it is essential that our offerings come from the depths of our own practice, that we use age-appropriate language, and that it be fun and engaging. To highlight these elements, Amy offers the following vignette:

> *At some point, my son began teaching his kindergarten teacher mindfulness. The teacher then asked me to share some practices with her class. So one morning several years ago, I found myself lying on the floor with nineteen*

five-year-olds. After the first practice, I asked the children to describe how they felt. As we went around the circle, children reported feeling "calm," "relaxed," and "happy." I felt pleased. Then one child said, "Dead." I watched the teacher's eyes become as big as saucers; she was panicked. I felt a momentary tightening within myself. The teacher had no mindfulness practice to provide her with either an understanding of the child's experience or a way of working with her fear. We continued around the circle, and as often happens in kindergarten, several children repeated some version of the previous answers, including "dead." After everyone had spoken, I returned to the children who said "dead," and asked, "What does dead feel like?" They answered, "like a swan," "like an angel," or "like floating."

Many children in our culture do not have words to describe feeling awake, alert, and still. "Dead" was as close as they could come to describing the experience of being in what we call the Still Quiet Place. This vignette illustrates several important points related to teaching children mindfulness:

- Teaching mindfulness must come from the depth of our own practice. Amy's practice allowed her to be aware of what was arising within her, to understand the children's and the classroom teacher's experience, and to respond to both. This is the essence of mindfulness. Mindfulness is simply paying attention in the present moment, with kindness and curiosity, and responding rather than reacting to the circumstances. In the previous example, Amy was aware of her brief attachment to the children having a relaxing experience, and of the sensations of concern and doubt as they arose. Simply noting these internal experiences without getting caught up in them enabled her to attend to the children. Years of mindfulness practice allowed her to "get" what the children really meant by "dead" and to respond accordingly.

- Teaching mindfulness is not the "see one, do one, teach one" model typically embraced in education. Rather, mindfulness requires that we practice it, live it, be it, and practice it some more before we offer it to others.

- Adult interpretations of words and experiences can be quite different from the interpretations of the children sitting in front of us. It is better to ask than to assume we know what the children mean when they use a particular word.

- Creative translation is essential when imparting the practice of mindfulness to children.

Still Quiet Place: Introduction and Translation

Below is the way that Amy typically introduces the Still Quiet Place and translates the essence of mindfulness so that even very young children can experience it:

> *Hello. My name is Amy, and I would like to share one of my favorite places with you. I call it Still Quiet Place. It's not a place you travel to in a car, or a train, or a plane. It is a place inside you that you can find just by closing your eyes. Let's find it now.*
>
> *Close your eyes and take some slow deep breaths. See if you can feel a kind of warm, happy smile in your body. Do you feel it? This is your Still Quiet Place. Take some more deep breaths and really snuggle in.*
>
> *The best thing about your Still Quiet Place is that it's always inside you. And you can visit it whenever you like. It is nice to visit your Still Quite Place and feel the love that is there. It is especially helpful to visit your Still Quiet Place if you are feeling angry, or sad, or afraid. The Still Quiet Place is a good place to talk with these feelings and to make friends with them. When you rest in your Still Quiet Place and talk to your feelings, you may find that your feelings are not as big and as powerful as they seem. Remember, you can come here whenever you want, and stay as long as you like.*

With skillful adaptation, the concept of Still Quiet Place can be used with students from ages three to ninety-three years old. The language above is for children ages three to seven, who are able to simply experience the Still Quiet Place and to feel it in their body-mind. With older children, the language can be more body focused with less emphasis on the Still Quiet Place as a location. Children ages five to nine can begin to remember to visit their Still Quiet Place when they are upset, and some may be able to use the practice to allow them to respond to upsetting circumstances. Most children ages nine to thirteen can apply the practices of mindfulness in much the same way as adults do; they can be aware of their thoughts, feelings, and physical sensations, and then practice responding rather than reacting to their life circumstances.

For younger children, a very simple twenty-minute weekly session—consisting of one practice, brief comments from some of the children, followed by another practice and comments from the remaining children—will support them in becoming familiar with the Still Quiet Place. For a single formal practice, a general rule of thumb is that children usually can practice one minute per their age in years. (For example, five-year-old children can generally do formal guided practice for about five minutes.) With a group of ten or more preschoolers or kindergartners, if each child speaks after each practice, the children may get restless and the experience of the practice may be long gone by the time it is the last child's turn to speak. Thus, we recommend that you hear from just some of the children after each practice. For slightly older children, let their comments and behavior guide you. With encouragement, some may be able to apply mindfulness in their daily lives. The course outline below is for children ages eight and up.

MBSR for Children: Course Outline

The primary intention of the course is to offer children an experience of the Still Quiet Place and to have them use mindfulness in their daily lives to respond rather than react to everyday events. Below are the basic features of the course:

- **Participants:** The course can be offered either to children only or to children and one or both parents.
- **Class size:** Eight to thirty participants is the usual class size.
- **Sessions:** The program is eight sessions (two the first week and one every week thereafter).
- **Session length:** The time varies from forty to ninety minutes per class, depending on the setting and class size.
- **Mindfulness practice:** The training consists of both formal practice (including body scan, sitting, eating, and walking exercises) and informal practice (focusing attention, attending to the present moment, choosing responses to everyday events). We use additional in-class exercises to enhance mindful awareness, artistic expression, and verbal communication.
- **Home practice:** In addition to the weekly group sessions, the participants are encouraged to engage in home practice to reinforce and deepen their in-class learning. Together the training and home practice involve exercises that focus on developing a familiarity with the Still Quiet Place and the application of mindfulness in daily life.
- **Materials:** Participants receive a workbook, a CD of twelve different short practices, and home-practice monitoring sheets to guide and support their home practice.

An overview of the mindfulness course we offer to children is presented in table 1 (a detailed child MBSR program manual will be published soon; Saltzman, in press). Due to page limitations for this chapter, we have chosen to describe one class in detail and to follow that with brief descriptions of the practices unique to this curriculum for children (see Additional Exercises and Practices, below). All of the formal guided practices can be found on the CDs *Still Quiet Place: Mindfulness for Young Children* (Saltzman, 2004) and *Still Quiet Place: Mindfulness for Teens* (Saltzman, forthcoming). For a description of practices that are shortened and adapted from the adult curriculum, please refer to *Full Catastrophe Living*, by Jon Kabat-Zinn (1990).

The outline below is a brief sketch of our program. Ultimately every group creates its own masterpiece—moving lines, adding shading and color to reveal depth and

Table 1. Overview of Eight-Week Mindfulness-Based Stress Reduction Course for Children

	Intentions	**Class Agenda**	**Home Practice**
Introduction to Program (parents only) 2 hours	■ Provide an experience of mindfulness ■ Introduce program to parents	■ Mindful Eating—raisin (see Mindful Eating) ■ Review data on benefits of mindfulness for adults and children ■ Review the rationale for offering MBSR to children ■ Discuss course structure and time commitment ■ Answer questions	■ None
Class 1	■ Provide definition of Still Quiet Place/ mindfulness ■ Establish ground rules ■ Offer an experience of mindfulness	■ Mindful Eating Practice ■ Introduce Still Quiet Place ■ Mindfulness as "paying attention to here and now" ■ Begin breath-based practices such as Jewel/Treasure (see Additional Exercises and Practices)	■ Jewel/Treasure Exercise ■ Monitor pleasant experiences using Pleasant Experiences Calendar ■ Engage in one mindful activity (e.g., brush teeth, shower, do a chore, care for a pet)
Class 2	■ Explore experience with formal and informal practice ■ Discuss how to make time for home practice ■ Examine how often our attention is in the past or future	■ Mindful Eating Practice ■ Review class 1 and home practice ■ Jewel/Treasure Exercise ■ Answer questions about the practice	■ Same as Class 1 ■ Eat a snack or meal mindfully

	Intentions	Class Agenda	Home Practice
Class 3	■ Continue to deepen the exploration of formal and informal practice ■ Cultivate the capacity to observe one's thoughts and feelings ■ Attend to the body	■ Mindful Eating Practice ■ Review class 2 and home practice ■ Introduce concept of "funny mind" (internal dialogue, see Home Practice section) ■ Body Scan Exercise (mindfulness of bodily experiences)	■ Body Scan Exercise (mindfulness of bodily experiences) ■ Monitor unpleasant experiences using the Unpleasant Experiences Calendar ■ Notice "funny mind" ■ Notice times when you feel stressed ■ Engage in mindful activity
Class 4	■ Examine thoughts and feelings associated with unpleasant experiences ■ Explore perceptions ■ Introduce yoga as one way to practice mindfulness	■ Mindful Eating Exercise ■ Review class 3 and home practice ■ Exercises to explore perception—how do we view ourselves and each other? ■ Exercises to investigate thoughts associated with difficult tasks ■ Yoga	■ Body Scan Exercise/Yoga (mindfulness of bodily experiences during yoga) ■ Monitor unpleasant experiences using the Unpleasant Experiences Calendar ■ Use awareness of breath to slow things down in everyday life ■ Engage in mindful activity
Class 5	■ Examine how resistance and how wanting circumstances, ourselves, or others to be different creates suffering ■ Explore how "funny minds" are often inaccurate, negative, or looking for trouble ■ Develop emotional fluency, or the ability to be aware of feelings without resisting or indulging them	■ Mindful Eating Practice ■ Review class 4 and home practice ■ Explore thoughts and feelings associated with unpleasant experience ■ Begin to develop concept of "funny mind" ■ Feelings Practice	■ Continue Feelings Practice, using haiku, other poetry, or art to depict feelings ■ Notice moments of reactivity and explore ways of responding ■ Engage in new mindful activity
Vacation	■ Maintain home practice without support of weekly class		■ Notice moments of reactivity and explore ways of responding ■ Engage in new mindful activity

	Intentions	**Class Agenda**	**Home Practice**
Class 6	■ Enhance the capacity to observe thoughts and feelings ■ Develop the capacity to respond rather than react	■ Mindful Eating Practice ■ Review previous class topics and home practice ■ Explore Feelings Practice through haiku, art, etc. ■ Thought Parade Exercise ■ Walking Practice (see brief description in Home Practice section) ■ Moving our practice into the world	■ Thought Parade Exercise ■ Take a "Thoreau walk" ■ Feelings Practice ■ Difficult Communication Calendar (see brief description in Home Practice section) ■ Continue responding to stressful situations and to "funny mind"
Class 7	■ Apply mindfulness during difficult communications ■ Continue to develop the capacity to respond rather than react ■ Begin Loving-Kindness Practice	■ Mindful Eating Exercise ■ Review class 6 and home practice ■ Communication dyads (one person describes a difficult communication; the other listens and reflects, then they reverse roles) ■ Share examples of responding, and role-play new responses to situations when the children reacted ■ Introduce Loving-Kindness Practice	■ Loving-Kindness Exercise ■ Continue responding to stressful situations and "funny mind" ■ New, more challenging mindful activity ■ Imagine the world from someone else's point of view ■ Bring something to share for the last session that represents what the class has meant to you
Class 8	■ Develop the capacity to send and receive love ■ Choose if and how you will use mindfulness in your life ■ Reiterate that instructors are available for ongoing support	■ Group choice ■ Review class 7 and home practice ■ Letter to a friend ■ Making the practice your own	■ Your choice ■ Flashlight Exercise ■ Make a commitment as to how you will continue

perspective. Each session, and the course overall, must be responsive to the individuals and experiences in the room. It is particularly important to attend to children's natural desire for movement. Sometimes it is skillful to let the children sit with their restlessness and notice the associated sensations, thoughts, and feelings. Other times it is skillful to let them be seaweed, or to dance, drum, or do hasty walking or energetic yoga.

Class Six: A Detailed Example

Class six is three-quarters of the way through the course. The children have become familiar with the Still Quiet Place, have some basic mindfulness vocabulary, have come to expect snacks, and are not shy about expressing their preferences. In class six, we continue Mindful Eating Practice and work with children on what we refer to as Feelings Practice. We begin Walking Practice (walking with mindful awareness, noticing your experience while placing one foot in front of the other) and move our practice to the outside world. Home practice involves continuing to practice activities and skills learned during class. We describe the key exercises in class six below.

Mindful Eating

In after-school settings, we always begin class with Mindful Eating, where children mindfully eat apples, tangerines, or Fig Newtons. Avoid snacks high in sugar and make sure to check for food allergies. In the beginning of the course, we have children look at the food offered and simply describe what they see—color, texture, stem (where it used to be connected to something else)—what they smell, and what is happening in their mouths as they look and smell. Then, in guided silence with their eyes closed, the children are instructed to take one bite.

> *Take one bite, paying attention to what is happening in your mouth, noticing the taste. Don't rush; take one bite at a time, noting how the taste changes, how your teeth and tongue work ... See if you can notice the urge to swallow, and then feel the swallow as the food moves down your throat ... After you have swallowed, when you are ready, take another bite. Take your time. Be curious about your experience. Before you open your eyes, notice how your body, mind, and heart feel now, in this moment.*

Eating a single bite mindfully may take a minute or more. This practice is a very concrete way for the children to practice bringing their attention into the present moment. At this point in the course, the children are familiar with mindful eating, and we may simply eat three to four bites in silence. After eating, we may use comments about expectations and preferences as springboards for exploring the inner experience of expectations, desire, and aversion.

Feelings Practice

The home practice for the preceding week included Feelings Practice and creating two artistic representations of the feelings the children experienced during the meditations. Feelings Practice involves becoming aware of and naming the current feeling state, and acknowledging that feelings may have ordinary names, like angry, happy, and sad, or more unusual names, like stormy, fiery, and empty. One boy playfully named his feeling "Herb." This exercise helps the children become more comfortable with identifying and expressing their emotions. It may be helpful for the facilitator to tell children that there may be layers of feelings or that the feelings may be subtle or somewhat shy.

After noting the feelings, the children are invited to notice where the feelings are experienced in the body (e.g., sitting in the chest, stirring in the belly, resting in the big toe). Then they are encouraged to notice if the feelings have colors (e.g., dark red, deep blue, bright green) or a sound (e.g., giggling, groaning, whining). We then encourage the children to ask the feelings what they want. Usually feelings need something simple, like attention, time, and space. We ask the children if they are willing to give the feelings what the feelings requested. This exercise decreases the tendency to overidentify with emotions, while enhancing a perspective of playfulness and curiosity toward emotions.

It is essential to give room for expression of the entire spectrum of experience. In general, this process allows children to really feel their feelings. Our experience suggests that unlike many adults, children do not tend to struggle with the guidance and overthink the practice. For example, a child will very matter-of-factly report that her feeling is purple with green spots, groans, and needs love. Occasionally the feeling will want something the child is unable to give, and we suggest that he or she ask the feeling if there is something else it wants. If a child repeatedly reports that he or she is bored, we have him or her look underneath the boredom, and often the child discovers sadness, anger, or fear.

In class six, we invite children to share their artistic representations of their feelings from the preceding week. Children always have the right to pass. However, we encourage them to stretch gently into any discomfort they may have about sharing; the discomfort represents another opportunity to practice mindfulness of feelings. With children who tend to be shy, we use the analogy of physical stretching in yoga. We suggest that they stretch toward sharing their experience and speaking up, while simultaneously honoring their limits. We remind them that, as with physical stretching, their capacity for being with their feelings and for sharing will change from day to day and moment to moment. In this way, we are cultivating the capacity to be with feelings without resisting or indulging them.

Children and adults tend to have habitual ways of interacting with their feelings. Without inquiry and insight, most of us tend to live within a fairly narrow range along the continuum of suppressing feelings or being overwhelmed by them. For those who tend toward suppression, the Feelings Practice described above may support them in becoming more emotionally fluent. For those who tend to be overwhelmed, they may benefit from having time to really anchor into the Still Quiet Place before meeting feelings. It can be helpful to clarify that we want to have our feelings without our feelings having us.

When the children are sharing their artistic representations of their feelings, we occasionally comment, responding to an individual child or a group theme, or offer a principle of mindfulness. At other times, we remain silent because someone has offered something profound that has touched everyone's heart.

Seaweed Practice

If the group is getting wiggly, we may do one of many brief movement practices, perhaps something as simple as "being seaweed." Each child is a strand of seaweed anchored to the floor. Initially we are in a strong current, making big rapid movements. Gradually the current decreases, and our movements become smaller and smaller until there is very gentle swaying and then stillness. Throughout the Seaweed Practice, the children are gently reminded to be aware of their physical sensations, thoughts, and feelings. This practice simultaneously honors the children's natural need for movement and continues to develop their capacity to pay attention; in this exercise the focus of attention is on the experience of moving.

Following the brief movement practice, we continue exploring stressful or difficult circumstances from the previous session. In earlier home practice (note that we do not call it "homework" to avoid any potential negative associations), the children have observed thoughts, feelings, and physical sensations that arise in stressful situations. They have also learned to use awareness of breathing to slow things down in everyday life. In class six, we discuss the preceding week's home practice of responding rather than reacting to life's circumstances.

Baseball Analogy

In one class, a boy described a frequent stressful interaction with his mother. The boy wanted attention, and his mother wanted some time and space. The boy also happened to love baseball. So we used the analogy that his mother threw him a curveball—meaning that she was not available. As a group, we explored what his "home run" responses might look like. Then we continued around the room, and each person was given the opportunity to describe a "curveball" scenario (difficult communication) in his or her life (e.g., spouses arriving late for dinner, parents wanting children to go hiking when the children didn't want to go). For the most part, the child or parent presenting the difficult communication offered his or her own "home run" response.

When the person presenting the scenario could not come up with a "home run" response, we had plenty of wise "batting coaches" in the room to offer ideas. For example, an older boy suggested to the boy mentioned above that he make an agreement with his mom to do his own thing for fifteen minutes, and then she would play with him for fifteen minutes. The boy and his mother both felt this was preferable to their usual mode of interacting. This particular exercise arose simply from knowing that the boy loved baseball and the intention to speak to him using an analogy that was meaningful to him. Because the boy presented the scenario, we focused the discussion and practice on exploring the range of responses available to him. There is also a parallel conversation to be had with his mother, exploring the variety of "home run" responses available for her.

Thought Parade Exercise

In the Thought Parade Exercise, children sit in chairs or lie on the floor, anchor their attention on the breath, and then begin to watch their thoughts go by as if they are watching a parade. They may notice that some thoughts are loud and brightly dressed, other thoughts are shy and lurk in the background, and still others come back again and again. When children notice they are marching with the parade (i.e., lost in thought), they are encouraged to return to the sidewalk and simply watch the thoughts go by. This practice supports children in watching their thoughts without believing them or taking them personally.

As an example of the Thought Parade Exercise, we offer the following story:

> *In one fifth-grade class, some of the boys were skeptical of mindfulness. One Wednesday when practicing the Thought Parade Exercise, they noticed that many of their thoughts related to their basketball game that afternoon. They had lost the previous game, and that afternoon they were playing a team that they thought was better than they were. They were worried about losing, playing poorly, and letting the team down. They wanted to win. The leader asked the boy who, in general, had been cool, funny, and less than participatory in the way that some ten-year-old boys can be, "If you are thinking about winning and losing, is your head in the game?" His eyes got big. His mouth hung open. He was in. Mindfulness is relevant. The leader reminded the class that two of the most successful teams in professional basketball, the Los Angeles Lakers and the Chicago Bulls, use mindfulness to bring their attention fully into the game, narrowing their focus to the ball, their teammates, and the opposing team, not getting distracted by the score or the noise of the crowd.*

Home Practice

An essential component of the course is home practice. Home practice includes both formal guided practices of resting in the Still Quiet Place and observing thoughts, feelings, and physical sensations, as well as informal practice exploring the applications of mindfulness in daily life. The home practice builds on the children's experiences from the preceding class and provides a starting point for the discussion in the following class.

When we teach the child-parent mindfulness course, both the children and the parents receive the same CD and workbook for home practice. At Stanford, we like to joke and tell the kids this is their first college course. The participants know that if a child picks up a parent's workbook or a parent picks up a child's workbook, they are exactly the same. This emphasizes that we are all in this together.

It is important to create the conditions that support the participants in doing the daily home practice. This involves identifying a regular time each day to practice; most children and families find that before homework or before bed works best. However, it is important to encourage families to be creative in when and how to implement the mindfulness practice in their daily lives. Supporting children and families to do the home practice involves a combination of encouraging, offering specific suggestions, nudging, and challenging, while simultaneously creating an environment that relies on evoking curiosity (rather than guilt) about what gets in the way of actually making time and doing the practice. Unlike home practice for adult MBSR courses, the guided formal practices for this course are just four to twelve minutes long.

At the end of each class, we review the home practice for the following week. We describe the practices for the upcoming week, address any potential obstacles, and reemphasize the importance of home practice. We explain that mindfulness is like learning a sport or learning to play a musical instrument. Mindfulness requires ongoing practice. Sample home practice exercises include the following:

- Practice the Thought Parade using the CD each day.
- Do Walking Practice at least three times during the week.
- Take a "Thoreau walk," giving your full attention to the experience of walking, feeling the movements of your body, seeing the colors, hearing the sounds, smelling the smells around you, and noting your thoughts and feelings. (This exercise was named after the American author Henry David Thoreau, who wrote about his experiences with practicing mindful awareness in daily life.)
- Complete the "Difficult Communication Calendar" [see below] for one difficult communication each day. This will help you understand the thoughts and feelings associated with difficult communications, notice your usual ways of reacting to situations, and explore new ways of responding. Practice responding to "funny mind" and stressful situations. ["Funny mind" refers to the negative internal dialogue of our minds. "Funny mind" includes thoughts that may be inaccurate, that may argue with reality, and that may be painful.] For example, you might notice the following "funny mind" thought sequence: "I can't do this problem. I can't do math. I am going to fail. I am stupid." Noticing these "funny mind" thoughts helps you remember that thoughts are just thoughts. Then you can return your attention to actually doing the math. Complete the Practice Page with kindness, curiosity, and freedom from guilt. [The Practice Page is a daily log that children use to document their formal and informal mindfulness practice over the week.]
- Call or e-mail us with comments, questions, or concerns.

Additional Exercises and Practices

Now let's look at some additional exercises and practices that can be incorporated into various sessions. Together the practices below represent developmental adaptations and truncated practices from standard adult MBSR curricula.

Jewel/Treasure Exercise. Bring a basket of medium-sized stones and have each participant choose one. Ask everyone to lie down on their backs and place the stone on their belly button, either inside or outside their clothing. Invite the children to feel the stone move up with the in-breath and down with the out-breath. Invite them to notice the space between the in-breath and the out-breath, and a second space between the out-breath and the in-breath. Let them notice how it feels to rest their attention on the breath and the Still Quiet Place between the breaths.

Loving-Kindness Practice. Ask participants to remember a time when they felt loved by someone, such as a parent, grandparent, teacher, friend, or pet. It may be helpful to suggest that this can be a very simple moment such as a hug or a smile. Then invite the children to really feel this loving moment, to open their hearts, and to receive the love of this moment. Ask the children to send love to the person or animal who loves them. Very young children enjoy blowing kisses. Older children can simply imagine receiving and sending love. Have them feel the love flowing between themselves and the person or animal who loves them. This sequence can be repeated for others who love them. Children can experiment with sending love to someone they don't know well, such as the server in the school cafeteria or the person who delivers their mail. Children might then think about someone they are having difficulty loving, such as their "ex–best friend" or their sibling. This exercise can be closed by asking the children to send love to themselves, and to feel their love returning to them, and then to send love to the whole world and feel the whole world's love returning to them.

Flashlight Exercise. Invite the participants to sit or lie in a comfortable position and play with the "flashlight of their attention." Ask participants to focus the flashlight in turn on thoughts, emotions, sounds, sensations, and their breath. Then focus on whatever drifts through the light and then focus back on the breath again. Ask participants to expand their attention to include everything and then have them narrow their attention to just one object (and so on).

The exercises above represent some of the curriculum on which our research is based. We now review preliminary research results documenting the impact of our curriculum for children in fourth through sixth grades and their parents.

Difficult Communication Calendar

Describe the communication, with whom? The subject?	How did the difficulty come about?	What did you *really* want from the person or situation? What did you actually get?	What did the other person(s) want? What did they get?	How did you feel during and after this time?	Have you resolved this issue yet? How?

Research Findings

To evaluate the impact of the child-parent MBSR course, we are conducting a study of children and their parents. We have two main goals for our project: (1) to examine the feasibility of training families in mindfulness practice, and (2) to measure specific dimensions of psychological functioning that we hypothesized would change with mindfulness training.

The preliminary results presented below are based on a self-referred nonclinical community sample of twenty-four families (thirty-one children and twenty-seven parents) who enrolled in our child-parent MBSR program, and eight families (eight children and eight parents) who completed the waitlist control condition. We are in the process of analyzing the additional waitlist control data. The sample consisted of high-functioning, middle-class families with children in grades 4 through 6, who were primarily European Americans from the area around Stanford University. Participants in the MBSR course attended in a variety of combinations: one child and one parent; two children and one parent; two parents and one child; and five families of four. Of the twenty-four families who began the course, only four families dropped out, a 17 percent attrition rate. Given the complexities of juggling child and parent schedules as well as scheduling child care for siblings, we were happily surprised that so many families sustained their participation in the eight-session MBSR course. This suggests that a family format of MBSR can be implemented.

With respect to MBSR-related changes in functioning, we measured targeted domains previously shown to be influenced by mindfulness training. Based on reviews of MBSR-related changes in adults (Allen, Chambers, & Knight, 2006; Baer, 2003; Grossman, Niemann, Schmidt, & Walach, 2004) and models of mindfulness mechanisms (Shapiro, Carlson, Astin, & Freedman, 2006), we investigated attention (i.e., alertness, switching, cognitive control), emotional reactivity and regulation, anxiety and depression symptoms, and metacognitive functioning (i.e., self-compassion, self-criticism, mindfulness skills). We used a battery of self-report questionnaires with child and adult versions, and computer-administered cognitive-affective tasks to measure changes in functioning from pre- to postmindfulness training.

Differences in Child-Parent Baseline Functioning

To better understand our sample, we examined whether children and their parents demonstrated any differences in psychological functioning at baseline. Compared to their children, parents demonstrated better attention skills, including alertness and cognitive control, based on the Attention Network Task (Fan, McCandliss, Sommer, Raz, & Posner, 2002), as well as greater critical self-judgment and overidentification with negative beliefs on the Self-Compassion Scale (Neff, 2003). Compared to their children, parents in this sample have more developed attentional capacities and appear to be more critical of themselves.

Because previous studies with adults have shown reliable reductions of mood and anxiety symptoms after mindfulness training (Ramel et al., 2004; Segal et al., 2002), we examined the relationship of state anxiety with psychological functioning in children and their parents at baseline. We found that state anxiety was associated with greater depressive symptoms in children (Children's Depression Inventory [Kovacs, 1992; $r = 0.44$, $p < 0.05$]) and their parents (Beck Depression Inventory-II [Beck, Steer, & Brown, 1996], $r = 0.39$, $p < 0.06$). In parents, state anxiety was strongly associated with lesser mindful awareness (Cognitive Affective Mindfulness Scale–Revised [Feldman, Hayes, Kumar, & Greeson, 2003], $r = -0.69$, $p < 0.0005$) and self-compassion (Self-Compassion Scale, $r = -0.64$, $p < 0.001$). Children's state anxiety was associated with greater self-endorsement of negative social traits (Self-Referential Processing Task, $r = 0.62$, $p < 0.01$) and with poorer cognitive control of attention (Attention Network Task, cognitive control component, $r = 0.53$, $p < 0.05$). This suggests that there may be an important link between anxiety and poorer psychological functioning in both the children and their parents. At the beginning of the study, the most anxious children were also more depressed, more likely to describe themselves in negative terms, and less able to control their attention. The most anxious parents were also more depressed, less compassionate with themselves, and less mindful (aware in the present moment).

Changes from Pre- to Post-MBSR

In the domain of attention, we found an interaction between group and time such that MBSR versus waitlist participants showed a significantly greater improvement on the cognitive control of attention component of the Attention Network Task. Both children and parents in the MBSR program demonstrated the same pattern of improvement from pre- to post-MBSR. Compared to families on the waitlist, children and parents who participated in the MBSR group demonstrated increased ability to direct their attention in the presence of distracters that usually induce conflict. Cognitive control of attention is the last to reach maturity during the developmental trajectory and is also most tightly coupled with academic success.

In regard to emotional reactivity, we found that participants in the MBSR group versus the waitlist group reported significantly less negative emotion in response to physical and social threat scenarios. This effect was stronger in parents than children. With respect to positive or negative self-view, we found no evidence of change in either the MBSR or waitlist participants.

For mood symptoms, while children did not show a change, their parents reported significant reductions in both anxiety symptoms and depression symptoms from pre- to post-MBSR. In the domain of metacognitive functioning, children and their parents both reported improvement for self-judgment and self-compassion. Only parents however, showed significant reduction in isolation and overidentification with negative beliefs. After MBSR, children were more compassionate and less judgmental with themselves, and parents were more compassionate and less depressed, anxious, and judgmental with themselves. Considered together, these results suggest that both children and their parents may improve in attention, emotion, and metacognitive processes following mindfulness training.

Analysis of Potential Mediators of Change

We examined average weekly home mindfulness practice as a potential mediator of MBSR effects on psychological functioning. First, we looked at group differences in two types of home practice: formal (e.g., guided sitting, body scan) and informal (e.g., a meaningful pause, mindfulness in daily life). Because children and parents listened to the guided practices together, they reported the same amount of formal practice. However, parents demonstrated a near-significant trend toward a greater amount of informal practice (integrating mindfulness into their daily lives) than their children ($p = 0.07$).

Next, we investigated whether amount and type of home practice was a potential predictor of MBSR treatment outcomes. We employed a hierarchical linear regression model to determine if a significant baseline predictor of post-MBSR response was no longer significant when average meditation practice was entered into the model. After removing variance in post-MBSR depressive symptoms related to baseline depressive symptoms, we found that average weekly practice accounted for a significant amount of the variance in post-MBSR depressive symptoms (R^2 change = 0.16, $F[2, 24] = 4.10$, $p < 0.05$). While formal practice was not a significant predictor ($p > 0.2$), informal practice alone did significantly predict improvement in depressive symptoms ($\beta = -0.30$, $t = -2.06$, $p < 0.05$). Thus, after accounting for depression at baseline, we found that informal practice predicted improvement in depressive symptoms in adults.

The same analysis applied to the cognitive control component of the Attention Network Task indicated that neither overall amount of mindfulness practice nor informal practice significantly predicted post-MBSR cognitive control of attention (overall $p > 0.09$, informal only $p > 0.15$). However, formal practice, did significantly explain a significant amount of variance in post-MBSR cognitive control of attention, after accounting for baseline cognitive control ($\beta = 0.44$, $t = 2.16$, $p < 0.05$). These data suggest that participants who did more formal guided practice showed greater improvements in their ability to control their attention.

Considered together, these preliminary results suggest that following completion of mindfulness training, children and their parents may demonstrate beneficial changes in attention, mood, and metacognitive domains (compassion and mindfulness), and that considering the effects of formal and informal practice on different treatment outcome variables may be helpful in understanding components and mechanisms of mindfulness practice.

Teaching Mindfulness to Children and Their Parents Simultaneously

Our ongoing research—both the quantitative data, reported above, and our qualitative experience working with families—indicates that this mindfulness curriculum benefits children and their parents. We modified the standard adult MBSR curriculum in several ways to facilitate working with children and their parents. First, for home practice, we asked the parents to choose mindful activities that involved their children—for example, kissing them good-bye in the morning, greeting them after school, and tucking them in at night.

With a large group, the majority of the discussion is focused on the children. Often if the kids are wiggly and need to do some movement, we will take them outside for a movement practice and leave the parents with a discussion question such as "What subtle feelings did you notice over the week?" During the last fifteen minutes of class, parents are given time to ask questions and have adult discussion, while the children draw pictures of their experience of the Still Quiet Place, write haiku or other poems, play outside, or play games that engage mindfulness, such as pick up sticks and Jenga (a game where blocks are placed in a stack and each player in turn pulls a block from anywhere in the stack and places the block on the top of the stack, with the object being not to topple the stack). Parents really appreciate this time to explore how they can apply the principles of mindfulness to their parenting. They often want to stay well past the end of class and the end of their children's willingness to stay.

Perhaps the most challenging aspect of working with children and parents together is that the parents often have an agenda. Frequently parents have brought their child to our MBSR class seeking the exact benefits we are documenting in our research; thus they can get quite attached to the outcome. In the first course for the child-parent study, one mother asked, "What if my child doesn't want to come?" Implicit in how she asked the question was her hope that we would "make" her child come. This particular course was in the context of a research study, and research doesn't like dropouts. However, our response in the moment was "Mindfulness is about accepting what is so, and not about forcing anything; thus it is antithetical to the practice to force someone to participate."

Her question prompted us to ask for suggestions from both children and parents about the class format. The children suggested more movement and less talk. As a group, we agreed that the suggestions would be incorporated into the upcoming classes, that the children who felt they did not want to continue would attend two more sessions, and if at that point they no longer wished to participate, they would stop coming to class.

In the ensuing discussion with just the parents, we shared the following thoughts:

- As parents, our practice is to notice when we want our children to be other than they are, when we have an agenda, and when we are trying to fix or change them. There is a distinction between forcing and supporting. Once we realize our true intentions, we can choose a skillful path. Perhaps living mindfully, being present with and responsive to our children moment by moment, is more important than getting them to practice mindfulness.

- The first two sessions provided children with an experience of the Still Quiet Place and the basic vocabulary of mindfulness. Before starting the course, the children did not know that they had a Still Quiet Place inside. This new knowing is a meaningful learning experience in and of itself, and perhaps it is enough for now.
- Introducing mindfulness to children and parents is like planting seeds, and seeds germinate in their own time. A child who is uninterested in mindfulness now may choose to use apply what has been learned in six weeks; before an important test, game, or performance; during a particularly difficult time in college; or not at all.

In closing, we reminded parents that although they may have enrolled in the mindfulness class "for Susie or Patrick," their children would benefit if the parents developed their own practice. In fact, research from Dr. Georgia Watkins at Mount Sinai School of Medicine has shown that the greatest source of children's stress is not academic stress, peer pressure, or overscheduling, but rather parental stress. Thus, if parents practice mindfulness and reduce their stress, they may simultaneously reduce their children's stress and provide a living demonstration of mindfulness. These comments helped the parents remember that in the initial session many of them had acknowledged that they were taking the mindfulness course not only for their child, but also to cultivate patience, kindness, clarity, gentleness, and wisdom within themselves.

Teaching Mindfulness in the Classroom

Some innocent missteps have taught us that when bringing MBSR into a school setting, it is essential to clearly convey the secular and universal nature of mindfulness and to be proactive in eliciting support of the school administration, teachers, and parents. One or two confused or frightened parents can end a program, or an unreceptive teacher can severely impact the children's experience. Here is a brief example:

> *With the full support of the head of the school and the assistant head, Amy offered a mindfulness course to the two fifth-grade classes on an every-other-week basis. Both fifth-grade teachers were new to teaching fifth grade and were working with new curricula. The experience in the two classrooms was entirely different. In the first room, the teacher intuitively got the practice and said, "I did something similar as a child; I just didn't have a name for it." In the second room, the teacher's response was much cooler, and it wasn't until midyear that*

she verbalized her feelings. While Amy had sensed her feelings, she certainly had not understood their depth. The second teacher said she resented Amy being in the room, she felt mindfulness had been inserted into her curriculum, and she wanted those forty minutes to teach. She also felt that the school as a whole was overly focused on communication and children's stress. She said that when she was young, children just dealt with stress, and that the school was making "too big a deal out of it." This may well have explained the different outcomes in the two rooms. In the first room, a majority of the children enjoyed mindfulness and found it beneficial. In the second room, many children did not enjoy mindfulness or find it beneficial, or if they did, they were reluctant to say so in the presence of their teacher.

If you are exploring the possibility of bringing mindfulness into a school setting, you may have connections with one or more individuals. However, if you want the children to have the greatest chance of reaping the benefits of mindfulness practice and for the program to flourish, be sure to create an opportunity for school administrators, classroom teachers, and parents to experience mindfulness practice and ask questions so misconceptions do not arise and gain momentum.

Conclusion

Our experience and data suggest that children and their parents may benefit from an eight-week curriculum in mindfulness-based stress reduction in ways that are both measurable and meaningful. We continue to measure outcomes from baseline to post-treatment for families taking the MBSR course and those not taking the course. Our findings to date support the usefulness of MBSR and indicate significant improvements both in scientific terms and also in terms of meaningful outcomes in the daily lives of children, parents, and teachers. Our experience suggests a profound difference both at home and in the classroom when a child is more able to control his or her attention and is less emotionally reactive. The impact on the social relations and learning environment cannot be underestimated. Perhaps most importantly, the MBSR course appears to be meaningful for both children and their parents. In closing, we will let the children speak for themselves. At the end of each MBSR course, we ask participants to write a brief note to a friend who knows nothing about mindfulness describing how it feels to rest in the Still Quiet Place, and how he or she uses mindfulness in daily life. The comments below are taken verbatim from the children's notes, misspellings and all:

- Dear Invisible Bob: Resting in the Still Quiet Place is very relaxing. It helps you get in touch with your inner self. And find out how you are actually feeling.
- Dear Keith: I am doing this thing called mindfulness. It is a way of understanding and being aware of feelings. One thing you do is go to the

Still Quiet Place. It feels relaxing to be there. Mindfulness has helped me before homework because it relaxes me so I do a good job with my homework.

- It feels sort of strange but peaceful. I can't really tell how I use mindfulness at home, but I do know it helps me when I am mad at my brother.
- Mindfulness is a great class because you can chill out, and relax. It will cool you down and make you less stressed. You should try it if you are mad or sad or just want to feel better. That's what I do. Try it!
- Still quiet place has given me a lot of stress relief. I use mindfulness when I'm upset or stressed out. Mindfulness Rocks! Thank you Dr. Saltzman for introducing this wonderful program to me.
- Dear Friend: Mindfulness is a class I am taking at school. It is a time when we breathe and think about our thoughts, about NOW, not the past or the future. When we settle in breathing we go to our "still quiet place." It feels calming in the "still quiet place." I use mindfulness when I am nervous about something.

References

Allen, N. B., Chambers, R., & Knight, W. (2006). Mindfulness-based psychotherapies: A review of conceptual foundations, empirical evidence and practical considerations. *Australian and New Zealand Journal of Psychiatry, 40*, 285–294.

Baer, R. A. (2003). Mindfulness training as a clinical intervention: A conceptual and empirical review. *Clinical Psychology: Science and Practice, 10*, 125–143.

Beck, A. T., Steer, R. A., & Brown, G. K. (1996). *Beck Depression Inventory–second edition manual.* San Antonio, TX: The Psychological Corporation.

Brown, K. W., & Ryan, R. M. (2003). The benefits of being present: Mindfulness and its role in psychological well-being. *Journal of Personality and Social Psychology, 84*, 822–848.

Fan, J., McCandliss, B. D., Sommer, T., Raz, A., & Posner, M. I. (2002). Testing the efficiency and independence of attentional networks. *Journal of Cognitive Neuroscience, 14*, 340–347.

Feldman, G. C., Hayes, A. M., Kumar, S. M., & Greeson, J. M. (2003, November). Clarifying the construct of mindfulness: Relations with emotional avoidance, over-engagement, and change with mindfulness training. Paper presented at the Association for the Advancement of Behavior Therapy, Boston, MA.

Grossman, P., Niemann, L., Schmidt, S., & Walach, H. (2004). Mindfulness-based stress reduction and health benefits. A meta-analysis. *Journal of Psychosomatic Research, 57,* 35–43.

Kabat-Zinn, J. (1990). *Full catastrophe living: Using the wisdom of your body and mind to face stress, pain, and illness.* New York: Dell Publishing.

Kovacs, M. (1992). *Children's Depression Inventory.* New York: Multi-Health Systems.

Neff, K. D. (2003). The development and validation of a scale to measure self-compassion. *Self and Identity, 2,* 223–228.

Ramel, W., Goldin, P. R., Carmona, P. E., & McQuaid, J. R. (2004). The effects of mindfulness meditation on cognitive processes and affect in patients with past depression. *Cognitive Therapy and Research, 28,* 433.

Saltzman, A. (2004). *Still Quiet Place: Mindfulness for young children.* Audio CD contains many of the practices used in the Still Quiet Place curriculum. Available from www.stillquietplace.com.

Saltzman, A. (in press). *Still Quiet Place: Manual for teaching mindfulness-based stress reduction to children.* Will be available in the context of workshops and trainings through www.stillquietplace.com.

Saltzman, A. (forthcoming). *Still Quiet Place: Mindfulness for teens.* Audio CD contains many of the practices used in the Still Quiet Place curriculum. Will be available in the context of workshops and trainings through www.stillquietplace.com.

Segal, Z. V., Williams, J. M. G., & Teasdale, J. D. (2002). *Mindfulness-based cognitive therapy for depression: A new approach to preventing relapse.* New York: Guilford.

Shapiro, S. L., Carlson, L. E., Astin, J. A., & Freedman, B. (2006). Mechanisms of mindfulness. *Journal of Clinical Psychology, 62,* 373–386.

Chapter 8

Acceptance and Commitment Therapy for Childhood Externalizing Disorders

Michael P. Twohig, Ph.D., Utah State University;
Steven C. Hayes, Ph.D., University of Nevada, Reno;
and Kristoffer S. Berlin, Ph.D., Brown Medical School

Clinicians working with children with externalizing problems have many options in the treatment approach they use. Nearly twenty evidenced-based options are currently available for externalizing problems (attention-deficit/hyperactivity, oppositional defiant, and conduct disorders) as listed on the Society of Clinical Child and Adolescent Psychology Web site (www.clinicalchildpsychology.org). Most of these options fall under the general rubric of behavior therapy, including cognitive behavioral therapies (CBT) and behavioral parent training. Both approaches appear to be worthwhile, although their effects tend to vary based on the child's developmental level. Behavioral parent training generally yields stronger effects for preschool and school-age youth, whereas cognitive-behavioral interventions generally have stronger effect for adolescents (McCart, Priester, Davies, & Azen, 2006). Behavioral parent training programs address externalizing problems by training adults in the child's life (e.g., parents, teachers, other relatives) to use effective behavioral management strategies. These strategies include increased monitoring of child behavior, positively reinforcing prosocial behavior, and developmentally appropriate consequences for problem behavior such as defiance, temper tantrums, and fighting. These therapies are usually conducted in group or individual formats and include a mixture of didactic instruction, live or videotaped modeling, and role plays (Eyberg & Boggs, 1998; Webster-Stratton & Hammond, 1997).

As children grow older, many of these therapies begin to include more cognitive-based and emotionally focused techniques. Clinical researchers embracing a cognitive perspective have identified a variety of impaired "social-cognitive" skills among youth with antisocial behavior problems (Crick & Dodge, 1994; de Castro, Veerman, Koops, Bosch, & Monshouwer, 2002; Lochman & Dodge, 1994; Perry, Perry, & Rasmussen, 1986). Within a social-cognitive framework, antisocial youth have been found to hold hostile attributional biases, make errors in the interpretation of social cues, and have stronger expectations that aggression will lead to positive outcomes. Generally, cognitive behavioral interventions seek to teach youth to attend to social cues more effectively, to generate multiple interpretations for others' behavior, and to engage in nonviolent problem-solving strategies. Youth are also taught about the short- and long-term consequences of antisocial behavior, and they learn how to manage their negative affect. Examples of these empirically supported approaches include anger coping therapy (Lochman, Burch, Curry, & Lampron, 1984), assertiveness training (Huey & Rank, 1984), and problem-solving skills training (Kazdin, Esveldt-Dawson, French, & Unis, 1987).

The majority of families who complete evidence-based treatments for externalizing problems experience both short- and long-term benefits (Brestan & Eyberg, 1998; Lonigan, Elbert, & Johnson, 1998). However, evaluation of the literature consistently reveals poor outcomes of these programs among a sizable minority of families (e.g., Eyberg & Boggs, 1998; Webster-Stratton & Hammond, 1997). These negative outcomes include high rates of premature family dropout, parental failure to engage in the treatment process, and failure of the child and parents to maintain positive changes at follow-up (Miller & Prinz, 1990). Even iatrogenic effects have been documented. For example, group-based interventions for deviant youth can lead to worse psychosocial outcomes (Dishion & Andrews, 1995).

Thus there is a need for further treatment development focused both on the child and the important adults in the child's life (e.g., parents and teachers). In the case of younger children, most of the treatment failures seem to be due to problems in parental or teacher treatment implementation. In the case of older children, there appears to be a need for additional ways to address their behavioral, cognitive, and emotional problems. Behavior therapy and behavioral principles are the cornerstones of treatment for childhood externalizing disorders, but behavior analytic researchers are only now developing the conceptual tools needed to address human cognition. In the next section, we will briefly present this work.

Behavioral Approach to Cognition: Relational Frame Theory

Relational frame theory (RFT; for a book-length treatment, see Hayes, Barnes-Holmes, & Roche, 2001) is a modern behavior analytic approach to human language and cognition. When a child is taught that a picture of an elephant is called "elephant" and goes with the written word E-L-E-P-H-A-N-T, the child will likely derive relations among all three of these events. If a child were given three choices of written words where one is E-L-E-P-H-A-N-T, he or she will choose it when the word "elephant" is said even though these two stimuli were never trained together. This response was verbally "derived" rather than learned through direct training.

This might not sound all that surprising, but those who are more familiar with behavioral theory will note that a stimulus just acquired a function, apparently with no history of training. From an RFT point of view, this occurred because the child learned similar relations with other exemplars, an idea that has recently been confirmed with infants (Luciano, Becerra, & Valverde, 2007). Like generalized imitation, with enough training, a "frame" can be placed on any event (not just elephants, but dogs, cats, balls, cars, and so on). Moreover, by training just a few relations, an entire network can be derived.

If relations of similarity (or what RFT theorists call "frames of coordination") can be learned through multiple exemplars, there is no reason that other relations, such as relations of opposition, difference, comparison, and so on, cannot also be learned through multiple exemplars. This too has been confirmed in research with children (Barnes-Holmes, Barnes-Holmes, & Smeets, 2004; Barnes-Holmes, Barnes-Holmes, Smeets, Strand, & Friman, 2004; Berens & Hayes, 2007).

Children also apparently learn to distinguish themselves from others through relational training. These "deictic relations," such as I-you, here-there, and now-then, are not defined by formal (or physical) properties but by their relation to the speaker. Evidence from RFT laboratories shows that these relations develop over time (McHugh, Barnes-Holmes, & Barnes-Holmes, 2004), are deficient in some children such as autistic spectrum disordered children (Heagle & Rehfeldt, 2006), seem to correlate with social communication abilities (Rehfeldt, Dillen, Ziomek, & Kowalchuk, 2007), and can be trained (Heagle & Rehfeldt, 2006; Rehfeldt et al., 2007; Weil, 2007). Furthermore, there is growing evidence that deictic relations underlie the ability to take the perspective of others and the ability to show empathy (Weil, 2007). Children trained on deictic framing, for example, demonstrate significant improvements in their theory of mind performances (Weil, 2007), which measure the ability to understand the perspectives of others.

These relational processes present both challenges and opportunities in the treatment of children, and there is increasing evidence that it is necessary to deal with them for this simple reason: relational operants operate on other behavioral processes. The functions of events in relational frames can change based on the functions of other related events. For example, if X is the opposite of Y, and Y is a reinforcer, then we can derive without direct training that X may now be a punisher (for an empirical example of such effects see Whelan & Barnes-Holmes, 2004). Similarly, if X is greater than Y, and Y is paired with shock, then X may now be more fearful and arousing than Y, even though it was never paired with shock (Dougher, Hamilton, Fink, & Harrington, 2007). Another reason to deal with relational processes is that both clinical problems and opportunities for their treatment emerge at the level of these processes. Some of these are directly relevant for the analysis of externalizing disorders and perhaps their treatment as well.

Humans do not just respond to the physical characteristics of stimuli or to the direct history related to them. Some responding is based instead on derived relations between events. A child does not simply get a grade on a homework assignment, he or she gets a "good," "okay," or "bad" grade. These grades are not just numbers or letters, they are "important" and "can affect one's future" or, given other histories, they may be "no big deal." Similarly a child with attention-deficit/hyperactivity disorder (ADHD) does not have just an "urge" to get out of his seat, he has an "annoying" or a "bad" urge. Thus no account of childhood problems is likely to be complete without an analysis of the role of these verbal/cognitive processes.

Effects of Relational Framing: Behavioral Inflexibility

We will begin in a general way, and then provide evidence that our approach applies to what is known about externalizing disorders. As a kind of behavioral experiment, look at a nearby object and see if it is possible for thirty seconds or so not to have any idea what its name is, and try not to label the object by color, size, material, beauty, preference, and the like. For most people, this is an impossible task. Verbal humans label, judge, and evaluate everything—almost without being conscious of it.

This is an example of how stimulus functions from relational framing tend to dominate over other sources of behavioral regulation. Relational framing is impossible to fully stop, and in terms of functional utility, there would be no benefit in doing so. *Cognitive fusion* refers to when verbal processes dominate over the natural environmental functions (Hayes, 2004). For example, a child who experiences an urge get out of his seat as just a feeling, and nothing more, would be less cognitively fused; a child who experiences the same urge as "very annoying" and struggles with it would be more verbally fused—the second child has no psychological separation from his urge. Verbal humans seldom experience the world as it actually is. We do not respond only to the actual environment. We respond in part to a verbally constructed version of it, and our verbal version often does not correspond to what is actually occurring. As people interact with the world, they develop rules for how it works; this process can be helpful, but it can also be problematic when it is an inaccurate representation of what is occurring. Once verbal rules are developed, they are very difficult to challenge, even in the face of contrary evidence. Once they are derived, they never seem to go away (Hayes, et al., 2001; Wilson & Hayes, 1996).

Thus there is a light and a dark side to our verbal abilities. On the one hand, we can interact more effectively with our worlds because we do not need to learn everything by direct experience, but on the other hand, we can judge and evaluate everything—even our own thoughts and feelings. This means that the same cognitive abilities that allow children to solve problems verbally through frames of coordination, time, and comparison also allow them to label to their private events, predict them, evaluate them, and attempt to avoid or control them. A central clinical problem from this perspective is that children and adults usually focus on ways to control these reactions when control is not a helpful solution.

Experiential avoidance (Hayes, Wilson, Gifford, Follette, & Strosahl, 1996) involves attempting to alter or alleviate the occurrence, intensity, or situational sensitivity of private events when doing so causes behavioral harm. This is largely a product of an inaccurate rule that uncomfortable private events are bad and work should be done to control them. Experiential avoidance is harmful both in adults (Hayes, Luoma, Bond, Masuda, & Lillis, 2006) and in children (Greco, Lambert, & Baer, in press), accounting for 20 to 25 percent of the variance in many problem areas. Experiential avoidance or control can present itself in many ways in children. Youth with externalizing problems may, for example, act out in class and fight with their peers to counteract thoughts of not being liked or to suppress their fear of rejection and feelings of insecurity. The repertoire-narrowing effect of experiential avoidance and cognitive fusion create *psychological inflexibility*, or the inability to modulate persistence and change in order to accomplish valued ends (Hayes et al., 2006).

There is a significant body of evidence that points to such processes in externalizing disorders. These children tend to have significant problems with social perspective-taking tasks, theory of mind tasks, and empathy (Happe & Frith, 1996). Even preschoolers with behavior problems show poorer understanding of others' emotions, as indicated by poorer performance on theory of mind tasks compared to their same-aged peers (Hughes, Dunn, & White, 1998). Children with conduct disorder also show less empathy toward others relative to diagnosis-free youth (Cohen & Strayer, 1996), and appear to regulate their emotions in different ways. For example, conduct-disordered youth tend to be less overtly expressive, despite exhibiting significantly higher levels of physiological arousal on mood induction tasks compared to their peers (Cole, Zahn-Waxler, Fox, Usher, & Welsh, 1996), who tend to be more expressive and less physiologically reactive. This experiential-avoidant style is supported in part by the fact that these children also tended to have high rates of anxiety and depression at a subsequent follow-up than more emotionally expressive peers. Furthermore, children with ADHD also show less psychological flexibility as demonstrated by their poor performance on tasks such as the Wisconsin Card Sorting Task, which measures the ability to display flexibility in the face of changing schedules of reinforcement (Seidman, Biederman, Faraone, Weber, & Ouellette, 1997).

These patterns seem to relate in part to parenting practices. Oppositional, aggressive, hyperactive, and inattentive patterns in children have been linked with parenting practices characterized as unresponsive, overly harsh, and punitive (Burke, Loeber, & Birmaher, 2002; Reid, Patterson, & Snyder, 2002). Moreover, lack of emotional warmth within the parent-child relationship is associated with oppositional child behavior (Stormshak, Bierman, McMahon, & Lengua, 2000). Direct observations of parenting patterns suggest that children's antisocial behavior can be predicted at least in part by parent displays of anger. In contrast, the parents of more well-adjusted children established a supportive presence, gave clear instructions, and set clear limits during parent-child interaction tasks.

Aggregate findings suggest the following about youth with externalizing problems: (1) they tend to express a limited range of affect despite showing high physiological reactivity to negative mood-inducing stimuli; (2) they tend to be less able to understand the emotional life and psychological perspectives of others; (3) they appear to feel less empathy toward others; (4) they are less psychologically flexible; and (5) they experience more punitive and unresponsive interactions from their parents, higher levels of parental anger, and less emotional warmth within the parent-child relationship. This list maps onto the core perspective of acceptance and commitment therapy (ACT, said as one word, not initials; Hayes, Strosahl, & Wilson, 1999) to a remarkable degree. ACT targets harmful effects of experiential avoidance, cognitive fusion, and psychological inflexibility while adhering to the sensibilities of behavioral interventions.

It is also worth considering the role of parents in applying treatments for externalizing disorders. Dropout from parent-focused treatment is often predicted by parental (especially maternal) stress or poor mental health (e.g., Werba, Eyberg, Boggs, & Algina, 2006). A meta-analysis of parent training for child externalizing behavior problems (Reyno & McGrath, 2006) concluded that only maternal mental health predicted both response to treatment and dropout. Further, it is known that parental experiential avoidance predicts parenting-related stress and difficulty in dealing with caregiver challenges (Greco, et al., 2005), and that stress, anxiety, and depression are significantly correlated with experiential avoidance.

ACT is known to be broadly useful with mental health problems, stress, anxiety, and depression (Hayes et al., 2006), and to assist with the mental health challenges of difficult parenting situations (Blackledge & Hayes, 2006). Furthermore, ACT methods can be added to behavioral and educational interventions to produce greater compliance, engagement, willingness to learn, and willingness to use new skills or parenting skills. For example, ACT methods produce more willingness to use exposure methods in people with anxiety disorders (Levitt, Brown, Orsillo, & Barlow, 2004); they produce greater willingness to take advantage of new learning (Luoma et al., 2007; Varra, 2006); they increase the ability to do difficult things behaviorally (Dahl, Wilson, & Nilsson, 2004; Forman et al., 2007; Gifford et al., 2004; Gregg, Callaghan, Hayes, & Glenn-Lawson, 2007); they empower people to take charge of their environments (Bond & Bunce, 2000); and they decrease burnout and emotional exhaustion (Hayes, Masuda, Bissett, Luoma, & Guerro, 2004). Importantly, many of these changes in outcomes occurred because of changes in ACT processes (see Hayes et al., 2006, for a review). This finding is now so common that when clinicians identify problems with experiential avoidance or psychological flexibility in particular populations, and see that they are related to important clinical outcomes, it is reasonable to consider the use of ACT as at least broadly empirically supported, even before specific outcome trials have been performed with the specific outcome targets.

Given the entire set of findings just reviewed, acceptance-based approaches may also enhance outcomes of behavioral parent training (Coyne & Wilson, 2004; Greco & Eifert, 2004). The parents' own struggle may contribute to the family's presenting problems by directly affecting their parenting practices, which in turn may exacerbate child behavior problems. For example, parents may be inconsistent in their use of disciplinary techniques, or they may lessen the severity of consequences, in an attempt to assuage their guilt or discomfort occasioned by setting firm limits and enforcing behavior plans. Parental experiential avoidance may similarly lead to decreases in adequate parental involvement and monitoring in an attempt to avoid stressful situations and fear of potential conflict with the child.

Using ACT for Children with Externalizing Behavior Problems

ACT is not a structured clinical intervention; it is a model of how to do behavior therapy. Given the literature, it makes sense that intervention with externalizing disorders should entail not just specific behavioral methods but also methods to ensure parental engagement, to address parental mental health issues, and to address children's deficits in the areas of perspective taking, empathy, emotional regulation, psychological flexibility, and patterns of experiential avoidance. ACT targets these clinically relevant processes in youth and at the same time does not diminish or eliminate any of the existing empirically supported behavioral methods from inclusion in the treatment protocol. Therefore, even without specific data in the area of childhood externalizing disorders, it makes sense to describe an ACT approach for this clinical population so that its impact might be explored. Of note, there is a growing body of research on the application of ACT to children (see chapters 2, 5, 9, 11, and 12 in this volume), and some theoretical direction has been provided (Greco & Eifert, 2004; Murrell, Coyne, & Wilson, 2004; Twohig, Hayes, & Berens, in press).

Functional Analysis

From a behavioral point of view, it is not necessarily important what the particular behavior is, but more what variables are maintaining it and how the therapist can successfully influence them. For example, if a child diagnosed with ADHD will not stay in her seat during class, it needs to be determined why this is so. It could be because the child is struggling with her studies and is avoiding them, the boy behind her is picking on her, the chair hurts her back, she feels an incredible amount of energy and only knows one way to expel it, and/or she could get attention from the class for her behavior. Knowing these variables makes it possible to appropriately address the problem behavior. Behavioral psychologists have long focused on functional assessment procedures to achieve this end. Functional assessments can include a variety of procedures such as questioning the child, interviewing parents and teachers, observing the child, or setting up experimental procedures to test the effects of certain conditions. The use of more formal experimental procedures has generally been called a "functional analysis" and has been well researched in behavioral psychology.

Functional assessments will help the therapist understand the variables that might be maintaining the problem behavior. The findings from the functional assessments can lead to different intervention possibilities, such as instructing adults in contingency management procedures, conducting some skills training, or targeting the function of thoughts and feelings. It would be evident if the child's environment is set up in such a way to maintain her problematic behavior when slight manipulations of the environment result in significant changes in the target behavior. This type of issue is more easily remedied by appropriate alterations to the child's environment. Contingency management procedures are often coupled with skills training procedures. In some situations, basic skills training is sufficient to alleviate problem behaviors. This could be seen in a child who acts out while completing multiplication problems. It might be the case that the child is behind his peers in math and that the acting out would decrease if the child did not have as much difficulty with the math problems. Thus the most prudent treatment would be additional training in multiplication.

An ACT approach is not necessary in all situations, but might be a worthwhile avenue in some. As a clinical example, take a child who experiences great levels of frustration with her peers and constantly fights with them. If the peers are not behaving inappropriately and this is not solely a particular skills deficit, then it has more to do with the ways in which the child responds to her own thoughts and emotions. It may be that this child believes her peers are behaving in a hostile or threatening manner, or perhaps the child attacks others to alleviate her aversive emotional states (e.g., thoughts that no one likes her; fear that she will be ridiculed). In this type of situation, ACT may help round out the behavioral methods commonly used.

Clinicians might identify the following variables to assist with an ACT-based case conceptualization: (1) the form, frequency, and intensity of the problematic behavior; (2) the situational triggers for these behaviors, both internal private experiences and external events; (3) the distressing thoughts, feelings, memories, sensations, or events that the problematic behavior pattern is helping the child avoid; (4) the specific experiential avoidance or control strategies used to manage painful psychological content; (5) the short-term reinforcers (e.g., feeling less anxiety, feeling more accepted) that maintain these unworkable control strategies; (6) the client's valued directions in school, recreation, friendship, and family, among other domains; and (7) the extent to which problematic behaviors are interfering with the child's desired life outcomes (Murrell et al., 2004, p. 250).

ACT for the Parents of the Client

The role of negative reinforcement (and coercion) in the development and maintenance of externalizing problems is not a new idea. Beginning in the early 1970s, Patterson and colleagues began documenting the process by which family members use aversive reactions to exert short-term control over others in the service of terminating conflict (Patterson, Reid, & Eddy, 2002). Parental experiential avoidance is associated with passive or acquiescent parenting behaviors and youth behavior problems. Parenting practices, adolescent behavior problems, and parent experiential avoidance were assessed in nearly two hundred nonclinical parents. It was found that the parent's inability to take action in the face of unwanted internal events (experiential avoidance) was positively related to inconsistent discipline, poor monitoring, and decreased parental involvement, with these parenting practices in turn relating to adolescent behavior problems (Berlin, Sato, Jastrowski, Woods, & Davies, 2006). Traditional behavioral parent training programs typically address only the parenting behaviors, like the consistency of discipline and the quality of involvement and monitoring of children. Most interventions do not directly target the factors that influence these parenting behaviors, like experiential avoidance.

Clinicians who wish to enhance behavioral parent training with acceptance-based strategies would likely target the parents' own experiential avoidance that interferes with their ability to implement the behavioral interventions. Similar to work with children, the key to successfully working with caregivers relies on clinicians conducting a functional assessment of the barriers to engaging in valued parenting and to implementing parenting skills and agreed-upon behavior plans. This assessment should be an ongoing process throughout treatment. For some parents, difficulties in implementing behavior plans may arise related to a skill deficit, in that they are unsure about the techniques or how to generalize behavioral principles to novel situations and behaviors. For other parents, the conflict and escalation in problematic behaviors that often arises when contingencies are changed with children may be "too much to bear." The caregiver's perspective that he or she was unable to tolerate the associated distress may provide the clinician with an opportunity to use acceptance-based strategies.

Another possibility is that parents fail to implement behavior plans due to the meaning they ascribe to their child's or their own behavior. For example, a critical ingredient to behavioral parent training is differential reinforcement that involves ignoring problematic child behavior and praising appropriate behavior. For some parents, the idea of ignoring a child who talks back, rather than verbally or physically reprimanding her, may reflect the actions of a "weak parent." Likewise, caregivers may also strongly believe that they are "horrible parents" because of their child's problematic behavior. These last two examples could be addressed from an ACT perspective with defusion exercises that seek to weaken the literality of painful thoughts and feelings. Through defusion work, parents would learn to experience their feelings and thoughts as less compelling.

ACT for Children

ACT is somewhat unique because of its emphasis on healthy functioning over a particular type of symptom reduction. Symptom reduction in a particular domain is a goal to the extent that it supports larger values-based activities. The dominance of verbal fusion and experiential avoidance can interfere with healthy functioning and exacerbate parenting difficulties and child behavior problems. These potentially harmful processes are targeted in ACT, and core clinical methods are used to promote psychological flexibility, which is created through six processes: acceptance, defusion, self as context, contact with the present moment, values, and committed action (see chapter 3, figure 1). The first four are mindfulness processes; the last four are commitment and behavior change processes.

Therapeutic Stance

Children seldom present for therapy on their own. They are usually assigned to work with someone because an adult in their life has identified some behavioral problem of significance. Thus motivation to participate in treatment is often limited. Most child psychologists are already sensitive to this issue and are good at managing it. The difficult part for many therapists will be to understand and adopt the theoretical framework that underlies ACT. One area where people often stray from ACT is by adhering to a more traditional "control of private events" framework and then attempting to use ACT as another method within this framework. The content or form of a particular private event is not the treatment target as it is in other therapeutic approaches. For example, "urges" are not the problem for a child with ADHD, nor is "anger" for a child with oppositional problems. The problem is how the child responds to these events when they occur. The thought or feeling itself does not need to change before the overt behavior changes.

Therefore a social context needs to be created in therapy in which the child truly feels that thoughts and emotions are acceptable and do not need to be regulated simply because of their form or frequency. This is accomplished in part by creating a therapeutic context in which these events are normalized. Thus the therapist might express that he or she is feeling different emotions and model how to continue behaving effectively while they are there. Additionally, an ACT therapist would want to avoid talk about "causes" of disorders or other types of storytelling of how the disorder developed. Any talk that would strengthen the fusion with these thoughts would ultimately be harmful from this therapeutic stance. The client is taught to trust his or her experience rather than what his or her mind suggests.

Therapeutically, the goal of ACT is to help the client experience thoughts and feelings as just that, thoughts and feelings, but only as much as it helps the person move in a better direction in life. When meaningful areas of life are linked up to the work done in therapy, there will be an increase in motivation to participate in treatment and it will give meaning to participating in treatment.

Therapists who are familiar with ACT but less familiar with working with children have expressed concerns that ACT will be difficult to do with children. This could be part of the reason that there has been considerably less ACT work with children than with adults. There also seems to be confusion between understanding the theory, the model, or how to implement the therapy and what it is like to actually participate in the therapy. Functional contextualism, RFT, and the techniques, assumptions, and principles of ACT would be difficult for a child to understand, but that is very different than participating in ACT as a therapy. ACT relies heavily on less literal methods such as metaphors, exercises, and stories because literal discussion can inadvertently support normative language processes that give way to cognitive fusion and experiential avoidance. This also means that ACT methods are more similar to methods commonly used with children. Logical, straightforward discussion has its role in ACT, but it is a rather limited one because logical processes are often assumed to be problematic within this framework. Again, this means that ACT methods are less complicated and abstract than most approaches and, for these reasons, may be very well suited for children and adolescents.

Acceptance

Acceptance is a core component of ACT. It is, in a sense, what an ACT therapist teaches the child to do with problematic thoughts, feelings, and bodily sensations: to experience them fully and without unnecessary defense. Acceptance has multiple meanings in the field of psychology. In ACT, *acceptance* refers to the way in which one responds to private events. There might be some situations that require acceptance of one's situation or the actions of others, but this is not usually what is meant by acceptance in ACT. Acceptance is best thought of as a behavior rather than an attitude. It is a skill; it is something that the child learns to do. There are a variety of exercises or statements that could foster acceptance in a child. The following is an example of an ACT exercise that might foster acceptance over controlling a thought or a feeling. It is described as though it was being said to a child diagnosed with conduct disorder who regularly argues with his teachers.

Therapist: Tommy, you said that you argue with your teacher because she is so "dumb."

Client: Yeah, she is always getting on my case and asking me to do such stupid things, like clean up or fix stupid things on my papers. I like to do things my way.

Therapist: Fair enough. But this arguing is getting you in trouble, right?

Client: Yeah. Sometimes I have to miss recess, or I get extra homework.

Therapist: I want to help you get recess and not have to do that extra homework. There are some skills that might help you. I bet it bothers you when she asks you to do these things.

Client: Yeah, I get angry.

Therapist: Does arguing make you less angry?

Client: A little.

Therapist: And it also gets you in trouble. I know you like to do things your way, but what if I taught you another way to deal with your "angry" feelings that might keep you out of trouble?

Client: Okay.

Therapist: You know how it itches when you are bitten by a mosquito or if you get into a plant that you are allergic to? You can do things to make the itch go down like scratching it, but those things only work for a couple seconds and then the itch comes back. You keep doing this and eventually your skin will turn red and become irritated. I think you are doing the same thing with your anger. You "scratch" it to make it go away each time it shows up. You yell or fight so that you feel less angry. But this ends up getting you in trouble instead of making the anger go away—a lot like scratching makes your skin red rather than making the itch go away. Sometimes the best thing to do with an itch is to let it be. It will not make it go away, but it will keep your arm from turning red and irritated. Sort of how arguing to make your anger go away leads to not getting to go out for recess. So do you think you could let your anger be there without trying to make it go away, like you would let a mosquito itch just be there?

In this situation the therapist would likely be in contact with the school and the teacher while implementing ACT individually with the child. Consistent with traditional behavioral interventions, the teacher would be encouraged to use differential reinforcement with the child to help him learn greater acceptance.

It can also be helpful to be very concrete and to use experiential methods such as role play when working with children. For example, if working with a young boy who fights and teases other children because he does not feel "tough" otherwise, the following acceptance intervention could be useful. The therapist and the client can role-play situations where the boy feels "weak." The therapist can do things better than the client, the client can purposefully fail at things he is usually good at, the therapist can pretend to tease the boy, or the boy can say nice things to the therapist instead of his usual tough things. Doing these types of exercises will likely evoke the feeling of being "weak," which he will want to replace with feeling "tough." The therapist can work with the child to let these feelings be there—without fighting with them. The child can describe them, or act in ways opposite to them, and just generally "open up" to them. The therapist needs to be careful not to tell the child that doing this is in the service of lessening or controlling the emotions; it is done so that the client can get better at having these emotions without acting on them. This type of exercise can also be done with other emotions that clients struggle with. For example, if a child struggles with sitting through a whole class because of urges to get out of her chair, the therapist and the client can make games out of who can be more accepting of boredom. They can do repetitive tasks or sit quietly while practicing acceptance of boredom.

In addition to exercises, acceptance is one skill that is often modeled in ACT. There are many instances in which the therapist can show the client that it is fine to feel whatever feeling or have whatever thought that shows up during the therapy session. This can be very useful for children because they generally learn from adults and may look up to their therapists. For example, when a therapist forgets what he or she was going to say or is not sure of the answer, it shows acceptance to share with the child, "Wow, I feel embarrassed; I forgot what I was going to say." The therapist should illustrate that he or she is welcoming of these types of feelings when it is useful for the client. If it is therapeutically useful, the therapist can also model emotional acceptance by showing emotion at an appropriate instance.

Defusion

Children avoid things that are real and can harm them. If you ask a child if she needs to be afraid of a picture of a monster or a real monster, the child will likely pick the real monster. From an early age, however, children start to respond to their thoughts and feelings as though they were real things. Thoughts are useful when doing homework or taxes, but they are less helpful when constantly struggling with thoughts like "being good enough" or "being tough enough." ACT works to alter the context under which private events are experienced and changes them from purely literal events to ongoing processes of thinking and feeling, which increases the flexibility of behavioral regulation. Cognitive defusion processes should increase the likelihood of acceptance behaviors and vice versa because it is easier to accept nonliteral events. There are numerous practices or exercises that can foster seeing thoughts, feelings, and bodily sensations for what they are. The following exercise involves an active approach that may be helpful for children, as they tend to learn better from practice rather than didactic training. It is called Thoughts in Flight. This exercise also supports other ACT processes such as acceptance and self as context (described below). The exercise can be introduced by saying the following:

> *We are going to play a little game with the thoughts that bother you at school. Usually when the thoughts start to show up, you grab onto them and struggle with them. You really get involved with them. We are going to do something—not to make them go away—but to play with them a little differently. We are going to make paper airplanes and use the thoughts that get in your way as the names for the planes. We will write those thoughts on the side of the planes.*

The therapist helps the client make a couple planes. Next, the therapist and the client determine what thoughts have been interfering with the child and write those thoughts on the side of the airplanes. Next, the child is told that it is her job to watch the airplanes as they fly by without trying to grab the thought-plane or trying to keep it in the air. The therapist and the child can play with the planes and throw them around the room. This exercise should help the child see her thoughts in a different, less threatening way. It can also be modified to promote acceptance. For example, the planes can be thrown at the child (safely), and the child can compare fighting against them versus just letting them land in her lap. Then she can be asked which one takes more work, trying to stop the thought-planes, or just letting them land on her lap?

The following exercise, called Taking Your Mind for a Walk (Hayes et al., 1999, pp. 162–163), can be altered for use with children.

> *Before we start today, it is important for us to identify who all is in the room. By my count, there are four of us: Me, You, Your Mind, and My Mind. Let's just set out to notice how our minds get in the way. To do this I want us to do a little exercise. One of us will be a Person, the other will be that person's Mind. We are going outside for a walk, using a special set of rules: The Person may go where he or she chooses; the Mind must follow. The Mind must talk all the time about anything and everything: describe, analyze, encourage, evaluate, compare, predict, summarize, warn, and so on. The Person cannot talk with the Mind. If the Person tries to talk to the Mind, the Mind should say "not your turn." The Person should listen to the Mind without "minding back," or necessarily doing what the Mind says to do. Instead, the Person should go wherever he or she chooses to go no matter what the Mind says. After at least five minutes, we will switch roles. The Person becomes the Mind and the Mind becomes the Person. The same rules will apply for another five minutes.*

At this point, the therapist and the client can go for a walk around the clinic or outside if possible. The therapist speaks into the client's ear as if he or she was the client's mind. The two switch and let the child be the mind for the therapist. This exercise should help the client experience his or her mind in a different—less literal—way.

Being Present

Exercises that are focused on being present are particularly important for children who struggle with attention in general or who struggle with recognizing that their emotions and thoughts are occurring and affect their behavior. The function of these exercises is to help clients notice that they are thinking, feeling, and experiencing different sensations, and that there are events in their environments that influence them. Recognizing one's private events is an important first step in responding in the presence of them. This section includes a variety of exercises that children can do to be more present with their private events.

The therapist can get a particular food such as a candy that the child really likes and instruct him to eat this piece of candy about ten times slower than he usually does. The therapist can then ask him to pay close attention to each phase of eating the candy. After the first bite, the therapist might have him describe all the different aspects of the candy: What it is like to eat the candy? What does it feel like in your hands? How does it feel in your mouth and on your tongue? What processes are involved in eating the candy? What does it feel like to chew the candy? What does it feel like to swallow it? What does the candy taste like? There will be many qualities to eating it that he will not have noticed before.

This exercise can be done with many different activities, including those that the child really enjoys. Many young children like playing games or playing on swings and slides. For example, a child can slide down a slide or jump off a couple stairs and pay very close attention to the different feelings and sensations that are involved in doing so. There are feelings in the stomach and in the head that are involved in jumping off of something. Finally, the child should be told to practice this same exercise when in class or in other situations where he has trouble paying attention. For example, the child can be instructed to pay attention to all the different qualities that are involved in the teacher giving a lecture. He should pay attention to the way that she writes, the way that her mouth moves, what she does with her hands, and so on. The child may find it entertaining, and this mindfulness exercise will help him to be more present with what is occurring in a situation where he usually is not present.

Self as Context

Self as context involves experiencing oneself as the place, perspective, or context in which private events occur, as opposed to the "conceptualized self" where oneself is experienced as being these private events (e.g., self-judgments). Self as context is essential to understanding the distinction between one's experiences and the person experiencing or being aware of these experiences. Self as context is assuming increasing importance in ACT work with children because of the evidence reviewed earlier relating deictic frames to perspective taking, theory of mind, and empathy skills. Self as context is also a useful process to address when a child is attached to a conceptualization of himself or herself that is problematic. For example, a child may see himself as the "bully" or herself as the "class goofball" and only behave in ways that support that conceptualization of self.

For some externalizing disorders, such as conduct disorder, there may be clinical benefits to the child being able to take the perspective of his or her peers. Some behavioral deficits are not in particular overt responses but rather are in one's ability to respond relationally, which is a higher-order "cognitive" deficit. The relational abilities necessary to take another's perspective can be modified through "deictic relations," such as I-you, here-there, and now-then. If a child has these relational abilities, then he will be better able to respond from another's perspective, thus showing greater empathy and social sensitivity. Technologies from RFT have been shown to be useful in training these abilities. The procedures necessary to train these relational frames are generally straightforward: the relational operant needs to be trained across many contexts, with many stimuli, and the operant should not be based off of formal features of the stimuli—thus making it generalizable. For example, the deictic frame I-you should be trained across many different people where the "I" stays constant and the "you" changes. After training this relation across many different people, the client learns that the "you" is not formally defined in an absolute sense but is based on arbitrary contexts.

The client can also be trained to apply the deictic frame "I-you" to other people having a conversation. After multiple exemplars, the client learns that "I" is context dependent and does not always refer to the client. To increase generalization, this frame can also be applied to other animals such as cats or dogs or to pictures of people. Similarly, the flexibility of deictic frames should be targeted (e.g., "if here were there and there were here, what would be here?"). Empirical support for this type of work exists (Heagle & Rehfeldt, 2006; Weil, 2007). Similarly, it has been proposed that deficits in relational abilities also play a part in ADHD (Twohig, et al., in press). For example, children with ADHD may lack the relational abilities necessary to "understand" a self-control task. Specifically, relational frames of coordination, temporal (time or contingency), and comparison are necessary to understand and follow a rule. Similar training procedures would be used to train these types of relational responding abilities in children with ADHD.

The second way that self as context can be useful when treating childhood conduct disorders is when there is a behavioral excess of seeing one's private events as representations of themselves. It can be difficult for a child to let go of a particular thought or feeling when that child sees that private event as a part of who she is. It might be hard on the child's "pride" to be told what to do by the teacher if that child sees her pride and herself as the same thing. Thus a context where it is safe to experience such feelings and thoughts needs to be created. This constant sense of being in the present as a whole person that can't be damaged sets the context where "dangerous" thoughts and feelings can be safely experienced. This is evidenced by the way that many children speak of their thoughts and feelings, such as "I am angry" or "I just have too much energy," as though the person and these feelings are linked in such a way that the feelings have power over the child's behavior. Self as context helps the child experience thoughts and feelings as events that occur within the individual but do not define the individual—they are events that come and go just as all other events in life. They are not more important or less important than other events throughout the day. The child is not defined by these thoughts or feelings; they are part of the whole. The child is taught to experience these events in different ways. This helps the client experience events with less evaluation and more as they really are. This practice shares some similarities to mindfulness and meditation practices, but only in the way that these skills teach the child to experience thoughts as thoughts and feelings as feelings, not as defining characteristics of her as a person.

Self as context training to date has focused on the flexibility of deictic frames (e.g., "If I were you, what would I be seeing?"), but it is easy to extend the concept in other frames. For example, a clinician might ask the child to describe a number of different qualities of the therapist, assuring the client she can say whatever she wants. The client will likely say things such as male/female, old/young, rich/poor, smart/dumb, funny/boring, nice/mean, and so on. The therapist can help the child recognize which qualities are more stable and concrete, such as male/female, and which are arguable, such as funny/boring and nice/mean. Next, the therapist can ask the child to come up with similar characteristics for herself. The child will likely come up with similar qualities such as young, good at sports, funny, smart, popular, girl, and so on. Together the therapist and child can note the identities that they do not have to work hard to keep, such as male/female and age, and contrast these with the ones that they struggle with, such as "smart" or "popular." The clinician should help the child talk about the things that she does to support the self concepts of "smart" and "popular"—or whatever it is for the child.

At this point, it may be useful to engage in flexibility training around the changeable concepts. The clinician might role-play with the child how he might act if each of these features were changed in either a positive or negative way. With negative self-concepts in particular, they can explore ways in which the child does in fact act that contradict this concept at times. The point is to show how fluid self-concept behaviors can be, even though they tend to be "sticky" conceptually. We suggest returning to key concepts that are especially troublesome to the youth (e.g., tough guy, bad son, stupid) and explore with the child how he will still be himself even without those particular concepts. He will still have the thousands of other properties of value if he lets certain ones go. After all, these concepts are not him in the same way that he is male.

Values

There are many things that are important to children: family, sports, friends, school, and so on. *Values* in ACT are areas of life that one cares about. They are different from goals. Goals are generally temporary events that have a final outcome, whereas values are elements of life that are important to the person and that he or she is willing to work on. This is the part of therapy that adds meaning to the processes that were previously attended to, such as experiencing difficult emotions and thoughts. In turn, linking these previous ACT processes up to valued actions can alter their function. This is the only area in ACT where specific relations are targeted. In all other processes, there is great caution in altering cognitions directly. This is an area where being literal is less problematic. For example, a child diagnosed with ADHD may value being in school and being part of a class, but acting on his urges to get out his seat and yell out in class is interfering with his values. Reminding the child of how attempts at controlling emotions may take him away from his values can make it more rewarding to experience the emotions rather than try to control them. The therapist might say to the child, "Staying in your chair all the way through class and only talking when the teacher calls on you would make you more part of your class and would allow you to attend all recesses." It changes the function of the urges to get out of the chair from feelings that get in the way to opportunities for doing things that are important to the child.

In some instances, a child will not be able to specify or come into contact with larger values. This is not an issue, because each child is at a different place developmentally. Because values work is functional, it can still be done and is of use to therapists. The client may not be able to specify larger values, but he or she will likely value participating in recess or not having detention. Clarifying these relationships can be just as useful as clarifying the relationship between acceptance and larger processes. There will be a time later in therapy when the client can work on specifying larger values. When working on values clarification with youth, it can help to describe "valuing" as moving in chosen directions in life. The therapist and child might work together to create a "values compass" in which the child's values are written in an area representing his or her chosen life directions. For example, a recent client reported that he cared most about family and friends. He said that getting in trouble at school hurts his relationship with his mother, and that yelling and being aggressive hurts his friendships. Being helpful at home, not fighting and yelling, and staying out of trouble at school results in a better relationship with his mother. Similarly, not yelling and being more patient results in better relationships with his friends. A list of values-consistent behaviors such as helping at home and doing well in school was easily created in conjunction with a list of values-inconsistent behaviors such as fighting and yelling. When asked to think of internal barriers to following his values, the child noted that he engages in values-inconsistent behaviors when he feels angry. He was assisted in seeing that fighting and yelling were often attempts to control the feeling of anger, and acceptance was offered as an alternative.

When working with children who are a little older, such as in their teenage years, they can be asked to imagine their high school graduation. Clients can be asked to close their eyes and to imagine two outcomes for their high school graduation—the first based on how they are living their lives right now, and the second based on a world where anything is possible and they are able to choose the graduation they really want. Children can also talk about the qualities of the people they look up to and ways that they want to be more like them. For example, a child may look up to her parent or a famous athlete. The therapist might ask the child to describe those qualities of the parent that she looks up to and then help the child see how those attributes can be pursued in her own life.

Behavioral Commitments

Behavioral commitments involve choosing and engaging in actions that are consistent with one's values while practicing the other components of ACT. This phase of treatment could also be called the "behavior change phase" and is where more traditional behavior change procedures are utilized. What makes it different than straight behavior therapy is that all behavior change procedures are done from an ACT approach. The client learns to practice acceptance and defusion from problematic thoughts and feelings when the thoughts occur during the exercises. Also, the use of these procedures is always linked up to the client's values. It is assumed that larger and larger behavior patterns will develop and that the client's repertoire will expand in terms of both overt skills and psychological flexibility.

The exercises and behavioral commitments will vary greatly depending on the particular behavior problem. The exercises could involve using more behaviorally based treatment procedures from other validated treatment protocols or, if appropriate, asking children to commit to change areas of their lives. Here are a few examples: A child with ADHD could sit through class for longer and longer periods. A child with oppositional defiant disorder could practice giving a compliment to a peer whom he usually bullies, or he might go longer and longer periods of time without arguing. A child diagnosed with conduct disorder could similarly make commitments to not engage in harmful behaviors for specified periods of time while engaging in acceptance and defusion. For example, when making behavioral commitments or engaging in values-based exercises, the child might be encouraged to experience "discomfort" openly and to notice his thoughts and feelings as just that—thoughts and feelings.

Conclusion

In summary, there are many empirically supported approaches clinicians can use when working with children who struggle with externalizing problems. The present chapter has highlighted how traditional behavior therapies based on functional assessments can be augmented by integrating ACT-based conceptualizations and strategies with children, their caregivers, or both. In particular, ACT seems to target some of the mechanisms that research suggests contribute to the maintenance of externalizing problems. Moreover, the methods that derive from an ACT conceptualization seem to go beyond contingency management or cognitive behavioral procedures. In general, ACT involves learning to accept the presence of private events, seeing them for what they are, and making commitments to engage in behaviors that are linked to larger valued behaviors. Whether this approach is empirically useful with preventing or treating externalizing disorders will require well-crafted research. The purpose of our chapter was to orient clinicians and researchers to some ways these approaches might be developed and tested.

References

Barnes-Holmes, Y., Barnes-Holmes, D., & Smeets, P. M. (2004). Establishing relational responding in accordance with opposite as generalized operant behavior in young children. *International Journal of Psychology and Psychological Therapy, 4*, 559–586.

Barnes-Holmes, Y., Barnes-Holmes, D., Smeets, P. M., Strand, P., & Friman, P. (2004). Establishing relational responding in accordance with more-than and less-than as generalized operant behavior in young children. *International Journal of Psychology and Psychological Therapy, 4*, 531–558.

Berens, N. M., & Hayes, S. C. (2007). Arbitrarily applicable comparative relations: Experimental evidence for a relational operant. *Journal of Applied Behavior Analysis, 40*, 45–71.

Berlin, K. S., Sato, A. F., Jastrowski, K. E., Woods, D. W., & Davies, W. H. (2006, November). *Effects of experiential avoidance on parenting practices and adolescent outcomes.* In K. S. Berlin & A. R. Murrell (Chairs), *Extending acceptance and mindfulness research to parents, families, and adolescents: Process, empirical findings, clinical implications, and future directions.* Symposium presented to the Association for Behavioral and Cognitive Therapies, Chicago, IL.

Blackledge, J. T., & Hayes, S. C. (2006). Using acceptance and commitment therapy in the support of parents of children diagnosed with autism. *Child and Family Behavior Therapy, 28,* 1–18.

Bond, F. W., & Bunce, D. (2000). Mediators of change in emotion-focused and problem-focused worksite stress management interventions. *Journal of Occupational Health Psychology, 5,* 156–163.

Brestan, E. V., & Eyberg, S. M. (1998). Effective psychosocial treatments for conduct-disordered children and adolescents: 29 years, 82 studies, and 5,272 kids. *Journal of Clinical Child Psychology, 27,* 180–189.

Burke, J., Loeber, R., & Birmaher, B. (2002). Oppositional defiant disorder and conduct disorder: A review of the past 10 years, part II. *Journal of the American Academy of Child and Adolescent Psychiatry, 41,* 1275–1293.

Cohen, D., & Strayer, J. (1996). Empathy in conduct disordered and comparison youth. *Developmental Psychology, 32,* 988–998.

Cole, P. M., Zahn-Waxler, C., Fox, N. A., Usher, B. A., & Welsh, J. D. (1996). Individual differences in emotion regulation and behavior problems in preschool children. *Journal of Abnormal Psychology, 105,* 518–529.

Coyne, L. W., & Wilson, K. G. (2004). The role of cognitive fusion in impaired parenting: An RFT analysis. *International Journal of Psychology and Psychological Therapy, 4,* 469–486.

Crick, N. R., & Dodge, K. A. (1994). A review and reformulation of social information-processing mechanisms in children's social adjustment. *Psychological Bulletin, 115,* 74–101.

Dahl, J., Wilson, K. G., & Nilsson, A. (2004). Acceptance and commitment therapy and the treatment of persons at risk for long-term disability resulting from stress and pain symptoms: A preliminary randomized trial. *Behavior Therapy, 35,* 785–802.

de Castro, B. O., Veerman, J. W., Koops, W., Bosch, J. D., & Monshouwer, H. J. (2002). Hostile attribution of intent and aggressive behavior: A meta-analysis. *Child Development, 73,* 916–934.

Dishion, T. J., & Andrews, D. W. (1995). Preventing escalation in problem behaviors with high-risk young adolescents: Immediate and 1-year outcomes. *Journal of Consulting and Clinical Psychology,* 63, 538–548.

Dougher, M. J., Hamilton, D., Fink, B., & Harrington, J. (2007). Transformation of the discriminative and eliciting functions of generalized relational stimuli. *Journal of the Experimental Analysis of Behavior, 88,* 179-197.

Eyberg, S. M., & Boggs, S. R. (1998). Parent-child interaction therapy for oppositional preschoolers. In C. E. Schaefer & J. M. Briesmeister (Eds.), *Handbook of parent training: Parents as co-therapists for children's behavior problems* (2nd ed., pp. 61–97). New York: Wiley.

Forman, E. M., Hoffman, K. L., McGrath, K. B., Herbert, J. D., Bradsma, L. L., & Lowe, M. R. (2007). A comparison of acceptance- and control-based strategies for coping with food cravings: An analog study. *Behaviour Research and Therapy, 45,* 2372-2386.

Gifford, E. V., Kohlenberg, B. S., Hayes, S. C., Antonuccio, D. O., Piasecki, M. M., Rasmussen-Hall, M. L., et al. (2004). Acceptance theory–based treatment for smoking cessation: An initial trial of acceptance and commitment therapy. *Behavior Therapy, 35,* 689–705.

Greco, L. A., & Eifert, G. H. (2004). Treating parent-adolescent conflict: Is acceptance the missing link for an integrative family therapy? *Cognitive and Behavioral Practice, 11,* 305–314.

Greco, L. A., Heffner, M., Poe, S., Ritchie, S., Polak, M., & Lynch, S. K. (2005). Maternal adjustment following preterm birth: Contributions of experiential avoidance. *Behavior Therapy, 36,* 177–184.

Greco, L. A., Lambert, W., & Baer, R. A. (in press). Psychological inflexibility in childhood and adolescence: Development and evaluation of the Avoidance and Fusion Questionnaire for Youth. *Psychological Assessment.*

Gregg, J. A., Callaghan, G. M., Hayes, S. C., & Glenn-Lawson, J. L. (2007). Improving diabetes self-management through acceptance, mindfulness, and values: A randomized controlled trial. *Journal of Consulting and Clinical Psychology, 75,* 336–343.

Happe, F., & Frith, U. (1996). Theory of mind and social impairment in children with conduct disorder. *British Journal of Developmental Psychology, 14,* 385–398.

Hayes, S. C. (2004). Acceptance and commitment therapy, relational frame theory, and the third wave of behavior therapy. *Behavior Therapy, 35,* 639–665.

Hayes, S. C., Barnes-Holmes, D., & Roche, B. (Eds.). (2001). *Relational frame theory: A post-Skinnerian account of human language and cognition.* New York: Plenum.

Hayes, S. C., Luoma, J., Bond, F., Masuda, A., & Lillis, J. (2006). Acceptance and commitment therapy: Model, processes, and outcomes. *Behaviour Research and Therapy, 44,* 1–25.

Hayes, S. C., Masuda, A., Bissett, R., Luoma, J., & Guerrero, L. F. (2004). DBT, FAP, and ACT: How empirically oriented are the new behavior therapy technologies? *Behavior Therapy, 35,* 35–54.

Hayes, S. C., Strosahl, K. D., & Wilson, K. G. (1999). *Acceptance and commitment therapy: An experiential approach to behavior change.* New York: Guilford.

Hayes, S. C., Wilson, K. G., Gifford, E. V., Follette, V. M., & Strosahl, K. (1996). Emotional avoidance and behavioral disorders: A functional dimensional approach to diagnosis and treatment. *Journal of Consulting and Clinical Psychology, 64,* 1152–1168.

Heagle, A., & Rehfeldt, R. A. (2006). Teaching perspective-taking skills to typically developing children through derived relational responding. *The Journal of Intensive Early Behavioral Intervention, 3,* 8–34.

Huey, W. C., & Rank, R. C. (1984). Effects of counselor and peer-led group assertive training on black adolescent aggression. *Journal of Counseling Psychology, 31,* 95–98.

Hughes, C., Dunn, J., & White, A. (1998). Trick or treat?: Uneven understanding of mind and emotion and executive dysfunction in "hard-to-manage" preschoolers. *Journal of Child Psychology and Psychiatry and Allied Disciplines, 39,* 981–994.

Kazdin, A. E., Esveldt-Dawson, K., French, N. H., & Unis, A. S. (1987). Problem-solving skills training and relationship therapy in the treatment of antisocial child behavior. *Journal of Consulting and Clinical Psychology, 55,* 76–85.

Levitt, J. T., Brown, T. A., Orsillo, S. M., & Barlow, D. H. (2004). The effects of acceptance versus suppression of emotion on subjective and psychophysiological response to carbon dioxide challenge in patients with panic disorder. *Behavior Therapy, 35,* 747–766.

Lochman, J. E., Burch, P. R., Curry, J. F., & Lampron, L. B. (1984). Treatment and generalization effects of cognitive-behavioral and goal-setting interventions with aggressive boys. *Journal of Consulting and Clinical Psychology, 52,* 915–916.

Lochman, J. E., & Dodge, K. A. (1994) Social cognitive processes of severely violent, moderately aggressive, and nonaggressive boys. *Journal of Consulting and Clinical Psychology, 62,* 366–374.

Lonigan, C. J., Elbert, J. C., & Johnson, S. B. (1998). Empirically supported psychosocial interventions for children: An overview. *Journal of Clinical Child Psychology, 27,* 138–145.

Luciano, C., Becerra, I. G., & Valverde, M. R. (2007). The role of multiple-exemplar training and naming in establishing derived equivalence in an infant. *Journal of the Experimental Analysis of Behavior, 87,* 349–365.

Luoma, J. B., Hayes, S. C., Twohig, M. P., Roget, N., Fisher, G., Padilla, M., Bissett, R., et al. (2007). Augmenting continuing education with psychologically focused group consultation: Effects on adoption of group drug counseling. *Psychotherapy Theory, Research, Practice, Training, 44,* 463-469.

McCart, M. R., Priester, P. E., Davies, W. H., & Azen, R. (2006). Differential effectiveness of behavioral parent-training and cognitive-behavioral therapy for antisocial youth: A meta-analysis. *Journal of Abnormal Child Psychology, 34,* 527–543.

McHugh, L., Barnes-Holmes Y., & Barnes-Holmes, D. (2004). Perspective taking as relational responding: A developmental profile. *Psychological Record, 54,* 115–144.

Miller, G. E., & Prinz, R. J. (1990). Enhancement of social learning family interventions for childhood conduct disorder. *Psychological Bulletin, 108,* 291–307.

Murrell, A. R., Coyne, L. W., & Wilson, K. G. (2004). ACT with children, adolescents, and their parents. In S. C. Hayes and K. D. Strosahl (Eds.), *A practical guide to acceptance and commitment therapy* (pp. 249–274). New York: Springer.

Patterson, G. R., Reid, J. B., & Eddy, J. M. (2002). A brief history of the Oregon Model. In J. B. Reid, G. R. Patterson, & J. Snyder (Eds.), *Antisocial behavior in children: Developmental theories and models for intervention.* Washington, DC: American Psychological Association.

Perry, D. G., Perry, L. C., & Rasmussen, P. (1986). Cognitive social learning mediators of aggression. *Child Development, 57,* 700–711.

Rehfeldt, R. A., Dillen, J. E., Ziomek, M. M., & Kowalchuk, R. K. (2007). Assessing relational learning deficits in perspective-taking in children with high-functioning autism spectrum disorder. *Psychological Record, 57,* 23–47.

Reid, J. B., Patterson, G. R., & Snyder, J. (2002). *Antisocial behavior in children and adolescents: A developmental analysis and model for intervention.* Washington, DC: American Psychological Association.

Reyno, S. M., & McGrath, P. J. (2006). Predictors of parent training efficacy for child externalizing behavior problems: A meta-analytic review. *Journal of Child Psychology and Psychiatry, 47,* 99–111.

Seidman, L. J., Biederman, J., Faraone, S. V., Weber, W., & Ouellette, C. (1997). Toward defining a neuropsychology of attention deficit–hyperactivity disorder: Performance of children and adolescents from a large clinically referred sample. *Journal of Consulting and Clinical Psychology, 65,* 150–160.

Stormshak, E. A., Bierman, K. L., McMahon, R. J., & Lengua, L. J. (2000). Parenting practices and child disruptive behavior problems in early elementary school. *Journal of Clinical Child Psychology, 29,* 17–29.

Twohig, M. P., Hayes, S. C., & Berens, N. M. (in press). A contemporary behavioral analysis of childhood behavior problems. In D. W. Woods & J. Kantor (Eds.), *A modern behavioral analysis of clinical problems.* Reno, NV: Context Press.

Varra, A. A. (2006). The effect of acceptance and commitment training on clinician willingness to use empirically-supported pharmacotherapy for drug and alcohol abuse. Unpublished doctoral dissertation, University of Nevada, Reno.

Webster-Stratton, C., & Hammond, M. (1997). Treating children with early-onset conduct problems: A comparison of child and parent training interventions. *Journal of Consulting and Clinical Psychology, 65,* 93–109.

Weil, T. M. (2007). The impact of training deictic frames on perspective taking with young children: A relational frame approach to theory of mind. Unpublished doctoral dissertation, University of Nevada, Reno.

Werba, B. E., Eyberg, S. M., Boggs, S. R., & Algina, J. (2006). Predicting outcome in parent-child interaction therapy: Success and attrition. *Behavior Modification, 30,* 618–646.

Whelan, R., & Barnes-Holmes, D. (2004). The transformation of consequential functions in accordance with the relational frames of same and opposite. *Journal of the Experimental Analysis of Behavior, 82,* 177–195.

Wilson, K. G., & Hayes, S. C. (1996). Resurgence of derived stimulus relations. *Journal of the Experimental Analysis of Behavior,* 66, 267–281.

Authors' Note

The authors would like to thank Lisa Coyne, Ph.D., for sharing her clinical knowledge of this area.

Chapter 9

Acceptance, Body Image, and Health in Adolescence

Laurie A. Greco, Ph.D., University of Missouri, St. Louis;
Erin R. Barnett, MA, University of Missouri, St. Louis;
Kerstin K. Blomquist, MS, Vanderbilt University;
and Anik Gevers, BA, University of Missouri, St. Louis

Many of us struggle with our body image and wish to change something about our appearance. Unfortunately, feeling good about the way we look may be nearly impossible in a society that promotes unattainable and at times unhealthy attractiveness ideals for both sexes. Currently mass media glamorizes an ultrathin body type for women and a lean, muscular build for men. Succumbing to societal pressures, men, women, boys, and girls of all shapes and sizes take great pains in altering and maintaining their appearance. We invest in the latest dieting fads, weight-loss pills, sports and fitness magazines, push-up bras, protein shakes, steroids, personal trainers, and medical procedures that range from liposuction to breast implants for women and pectoral implants for men. We work hard, attaching to the notion that good looks will promote our future happiness and success. Yet, despite all of this hard work, do we truly feel better about ourselves and our bodies? More importantly, what does this investment cost in the way of personal freedom and life vitality? And what might we, as mental health professionals, do to alleviate the unnecessary suffering that comes from these futile pursuits to achieve society's attractiveness ideals?

In this chapter, we present acceptance and commitment therapy (ACT; Hayes, Strosahl, & Wilson, 1999) as a potentially beneficial approach for adolescent girls whose struggle with body image does indeed come at significant personal costs. Although most of us share in this struggle, body dissatisfaction typically begins or intensifies in adolescence and is most strongly associated with perceived self-worth during this stage of development (e.g., Neumark-Sztainer, 2005). An estimated 60 percent of adolescent boys and 75 percent of adolescent girls believe that their appearance affects their happiness (O'Dea & Abraham, 1999). Although physical appearance is clearly important to adolescents of both sexes, girls appear to be more susceptible to body dissatisfaction and its detrimental correlates (e.g., Bearman, Presnell, Martinez, & Stice, 2006; O'Dea & Abraham, 1999; Urla & Swedbund, 2000). For these reasons, our chapter focuses primarily on adolescent girls. We begin by situating body image and weight concerns within a developmental framework, suggesting possible pathways to eating- and weight-related problems. We then summarize clinically relevant processes in ACT and conceptualize "the body-image problem" from an ACT perspective. Finally, we describe the ACT for Health program, a school-based intervention for adolescent girls who may be at risk for serious clinical problems such as obesity, bulimia, and binge-eating disorder.

Eating- and Weight-Related Problems in Adolescence

Adolescence is a developmental period marked by transition and change: Hormones are in flux as the capacity for abstract thinking emerges and the quest for autonomy and independence begins. Questions of "Who am I?" and "What do I want out of life?" become central as adolescents strive to identify personal values that may very well differ from those of parents, teachers, peers, and society at large. Subsets of youth experience notable adjustment problems and elevations in anxiety, depression, and substance use as social and academic demands escalate. Most relevant to our chapter, body dissatisfaction and eating pathology have a peak age of onset in adolescence and are especially prevalent among girls (e.g., Bearman et al., 2006). This is perhaps unsurprising, as young women and girls are aggressively targeted by mainstream media and are exposed to unattainable attractiveness ideals beginning in early childhood (Urla & Swedbund, 2000). Girls as young as seven years express body-image concerns and begin to internalize attractiveness ideals communicated by family, peers, media, and other outside sources (Sands & Wardle, 2003; Thompson, Rafiroiu, & Sargent, 2003). Unfortunately, striving to achieve the current thin ideal may be a self-defeating battle for adolescent girls, who typically exhibit weight gain and structural body changes (e.g., widening hips) within the context of pubertal development.

Possible Developmental Pathways

Adolescent girls who buy into societal expectations and rules surrounding appearance and weight may be at risk for body dissatisfaction and related clinical problems (Eifert, Greco, & Heffner, in press; Levine & Harrison, 2001). Research on the developmental pathways of eating pathology suggests that sociocultural pressures to be thin may elicit heightened body dissatisfaction and negative affectivity (Stice, 2001; Stice, Presnell, Shaw, & Rohde, 2005). A sizable proportion of adolescent girls respond by dieting or engaging in other forms of weight-control behavior. However, these attempts to lose weight predict future episodes of overeating and subsequent weight gain, setting in motion an insidious cycle of dieting, overeating, dietary failure, affective distress, and unworkable attempts at emotional regulation. Thus, paradoxically, dieting and other forms of weight control may increase risk for overweight and obesity, as well as associated eating disorders such as bulimia and binge-eating disorder (e.g., Stice, Shaw, & Nemeroff, 1998; Stice et al., 2005; Wardle, Waller, & Rapoport, 2001).

Deficiencies in interoceptive awareness may further contribute to unhealthy eating and weight control patterns. Specifically, young women and girls prone to disordered eating may have trouble identifying or distinguishing between various types of private events including thoughts, emotions, and the physical sensations of hunger and fullness (e.g., Leon, Fulkerson, Perry, & Early-Zald, 1995; Sim & Zeman, 2004, 2006). As a result, girls may demonstrate insensitivity or unresponsiveness to eating-related cues: instead of eating when hungry and stopping when full, eating behavior is regulated by external stimuli (e.g., presence of food) and emotional experiences unrelated to appetite. Evidence also supports affect regulation models of obesity, bulimia, and binge eating. These models suggest that girls who struggle with body image and weight may use food to soothe or distract themselves from uncomfortable private experiences such as feelings of boredom, sadness, and emptiness (e.g., Greeno & Wing, 1994; Sim & Zeman, 2006; Stice, 2001).

In summary, girls with eating- and weight-related problems may attach to sociocultural rules surrounding beauty and weight and engage in futile weight control efforts in pursuit of socially prescribed attractiveness ideals. Many of these girls struggle with interoceptive awareness; demonstrate insensitivity to appetite cues; and use eating and weight-control behavior to regulate internal discomfort (e.g., weight-related thoughts, urges to binge, and feelings of guilt). In our experience, an ACT approach addresses each of these risk factors and, as a result, may offset developmental pathways associated with serious health problems such as obesity, bulimia, and binge-eating disorder.

Overview of ACT

ACT is an evidence-based behavior therapy that has been used successfully with children and adults exhibiting a broad array of clinical problems such as anxiety, depression, eating disorders, substance use, chronic pain, and thought disorders (see Hayes, Luoma, Bond, Masuda, & Lillis, 2006; see also chapters 5, 8, 11, and 12 in this volume). Across populations and presenting concerns, ACT methods are used to weaken psychological inflexibility characterized by elevated cognitive fusion and experiential avoidance. *Cognitive fusion* refers to the tendency for human beings to mistake private events (e.g., thoughts, feelings, images, physical-bodily sensations) as actual representations of reality.

Rather than simply noticing the ongoing process of thinking and feeling, our ability to use language allows us to fuse with (or attach to) the content of private events (Hayes et al., 1999). Even in small doses, cognitive fusion breeds inflexibility and may give rise to *experiential avoidance*, or the unwillingness to experience certain private events, along with attempts to manage, alter, avoid, or otherwise control the nature of these internal experiences (Hayes & Gifford, 1997).

From an ACT perspective, it is normal and psychologically healthy to experience a full range of thoughts and feelings, including body-image concerns, negative self-evaluations, and related emotional distress. In ACT, the content of thoughts and feelings is not evaluated in any absolute sense as "good/bad," "rational/irrational," "right/wrong," "healthy/disordered," and so on. Instead private events are viewed as transient internal experiences that will come and go for the rest of our lives. No matter how painful and unwanted, private events are not in themselves problematic or harmful. The real harm comes from our tendency as human beings to respond in ways that produce short-term relief to the detriment of our long-term personal values and goals. Thus, how we choose to respond, such as with our hands and our feet, is of utmost importance in ACT and dictates the degree to which painful private experiences will impact our lives.

In ACT, acceptance-based methods are used to weaken cognitive fusion and unworkable levels of experiential avoidance. At the same time, intensive values work and more traditional behavioral procedures such as goal setting and exposure are integral to promoting *psychological flexibility*, or "the ability to contact the present moment more fully as a conscious human being and to change or persist in behavior when doing so serves valued ends" (Hayes et al., 2006, p. 7). In contrast to some other evidence-based behavioral treatments, the central goal in ACT is to promote psychological flexibility and values-consistent behavior, no matter how one feels at the time. Alleviation of internal experiences (e.g., anxiety, depression, body-image concerns) is not explicitly sought and, if it occurs at all, it is viewed as a welcomed and often transitory by-product of therapy.

The "Language Disease"

Consistent with Eastern spiritual traditions such as Buddhism, language is conceptualized within ACT as a double-edged sword that greatly increases the potential for human suffering (Hayes et al., 1999). Language affords humans remarkable evolutionary advantages; for example, human beings are able "to language" in such a way that allows us to solve complex problems, advance technology, and educate future generations at levels far surpassing those of any other species. Notably, however, these very same verbal capabilities enable us to criticize, evaluate, and compare ourselves, each other, and the world in which we live (indeed, our minds do this all the time). Language further fuels our ability to worry about the future, ruminate over past events, and fuse rigidly with even the most unworkable beliefs, expectations, and rules. Unfortunately, what has been referred to as the "language disease" is pervasive and affects virtually all human beings who live in and with a social-verbal community.

In our view, the girls we work with are afflicted with the language disease that we all share but may manifest or express in different ways. Most of the girls in our program are fused with negative self-evaluations and rules surrounding feminine beauty and weight (e.g., "I must lose weight"; "Skinny is beautiful"; "I am fat and worthless"; "My life won't be good until I lose weight"; "I'm ugly and therefore unacceptable"). These girls often respond to their painful thoughts and feelings by engaging in unworkable forms of experiential avoidance such as binge eating to alleviate emotional discomfort or dieting to counteract weight-related thoughts. The bingeing and dieting are a reflection of excessive cognitive fusion and experiential avoidance, both of which stem from the ubiquitous language disease.

Working with Adolescents

Developmentally speaking, an ACT approach may be particularly well-suited for adolescents. ACT clinical methods such as metaphor and experiential exercises are inherently less didactic and are therefore more difficult to obey or disobey. Most of the adolescents we work with appear to welcome ACT's explicit focus on personal responsibility, values, and choice—all of which reflect important developmental tasks such as identity formation and the pursuit of autonomy and independence (Greco & Eifert, 2004). Adolescents also tend to be highly receptive to ACT's emphasis on radical acceptance, genuineness, and a common or shared humanity. Toward this end, group leaders acknowledge that we all suffer. They normalize the adolescent's pain and suffering by self-disclosing some of their own vulnerabilities and making deliberate efforts to diminish any of the "us-them" formulations that show up in session (e.g., "us," the seemingly all-knowing, happy, and put-together therapists; "them," the troubled or disordered adolescents). Working with diverse groups may also be useful in normalizing and validating pain, as girls of all shapes, sizes, and backgrounds begin to realize that they are interconnected and share in this common human struggle.

When working with adolescents, it is important to adapt clinical methods in ways that enhance their acceptability and developmental relevance. For example, in the ACT for Health program, group leaders use teen magazines and music videos to teach skills for thinking critically about media messages. Instead of using adult-generated directives, metaphors and poetry are used to evoke and intensify emotional experience as well as to illustrate important ACT principles. Similarly, adolescents are invited throughout the program to express themselves through less verbal mediums such as art, music, and movement. As described below, it may also be useful to modify certain terminology within the treatment context.

LIFE Exercises

LIFE exercises are incorporated throughout the program to promote out-of-session practice, generalization of skills, and ongoing personal growth. Drawing from the clinical innovations of Eifert and Forsyth (2005), the acronym LIFE stands for "living in full experience" and is precisely what clinicians seek to model and teach in any ACT program. Developmentally speaking, it may be helpful to conceptualize out-of-session practice as opportunities to live in full experience rather than as "homework" that will be reviewed in the next week's session. Reasons for this are simple: Adolescents are assigned homework all the time. They must complete it to earn passing marks; failure to do so results in adult disapproval and negative academic consequences. Thus assigning "homework" may evoke aversive reactions from group members, compliance based on aversive control, or perhaps even noncompliance. Incidentally, most of the girls we work with choose to participate fully in LIFE exercises. To foster engagement, we recommend tailoring exercises to ensure that activities are personally relevant and linked with meaningful long-term outcomes (i.e., values).

Overview of the ACT for Health Program

ACT for Health is a prevention program for girls eleven to eighteen years of age who exhibit at least one of the following risk factors: (1) elevated body dissatisfaction; (2) body mass index (BMI) $\geq$ 25 kg/m^2; (3) episodes of binge eating; (4) current or recent dieting attempts; and/or (5) radical weight-control behavior such as fasting, vomiting, or laxative use. Notably, the ACT for Health program was developed for at-risk girls who do not yet demonstrate full clinical syndromes. As such, we provide appropriate referrals for adolescents who are clinically obese (BMI $\geq$ 30) or meet diagnostic criteria for any of the three major eating disorders (anorexia, bulimia, and binge-eating disorder).

Program Format and Goals

ACT for Health is delivered in school settings and generally consists of six to ten sessions, with number of sessions contingent upon the unique needs of each group. Depending on administrator and teacher preferences, sessions are held once or twice a week during or after school hours and last between sixty and ninety minutes. Most groups are comprised of two female cotherapists ("group leaders") and eight to fifteen girls who are relatively close in age. Ideally, group composition is diverse and includes girls of all shapes and sizes who are at varying levels of risk and who come from a range of ethnic and socioeconomic backgrounds. This is most often the case in our city schools and sets the stage for creating a sense of common or shared humanity, which is foundational in ACT and critical to working effectively with the target population.

An overarching goal of ACT for Health is to empower adolescent girls to live with "fidelity to oneself" in a society that is unlikely to change in the foreseeable future—a society that promotes gender-role stereotypes, objectification of women's bodies, and an often unobtainable thin ideal. Integrating feminist principles of empowerment into an ACT clinical model, the primary goals of this program are to: (1) weaken attachment to sociocultural expectations and rules surrounding gender-role stereotypes, appearance, and weight; (2) enhance acceptance and mindfulness of private experiences; (3) disrupt habitual and potentially harmful patterns of consumption while fostering healthy lifestyle habits; (4) empower girls to take responsibility for their lives and to live in accord with their personal values irrespective of internal and external barriers; and (5) promote self-compassion and forgiveness toward oneself, especially during times of heightened stress and when mistakes are made. The next section describes core facets of the ACT for Health program and provides examples of clinical interventions used to achieve the above-mentioned goals.

ACT for Health Interventions

Although this chapter focuses on applications for high-risk girls, the interventions summarized herein have been adapted from our work and other people's work with human beings of both sexes, many of whom have presented with full clinical syndromes in medical settings and more traditional outpatient clinics. We have applied these interventions in the context of individual and family therapy with adolescents and young adults who exhibit clinical problems ranging from anorexia nervosa to morbid obesity. Thus we encourage clinicians to be creative in using these and other ACT methods with the diverse range of human beings who suffer from the language disease.

Psychoeducation and Health Promotion

Consistent with the egalitarian posturing of ACT and feminist psychotherapy, group leaders make deliberate efforts to minimize hierarchical roles such as "teacher-student" that may arise during didactic portions of the program. Girls' struggles with body image and weight are often not due to lack of information. Many of the girls we work with have been exposed to similar content in health class or from alternate sources such as parents, physicians, fitness magazines, and television. For these reasons, educational content is introduced later in the program and is integrated into only a few sessions. In these sessions, we prioritize as follows: common humanity and therapeutic process first; provision of information second. Further, to increase personal relevance and motivation for enacting healthy lifestyle goals, group leaders link health-related information with individual and group values that have already been identified. In this way, we are not simply presenting instructions or rules for how to live "right"; educational material is now relevant to every girl in the room and may provide direction for pursuing personal values related to health, wellness, and self-care.

Media critical-thinking skills. Both in and out of session, girls practice identifying messages and images sold to them by others. This may be done through the mindful consumption of music videos, commercials, and magazines. Group members learn to recognize salient messages directed at young women and girls, as well as the sources and possible motivations behind these messages. Media critical-thinking exercises can be done in conjunction with creative hopelessness, defusion, and mindfulness interventions (described below). In this way, girls may concurrently identify the costs of pursuing societal ideals; defuse from rules surrounding gender role stereotypes, beauty, and weight; and practice nonjudgmental awareness when exposed to media images that elicit painful emotional reactions.

Health promotion. To facilitate values-consistent health behavior, group members work collaboratively to generate ideas for: (1) making healthy food choices (e.g., packing a well-balanced lunch rather than eating fast food); (2) meeting nutritional needs (e.g., replacing soda with milk, increasing intake of fruits and vegetables); (3) engaging in moderate levels of consumption (e.g., limiting meals to one serving size); and (4) incorporating moderate physical activity into daily routines (e.g., walking or riding a bike to school; organizing "social walks" with group members or other supportive peers). Opportunities for health promotion are then provided, either as out-of-session LIFE exercises or as in-session activities. For example, mindfulness of eating exercises may be used in session to facilitate the practice of moderate consumption, and group walks can be organized in sessions that address physical activity and values-consistent health behavior.

Creative Hopelessness: Letting Go of the Futile Struggle

The purpose of creative hopelessness is to bring group members into experiential contact with their psychological pain and the experienced workability or unworkability of their efforts to manage or control this pain (Hayes et al., 1999). Group leaders deliberately include themselves in the human suffering boat and may self-disclose some of their own painful experiences to model acceptance, vulnerability, and "owning" of these shared human experiences. For example, a group leader might share her struggle with thoughts such as "I'm not good enough" as well as feelings of sadness and loneliness. Using the images of a protective shield and a mask, group leaders might share the ways in which they "hide out" to keep themselves psychologically safe (or, more accurately, to create the illusion of safety). One way of initiating the creative hopelessness process is as follows:

> *All of us in this room know what it's like to hurt and to suffer, yet we often work so hard to keep our pain hidden. We carry around our "protective shields" to keep others out; we hide behind our "masks" so other people cannot truly see us. What we are asking from each of you and ourselves is really big—perhaps terrifying. Instead of fighting to "stay safe," we're asking everyone in this room to lower the shields and take off the masks that we've worked so hard to create. This is an important first step in our work together, and it requires a good deal of courage. It means opening ourselves up to painful experiences and sharing in each other's pain. We would like to assure you that we would not ask you to open up to your pain and other people's pain for no reason. There certainly is a purpose; the hard work that we will do in here is 100 percent for you, your life, and what you truly care about—your values. As we work together today, remember that we are all responsible for creating an environment that is open and safe. For this to happen, it is important that we respect the privacy of everybody in this room. This means that whatever we talk about in this room stays here.*

It is important to keep creative hopelessness connected with personal values and life purposes such as by using the Swamp Metaphor (Hayes et al., 1999). The gist of this metaphor is that we do not choose to get in and wade around the smelly swamp for no reason. We get in the swamp when it truly matters to do so: when the swamp stands between us and where we most want to go in life (i.e., our valued directions). Repeatedly linking the painful work of treatment to adolescents' personal values may enhance their willingness to participate fully in the program.

After identifying painful content, adolescents are asked to list (without evaluation) everything they have tried in an attempt to alleviate, manage, or otherwise control their pain and discomfort (e.g., isolating oneself, dieting, binge eating, exercising, shopping, studying, making jokes, or using alcohol). Once a list of "control strategies" has been developed, adolescents identify the short- and long-term workability of trying to control painful thoughts and feelings. Most of the girls we work with are able to identify one short-term benefit of these strategies, namely the momentary relief from painful thoughts and feelings. The benefits of striving to "look good" also tend to be small and short-lived and may include feeling better about oneself for a time, reaching a certain weight-loss goal, or being able to fit into a desired piece of clothing. In contrast to these transient successes, the costs of experiential avoidance and control tend to be large and long lasting. Most girls conclude that their control efforts, no matter how well intentioned or seemingly benign, are fundamentally unworkable and may be costing them their lives (literally, for some).

Figure 1. Creative Hopelessness Supplement: What Do You/We Struggle with in the World Inside and Outside of Our Skin?

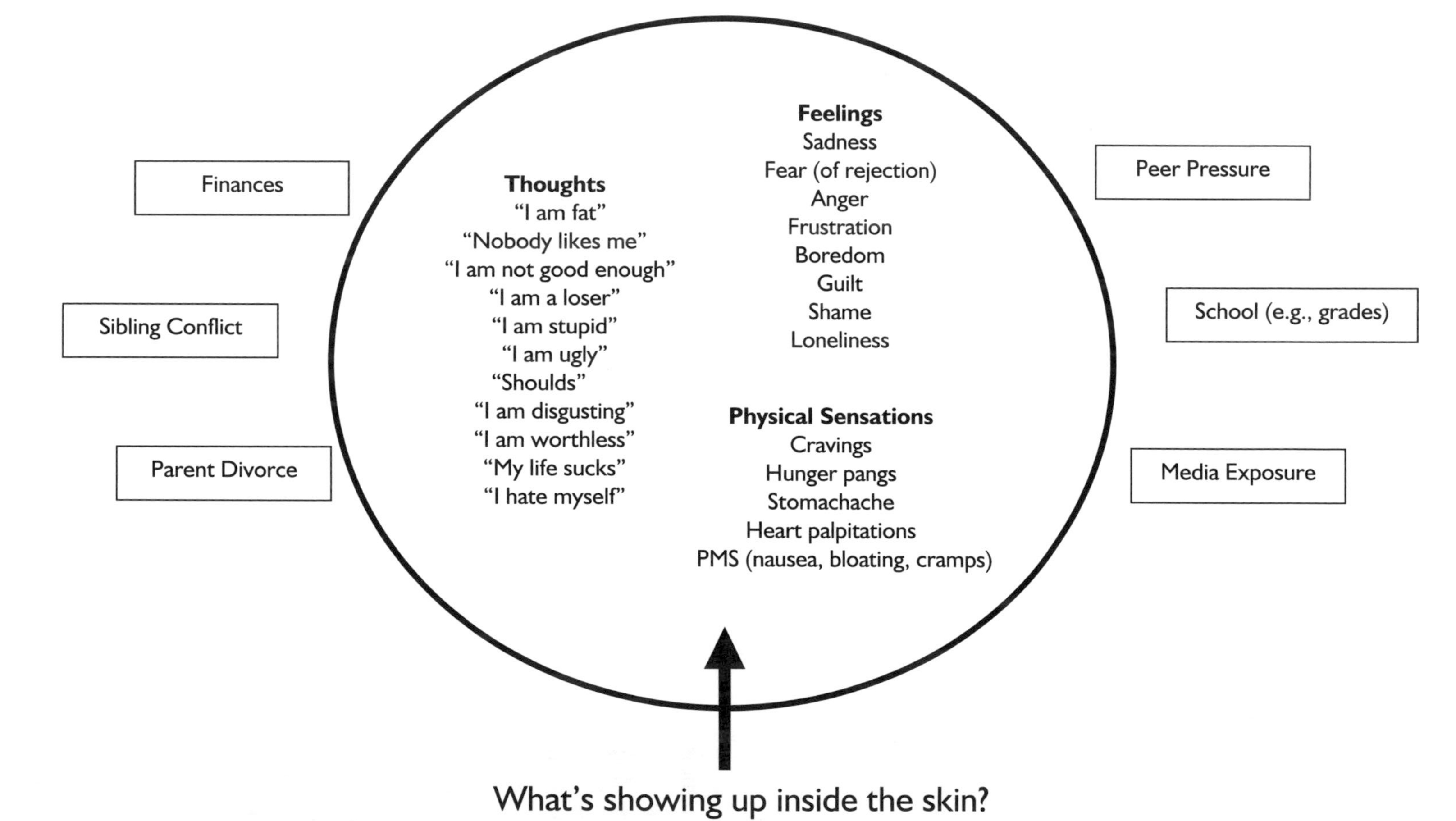

Creative hopelessness circle. When doing creative hopelessness, we suggest writing out the collective struggle on a dry erase board or (preferably) a large piece of paper or poster board that can be used in future sessions. As shown in figure 1, clinicians might begin by drawing a large circle and explaining that everything written inside the circle reflects internal experiences or the "world beneath our skin." External struggles such as financial hardship, family conflict, and academic problems are written outside of the circle to denote the external world "outside the skin." When external struggles are provided, clinicians can link them to the world beneath the skin by asking questions such as "What thoughts and feelings do you experience when you and your parents fight?" Throughout the course of treatment, we recommend revisiting the work done in creative hopelessness. As new experiences are shared, clinicians can add them to the list of painful content, control strategies, and experienced workability of these strategies.

There are several advantages of using the circle visual aid during creative hopelessness. Drawing out the adolescent's struggle helps both the clinician and the adolescent to conceptualize "the problem" (i.e., excessive fusion and experiential avoidance). The creative hopelessness circle can also be used to enhance interoceptive awareness and to facilitate discrimination training. Clinicians might explicitly label the various types of private events listed inside of the circle (e.g., "I am fat" is a thought; sadness is a feeling; cravings are physical-bodily sensations that may be experienced in the stomach area). The creative hopelessness circle can also be used to make concrete distinctions between experiences that occur "inside" versus "outside" of the skin.

You are response-able. Early in the program, adolescents are relieved of the responsibility of having to control events that take place inside of the circle. Thus adolescents learn at the outset that they are no longer responsible for trying to manage, control, or fix experiences that occur beneath their skin. They are, however, 100 percent response-able (literally, "able to respond") in the outside world. Group leaders emphasize that naturally occurring private experiences such as those listed inside the circle will come and go for the rest of our lives, whether we like it or not. Thus, instead of depleting energy and life resources on the internal war (which ultimately is a war waged against one's own self), adolescents learn to take personal responsibility for the one thing that they have direct control over—their overt behavior, or what they choose to do with their hands, feet, and mouths. Throughout the program, girls will have opportunities to create "valued footprints" across meaningful areas of life. In doing so, they must redirect their efforts to the outside world in areas of life that truly are amenable to change.

LIFE exercises. As a supplement to creative hopelessness done in session, group leaders might ask girls to self-monitor (1) when and how they use control strategies, and (2) the short- and long-term consequences of these strategies. The protective shield and mask exercise can also be done as an out-of-session LIFE exercise. Group members are asked to give some form to the protective shields and masks that they use to gain social acceptance, to protect themselves from pain or discomfort, and to hide out from others.

Shields and masks can be constructed using art supplies, or group members might bring in an object from home that symbolizes their struggle. We sometimes hold a "willingness ceremony" during which each person symbolically puts down her shield or takes off her mask while making a public commitment to stay present and open throughout our work together. Commitments can also be made to support one another during difficult times when we once again raise our shields and put on our masks.

Cognitive Defusion: The Art of Demoting Language

Cognitive defusion exercises are used to undermine excessive fusion by weakening the literal and evaluative functions of language in certain contexts (Hayes et al., 1999). To illustrate critical distinctions between the person who is thinking and the content of thought, group leaders begin right away to model and encourage defused languaging, such as "I am having the thought that I am fat" (rather than "I am fat") or "My mind is telling me that I can't do this" (rather than "I can't do this"). Clinicians can also introduce the practice of "thanking your mind" for the painful and unpleasant thoughts that it gives. Instead of challenging and trying to change the thought "I am disgusting and unlovable," an adolescent might simply thank her mind for sharing that particular thought. Group leaders acknowledge the universality of painful thoughts and note that this is simply what our chattering minds do—they generate content incessantly, often without our input or approval.

The good news is that our "mindstuff," no matter how painful, is incidental at best. What is truly important is how we choose to respond to these private experiences. For example, we can treat internal content as literal truths that must be taken very seriously and obeyed. Alternatively, we can learn to experience thoughts and feelings as less compelling by treating them as temporary houseguests. Inevitably some of these guests will be unwanted or even disliked; yet we can continue to welcome them in. In doing so, we recognize that even our most painful thoughts and feelings cannot literally harm us; rather, the potential for harm comes from our overt reactions and attempts to control these experiences.

Name your mind. Group leaders and adolescents name their minds as a way of inviting playfulness and augmenting defusion throughout the program. Creating personalized names for our mischievous minds provides a playful way of talking about and relating to painful content. Adolescents tend to enjoy this exercise and may demonstrate increased willingness to live with their mindstuff when its source is treated as a separate, external entity that comes to be known quite well. In group settings, the process and outcome of naming one's mind can itself be defusing and entertaining. Some of our favorite mind names include Captain Smash, Lizard Breath, the Joker, and of course our own: Ocerg, Nalp, Eneek, and Princess. No matter how dreadful the content, thoughts suddenly seem less powerful and serious when we notice who is providing them (e.g., "Captain

Smash is at it again, telling me I shouldn't even bother with this"; "Ocerg was ragging on me the whole time I was jogging; I wanted to leave her on the side of the road, but I get that she has to come with me"). Other defusion exercises such as Take Your Mind for a Walk (see Hayes et al., 1999; also see chapter 8 in this volume) might then be done with Captain Smash and Ocerg. In this exercise, adolescents practice the act of choosing what to do and where to go, no matter what their external, chattering minds say.

Milk, milk, milk. Another popular defusion intervention in adolescent groups is Titchener's (1916) milk exercise, which is used to demonstrate how the psychological meanings we attach to a word can be weakened as other, more direct properties of the word are noticed. In this exercise, group members rapidly repeat the word "milk" over and over until its literal meaning (e.g., "white, cold, creamy drink") quickly dissolves, and the direct stimulus functions of "milk" become more salient. For example, adolescents might begin to experience "milk" as a string of letters that produce a strange birdlike sound when uttered in rapid succession. They might also notice how their lips press together when making this funny noise. This exercise is repeated with personally relevant words or phrases that elicit significant emotional distress (e.g., "I'm fat," "Loser," "Ugly"). When working with groups, we often repeat each person's painful content together until its literal meaning dissipates for the person struggling with that particular thought. By the end of a single defusion session, group members may begin to experience their painful thoughts in a more flexible, less literal way. Although the thoughts may continue to elicit pain, it is now possible to experience them as mere words or sounds that cause one to spit or giggle when repeated quickly over and over again. This exercise sets the stage for future defusion interventions in which adolescents learn to interact with unwanted thoughts and feelings in a fundamentally different way—with curiosity, playfulness, and nonattachment.

Musical theater. In one of our favorite group exercises, adolescents and group leaders work individually and in collaboration to create a "musical of pain and suffering" (the name of course can be tailored to fit dominant themes and content expressed by the group). The exercise begins with each person selecting a musical instrument; we often bring in hand-crafted drums, maracas, rattles, tambourines, and cymbals. Another option is for participants to create their own instruments using art supplies, natural materials, or objects in the room. After selecting an instrument, each person identifies an especially painful thought that they struggle with such as "I'm fat and worthless." Group members are then asked to come up with movements and music to express this thought. Each person then sings her painful thought with the chosen movements, gestures, and musical accompaniments. Depending on the size of the group, girls may be divided into pairs or smaller subgroups to choreograph their musicals. When the full group reconvenes, each of the smaller groups is invited to share their experiences and (if willing) to perform their "routines" for the larger group.

A modification of this exercise described by Hayes and colleagues (1999) is for group members to practice singing or saying painful thoughts in silly voices. For example, adolescents might take turns saying "I hate myself" as a drunk, an old woman, Donald Duck, an opera singer, and a telephone operator. If done in pairs or smaller groups, we suggest reconvening to share individual experiences as well as some of the favorite voice animations. The inherent silliness of these exercises may help participants experience the content of their thoughts and feelings in a less literal, nonattached way. Of note, we have used these same interventions with older adolescents and adults in treatment settings, teaching seminars, and professional workshops. In our experience, children and adults alike enjoy creating their "musicals of pain and suffering" and seem to welcome the opportunity to interact with their psychological pain in ways that are playful, unconventional, and, in a sense, liberating.

Exercise 1: Weakening Sociocultural Messages Through Mindfulness of Media and Defusion

Instructions: In the first (left) column, write down the media sources you come across during the week. In the second column, write down any messages or rules that you learned through the various types of media. In the third column, write down your thoughts and feelings after hearing these messages. In the fourth column, rate how believable or true your thoughts and feelings first seemed to you. In the fifth column, write down what you did to "play with words" to make them less serious and less powerful. In the last column, rate how believable or true your thoughts and feelings seemed to you *after* you practiced "playing with words."

Media sources	Messages/ rules that we learn from these sources	My thoughts & feelings after hearing these messages	Believability rating 1–100	Ways that I played with words to make them less powerful	Believability rating 1–100
Teen magazine	*Makeup makes you prettier. Guys like skinny girls with big boobs. You can't be happy unless you look good.*	*No wonder I don't have a boyfriend; I'm ugly; sadness; shame; loneliness*	*85*	*Sing thoughts. Say "I'm ugly" in a silly voice. Say "loser" a whole bunch of times really, really fast.*	*40*

LIFE exercises. In one out-of-session exercise, group members identify messages in the mass media aimed at young women and girls. These messages might be embedded within music videos, television programs, commercials, magazine ads, and so forth. As shown in exercise 2, girls identify the source of these messages, as well as any rules that they or other girls their age might derive from them (e.g., "Successful women are beautiful and thin"; "I need to work harder to get my body in shape"; "I need to lose weight so that others will like me"). Adolescents then rate the believability of these messages both before and after defusion. Group leaders encourage girls to interact playfully with the content of these messages and rules such as by chanting them in concert with dramatic arm motions or by saying them with exaggerated slowness and facial distortions while looking in a mirror. In the following session, adolescents are invited to share their defusion strategies and their internal experiences before and after defusion.

Mindfulness and Exposure

Mindfulness is an acceptance-based method and process that, in its simplest form, involves paying attention to internal experiences and external stimuli in a way that is accepting, compassionate, and nonattached (e.g., Baer, 2003). In the ACT for Health program, mindfulness methods are used to enhance interoceptive awareness, to promote acceptance of private events, and to disrupt unworkable patterns of behavior (e.g., mindless consumption of junk food when feeling bored; binge eating to alleviate emotional discomfort). Mindfulness is used alone and in conjunction with exposure procedures to provide opportunities for acceptance during critical (and often the most painful) moments.

Targets and metaphors. In the first few sessions, mindfulness interventions might focus on relatively benign targets such as the breath, sounds, smells, and tactile sensations (e.g., the temperature of the room; how the air or one's clothes feel against the skin; how one's back touches the fabric of the chair, etc.). Gradually group leaders move to more challenging experiences such as noticing the content of thoughts, the ongoing process of thinking, and the "observer you" who is conscious and aware of noticing these experiences (see Hayes et al., 1999). Other targets of mindfulness and exposure include emotional experience and physical sensations related to eating, such as hunger, satiation, cravings, and urges to binge.

Group leaders often use metaphors to facilitate mindfulness training. For example, adolescents might be instructed to experience thoughts and emotions as a continuous flow of bubbles floating in front of their face. As private events come up, they are placed in a bubble and observed with gentle curiosity and compassion. The goal is simply to notice the private content without popping any of the bubbles. Attempting to grasp or hold onto desirable content will result in popping, as will pushing or blowing away unwanted content. Another suggestion is to introduce the observer perspective using the metaphor of a curious scientist who looks down through a microscope to observe her subject matter. Even though the specimen is important to the scientist, she is able to observe and describe its properties fully from a healthy distance. Adolescents can be asked to notice their experiences from an observer perspective, much as a scientist would observe an amoeba with curiosity through a microscope. Similar to a scientist becoming an expert on her subject matter, adolescents work toward becoming their very own experience experts through regular mindfulness practice (Greco, Blackledge, Coyne, & Ehrenreich, 2005).

Mindful consumption. As noted above, young women and girls with body-image and weight concerns often struggle with interoceptive awareness and may therefore demonstrate insensitivity to internal cues such as hunger and satiation. Moreover, most of the girls in our program use eating and weight-loss efforts to regulate emotional experiences. Mindfulness of eating is integral to addressing these clinical issues and is therefore practiced on a regular basis, both in and out of session. As with other ACT methods, there are many different ways to teach mindful eating. It may be useful to begin with discrimination training to make explicit distinctions between thoughts, feelings, and eating-related experiences such as hunger, fullness, cravings, and urges. Lunch or snacks may be consumed during session to elicit relevant appetite cues. Through ongoing mindfulness practice, adolescents learn to notice a host of internal and external stimuli before, during, and after consumption. To begin with, attention might be directed toward the food's texture, smell, color, shape, temperature, and taste, as well as the physical sensations of chewing and swallowing. Internal experiences such as thoughts, feelings, hunger, and urges to binge are labeled in turn and observed with nonjudgmental awareness. Instead of reacting impulsively, adolescents learn to sit, breathe, and ride the wave of experience.

Mirror exercise. Another application of mindfulness is to observe internal experiences during body-related exposure exercises. The mirror exposure exercise can be done individually or in small groups using full-length or relatively large mirrors such as those found in some school restrooms. This exercise involves having group members observe nearly every aspect of their appearance for prolonged periods, with an emphasis on body parts that elicit the highest levels of distress (e.g., stomach, hips, legs, breasts). For girls in our program, this often means coming face-to-face (literally) with tremendously difficult types of psychological pain such as guilt, shame, self-loathing, and perceived inadequacies. For this reason, we recommend integrating defusion, mindfulness, self-compassion, and values methods to promote acceptance and to dignify the adolescent's experience of pain. This is particularly important in later sessions when exposure exercises may be intensified by having adolescents wear "feared" articles of clothing such as bodysuits or gym clothes.

LIFE exercises. All of the mindfulness exercises done in group can be adapted for home practice. The notion of "mindful consumption," for example, can be broadened to include sociocultural messages and rules provided by family, peers, and advertising in the mass media. Adolescents can assume the posture of a curious scientist as they are inundated with messages from outside sources; as with other mindfulness interventions, adolescents attend to the content of these messages as well as to their private experiences without necessarily acting on either one. As another example, the mirror exercise can be intensified at home such that adolescents practice acceptance, mindfulness, and self-compassion while completely nude in front of a full-length mirror. They might begin by standing and looking at each body part in turn and gradually move to more "risky" and playful types of behavior such as jumping up and down or dancing in front of the mirror. Finally, we encourage adolescents to organize and attend group mindfulness sessions outside of the program. This can be done with other group members, though we also encourage adolescents to teach mindfulness skills to family members and friends who may be more permanent supports in their lives.

Values Identification and Clarification

Given some of the key developmental tasks during adolescence, the teenage years present an ideal window of opportunity for clinicians to promote acceptance in the service of values-based living (Greco & Eifert, 2004). For this reason, values work is introduced in the first session and is continued over the course of treatment (and life). When introducing the program, group leaders convey that one of our central goals is to support adolescents in living consistently with their chosen values. It is important to clarify that ACT for Health does not seek to improve body image, reduce emotional distress, or generate weight loss. Instead this program teaches adolescents to take personal responsibility for their lives, including their physical health. In essence, group leaders seek to empower girls to live in accord with their personal values no matter how they feel at the time and irrespective of external pressures to do otherwise. Almost uniformly, the adolescents with whom we work express willingness to participate in the program, even if its goals differ from what they had initially expected or hoped for.

Nature of valuing. Identifying and living in accord with one's values—or "valuing"—is a lifelong process that necessitates personal responsibility, commitment, and choice. The Going West Metaphor can be used to illustrate the nature of valuing (Hayes et al., 1999). In an important sense, valuing is like choosing to go west (or your direction of choice). We might travel west for days, months, and years. Yet we never truly arrive at west as we might arrive at a specific destination or goal. It is always possible to take one more step, moving further along the path of our chosen direction. In an important sense, values represent our personally chosen life directions; they function as guideposts that help organize our behavior but are not attainable in an absolute sense. Another important aspect of valuing is that we can never fail at our values. Even if we fall face down toward east, we can always choose to stand back up, reorient ourselves toward west, and take another step.

Letting go of our cover stories. In adolescence and adulthood, many of us experience social pressures and intensive self-doubts that interfere with our ability to be "real" or genuine with other people and even with ourselves. Throughout the program, group leaders and adolescents support each other in choosing authenticity and fidelity to oneself over social acceptance. This can be done in a number of ways, such as through group-designed ceremonies in which everyone symbolically takes off their masks, puts down their protective shields, and stands unguarded with themselves and with each other. Ceremonies and other symbolic "coming out" exercises can be used to celebrate and honor our pain, vulnerabilities, values, and dreams as human beings. Useful questions that we continually ask ourselves and the adolescents with whom we work include the following:

- What if we abandoned the pursuit of attractiveness ideals and lifestyles sold by others and we chose to focus instead on creating healthy, authentic, meaningful lives that have little to do with the way we look or how others might judge us?
- How do we live with fidelity to ourselves in a world that has such a harsh need to change us?
- Are we willing to let go of being "important" and "right" even if this means risking our significance as human beings? Are we willing to let go and risk our significance to have the lives that we truly long for? If the answer is no, what might we gain and lose along the way? If the answer is yes, what might we gain and lose along the way?

In an ongoing exercise, group members are supported in letting go of their "cover stories" (more on this below) so that they might be free to hurt *and* to love more fully. Each adolescent creates a "life book" depicting her personal values and the pain that inevitably accompanies these values (after all, it hurts to care). Pictures, images, and written narratives can be used to portray one's pain and values, as well as the internal and external barriers that interfere with moving in valued directions. The content or inside pages can be constructed gradually throughout the program, either in session or as out-of-session LIFE exercises. Adolescents are also given opportunities near the beginning and end of treatment to create two very different book covers. The first represents the adolescent's public face or "cover story" that other people are permitted to see. The second cover reflects a more open and genuine look into the essence of each person's deepest values and sufferings. At the end of treatment, adolescents may choose to share their books and make a commitment to letting go of the cover stories that are easier and more socially acceptable, yet at the same time inauthentic and life deadening.

Two sides of the same coin. We can almost always find a value behind our pain. Simply put: If we did not care, then it would not hurt so much. To represent the intimate connection between values and pain, adolescents are asked to construct a personalized "coin" (Follette & Pistorello, 2007) that symbolizes their current life struggles. (This can be done using cardboard or construction paper cut in a circle the size of one's palm.) On one side of the coin, group members describe their most painful internal experiences, such as fear of rejection, loneliness, and thoughts about not fitting in. Core personal values underlying these experiences are then written on the other side of the coin. For example, the adolescent might have strong relationship values characterized by a desire for closeness, intimacy, mutual acceptance, and respect. Group leaders point out that the coin has two sides, and it is impossible to have one without the other. Adolescents are asked whether they are willing to make room for the pain if it means that they can keep the value. Out-of-session LIFE exercises might involve holding the two-sided coin while engaging in meaningful activities that evoke both the values and the pain.

In a related exercise, group members are asked to write down something that "haunts them" on one side of an index card. This can be a painful thought that they have struggled with for a long time, something unspeakable or shameful that they have done, or perhaps a traumatic event from their past. In a guided mindfulness exercise, adolescents are asked to lower their shields, take off their masks, and sit undefended with this painful content (relevant music or poetry can be used to enhance the emotional salience of this exercise). After sitting with their pain for some time (perhaps 10–15 minutes), adolescents write down the value(s) underlying this enduring pain on the other side of the index card. Group leaders can ask evocative questions such as "In order to have the life you truly want, what do you need to let go of, make space for, and open up to?" Acceptance methods and goal setting linked with personal values may then be used to facilitate the process of letting go, making space, and opening up.

LIFE Exercises. A primary goal of ACT for Health is to promote acceptance in the service of life vitality and values-consistent living. As such, nearly all of the LIFE exercises in this program are presented within the context of the adolescent's personally chosen values. Two LIFE exercises that may be done to clarify some of these core values are the Eulogy Exercise and the Values Compass Exercise (see Hayes et al., 1999; and Heffner & Eifert, 2004). In the Eulogy Exercise, adolescents are asked to write a eulogy for themselves that reflects what they would like their life to stand for and how they would most want to be remembered. In essence, the eulogy is the adolescent's chosen legacy and embodies her most cherished values, passions, life goals, and dreams. Based on this exercise, adolescents can develop values statements to provide life direction, as well as more specific goals and concrete action steps that can be enacted in the service of these values. Group leaders can then introduce the valued footprints exercise. This exercise encourages the girls to engage in "valued footprints" (or values-consistent behavior) over the week (see exercise 2).

Exercise 2: Making Valued Footprints in Life

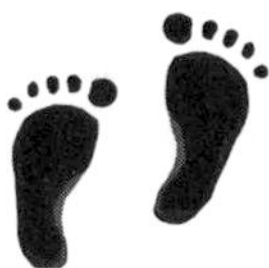

Making Valued Footprints in Life

Valued area that I will work on this week:

____

My values in this area:

____

____

____

Goals I can set to help me move toward my values:	Things I can do this week to move me toward my values and goals:
1.	1.
2.	2.
3.	3.

In the Values Compass Exercise shown in figure 4, girls identify and clarify their chosen life directions. This can be done visually by drawing out a values compass and writing out internal and external barriers that may arise throughout the journey. Acceptance methods such as mindfulness and defusion can be applied to internal barriers, and values-based change methods may be used to address external barriers.

Figure 2. Sample Values Compass

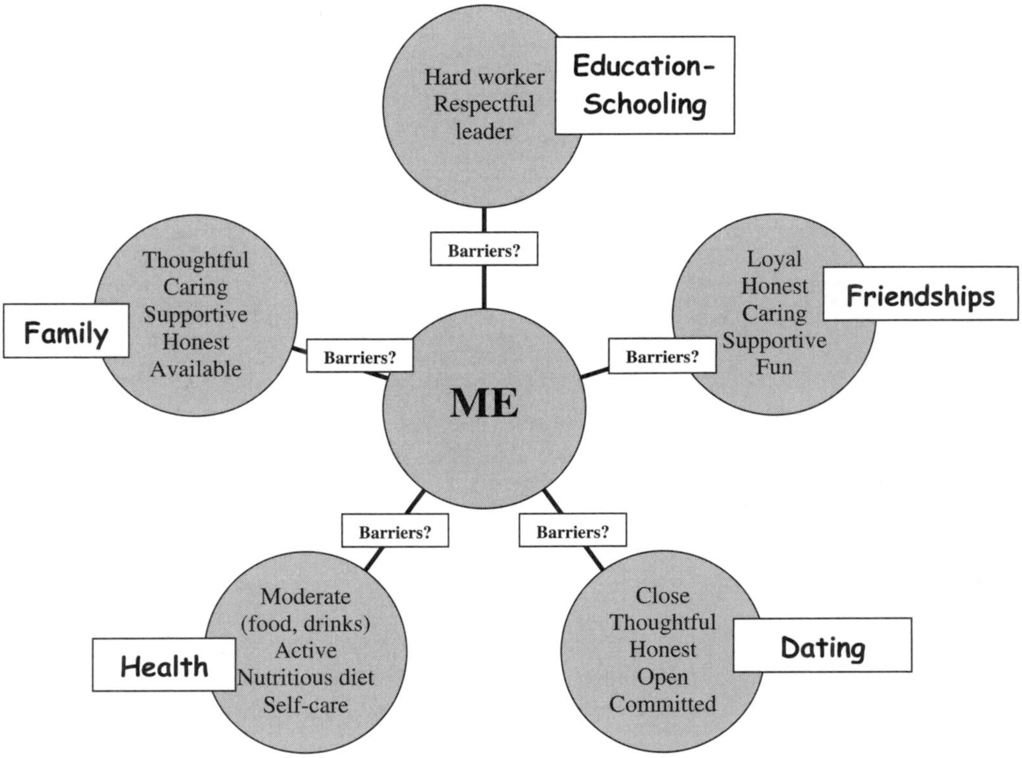

Education-Schooling
Hard worker
Respectful leader

Friendships
Loyal
Honest
Caring
Supportive
Fun

Dating
Close
Thoughtful
Honest
Open
Committed

Health
Moderate (food, drinks)
Active
Nutritious diet
Self-care

Family
Thoughtful
Caring
Supportive
Honest
Available

ME

Barriers?

Self-Compassion and Forgiveness

Girls with body-image and weight concerns frequently struggle with shame, guilt, self-loathing, and self-blame. We therefore make deliberate efforts throughout the program to engender compassion and forgiveness toward oneself. Acceptance-based methods such as those described above may be used to promote the three facets of self-compassion described by Kristin Neff (2003): (1) showing kindness and understanding toward oneself, especially during times of pain and suffering; (2) creating a common humanity in which the interconnectedness of all human beings is celebrated and embraced; and (3) holding painful thoughts and feelings in balanced awareness through mindfulness practice. Acceptance methods similarly can be used to foster forgiveness as conceptualized by Hayes and colleagues (1999). Etymologically, to "fore-give" means "allowing or giving that which came before." In essence, compassion and forgiveness are acts of willingness that involve choosing to let ourselves (and others) off the hook so that we might be free. By choosing acts of self-compassion and forgiveness, we are allowing our pain to be transient. Thus the gifts of self-compassion and forgiveness are ultimately for oneself.

Widening the Circle of Compassion. Throughout the program, compassion and forgiveness interventions are used to "widen the circle of compassion" to encompass our loves and our joys as well as our most painful experiences. In an eyes-closed exercise adapted from Pema Chödrön (1997), group leaders invite adolescents to sit comfortably in their chairs or to lie down on the floor. Mindfulness of breath is used to assist adolescents in getting present and releasing their grip on any distractions. Once psychologically present, group members are instructed to bring to mind an image of someone they care deeply about and perhaps love unconditionally. After the image of this person is clear, adolescents are asked to remember a time when they felt disappointed or hurt by the actions of this loved one. They might remember a time when their loved one betrayed them, let them down, or failed them in some other big way. Group members sit with their emotional experience and focus again on the breath. On each inhale, adolescents breathe the hurt and the loved one into their hearts. They allow their hearts to expand on each exhale, gradually making space for both the love and the hurt. This exercise is done slowly and repeated with different people: a friend, an acquaintance, an enemy, and finally oneself. At the start of treatment, many girls describe having the most trouble with opening their hearts up to themselves. As such, this exercise is often repeated and done in conjunction with other self-compassion and forgiveness exercises.

Eyes on Exercise with Self. In an exercise adapted from Hayes and colleagues (1999), adolescents are asked to sit with themselves as they make eye contact in a handheld mirror. For the majority of this exercise (which generally lasts 5–8 minutes), adolescents sit in silence with the intention of being fully open and present with themselves. During the first minute or so of this exercise, group leaders might facilitate the process of self-connectedness by reading a poem related to self-acceptance or by asking adolescents to notice the person behind their eyes:

> *See if you can notice, perhaps for the first time, the fact that there is an amazing human being behind those eyes. There is a human being in there who knows what it is like to feel joy and sorrow; who knows what it is like to love and to suffer deeply. At some point, she may have even considered taking her own life to escape all of life's miseries. And yet, here she is … behind those eyes, looking back at you. See if you can connect with the extraordinary fact that this human being has seen you through it all … the heartaches and sorrows, the happiness and joys. And she's still here, sitting with you and for you right now. As best you can, try to stay connected and present with this human being, the person behind those eyes. If you find yourself trying to hide or avoid her, then gently, lovingly, let go of the shield, take off the mask, and bring yourself back to right here, right now with the human being in the mirror.*

Loyal Soldiers. As group leaders and adolescents progress through the program, both will find themselves (at some point and in some form) reverting back to old control strategies. We see ourselves in real time picking up those well-worn shields and putting on those tired masks. The difference now is that we are fully aware of our hideout spots and have experienced the futility and pain of living there. Our evaluative minds are quick to point out that we "should know better by now." Self-compassion and forgiveness are essential in these moments and at other times when missteps and mistakes are inevitably made.

The Loyal Soldiers Metaphor (Plotkin, 2003) can be used to engender self-compassion and forgiveness when adolescents find themselves (once again) with shield in hand, ready to fight. Group leaders share the story of the Japanese soldiers in World War II who were stranded on deserted islands after their ships capsized or their planes crashed in the middle of the ocean. Many of these soldiers were not discovered for a long time; some were not located until months or years after the war had ended. When the soldiers were finally found, they took up their weapons ready to fight this war, still fully prepared to die for their country. After being told that the war was over and that Japan had lost, some of the soldiers remained insistent on fighting and continuing the war. The Japanese people responded by welcoming their soldiers home and expressing deep gratitude to them. The soldiers were publicly honored for their loyal service and commitment, and then reassigned to another honorable position within the community.

We all have loyal soldiers or self-protective ways of behaving that truly were adaptive and that kept us safe at some point in our lives. Group leaders assist adolescents in identifying such safety behaviors (e.g., isolating oneself, giving the silent treatment, acting smart, fading into the woodwork, pretending not to care, depending on others). In some cases, it may be useful to recast these familiar behaviors as loyal soldiers who have fought for some time now to keep the adolescent safe. When these behaviors are no longer serving valued ends, adolescents gently and with compassion tell their soldiers that the war has ended. They then express deep gratitude to these soldiers for working so hard for all of these years to keep them safe. Symbolically or using ceremony, group members may honor their soldiers and reassign them to a more functional post. In the reassignment process, it is important to identify contexts in which the soldier's efforts are not harmful and may in fact continue to be useful and serve valued ends. The following example is a brief illustration of this process:

> *Fifteen-year-old Julia identified forgiveness as an important relationship value and described a ten-year history of pushing people away whenever she feels threatened, hurt, or rejected in the relationship. Julia recognized this pattern as inconsistent with her values and experienced feelings of guilt and self-loathing every time she pushed another person out of her life. The therapist worked with Julia to identify possible loyal soldiers at work. Together they discovered a "pushing away soldier" that at one time served a very protective function: this soldier guarded Julia in childhood when she was molested repeatedly by her father. Within this context, pushing away was quite adaptive—it kept her safe from further harm.*

Now nine years later, Julia has minimal contact with her father, but she continues to push people away (especially those closest to her). With the therapist's guidance, Julia recognized that her loyal soldier fought to keep her safe for many years, even after the so-called war had ended. Self-compassion practice was initiated when Julia expressed heartfelt gratitude to the solider for keeping her safe at a time when she was vulnerable and in need of protection. In the reassignment process, Julia identified specific situations in which her loyal soldier may continue to serve useful purposes (e.g., when Julia is interacting with her father; when she is ignoring suggestive remarks made by a stranger; when she is responding to teasing and/or peer pressure from a group of acquaintances).

LIFE Exercises. The Loyal Soldier Metaphor is introduced in session and continued as an ongoing LIFE exercise. The entire process of identifying, honoring, and reassigning soldiers can be done symbolically, such as by having group members draw images or bring in objects that represent their soldiers. Adolescents might also choose to write a letter expressing heartfelt gratitude to their loyal soldiers for keeping them safe at a time of great need. In the letter, adolescents can explain with compassion that the war has ended, that they are safe now, and that it is time to stop fighting. Some group members choose to honor and reassign their soldiers by creating a special physical space for them in their rooms or outside in nature. For example, an adolescent girl created a "sacred corner" in her room for her most persistent soldiers. In this corner, she displayed the images and objects representing her loyal soldiers, along with letters of gratitude that she had written in session. With a little creativity on the part of the clinician and adolescent, there are many ways to work with our loyal soldiers.

Conclusion

In this chapter, we conceptualized eating- and weight-related problems from an ACT perspective and described a school-based program for adolescent girls with body-image and weight concerns. In the ACT for Health program, ACT's core clinical methods are used to: (1) weaken attachment to sociocultural expectations and rules surrounding gender-role stereotypes, appearance, and weight; (2) enhance acceptance and mindfulness of private experiences; (3) disrupt habitual and potentially harmful patterns of consumption; (4) empower girls to live with fidelity to themselves in a culture that is unlikely to change in the foreseeable future; and (5) promote self-compassion and forgiveness toward oneself. It is our hope that this chapter provides some guidance in working with adolescent girls and stimulates additional clinical innovations in this area.

Another hope is for this work to bring about empirical scrutiny and well-designed research on the development, maintenace, and treatment of eating pathology and weight problems. It will be important, for example, to investigate the nature and role of ACT processes in children and adolescents who struggle with body image and weight. Already there is evidence that cognitive fusion and experiential avoidance mediate the link between body-image concerns and unhealthy eating patterns among adolescent girls (Greco & Blomquist, 2006). In addition, preliminary investigations of the ACT for Health program are currently underway. If results are promising, an essential next step will be to conduct large-scale clinical trials comparing the impact of ACT relative to active control groups and "best practice" approaches. Finally, it will be essential for mental health professionals to partner with policy makers and administrators, with the long-term goal of implementing effective behavioral health programs into regular school programs and curricula so that more of our youth may be reached. This seems to us a critical future direction in light of the alarming obesity epidemic in Western societies, coupled with the high financial expenditures and mortality rates associated with obesity and related health conditions.

References

Baer, R. A. (2003). Mindfulness training as a clinical intervention: A conceptual and empirical review. *Clinical Psychology: Science and Practice, 10*, 125–143.

Bearman, S. K., Presnell, K., Martinez, E., & Stice, E. (2006). The skinny on body dissatisfaction: A longitudinal study of adolescent boys and girls. *Journal of Youth and Adolescence, 35*, 229–241.

Chödrön, P. (1997). *When things fall apart: Heart advice for difficult times*. Boston: Shambhala Publications.

Eifert, G. H., & Forsyth, J. P. (2005). *Acceptance and commitment therapy for anxiety disorders: A practitioner'streatment guide using mindful acceptance and values-based behavior change strategies*. Oakland, CA: New Harbinger.

Eifert, G. H., Greco, L. A., & Heffner, M. (in press). Accept, choose, and take action to move beyond the struggle with eating disorders. In J. Kanter (Ed.), *Behavior disorders from a contemporary behavioral perspective*. Reno, NV: Context Press.

Follette, V. M., & Pistorello, J. (2007). *Finding life beyond trauma: Using acceptance and commitment therapy to heal from post-traumatic stress and trauma-related problems*. Oakland, CA: New Harbinger.

Greco, L. A., Blackledge, J. T., Coyne, L. W., & Ehrenreich, J. (2005). Integrating acceptance and mindfulness into treatments for child and adolescent anxiety disorders: Acceptance and commitment therapy (ACT) as an example. In S. M. Orsillo & L. Roemer (Eds.), *Acceptance and mindfulness-based approaches to anxiety: Conceptualization and treatment* (pp. 301–324). New York: Springer.

Greco, L. A., & Blomquist, K. K. (2006, November). Body image, eating behavior, and quality of life among adolescent girls: Role of anxiety and acceptance processes in a school sample. In K. S. Berlin & A. R. Murrell (Cochairs), *Extending acceptance and mindfulness research to parents, families, and adolescents: Process, empirical findings, clinical implications, and future directions.* Paper presented at the Association for Behavior and Cognitive Therapies, Chicago, IL.

Greco, L. A., & Eifert, G. H. (2004). Treating parent-adolescent conflict: Is acceptance the missing link for an integrative family therapy? *Cognitive and Behavioral Practice, 11,* 305–314.

Greeno, C. G., & Wing, R. R. (1994). Stress-induced eating. *Psychological Bulletin, 115,* 444–464.

Hayes, S. C., & Gifford, E. V. (1997). The trouble with language: Experiential avoidance, rules, and the nature of private events. *Psychological Science, 8,* 170–175.

Hayes, S. C., Luoma, J. B., Bond, F. W., Masuda, A., & Lillis, J. (2006). Acceptance and commitment therapy: Model processes and outcomes. *Behaviour Research and Therapy, 44,* 1–25.

Hayes, S. C., Strosahl, K. D., & Wilson, K. G. (1999). *Acceptance and commitment therapy: An experiential approach to behavior change.* New York: Guilford.

Heffner, M., & Eifert, G. H. (2004). *The anorexia workbook: How to accept yourself, heal suffering, and reclaim your life.* Oakland, CA: New Harbinger.

Leon, G. R., Fulkerson, J. A., Perry, C. L., & Early-Zald, M. B. (1995). Prospective analysis of personality and behavioral vulnerabilities and gender influences in the later development of disordered eating. *Journal of Abnormal Psychology, 104,* 140–149.

Levine, M. P., & Harrison, K. (2001). Media's role in the perpetuation and prevention of negative body image and disordered eating. In J. K. Thompson (Ed.), *Handbook of eating disorders and obesity* (pp. 695–717). Hoboken, NJ: John Wiley.

Neff, K. D. (2003). Self-compassion: An alternative conceptualization of a healthy attitude toward oneself. *Self and Identity, 2,* 85–102.

Neumark-Sztainer, D. (2005). *"I'm, like, so fat!" Helping your teen make healthy choices about eating and exercise in a weight-obsessed world.* New York: Guilford.

O'Dea, J. A., & Abraham, S. (1999). Onset of disordered eating attitudes and behaviors in early adolescence: Interplay of pubertal status, gender, weight, and age. *Adolescence, 34,* 671–679.

Plotkin, B. (2003). *Soulcraft: Crossing into the mysteries of nature and the psyche.* Novato, CA: New World Library.

Sands, E. R., & Wardle, J. (2003). Internalization of ideal body shapes in 9-12-year-old-girls. *International Journal of Eating Disorders, 33,* 193–204.

Sim, L., & Zeman, J. (2004). Emotion awareness and identification skills in adolescent girls with bulimia nervosa. *Journal of Clinical Child and Adolescent Psychology, 33,* 760–771.

Sim, L., & Zeman, J. (2006). The contribution of emotion regulation to body dissatisfaction and disordered eating in early adolescent girls. *Journal of Youth and Adolescence, 33,* 219–228.

Stice, E. (2001). A prospective test of the dual pathway model of bulimic pathology: Mediating effects of dieting and negative affect. *Journal of Abnormal Psychology, 110,* 124–135.

Stice, E., Presnell, K., Shaw, H., & Rohde, P. (2005). Psychological and behavioral risk factors for obesity onset in adolescent girls: A prospective study. *Journal of Consulting and Clinical Psychology, 73,* 195–202.

Stice, E., Shaw, H., & Nemeroff, C. (1998). Dual pathway model of bulimia nervosa: Longitudinal support for dietary restraint and affect-regulation mechanisms. *Journal of Social and Clinical Psychology, 17,* 129–149.

Thompson, S. H., Rafiroiu, A. C., & Sargent, R. G. (2003). Examining gender, racial, and age differences in weight concern among third, fifth, eighth, and eleventh graders. *Eating Behaviors, 3,* 307–323.

Titchener, E. B. (1916). *A textbook of psychology.* New York: MacMillan.

Urla, J., & Swedbund, A. C. (2000). The anthropology of Barbie: Unsettling ideals of the feminine body in popular culture. In L. Schiebinger (Eds.), *Feminism and the body* (pp. 391–428). New York: Oxford University Press.

Wardle, J., Waller, J., & Rapoport, L. (2001). Body dissatisfaction and binge eating in obese women: The role of restraint and depression. *Obesity Research, 9,* 778–787.

Part 3

Integrating Acceptance and Mindfulness into Larger Social Contexts

Chapter 10

Mindful Parenting: An Inductive Search Process

Robert Wahler, Ph.D., Katherine Rowinski, BS, and Keith Williams, BS, University of Tennessee, Knoxville

It seems obvious that effective parenting begins with an objective observational study of that parent's child. What the child does and says amounts to a stream of stimuli requiring the watching and listening parent to sample and interpret these events and then to decide how to respond. Thus an effective parent must have a broad repertoire of responses to deliver the needed caregiving as the child behaves. But appropriate delivery depends on the parent's judgment calls on the myriad stimuli offered by the youngster over brief and lengthy time spans.

A parent's judgment calls about the significance of child actions and words is commonly termed "responsiveness" or "sensitivity" (Bakermans-Kranenburg, van IJzendoorn, & Juffer, 2003; Kochanska, 2002), a dimension ranging from appropriate to inappropriate parental reactions. Responsive/sensitive parents demonstrate this capability by consistently providing social reinforcement contingencies for their children's prosocial actions and words, along with clear limits on the youngsters' antisocial responses (e.g., warnings and time-out). Nonetheless, for a number of reasons, parents' ability to "do the right thing" is hard to maintain across children, situations, and time; most parents will readily acknowledge this problem (Holden, 1988; Wahler & Dumas, 1989). In fact, the meta-analysis by Holden and Miller (1999) of high-functioning child-parent dyads found parent responsiveness/sensitivity to be fairly situation specific but more or less stable over time. In other words, these effective parents were generally able to sustain their use of this capability, although they were temporarily disrupted when changes occurred in the environment (e.g., when company came, at the grocery store, during a family vacation). Imagine, then, what it is like to live in an environment where change is far more unpredictable, causing the parent to be fragmented in efforts to react appropriately (Dumas et al., 2005).

The process of learning and sustaining responsiveness/sensitivity is central to understanding effective parenting as well as in developing clinical strategies for those parents who are out of sync with their children. This chapter explores the construct "mindfulness" as it applies to a parent's acquisition and maintenance of appropriate reactions to child behavior. Mindfulness is a state of objectivity needed to observe the here-and-now stream of stimuli emanating from one's physical sensations, feelings, and thoughts, as well as from the environment (see the review and commentary section on mindfulness in *Clinical Psychology: Science and Practice*, Fall 2004, pp. 230–266). As we see it, teaching mindful parenting requires a parent's objective judgments of the larger patterns of child-parent social interactions as well as objective judgments of each social interaction. Thus our clinical strategy helps parents to study their own specific actions and words preceding and following the children's various responses and to study historical patterns of these child-parent social exchanges. The former strategy is implemented through behavioral parent training (BPT), while the latter strategy utilizes a new procedure we call "narrative restructuring therapy" (NRT)—a means of helping parents to improve the coherence of their narrative accounts of recent and long-past family interactions. We use mindfulness meditation to promote parents' objective study of the specific social interactions and the narrative accounts of these interaction patterns.

Our parenting clinic at the University of Tennessee is a service and research facility for low-income mothers who are seeking help for their behavior-disordered children. Most of our referrals are single mothers who report multiple sources of daily stress, including social isolation and extended family or boyfriend conflict, along with chronic difficulties with their referred children. These children are typically boys within the age range of eight to ten years, and most meet criteria for oppositional defiant disorder (ODD).

Our clinic service is cost free in return for the mothers' willingness to follow a research protocol involving their mindful participation in behavioral parent training and narrative restructuring therapy. Mothers and their children are expected to attend weekly videotaped clinic sessions, split into thirty-minute NRT experiences for the mother and subsequent thirty-minute BPT experiences for the mother and child. Mothers also complete self-report questionnaires at repeated intervals over six months of baseline, treatment (BPT plus NRT), and follow-up phases.

A mother's mindful participation in these dual treatment strategies includes our version of meditation practices similar to those outlined by Baer (2003), Bishop et al. (2004), and Kabat-Zinn (1994). Our version is aimed at inducing mothers' objective attention to the here-and-now playroom experiences with the children, as well as enhancing their objective study of their past experiences as they tell their life stories. This latter aim is based on Ellen Langer's conception of mindfulness as "an open, creative, probabilistic state of mind in which the individual might be led to finding differences among things thought similar and similarities among things thought different" (Langer, 1993, p. 44).

Applying this definition to a mother's mindful way of telling her story, we would want her account to be rich in detail and well organized. However, as Wahler, Rowinski, and Williams (2007b) found in their recent analysis of twenty-one clinic-referred mothers' baseline narratives, these stories were poorly organized and devoid of specific events. So, just as these mothers are hardly objective observers of their social interactions with their children, their skills in reviewing historical experiences at home are also lacking. While mindfulness meditation is usually considered as an intervention to promote one's review of here-and-now experiences, we have also found it useful in promoting mothers' retrieval of these specific autobiographical memories deemed crucial to helping them to restructure their narratives. Hayes and Shenk (2004) weighed in on this utility issue by pointing out the current diversity in procedural and theoretical conceptions of mindfulness, including their own functional contextual view of the phenomenon. As they put it, "[W]hat is critical is creating contexts in which new behaviors can be learned that are not normally fostered by the social/verbal contexts that surround day to day language and cognition" (p. 253). This statement captures our view of the first step in BPT and NRT as well as the essence of Langer's (1989) viewpoint.

What follows is a patchwork of research findings on responsive/sensitive parenting, parents' autobiographical memories, mindfulness meditation, and speculation on responsiveness/sensitivity through a mindfulness process close to the hearts of most parents—telling their stories of child care and family life. We will argue that these "patches" fit together fairly well in generating a new learning context in which parents might truly take a fresh look at what they and their children are doing. Then we will describe our early attempt to apply this perspective to parent training.

In some respects, this chapter is premature because of a dearth of published studies in which mindfulness was part of the parenting or parent-training study. However, there are numerous studies of mindfulness and its benefits for adults who practice the various procedures (Baer, 2003; Hayes & Wilson, 2003; Kabat-Zinn, 2003; Masuda, Hayes, Sackett, & Twohig, 2004; Segal, Williams, & Teasdale, 2002; Wells, 2002). All of these studies lend consistent support to mindfulness-induced improvements in the client's sense of well-being. Assuming that a sense of well-being includes the adult's open-minded contemplation of personal change, mindfulness could indeed facilitate a parent's responsiveness/sensitivity in child care.

A Matter of Perspective

Parents' capacities to be responsive/sensitive are correlated with their abilities to formulate personal perspectives about their children and relationships with their children (Aber, Belsky, Slade, & Crnic, 1999; Coyne, Low, Miller, Seifer, & Dickstein, 2007; Kochanska, 1997; Koren-Karie, Oppenheim, Dolev, Sher, & Etzion-Carasso, 2002; Slade, Belsky, Aber, & Phelps, 1999). These "perspectives" are verbal summaries offered by a parent who is asked to describe child behavior along with the social transactions comprising this parent's view of the parent-child relationship. Mothers have been the primary parents studied in this research, in which their verbal summaries are rated for affective content and organization. Slade et al. (1999) found a dimension described as joy-pleasure/coherence to best predict observed mothering, indicating that mothers who produced better organized perspectives with more positive affect were also likely to be more responsive/sensitive with their toddlers. Likewise, Coyne et al. (2007) and Koren-Karie et al. (2002) found coherent and rich summaries to reflect mothers' empathy as indexed by responsive/sensitive care of their respective toddlers and infants. This correlational connection was also found by Oppenheim, Goldsmith, and Koren-Karie (2004) in their intervention effort to improve mothers' accuracy and detail in perspectives of their preschoolers with behavior problems. From baseline to post-intervention, degree of improvement covaried inversely with measures of the children's behavior problems.

It would seem, then, that a mother's ability to provide a well-organized and detailed summary of her child and the qualities of their relationship is clearly associated with her ability to generate synchrony during observed interactions. Given that these maternal perspectives are based on recollections of recent and earlier child-care experiences, it seems reasonable to consider the perspectives as summaries of the mothers' autobiographical memories. The memories can be prompted by child-care interview questions (Aber et al., 1999) or by having the mothers view videotapes of their child-care episodes (Koren-Karie et al., 2002), but it is up to the mothers to provide the summarized content and the organization of that content.

In the adult clinical literature, the tendency to recall overgeneral memories, particularly those with negative affect, are correlated with clinical problems (e.g., Brittlebank, Scott, Williams, & Ferrier, 1993; Mackinger, Pachinger, Leibetseder, & Fartacek, 2000; Peeters, Wessel, Merckelbach, & Boon-Vermeeren, 2002; Raes et al., 2006; Williams, 1996). This seems to apply to sensitive parenting as well. If a mother's autobiographical memories are largely overgeneral, efforts to construct narrative perspectives of her life experiences are bound to lack coherence or relevance to the specifics of a situation. One's ability to formulate "chapters" of a life story (e.g., "living with my child") requires organization of specific events into a temporal pattern supporting the point of this story (e.g., "My child lacks confidence").

Our clinic-referred mothers seem to show overgeneral memories. Here is a story presented by a clinic-referred mother about "life with my child":

> *Like I said, it's hard. She is into her own thing a lot, and I don't have a place. She wants what she wants and I got to look everywhere. She's cute, but who knows where that's going to get her. Her dad's the same way, so I figure that there's not much I can do, really.*

When asked if she had more to tell, she said, "No, that's about it."

In contrast, here are the recollections offered by a nonclinical volunteer mother who was asked about her parenting problems:

> *Well, I remember the day last summer when Jimmy kicked a hole in the screen door and that really ticked me off. I grabbed the little dickens by his shirttail and paddled his butt. I knew better than to lose it like that. He cried and so did I.*

When asked about "life with my child," she said:

> *It's really hard work, but I like it. He's got ADD and I give him his pill each morning, but it didn't seem to do much for his hyper stuff. Him and me will look at each other, right in our eyes, and we both know what kind of day it's gonna be. Yesterday he said, while I had my hands on his head, "Mama, I just wanna stay with you!" His eyes shone like stars, and I hugged him. He was good all morning, but I knowed it wouldn't last and of course it didn't. That's Jimmy for you.*

Since there are no specific happenings in the first story, we are left wondering how events fit within this mother's accounts. The second mother gives us details of what happened, along with a clear picture of sequence in these occurrences. Van IJzendoorn's (1995) meta-analysis of mothers' narrative-based perspectives showed that mothers who could provide more succinct, detailed, and orderly narratives about their experiences were also apt to respond more appropriately when caring for their infants and toddlers.

Mindfulness Meditation and Effective Parenting

Nirbhay Singh (2001) has argued that mental health is best defined by one's holistic perspective of "fit" involving self and those people who comprise this person's social environment. The task of living, according to Singh, is to look for a "goodness of fit" in which one's strengths are aligned with the strengths of others. More recently Singh and colleagues (Singh et al., 2006) used this model to help three mothers of autistic children find this "goodness of fit" through training the mothers in mindfulness meditation. In a multiple baseline design, each mother completed a twelve-week course in the philosophy and practice of mindfulness; no parent training was conducted. Results showed marked increments in the mothers' parenting satisfaction from baseline through the mindfulness practice phase. In addition, objective observational measures of the children's home behavior revealed clear reductions from baseline in noncompliance, aggression, and self-injury over at least a year of weekly observations. Even more recently Singh et al. (in press) replicated and extended this experimental analysis with four mothers and their children who had developmental disabilities.

Since social contingencies offered by the mothers were not measured in both studies, we have no way of knowing if mindfulness meditation enhanced the mothers' responsive/sensitive parenting. Singh et al. (2006) offered the following speculation: "These positive changes seem to result from a transformation in the way the mindful person relates to events in his or her environment, rather than from learning a set of skills to specifically change behaviors. Although the exact ways in which mindfulness training produces these transformational effects can be determined definitively only with further studies, a number of possibilities can be considered" (p. 174).

One such possibility is highlighted in Singh's view of the "transformational" effects of mindfulness training. That term appears to capture both Hayes and Shenk's (2004) and Langer's (1989) notions that mindfulness equates to systemic change in one's perspective of life events. Langer might say that Singh's mothers were able to unravel the categories they formerly used to summarize their parenting experiences, and Hayes and Shenk might say that the mothers dissolved the linguistic context of their verbalized perspectives. If such transformations did occur, perhaps the effect could be seen in measures of a mother's perspective of her psychosocial experiences, including those involving her child. This is made more likely by the finding in adult clinical work that mindfulness meditation helps patients recall more specific and less overgeneral memories (Williams, Teasdale, Segal, & Soulsby, 2000), perhaps because they were less inclined to avoid processing negative events due to the accepting, nonjudgmental quality of mindfulness meditation (Kabat-Zinn, 2003).

Even when parents are in sync with their children, the maintenance of that synchrony cannot be entrusted to well-established parenting practices; the best of these practices must be tweaked as environments change and as children grow (Holden & Miller, 1999). Effective parents must also be flexible in how, when, and where they use their practices, meaning that they must somehow retain their sensitivity/responsiveness when they could easily trust the less effortful automaticity process. Perhaps regular mindfulness meditation would sustain their flexibility and might even enhance the coherence of their child-care perspectives. Should the latter enhancement occur, it might be easier for parents to maintain their effective parenting, which includes modifying their practices to ensure that "goodness of fit" described by Singh (2001).

This is the approach taken by Jean Dumas (2005) in his suggestions for "mindfulness-based parent training." Parents who practice meditation may be able to dissolve old habits and take the opportunity to reassess and learn what is needed to parent their children effectively. Continuous practice may be needed since, as Dumas states, "Automaticity is an integral part of our social and emotional functioning and a major guide to our interactions (Bargh & Chartrand, 1999). However, mindful practices are essential to take stock regularly of who we are and how we live, to avoid passing by life in the groove of habit" (pp. 789–790).

When Behavioral Parent Training Is Not Enough

In a meta-analysis of behavioral parent training, Bakermans-Kranenburg et al. (2003) showed that BPT alone can improve parents' responsiveness/sensitivity and secure parent-child attachments. Furthermore, Schwartzman and Wahler (2006) reanalyzed archival data on contingency management for parent training and found that narrative perspectives became progressively more coherent than control group mothers; they were more responsive/sensitive with their children during the parent training phase; and changes in narrative coherence were positively correlated with changes in the parents' responsiveness/sensitivity. No measures of the parents' mindfulness were obtained, and meditation was not part of the intervention package. Why then should parents and clinicians bother with mindfulness meditation and narrative restructuring?

The answer is that BPT is not always enough. It does not have durable effects on all families (Cavell & Strand, 2002; Serketich & Dumas, 1996), and the pathological process supporting parents' unresponsive/insensitive parenting appears to be broader than social contingencies produced through child-parent interaction (Wahler, 2007). There is a large "transmission gap" between parenting practices (i.e., responsiveness/ sensitivity) and quality of the child-parent relationship (van IJzendoorn, 1995). Meta-analyses show that only about a third of the variance in the mother-child attachment relationship relates to maternal responsiveness/sensitivity (Fearon et al., 2006; van IJzendoorn, 1995).

It seems likely that the child-parent relationship is also affected by child temperament (Crockenberg & Acredolo, 1983; Leerkes & Crockenberg, 2003). Mothers' ratings of infant and child temperament are, at best, only modestly correlated with impartial observers' ratings (Bates, 1980; Hubert, Wachs, Peters-Martin, & Gandour, 1982), suggesting that mothers might not recognize the potential influence of these child effects, apparently both due to mothers' personality characteristics (Vaughn, Taraldson, Cuchton, & Egeland, 2002) and because mothers' perceptions of their children's negativity and positivity are situation specific (Hane, Fox, Polak-Toste, Ghera, & Guner, 2006).

It is possible to imagine scenarios in which a mother is periodically responsive/ sensitive in providing social contingencies and yet oblivious to the pervasive influences of her child's temperament. Suppose for example, that a child's temperament includes impulsivity. This class of responses will diminish through the mother's appropriate contingency management comprised of sensitive discipline and positive reinforcement of the child's purposeful actions. If, due to temperament, the child still manifests occasional signs of impulsivity, the mother might wrongly assume that her contingency management strategy is not working. As a result, she may lose heart and no longer put forth the effort to maintain her newly acquired responsive/sensitive parenting practices. In our experience with BPT, this sort of dilemma is not uncommon.

This highlights the importance of helping clinic-referred parents attain a more objective perspective on their children's temperament. Otherwise it will prove difficult for a parent to hold the course when faced with child behavior problems that "shouldn't be there." This latter phrase was uttered twelve years ago by a father in our clinic who had done well in BPT with his ten-year-old daughter. He and his daughter were referred by the girl's pediatrician, who was concerned about "intense and frequent arguments between this divorced father and his daughter." During their intake interviews, both complained about the other party, with the girl stating that her father "never listens" and the father stating that "she thinks she's in charge." In BPT, both looked and listened to home videotapes of their interactions, aimed at pinpointing these complaints through their clinician's guidance. The dyad agreed to a general contract in which he would become a better listener and she would stop "bossing" him. The clinician assigned the father to be in charge of using time-out to curb arguments. The father was also assigned to serve as a listener whose goal was to set daily "talk sessions" in which he would simply prompt his daughter to elaborate her verbalizations. The home videotaping would become a mainstay part of weekly clinic sessions to teach these skills.

In our baseline testing of the father and daughter personalities, there was consistent evidence pointing to the father's passive nature and the girl's assertive nature. Thus we knew that the father and daughter were expected to learn social tactics that were incongruent with their basic temperaments. Nevertheless, the father did well in implementing the time-out strategy. According to the daughter, he also seemed to be genuinely interested in their conversations about her peer interactions and home life. Home videotapes were consistent with these self-reports in showing a reduction in arguments and increased mutually responsive/sensitive exchanges between the father and his daughter.

After the conclusion of BPT, three monthly home videotapes showed periodic arguments along with dips in child-parent synchrony, but this problem pattern was well below baseline levels. However, the dyad's separate self-reports became discrepant, with the father describing less satisfaction, in contrast to his daughter's sustained satisfaction. When the clinician telephoned the father to ask for elaboration, he begrudgingly noted his daughter's sustained improvement and also said, "I'm putting a lot of effort into this and still there's that attitude of hers that shouldn't be there—not after all this work." When asked about the girl's attitude, the father was at a loss to identify the source of his concern, but did offer the comment "You know, she is an awful lot like her mother."

When the clinician recommended a return to our clinic for further sessions, the father declined to do so, stating that he was in the process of talks with his ex-wife to change the current parenting plan. In essence, he had decided to give residential custody to the girl's mother in hopes that he could cope with this "mismatch" by limiting contact with his daughter to every other weekend. We had no further contact with this family.

Meditation and Restructuring Parents' Perspectives

Perhaps we could have helped this father to more fully appreciate the fruits of his work in BPT. He clearly told us that he was bothered by the quality of home life with his daughter, even though he could see improvement in their relationship. Just what was bothering him is open to conjecture: The girl's periodic assertiveness (i.e., her temperament)? Her similarity to her mother? His status as a single parent? His passive nature (i.e., his temperament)? Looking back on this case in the context of what we now understand from the literature, we should have helped this father to take a fresh look at his personal experiences.

This "fresh look" is an inductive look, a search process in which the searcher's judgment is suspended to allow an objective inspection of his or her memories, feelings, thoughts, physical sensations, and immediate environmental events. Our hypothesis is that mindfulness meditation is one way of helping parents to generate these objective inspections. As we stated in the last section of this chapter, mindfulness meditation appears to have generalized effects on the parent who both understands the philosophy behind this practice and regularly employs the practice (e.g., Singh et al., 2006; Singh et al., in press). While we don't know much about this generalization process, it does seem to produce improvements in children's behavior problems as well as improvements in the parents' satisfaction with their parenting. We have offered process speculations centering on parents' narrative perspectives of their children. Borrowing from Singh's speculation that meditation has "transformational" effects, we are hypothesizing that these effects occur within the composition of each parent's narrative perspective. As the perspective becomes more coherent and specific, the narrator's sensitivity/responsiveness is presumably enhanced.

Here is how we think it works: Mindfulness meditation temporarily suspends the parent's judgment of all sensations, both environmental and private (such as memories, thoughts, and feelings). Given this new inductive look, all sensations are closely examined as specific events stripped of their categorical meaning so that each is viewed as new. Thus, as Williams et al. (2000) demonstrated, meditation helps depression-prone adults to retrieve specific memories instead of the categoric memories involved in their ruminative thinking (Raes et al., 2006). Since these specific memories are new and unencumbered by earlier meaning, parents have an opportunity to reconstruct their perspectives on life with their children. If they do so in ways that preserve the specificity of remembered happenings, and these are organized into coherent narratives, this "fresh look" should be accompanied by responsive/sensitive parenting.

Because mindfulness meditation helps the meditator to suspend judgment of all experiences, the shift from deductive to inductive thinking includes the here and now as well as memories of the past. If we had helped the previously mentioned father through mindfulness meditation as well as BPT, he might have been able to suspend judgment of his daughter's assertive ("bossy") actions and words, along with his remembered comparisons of her temperament with that of his ex-wife and with his opposite temperament. It is this willingness to process all experiences fully that seems transformative when the parent adopts this "beginner's mind."

Of course inductive thinking usually ends when we formulate hypotheses about why things happen. Then we use our guiding powers of deduction to more efficiently pursue answers. In doing so, we no longer need to think about the questions we used to ask, such as "Why is parenting such hard work?" Once it is answered, the search is over, and even though environmental circumstances will change, they go unnoticed—in much the same way that our habits become automatic (Dumas, 2005).

If mindfulness meditation can help parents return to inductive thinking, they ought to ask new questions about their narrative perspectives of life with their children. This curiosity and willingness to wonder about one's perspective can perhaps be maintained by regular meditation. It is also possible that a parent's perspective of "life with my child" could be directly restructured through the guidance of a skilled listener (Schwartzman & Wahler, 2006). Since we know that meditation can help an adult to retrieve specific autobiographical memories (Williams et al., 2000), a first crucial step in NRT has occurred and the process could continue via listener prompts aimed at organizing these memories into coherent stories.

In essence, we are describing a parenting conundrum. Mindfulness meditation appears to dissolve categoric memories, ambiguous thinking, and undifferentiated feeling, allowing the mindful parent to take this "fresh look" at his or her specific experiences. However, NRT then helps parents to form new perspectives through intuition or more deliberate reconstruction efforts (narrative restructuring). The new perspective is both a blessing and a curse: Since it is newly formed, it is relevant to current circumstances and guides the parent's responsive/sensitive caregiving. If the new perspective works well as a parenting guide, the parent need not be mindful of its composition, and its function will soon become automatic. Keeping in mind the basic premise that children and environments change, all parents need to repeatedly return to the inductive search process to update their perspective. Those parents who cannot or will not update their perspectives are bound to experience varying degrees of trouble in parenting. Some will need the help of professionals when the trouble becomes chronic.

The Clinical Process: Mindfulness, NRT, and BPT

In our clinical work with troubled mothers, we combine principles of NRT (Wahler & Castlebury, 2002) with mindfulness meditation and BPT. The intake interview is scaffolded by four questions, the first two geared to hearing the mother's perspective about her child: (1) "Why did you bring your child to our clinic?" and (2) "What's it like to live with your child?" The next two questions ask the mother to tell about the more distant past: (3) "When your child was younger, what do you remember about being a parent?" and (4) "Tell me what you can remember about life with your parents." When the mother concludes each of her four narrative "chapters," she is simply asked if she has anything more to add. The interview is videotaped, transcribed, and rated for coherence following a manual by Wahler, Rowinski, and Williams (2007a). The mother also completes questionnaires measuring mindfulness, parenting style, insight regarding personal change, and view of her child's problems.

Next the clinician outlines our free clinic services as well as the research nature of these weekly services over a span of six months. The mother is told that the first three sessions are baseline in function, allowing us to get a picture of the playroom interactions and her life story. The "story" is prompted in thirty-minute sessions in which the clinician asks the same four questions used during the intake interview and no other guiding questions are asked. Immediately following this session, the parent-child dyad engages in thirty-minute playroom sessions. These playroom sessions are unstructured, and the clinician is not present. The mother is told to think of the playroom as her home and to interact with her child in any way she chooses.

The NRT ("life story") and playroom sessions are videotaped. The baseline videotapes are transcribed for the mother's narratives, and the playroom videotapes are observed and coded in fifteen-second intervals through standardized observation codes (Cerezo, 1988). The codes reflect specific prosocial, neutral, and antisocial child responses, along with generic mother responses, such as praise, disapproval, acknowledgement, and commands. Since the child and mother codes are scored in each time interval, we can quantify pictures of the child's disruptive as well as constructive behaviors and the mother's appropriate/inappropriate parenting (the percentage of appropriate mother responses constitute our index of sensitive/responsive parenting).

Transcripts of the mother's narratives following the four questions are considered to be four baseline "chapters" in her life story. Each chapter is rated on six dimensions of coherence as defined in Wahler, Rowinski, and Williams (2007a). The resulting profile depicts each dimension on a five-point Likert scale reflecting coherence of the central point, happenings, organization, orientation, internal states, and causality. As shown in the recent study of twenty-one clinic-referred mothers by Wahler, Rowinski, and Williams (2007b), their baseline narratives are noteworthy for ambiguous happenings, poor organization, and no consideration of causality. The most coherent aspect of these stories is the central point (i.e., the reason for telling the story).

The baseline pictures of child-mother interactions and the mother's narrative coherence profile will inform the clinician's use of NRT and BPT. Of course the BPT goal is to enhance the mother's sensitivity/responsiveness and the NRT goal is to enhance the coherence of her personal narrative. In starting these joint interventions, the clinician reviews with the mother during NRT sessions the most coherent part of her baseline narrative—the central point of her child-care chapters. The central point is the reason for telling her story: why she brought her child to the clinic and what it's like to live with this youngster. The clinician cites a phrase, sentence, or word frequently used by the mother in referencing that central point during the baseline sessions. One mother used the sentence "I feel like I am under my son Toby's thumb."

The clinician aims to promote the mother's mindful focus on this categoric memory ("I am under his thumb") to facilitate her retrieval of specific happenings. Obviously the clinician could simply ask for exemplars of the category (e.g., "Give me some examples of being under his thumb."). However, approaching the discovery of relevant memories in this manner leads the mother and clinician into a logical discussion of happenings that should fit this category (i.e., the child's coercive actions and words). In contrast, helping the mother to relax and then visualize the category encourages her free (and sometimes illogical) associations in the search process. In other words, we want to know, and we want the mother to know, the breadth of exemplars she has grouped under her chosen categoric memory.

Our version of mindfulness meditation incorporates some of the procedures described by Kabat-Zinn (1994), such as helping the mother to attend to her breathing and to allow her other physical, emotional, and mental sensations to flow freely through her mind. Then we ask her to visualize her categoric wording as if it were a door that she could open to other feelings, thoughts, and memories ("Just say them as they flow through your mind."). This latter facet of meditation is more akin to Langer's (1993) view of mindfulness, because our focus is on past happenings rather than the here and now. We want this mother to examine the full range of happenings she has grouped under her chosen category, "He's got me under his thumb," so that she can create "an open, creative, problematic state of mind in which [she] might be led to finding differences among things thought similar and similarities among things thought different" (Langer, 1993, p. 44). Of course, if the mother gets "stuck" and either ruminates about a remembered happening or loses her bodily relaxation, we help her to focus again on her breathing and allow her physical, emotional, and mental sensations to once again flow freely through her mind.

We have been impressed, and the mothers have been impressed, with the wide range of specific happenings they cite as exemplars of these child-referenced central points of their narratives. The mother we have illustrated started with "I can see and hear Toby [son] grabbing his PlayStation from me yesterday. He called me a bitch and spit on my hand. I cried and walked away." Later she noted a similar memory of her former husband: "When I told my ex-husband to pick up those potato chips he dropped, he threw a beer bottle at the front door."

As one might imagine, this widening range of diverse specific happenings under one categoric umbrella is confusing to the clinician as well to the mother. Her mindful study of this particular category produced an array of exemplars that lessened rather than enhanced the coherence of this chapter about Toby. The task of NRT is to help the mother organize these happenings, to put aside for the moment any happenings that now seem tangential to her, and to encourage the mother's enrichment of happenings that she sees as relevant to the current chapter. The enrichment occurs as she adds time and place, thoughts and feelings, and her view of causality (why the happenings occurred).

When the chapter attains coherence, the clinician will ask the mother to think about those happenings she later believed did not belong under the central point (e.g., the beer bottle incident). She is reminded that this happening occurred when she mindfully studies the categoric memory about her son, Toby. The clinician simply asks, "Does it belong or not?" We have found that most mothers, after restructuring the chapter in question, will prove to be insightful in Langer's (1993) sense of the term, by "seeing similarities in things thought different and differences among things thought similar" (p. 44). This mother answered that life with her former husband is related to Toby's problems but "is another story." Thus another central point is likely to emerge, either through the mother's spontaneous presentation of a new categoric memory, or through the clinician's recollections of the mother's words in her baseline chapters of the distant past (i.e., when your child was younger; life with your parents). This mother said, "I keep thinking about him [former husband] saying me and Toby was just alike. That blows my mind!"

New chapters begin when the mother and clinician initiate her mindful study of other categoric memories. Of course these become central points of new chapters comprised of happenings generated inductively through the meditation process described earlier (e.g., "Okay, now visualize and hear him saying you two are just alike. Open the door to other feelings, thoughts, and memories; just say them as they flow through your mind."). Her first recollection was "I can see him getting ready for bed the night after we was married. He was laughing and pointed at Toby's bedroom with one hand and at me with the other and said, 'I sure hope there's room for me between you two control freaks.'"

Other specific happenings quickly followed in her mindful study, and one of these so upset her that she and the clinician returned to the initial meditation process. As the mother put it, "I work as a supervisor at this mushroom plant, and years ago one of my girls told me, 'You tell us how to do our job but you won't let us do 'em—you're always in my way.'" After the mother regained her composure in this NRT session, she said, "I can see and hear me deny just that with Toby last week. I told him to pick up his comic books and for once he started to do it. I can't believe it, but I then started to change where he put 'em. He kicked over the stack and then we got into it big-time. You know what? That girl [at work] and Earl [ex-husband] was right. I am the damn superintendent who should be fired!"

After the mother and the clinician improved the coherence of this particular chapter, the mother noted its similarity to the first chapter about life with Toby. As she put it, "I done the same things with Earl, that girl, and Toby. I do know how to take charge, but then I can't close my big mouth. I pick at them and they come back at me. That's how I allow Toby to get me under his thumb."

Keep in mind that thirty-minute playroom sessions immediately follow the thirty-minute mindfulness/NRT sessions. The coded interactions between the mother and her son over baseline playroom sessions showed her sensitive/responsive parenting to average about 70 percent of her responses (we have norms set by volunteer mothers at around 90 percent). Toby's behavior was playful, interspersed with demands on his mother and refusals to comply with her instructions. These antisocial actions and words amounted to around 15 percent of his responses (our norm for volunteer children is at 5 percent). BFT is initiated as the mothers restructure their narrative chapters into more coherent perspectives of "life with my child." Since some of the specific happenings recalled through the mother's mindful study of categoric memories are those from earlier playroom sessions, the clinician and the mother can generate a plan for her parenting near the conclusion of each NRT session.

This mother's first BPT session was based on happenings derived from her categoric memory "He's got me under his thumb." One specific happening she retrieved during mindfulness study of this memory was this: "We went to the zoo with friends and while I was telling them about the elephant, he kept interrupting me." Since Toby periodically interrupted his mother's comments or explanations directed to him during baseline, the clinician outlined a plan of action in which she would warn him about her intended use of time-out for interruptions and then follow up by its use were Toby to interrupt her again. This plan was discussed near the end of an NRT session. During the playroom session, Toby did interrupt; she required him to sit behind a partition for five minutes of silence, but she also lectured him while he was silent. Toby, of course, ceased his silence, an argument ensued, and he knocked over the partition.

In a brief conversation between the mother and clinician after this session, the mother expressed her doubts about time-out and voiced her belief that she must tell Toby about his interruptions. In the next NRT session, the discussion continued and led to the review and enhanced coherence of her "life with Toby" chapter, culminating in her mindful study of the categoric memory "life with my former husband." The following BPT session was preceded by the mother's agreement to again use time-out and silence if Toby interrupted her. He did interrupt her, and the mother's performance was no better than during her last BPT session. While she did not lecture him when he was in time-out, she seemed angry on the videotape and threw a block of wood at the time-out partition, leading Toby to charge out yelling at her and the argument escalated. The clinician entered the playroom and ended the session. Surprisingly, the mother apologized to both Toby and the clinician.

It was during the mother's continued mindful study of "life with my former husband" that the mother retrieved the "mushroom plant" happening along with the home-based "pick up your comic books" happening with Toby. Of course she connected both chapters by constructing the larger central point "I am the damn superintendent who should be fired!" At the conclusion of this NRT session, she told the clinician, "I know what to do in the playroom with Toby." In fact, she handled the single time-out episode well, following Toby's interruption. Toby was also silent for five minutes, and the dyad was reasonably cooperative.

Over the next three months of NRT sessions, the mother developed a number of new chapters of her early and more recent life, with numerous specific happenings retrieved through the mindful study of categoric memories and the clinician's help in restructuring her narratives. The mother's BPT session focused on Toby's demands, his caustic remarks, and his prosocial interest in reviewing concerns about his peer relationships. All of the mother's playroom strategies emerged from the NRT sessions, along with the clinician's guidance about how the mother might enact the strategies in the playroom. The mother and her son did well.

During three monthly follow-up visits to our clinic, the mother continued to elaborate her various life story chapters and to discover overarching central points linking her chapters. Her overall coherence ratings from baseline lows of two on the five-point Likert scale averaged around four during three follow-up visits. Her playroom sensitivity/responsiveness scores increased from baseline lows of 70 percent to around 85 percent over the follow-up visits. Toby's antisocial scores decreased from 15 percent in baseline to less than 3 percent over follow-up. These three monthly visits are comparable to the baseline visits in the sense that the clinician only asks the four baseline questions and then only asks if the mother has more to add. The playroom sessions for mother-child interactions are unstructured. After session three, the mother again completes the same self-report questionnaire she completed after her intake interview.

Conclusion

Our clinical work is more informed by the previous review of research literature and theory than by our own empirical studies (i.e., Schwartzman & Wahler, 2006; Wahler, Rowinski, & Williams, 2007b). We hope to provide correlational evidence of expected baseline associations between clinic-referred mothers' parenting, mindfulness, and narrative coherence in the next few months; as we continue to use the same measures in our case studies, time-series analyses of these repeated measures may provide further correlational evidence of our subjective impressions.

We are a long way from offering experimental evidence for our clinical package as outlined in the just described case study. For those clinicians who wish to pursue this strategy with troubled mothers and their equally troubled children, we want to leave our readers with the following eight points based on our experiences:

1. Clinic-referred mothers want to tell their personal stories about parenting and other life experiences.
2. These stories can usefully guide a clinician's parent training strategy if the clinician will help mothers to improve their story coherence.
3. Clinical restructuring of a story chapter starts easily enough when the clinician hears the central point, usually expressed as a categoric memory.
4. Specific story happenings are summarized under the category, but the mother's wording of the category rarely fits the complete summary. For example, the categoric memory/central point "My child has me under his thumb" also included happenings that did not involve parenting or the child in question.
5. Mindfulness meditation is the strategy of choice to elicit a mother's retrieval of specific happenings, in contrast to directly prompting these exemplars. While the latter strategy will also yield specific happenings, the mother is likely to omit those that do not fit the categoric wording. These anomalous happenings become useful markers for new chapters that will prove to overlap with old chapters.
6. New central points or an expansion of a current central point will emerge as the mother is engaged in the process of restructuring her current chapter. New chapters are developed and are eventually connected to old chapters.
7. Specific chapter happenings are bound to occur during unstructured playroom interactions between the mother and her child. If a playroom

happening is targeted for BPT, the mother is more apt to cooperate if that happening is also set within the coherent context of her story.

8. The mother's story should retain its coherence if she continues to tell it to interested listeners. Restructuring the story will prove to be necessary as her life circumstances change. It is likely that she will need the occasional help of a skilled listener to do so.

References

Aber, J. L., Belsky, J., Slade, A., & Crnic, K. (1999). Stability and change in mothers' representations of their relationship with their toddlers. *Developmental Psychology, 35*, 1038–1047.

Baer, R. A. (2003). Mindfulness training as a clinical intervention: A conceptual and empirical review. *Clinical Psychology: Science and Practice, 10*, 125–143.

Bakermans-Kranenburg, M. J., van IJzendoorn, M. H., & Juffer, F. (2003). Less is more: Meta-analyses of sensitivity and attachment interventions in early childhood. *Psychological Bulletin, 129*, 195–215.

Bargh, J. A., & Chartrand, T. L. (1999). The unbearable automaticity of being. *American Psychologist, 54*, 462–479.

Bates, J. E. (1980). The concept of difficult temperament. *Merrill Palmer Quarterly, 26*, 299–319.

Bishop, S. R., Lau, M., Shapiro, S., Carlson, L., Anderson, N. D., Carmody, J., et al. (2004). Mindfulness: A proposed operational definition. *Clinical Psychology: Science and Practice, 11*, 230–241.

Brittlebank, A. D., Scott, J., Williams, J. M., & Ferrier, I. N. (1993). Autobiographical memory in depression: State or trait marker? *British Journal of Psychiatry, 162*, 118–121.

Cavell, T. A., & Strand, P. S. (2002). Parent-based interventions for aggressive, antisocial children: Adapting to a bilateral lens. In L. Kucynski (Ed.), *Handbook of dynamics in parent-child relations* (pp. 395–419). Thousand Oaks, CA: Sage.

Cerezo, M. A. (1988). Standardized observation codes. In M. Herson & A. S. Bellack (Eds.), *Dictionary of behavioral assessment techniques* (pp. 442–445). New York: Pergamon.

Clinical Psychology: Science and Practice, (Fall 2004), pp. 230–266.

Coyne, L. W., Low, C. M., Miller, A. L., Seifer, R., & Dickstein, S. (2007). Mothers' empathic understanding of their toddlers: Associations with maternal depression and sensitivity. *Journal of Child and Family Studies, 16*, 483–497.

Crockenberg, S., & Acredolo, C. (1983). Infant temperament ratings: A function of infants, of mothers, or both? *Infant Behavior and Development, 6*, 61–72.

Dumas, J. E. (2005). Mindfulness-based parent training: Strategies to lessen the grip of automaticity in families with disruptive children. *Journal of Clinical Child and Adolescent Psychology, 34*, 779–791.

Dumas, J. E., Nissley, J., Nordstrom, A., Smith, E. P., Prinz, R. J., & Levine, D. W. (2005). Home chaos: Sociodemographic, parenting, interactional, and child correlates. *Journal of Clinical Child and Adolescent Psychology, 34*, 93–104.

Fearon, R. M., van IJzendoorn, M. H., Fonagy, P., Bakermans-Kranenburg, M. J., Schuengel, C., & Bokhorst, C. L. (2006). In search of shared and nonshared environmental factors in security of attachment: A behavior-genetic study of the association between sensitivity and attachment security. *Developmental Psychology, 42*, 1026–1040.

Hane. A. A., Fox, N. A., Polak-Toste, C., Ghera, M. M., & Guner, B. M. (2006). Contextual basis of maternal perceptions of infant temperament. *Developmental Psychology, 42*, 1077–1088.

Hayes, S. C., & Shenk, C. (2004). Operationalizing mindfulness without unnecessary attachments. *Clinical Psychology: Science and Practice, 11*, 249–254.

Hayes, S. C., & Wilson, K. G. (2003). Mindfulness: Method and process. *Clinical Psychology: Science and Practice, 10*, 161–165.

Holden, G. W. (1988). Adults' thinking about a child-rearing problem: Effects of experience, parental status, and gender. *Child Development, 59*, 1623–1632.

Holden, G. W., & Miller, P. C. (1999). Enduring and different: A meta-analysis of the similarity in parents' child rearing. *Psychological Bulletin, 125*, 223–254.

Hubert, N. C., Wachs, T., Peters-Martin, P., & Gandour, M. J. (1982). The study of early temperament: Measurement and conceptual issues. *Child Development, 53*, 571–600.

Kabat-Zinn, J. (1994). *Wherever you go, there you are: Mindfulness meditation in everyday life*. New York: Hyperion.

Kabat-Zinn, J. (2003). Mindfulness-based interventions in context: Past, present, and future. *Clinical Psychology: Science and Practice, 10*, 144–156.

Kochanska, G. (1997). Mutually responsive orientation between mothers and their young children: Implications for early socialization. *Child Development, 68*, 94–112.

Kochanska, G. (2002). Mutually responsive orientation between mothers and their young children: A context for the early development of conscience. *Current Directions in Psychological Science, 11*, 191–195.

Koren-Karie, N., Oppenheim, D., Dolev, S., Sher, E., & Etzion-Carasso, A. (2002). Mother's insightfulness regarding their infants' internal experience: Relations with maternal sensitivity and infant attachment. *Developmental Psychology, 38*, 534–542.

Langer, E. J. (1989). *Mindfulness*. New York: Addison-Wesley.

Langer, E. J. (1993). A mindful education. *Educational Psychologist, 28*, 43–50.

Leerkes, E. M., & Crockenberg, S. C. (2003). The impact of maternal characteristics and sensitivity on the concordance between maternal reports and laboratory observations of infant negative emotionality. *Infancy, 4*, 517–539.

Mackinger, H. F., Pachinger, M. M., Leibetseder, M. M., & Fartacek, R. R. (2000). Autobiographical memories in women remitted from major depression. *Journal of Abnormal Psychology, 109*, 331–334.

Masuda, A., Hayes, S. C., Sackett, C. F., & Twohig, M. P. (2004). Cognitive defusion and self-relevant negative thoughts: Examining the impact of a ninety year old technique. *Behaviour Research and Therapy, 42*, 477–485.

Oppenheim, D., Goldsmith, D., & Koren-Karie, N. (2004). Maternal insightfulness and preschoolers' emotion and behavior problems: Reciprocal influences in a therapeutic preschool program. *Infant Mental Health Journal, 25*, 352–367.

Peeters, F., Wessel, I., Merckelbach, H., & Boon-Vermeeren, M. (2002). Autobiographical memory specificity and the course of major depressive disorder. *Comprehensive Psychiatry, 43*, 344–350.

Raes, F., Hermans, D., Williams, J. M., Beyers, W., Eelen, P., & Brunfaut, E. (2006). Reduced autobiographical memory specificity and rumination in predicting the course of depression. *Journal of Abnormal Psychology, 115*, 699–704.

Schwartzman, M. P., & Wahler, R. G. (2006). Enhancing the impact of parent training through narrative restructuring. *Child and Family Behavior Therapy, 28*, 49–65.

Segal, Z. V., Williams, J. M. G., & Teasdale, J. D. (2002). *Mindfulness-based cognitive therapy for depression: A new approach to preventing relapse*. New York: Guilford.

Serketich, W. J., & Dumas, J. E. (1996). The effectiveness of behavioral parent training to modify antisocial behavior in children: A meta-analysis. *Behavior Therapy, 27*, 171–186.

Singh, N. N. (2001). Holistic approaches to working with strengths: A goodness-of-fit wellness model. In A. Bridge, L. J. Gordon, P. Jivanjee, & J. M. King (Eds.), *Building on family strengths: Research and services in support of children and their families* (pp. 7–16). Portland, OR: Portland State University, Research and Training Center on Family Support and Children's Mental Health.

Singh, N. N., Lancioni, G. E., Winton, A. S., Fisher, B. C., Wahler, R. G., McAleavey, K. M., et al. (2006). Mindful parenting decreases aggression, noncompliance, and self-injury in children with autism. *Journal of Emotional and Behavioral Disorders, 14*, 169–177.

Singh, N. N., Lancioni, G. E., Winton, A. S., Singh, J., Curtis, W. J., Wahler, R. G., et al. (in press). Mindful parenting decreases aggression and increases social behavior in children with developmental disabilities. *Behavior Modification*.

Slade, A., Belsky, J., Aber, J. L., & Phelps, J. L. (1999). Mothers' representations of their relationships with their toddlers: Links to adult attachment and observed mothering. *Developmental Psychology, 35*, 611–619.

van IJzendoorn, M. H. (1995). Adult attachment representations, parental responsiveness, and infant attachment: A meta-analysis on the predictive validity of the Adult Attachment Interview. *Psychological Bulletin, 117*, 387–403.

Vaughn, B. E., Taraldson, B. J., Cuchton, L., & Egeland, B. (2002). The assessment of infant temperament: A critique of the Carey Infant Temperament Questionnaire. *Infant Behavior and Development, 25*, 98–112.

Wahler, R. G. (2007). Chaos, coincidence, and contingency in the behavior disorders of childhood and adolescence. In P. Sturney (Ed.), *Functional analyses in clinical treatment*. Burlington, MA: Elsevier.

Wahler, R. G., & Castlebury, F. D. (2002). Personal narratives as maps of the social ecosystem. *Clinical Psychology Review, 22*, 297–314.

Wahler, R. G., & Dumas, J. E. (1989). Attentional problems in dysfunctional mother-child interactions: An interbehavioral model. *Psychological Bulletin, 105*, 116–130.

Wahler, R. G., Rowinski, K. S., & Williams, K. L. (2007a). *Rating the personal narratives of parents*. University of Tennessee, Knoxville. Unpublished paper available from the first author.

Wahler, R. G., Rowinski, K. S., & Williams, K. L. (2007b, March). Clinic-referred mothers' monitoring capabilities: Mindfulness and narrative coherence? Paper Symposium, Society for Research in Child Development Conference, Boston.

Wells. A. (2002). GAD, metacognition, and mindfulness: An information processing analysis. *Clinical Psychology: Science and Practice, 9*, 95–100.

Williams, J. M. (1996). Depression and the specificity of autobiographical memory. In D. Rubin (Ed.), *Remembering our past: Studies in autobiographical memory* (pp. 244–267). New York: Cambridge University Press.

Williams, J. M., Teasdale, J. D., Segal, Z. V., & Soulsby, J. (2000). Mindfulness-based cognitive therapy reduces overgeneral autobiographical memory in formerly depressed patients. *Journal of Abnormal Psychology, 109*, 150–155.

Chapter 11

Integrating Acceptance and Commitment Therapy into Pediatric Primary Care

Patricia J. Robinson, Ph.D.,
Mountainview Consulting Group, Inc., Zillah, Washington

Use of acceptance and commitment therapy (ACT) in primary pediatric care requires the clinician to make numerous adaptations to practice style and use of ACT strategies. Practice success depends on skillful exploration of the new context for delivery of services and development of productive relationships with new colleagues. The primary care behavioral health (PCBH) model (Robinson & Reiter, 2007) helps the behaviorist develop a sustained focus on unique opportunities in primary care. Values that lead practitioners to care about children in primary care are the best source for inspiration in developing new clinical strategies and in making adaptations to practice details. These values underlie the mission of PCBH, which in the broadest sense is the desire to improve the health of children and bring them to adulthood with minds, bodies, and spirits capable of vital living. To pursue this mission, the behaviorist works as a team player who consults with primary care providers in an effort to further their delivery of services that protect and promote the health of patients from birth to adulthood.

In this chapter, I introduce readers to the primary care setting and illustrate how cognitive fusion and experiential avoidance may operate in common encounters between children and adolescents and their medical and behavioral health care providers. This chapter also offers translations of ACT core processes for use in interactions between children and their families and potential long-term primary care providers. The chapter concludes with the introduction of the use of ACT in population-based care programs for the costly health problem of childhood obesity. Before launching into the specifics of the ACT approach in primary care, a brief introduction of ACT and terms central to the ACT perspective is in order.

A Brief Introduction to ACT

ACT (Hayes, Strosahl, & Wilson, 1999) is a scientifically based approach to addressing the problems of human suffering. The goal of ACT is to help individuals develop greater psychological flexibility. Like physical flexibility, *psychological flexibility* is characterized by fluidity, greater range of motion or a wider range of behavioral action, and more resilience to injury and stress. Psychological flexibility requires the establishment of a valued direction and persistent movement toward this direction over time. Humans who subscribe most fervently to common cultural rules (e.g., "Doctors should be able to make my child normal!") tend to have less flexibility and to be vulnerable to greater suffering, both physical and mental.

Other important ACT processes include experiential avoidance and cognitive fusion. *Experiential avoidance* involves attempts to avoid or control private experiences (thoughts, feelings, sensations, etc.), even when avoidance does not work and perhaps leads to more serious problems. For example, the child who experiences a life-threatening motor-vehicle accident may avoid the memories of the accident by going to her parents' bed at night, even though they become frustrated with her and reprimand her for being a "baby."

Cognitive fusion occurs when we attach to our private experiences (thoughts, emotions, images, sensations) as though they were literally true. Let's assume that the little girl experienced thoughts and images of her mother dying at the time of the accident. When taken to be literally true, the young girl may begin to demonstrate experiential avoidance to rid herself (at least temporarily) of her painful private experience. Any thought of her mother dying can stimulate experiential avoidance, and the specific avoidance behaviors may be wide-ranging (e.g., stomachache at school prompts an early pickup by a child's mother; aggressive behavior leads to class dismissal, thereby allowing escape of a boring history lesson).

The alternatives to experiential avoidance and fusion are acceptance and defusion. Acceptance and defusion help us to create "breathing room" around painful aspects of living that have come to be avoided. The identification of values suggests behavioral directions that are of greater importance than persisting in avoidance patterns, which typically work only in the short term, if at all. Mindfulness practice figures prominently in developing acceptance and in facilitating values-driven behavior over time.

Pediatric Primary Care

An essential first step toward integrating ACT and other third-wave behavior therapies into pediatric primary care is to develop an understanding of the mission of primary care, the nature of services offered, the providers who offer them, and the barriers to integrating behavioral services. This section provides a brief introduction to these topics, and readers may want to consult other sources for more in-depth information (e.g., Robinson & Reiter, 2007; Strosahl & Robinson, 2007; Gatchel & Oordt, 2003).

The Mission of Primary Care

In 1996, the Institute of Medicine of the National Academies proposed the following definition of primary care: "Primary care is the provision of integrated, accessible health care services by clinicians who are accountable for addressing a large majority of personal health care needs, developing a sustained partnership with patients and practicing in the context of family and community" (Donaldson, Yordy, Lohr, & Vanselow, 1996, p. 32). This comprehensive definition suggests that primary care is the foundation for health care delivery and emphasizes the critical role of strong provider-patient relationships. Pediatric primary care is directed toward children, adolescents, and their families. The purpose or mission is to prevent illness and to maintain health for pediatric patients from birth to their entrance into adulthood. This necessarily means that the pediatric primary care provider is concerned also with the health of the families and communities that support the youngest members of society.

Pediatric Primary Care Services

In most communities throughout the United States, primary care is the child's first point of entry into the health care system and is the continuing focal point for health care services throughout adulthood. Patients receive a gamut of services in primary care, including well-child examinations, immunizations, health promotion and disease prevention, counseling, patient and parent education, and diagnosis and treatment of acute and chronic illnesses. Many of these patient-provider visit contexts are fertile ground for improving the health of children in general, particularly when medical and behavioral care are integrated and behavioral technology is applied to system issues.

The Pediatric Primary Care Team

A team of providers and staff members deliver primary care services. Members of the pediatric primary care team include pediatricians, family medicine physicians, and midlevel providers, such as nurse practitioners or physician assistants. When psychologists work in primary care, they are members of the primary care provider group. Pediatric primary care staff members include nurses and nursing assistants. In a single visit, patients typically receive services from two or three team members. Patients access team services in a variety of settings, including solo practices and clinics with multiple providers such as those found in some health maintenance organizations and in community health centers.

Challenges to Integrating Behavioral Health Services into Primary Care

Delivery of pediatric primary care services typically involves brief interactions, ranging between five and thirty minutes in length. Today pediatric primary care providers need to complete around thirty encounters per day with children and adolescents to make their practice financially sustainable. Since they typically schedule patients for 90 percent of their time in clinic, they are involved with direct patient care services 432 minutes or 7.2 hours in an eight-hour workday. Assuming contact with an average of thirty patients per day, the typical work pace allows the provider about fourteen minutes to welcome, diagnosis, treat, educate, and counsel each patient, as well as complete chart notes, make out lab orders, and write or transmit prescriptions.

In addition to the push for productivity, pediatric primary care providers struggle to meet the expectations of parents who have come to expect a "pneumonia-antibiotic" cure for numerous problems. "He's driving me crazy. Do you think he should be on medication?" "She stays in her room and won't do her chores. Do you think an antidepressant would help?" "He won't go to bed. Can you give him something for sleep?" Pediatric primary care is philosophically dedicated to the biopsychosocial model; however, the collision of time constraints with a "miracle medicine" approach pushes both patient and provider toward biomedical rather than biopsychosocial interactions.

The stress for patients and providers is palpable, and the result all too often is the development of a plan that might end the interaction in an amicable way but not support the child and family members in long-term health behavior change. Instead families may develop patterns of experiential avoidance that involve interactions with medical providers. Vulnerable families often have a variety of problems such as somatisizing or medically ill relatives, a family history of substance abuse problems or domestic violence, strained parent-child relationships, and intergenerational problems with depression and anxiety. Such high-risk families may further exhibit elevated illness behavior and present with vague physical complaints that primary care providers feel compelled to evaluate. Parents, in turn, may pursue additional visits for their child, and the provider continues to explore all medical possibilities. This unhappy series of events may go on for years.

The Primary Care Behavioral Health Model and ACT

In the 1990s, researchers began to look at models of integrated care that defined the behaviorist as a consultative member of the primary care team (Strosahl, 1997, 1998; Robinson, Wischman, & Del Vento, 1996). This model came to be known as the primary care behavioral health (PCBH) model. From its perspective of high-level integration, the primary customer for the behaviorist was the primary care provider rather than the patient. By consulting with patients in brief twenty- to thirty-minute contacts and teaching providers the key concepts and common interventions, the behaviorist began to experience more success in meeting the demand for behavioral services among primary care patients. ACT strategies figured prominently in these early efforts (see, for example, Robinson, 1996), and the term "acceptance and commitment therapy in primary care" (ACT-PC) was developed to represent the translation of core ACT strategies for use in primary care. This translation made ACT strategies more transparent to nonbehavioral primary care providers and fitted them to the time demands of primary care. Early studies suggested that the PCBH model was associated with better clinical outcomes, cost effectiveness, and patient satisfaction (Katon et al., 1996); thus the move to integrate gained momentum and spread from staff-model health maintenance organizations to the military and community health centers across the United States. The PCBH model quickly became the gold standard for integrating services (Strosahl & Robinson, 2007; Strosahl, 1996a, 1996b; Gatchel & Oordt, 2003). Its mission was not merely to provide direct patient care but also to improve the delivery of health care within the primary care system by empowering primary care providers to deliver effective behavioral interventions.

When working in the PCBH model, the behaviorist is commonly called a behavioral health consultant (BHC), as this term places appropriate emphasis on the consultative nature of clinical practice and provides an ongoing reminder of this for the behaviorist and primary care providers. *Behavioral Consulting and Primary Care: A Guide to Integrating Services* (Robinson & Reiter, 2007) provides detailed information about how to initiate a BHC practice, the core competencies for working in primary care, and practical tools for adjusting practice styles to suit the requirements of the setting and for influencing the practice habits of physicians and other members of the primary care team.

ACT and other contextual psychotherapies are particularly well suited to primary care practice (see Robinson & Reiter, 2007). The underpinnings of ACT fit well with the PCBH model philosophy, which directs attention to patient functioning rather than diagnosis. ACT principles and strategies are also empowering to system-level changes needed in primary care, as experiential avoidance and cognitive fusion figure prominently in unnecessary and costly use of services among some patients and underutilization of needed care among other patient groups (see Robinson & Hayes, 1997).

Several examples will provide readers with a taste for the ongoing process of experiential avoidance among pediatric patients and families who overutilize and underutilize care. Families that tend to somaticize psychological distress are often a high-utilizing and dissatisfied group of patients in primary care. Beginning early in life, children may learn to express psychological distress through somatic complaints. Their parents may then express concern about possible ("dangerous") physical explanations for unpleasant internal events. With these vulnerable patients, headache pain can lead providers to repeat costly scans and multiple medication trials, which are often associated with report of more side effects than beneficial effects. At the other end of the continuum, obese parents with overweight babies may avoid the early well-child examinations during the first year of life in order to avoid negative evaluation and reprimands from health care professionals. These parents, for example, may fear that the visit will be distressing and devoid of acceptance of what they've come to do (e.g., overfeed their babies in an effort to lower their babies' and their own distress).

ACT-PC offers a translation of core ACT strategies to support their use by BHCs and primary care providers who necessarily have more brief interactions with patients. While ACT developed originally in the context of hourlong patient contexts, the basic principles and strategies do not necessarily require extensive periods of contact or an ongoing relationship between the patient and provider. There is no evidence to suggest that an ordering of ACT strategies is an important aspect of treatment, and not all primary care patients need to experience all of the ACT core strategies in an episode of care. ACT-PC supports the BHC in choosing what seems to fit the patient's needs *and* the amount of time available for the interaction, whether that's five minutes or thirty minutes. In fact, there is an emphasis on using ACT interventions that are suited to ten-minute contacts, as these are the ones that physicians are most likely to learn and use with patients who are not referred for BHC services. Often it works best for a BHC or medical provider to suggest an ACT exercise to patients and recommend that they experiment with it or implement it with a trusted friend or relative. We use educational handouts extensively and have found that pictorial representations of ACT concepts are often well received by pediatric patients, their families, and their primary care providers. Examples of pictorial representations used to deliver ACT interventions and to teach primary care providers are presented later in this chapter.

ACT-PC encourages other changes to the ACT protocol to make it feasible in the primary care environment. For example, the patient's agreement to an exposure-based treatment is not solicited, and instead the possibility of additional discomfort is simply mentioned at the beginning of the consult as a part of introducing the service to the referred patient. Here's a sample introduction:

> *Hello. I am Dr. Jones, and I help the other doctors in this clinic help their patients. My expertise is in helping children and families find ways to improve their health and the quality of their lives. Today we'll look at the problem that your doctor wants us to explore. After ten or fifteen minutes of talking together, I'll probably offer a few recommendations for you and your doctor. What you do with the ideas I give you is really up to you. Your life experience probably tells you that short-term solutions to problems may not work in the long run, and many changes we make to improve the quality of our lives cause us discomfort.*

Finally, ACT-PC suggests ways to infuse ACT concepts into health care programs that focus on populations of patients and various aspects of the health care system. The next section suggests guidelines for practicing in the PCBH model and using ACT-PC methods.

Guidelines for Working in the PCBH Model and Using ACT-PC Methods

Three important guidelines for implementing ACT-PC are to: (1) provide the most potent behavioral interventions to as many patients as possible at the time of need, (2) adopt a consultative role where the primary care provider is the primary consumer of BHC services, and (3) view work activities from the lenses of a population-based health care provider rather than the traditional case-focused point of view.

Deliver Evidence-Based Care to Patients at the Time of Need

The PCBH model defines the BHC as a generalist who "takes all comers." This means that the BHC's workday may include the youngest patient in a clinic and the oldest. This requirement may be stressful for BHCs whose training has emphasized one age group to the exclusion of others. More important than mastery of empirically supported treatments for all possible conditions and age groups is the BHC's commitment to learning from primary care colleagues and to learning about evidence-based approaches "on the fly," as is characteristic of working in primary care settings.

The need for behavioral services is huge in the primary care setting, so the BHC needs to make changes to practice style that support extension of services to as many patients and families as possible. Challenging and necessary shifts in practice style include brief visits with a limited focus, fewer planned follow-up visits, and reliance on the primary care provider for ongoing support of behavior change plans. The BHC typically sees patients for fifteen to thirty minutes. In a typical eight-hour day of practice, the BHC will see twelve to fifteen patients. On days when the BHC sees patients in the context of group visits, this number may soar to thirty or forty contacts, all of which are charted. On average, the BHC sees patients for two or three follow-ups. However, more intensive contact is possible through group or class services for specific populations, such as for overweight children or pregnant women with gestational diabetes.

Rather than conduct a typical diagnosis-focused interview that includes an extensive psychosocial interview, the BHC limits exploration to the referral problem identified by the provider and patient. For example, a primary care provider might refer a teenager for a consultation concerning school attendance, and the BHC might discover that the patient is smoking cigarettes. To remain on time and to honor the primacy of patient-provider relationship, the BHC needs to focus on school attendance. However, the BHC could chart a recommendation that the provider address the smoking with the patient and perhaps refer the patient for a consultation targeting that particular health-risk behavior.

Use of an interview template (see figure 1) may help the BHC to complete a functional analysis of the referral problem and evaluate the workability of the patient's current coping strategies efficiently. Related to staying on time and ready for same-day referrals requires not only time-effective interviewing, but also a willingness to pass the patient back to the provider for ongoing support as soon as possible. Without the ability to translate ACT and other behavioral interventions to user-friendly formats for physicians and staff, the BHC will fall into the trap of seeing patients back more often, perhaps eliminating same-day slots in the BHC's schedule.

Figure 1. Interview Template for Initial Behavioral Health Consult Visit

Primary Care Provider:

Functional Analysis of Referral Problem/Question/Concern:

Target Behavior (frequency, duration): **Antecedents**: **Consequences:**

Avoided Feelings/Thoughts/Sensations:

Avoidance Strategies (include short- and long-term results):

1.

2.

Important Life Values:

Workability of Avoidance Strategies in Light of Valued Directions:

Mindfulness Skills:

Healthy Lifestyle Behaviors:

-Family -Friends

-School/Grades -Work/Career Direction

-Sleep/Exercise -Drugs/Alcohol/Misuse of Food

Plan: (For example: Patient will practice Clouds in the Sky Exercise with his mother on a daily basis.)

Recommendations:

To patient/family: (For example: Family will practice Pass the Heart game to increase values focus in weekly family meetings.)

To primary care provider: (For example: Please inquire about and support patient and family use of recommended exercises/games in follow-up with you in two weeks.)

Many new BHCs find it difficult to complete care with patients in four contacts or less on average. Therefore the BHC needs to monitor this statistic and use it to evaluate and shape his or her practice. While some high-risk patients do warrant more than three follow-ups, many benefit from single consults or an initial consult with a single follow-up. A single visit focused on learning the use of a specific skill (such as mindfulness) with a troubling situation (such as a child's regression in toileting skills after a period of separation from the parents) may be all that is needed. As a rule, the BHC invites the patient to return only if further intervention is needed. Otherwise, like the medical provider, the BHC simply encourages the patient to return in the future if the need arises.

Assume a Consultative Role

In primary care, the role of the BHC is that of a consultant. This requires the BHC to recognize and consistently honor the primacy of the relationship between the provider and the patient and the patient's family. This relationship often started at birth, as many family medicine providers deliver babies. Thus the primary care provider often has a wealth of information about the patient and family, and the BHC is wise to acknowledge and use this information. Most families tend to accept the provider's recommendation of involving the BHC temporarily in their care. Families appear most receptive when primary care providers make the referral by asking the child and parent to see another member of the primary care team whose area of expertise is that of behavior change.

As a consultant, the BHC provides recommendations to both patients and the pediatric primary care provider. One of the more interesting challenges of being a BHC is finding ways to communicate recommendations (including ACT interventions) so that they are transparent and have the depth necessary for the provider to understand how to adjust the intervention for a wide range of current and future patients. For example, a BHC might teach a socially anxious seventh-grader to hold her various thoughts (about her social skills, attractiveness, etc.) as she might hold vegetables in a bowl of soup and to: (1) simply watch them as they float, (2) notice how her mind evaluates them (thinking that I'm pretty is a "good thought"; potatoes are "nice"; noticing that my voice is shaky is "bad"; okra is "awful"), and (3) allow the soup/mind to be what it is without retreating from a planned social interaction. To attain a balance between the transparency requirement and the need for depth, the BHC needs to offer a variety of educational opportunities for primary care providers. These instructive interactions, of course, begin with providing specific yet brief feedback concerning the referred patient. Ideally this feedback is given on the day the patient is referred and seen by the BHC, as this is the most teachable moment for the provider.

The BHC can also use chart notes to communicate recommendations and to teach primary care providers about ACT interventions. The SOAP format—subjective objective assessment plan—is common in primary care, and the BHC should use this format as a starting point and limit the length of the note to one page. Brevity helps assure that the provider will read the note. Specificity in the "plan" section improves the provider's ability to support and thus amplify the impact of the intervention initiated by the BHC. Figure 2 provides an example of a SOAP note.

Figure 2. An Example of a SOAP Note

Subjective: Dr. Ramos-Diaz refers this eight-year-old male Latino for a consultation concerning sleep problems and symptoms of traumatic stress. Six days ago, patient was accidentally struck in the back by a poorly aimed taser gun fired by a security officer in a dance hall. Patient was playing with his older brother at a table near the exit while his parents were dancing. He was taken to the hospital for emergency care and is now recovered physically. Since the accident, patient is hypervigilant when away from home and becomes distressed when he sees security or police officers. Sleep onset is slow. Patient reports waking up nightly with bad dreams, some of which are about the accident. Patient doesn't want to talk about the accident and has missed two days of school since the accident due to stomachaches and "just feeling bad." Patient is an above-average student who likes school and seeing his friends. He gets along well with his parents, brother, teachers, and friends. He has asthma.

Objective: Patient's mother completed the Pediatric Symptom Checklist today; total score of 21 suggests significant psychosocial dysfunction. Patient played with toys throughout the visit and limited responses to questions about the accident to nodding his head.

Assessment/Plan: Sleep problems, traumatic stress symptoms. Patient and his mother learned the Past-Present-Future Exercise to enhance skills for experiencing the present moment and the Rag Doll Relaxation Exercise to decrease hypervigilance. They will practice these exercises several times daily. At bedtime, they will practice the Rag Doll procedure, and the mother will provide light massage to patient's back if requested. Recommend that Dr. Ramos-Diaz see patient in one week and support his consistent attendance of school, even with stomachaches.

Many medical providers will ask for an explanation concerning specific interventions mentioned in chart notes. Still, it is often useful for the BHC to provide additional training so providers learn to apply behavioral technology flexibly in their patient interactions. Additional potential venues for sharing ACT and other behavioral techniques with providers include lunch-hour presentations and provision of written materials. Most pediatric physicians will welcome one-page newsletters that provide further explanation and examples of frequently used interventions, and many will read short chapters on ACT. Once versed in the basics, primary care providers may become a source of new metaphors that are particularly well suited to the practice context. Training programs that offer experiential opportunities in ACT may deepen primary care provider and staff understanding of ACT concepts and enhance their ability to use ACT strategies.

Practice in a Population Health Model

The principles of population-based care underlie much of the rationale for the PCBH model, and most are new to BHCs who enter the primary care setting. The case model that is typical of traditional mental health treatment has different goals from the population health model. Population-based care facilitates a systematic approach to preventive and acute care, as well as to the growing problem of chronic disease management (Lipkin & Lybrand, 1982). Interventions based on this model might, for example, direct providers to use a screening procedure to better identify members of a population (e.g., six- to twelve-year-old children with ADHD) with a certain problem (behavior problems at home and in school) for referral to the BHC for delivery of a specific intervention protocol. Alternatively, a population health program might call for dissemination of educational information (e.g., health risks of alcohol and drug use, use of seat belts) to a population (teenagers), in hopes of lowering the incidence of related medical problems (motor-vehicle injuries). Programs for high-impact problems (such as relationship problems between teenagers with attention deficit disorder and conduct disorder and their parents) also benefit from a population focus.

The hallmark of population-based care is an approach of making a limited number of services available to many members of the population rather than providing intensive services to a select few. While intensive specialty interventions offer significant help to a small number of identified individuals, the majority of individuals needing help in the population go unidentified and/or underserved. These individuals, in turn, increase the health burden on the population and use up valuable health care resources. Population-based approaches thus attempt to reach more members of the population, if in a more limited manner, in hopes that small improvements in many may lift the overall health of the population. In a very fundamental way, the approach seeks to use available research to design optimal methods for using limited health care resources to benefit as much of the population as possible.

An ACT-PC population program can often be incorporated into a "clinical pathway," which provides specific instructions to providers concerning the specific target population. Robinson (2005) suggests a template for design of population-based care initiatives concerning common problems in primary care, and provides an example of applying such to the problem of depression in primary care (Robinson, 2003). *Behavioral Health as Primary Care: Beyond Efficacy to Effectiveness* (Cummings, O'Donohue, & Ferguson, 2003) also offers helpful information on this topic, and Rivo (1998) offers a concise summary of population care.

ACT-PC Consultation Services for Patients and Families

I conclude this chapter with suggestions for developing and sustaining a focus on a specific pediatric primary care population. ACT strategies and concepts have the potential for improving outcomes for children, their families, and pediatric providers. Technologies suggested by ACT, however, need to be adapted and applied in ways that respect the time constraints and the varying interest levels among providers. This list offers six principles to help BHCs be imaginative and effective in their use of ACT in primary care. The following principles may be used for creating and applying ACT materials in pediatric primary care:

1. Develop materials that have broad applicability.
2. Develop materials that are portable.
3. Develop materials that can be explained and used in less than fifteen minutes.
4. Develop materials that make ACT interventions transparent for providers.
5. Develop materials that work in individual and group settings.
6. Measure concepts that reflect the ACT perspective and that are feasible for the setting.

One or more examples are offered below to illustrate each of the principles. The best pediatric primary care variations of ACT come from collaborative efforts between BHCs and pediatric providers, and the examples offered in this section grew out of teamwork.

Develop Materials with Broad Applicability

There is precious little time in primary care, and using separate handouts for every possible presenting complaint will impede the BHC's effort to stay current and be present in a busy schedule. Primary care providers are also more likely to use a few handouts that are all encompassing. We have created the Human Shell and the Castle handout to meet this criterion (see exercise 1). Predrawn handouts may support pictorial approaches, and most of the ACT core processes can be taught to providers and patients with the support of the picture. The following explanation of how to use the Human Shell and the Castle comes from a dialogue with a ten-year-old boy:

> *Okay. Let's pretend that this guy's name is Swallow [the name of the child's favorite video game character]. Like you, he has all these thoughts in his head that he doesn't like that much. Let's write them here [in section I: Unwanted*

Thoughts and Feelings]. What do you think Swallow does when he's thinking these thoughts? [This request seeks to define the child's experiential avoidance moves.] Let's write these down here [in section II: Ways to Avoid: Work?/Cost?]. We'll talk about these in a minute—try to figure out if they work the way you want them to.

Now, let's look at the Castle of the Mind, Body, and Spirit. This is the kind of castle where the very best hopes and dreams live. They are the really important things in life—like having friends, getting along with your family, learning, exploring. What do you think belongs in the castle for you and Swallow? Let's write these here [in section III: Castle of the Mind, Body, and Spirit.)

Now let's look at this path and think of it as the road that Swallow wants to take to the castle. Sometimes some of the things up here in this box [II. Ways to Avoid] pop up and block the road. Let's look at each of these and decide if they do this for you. Does doing X work for Swallow in the short term, like for five or ten minutes? What is the cost of doing this in the long term? [BHC continues to make notes about the patient's responses for each item that could block the road and then summarizes the short- and long-term effectiveness of each.]

Well, it looks like a mixed situation here [as it is usually the case that some types of avoidance work and some do not]. When the situation is like this, it's hard for Swallow to travel toward the castle. He gets trapped by some of the things in the roadblock and may not keep trying to get to the castle. I have an idea. Let's draw a circle around everything, because it's all more or less you—the boy, the road, the roadblock, and the castle. [BHC draws a circle around the entire graphic.] Then I'll tell you what lessons I think might help you and Swallow stay on the road to the castle even with the yucky thoughts, feelings, and roadblocks. We will write them here at the bottom of the page, and I'll teach you one lesson today.

The BHC can adjust the specifics in the story to the child. If possible, the BHC can use a favorite character to increase children's willingness to experience and explore unwanted private events. The BHC can also name the exercise so that it fits the child. Possible examples include the Courageous Child, the Brave Boy, and You Go Girl.

A variation of the Human Shell and the Castle is the Child with a Crown Exercise (see exercise 2). The pictorial support is simply a human form with a crown. The BHC can begin by suggesting to the child that the crown has jewels that can serve as guides for the child. The jewels can help guide the child in visualizing what he or she wants to be like at school and at home in his or her best moments. The BHC can write down words or phrases that represent the jewels in section I, "What are the jewels in my crown?" Then, the BHC can help the child verbalize what he or she has inside his or her head, what thoughts and feelings he or she wants to get rid of or ignore. The BHC records the child's responses in section II, "What are the thoughts and feelings that I

Exercise 1. The Human Shell and the Castle

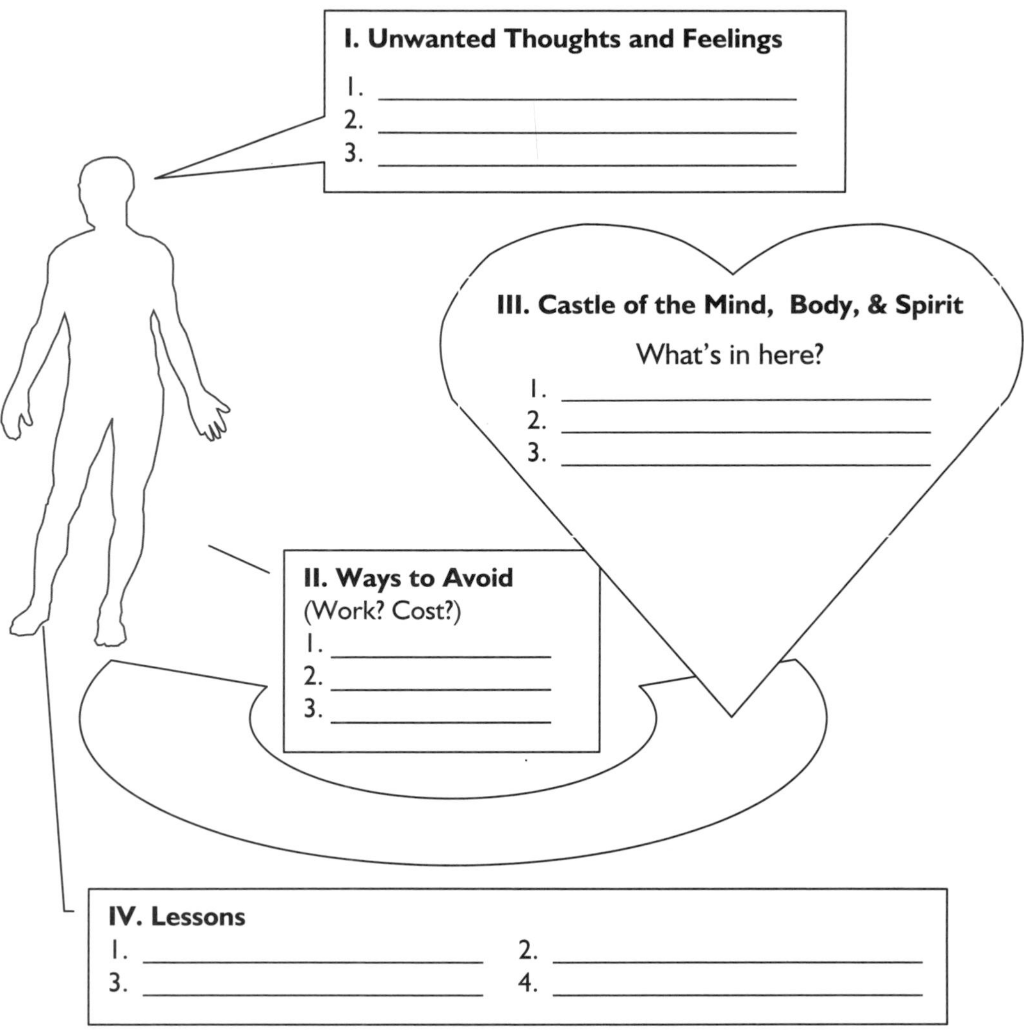

don't like?" If time allows, the BHC can move the child into responding to section III, "How do I try to avoid them?" and perhaps engage the child in a discussion of how control works sometimes and not other times (like when one tries to hold an ice cube and keep it from melting).

The BHC may also use a willingness strategy to help the child develop more willingness and acceptance of unwanted private events. For example, the BHC might suggest that the child and BHC take a thought or image from the head and hold it gently in their hands, watching to see how the hands feel about this … and the heart and head as well. In such a willingness exercise, the BHC and child can take turns sharing their current thoughts and feelings about the "thought in the hands." The BHC might also engage the child in a discussion about what might help the child make the jewels shine

Exercise 2. Child with a Crown

I. What are the jewels in my crown?

1. ______________________________
2. ______________________________
3. ______________________________

II. What are the thoughts and feelings I don't like?
1. ______________________________
2. ______________________________
3. ______________________________
III. How do I try to avoid them?
1. ______________________________
2. ______________________________
3. ______________________________

IV. How can I make the jewels in my crown shine?

1. ______________________________
2. ______________________________
3. ______________________________

more brightly every day (and note responses in section IV, "How can I make the jewels in my crown shine"). As with the Human Shell and the Castle, the BHC can draw a circle around the child, the unwanted private events, and the lessons (or skills the child agrees to learn) as a way of modeling acceptance.

Develop Materials That Are Portable

Handouts may support primary care providers in learning and applying ACT consistently. Nonetheless, handouts can also slow work flow. BHCs are in and out of exam rooms quickly with same-day patients and may not always have ready access to handouts. Likewise, providers may not take time or remember to use handouts with children who may benefit from psychological intervention. When possible, it is best to design materials to support ACT interventions in a way that they can be created with available materials in the place of care at the moment of need. For example, the Human Shell and the Castle and the Child with a Crown can be drawn out on a paper exam room table cover or a prescription pad. Drawing these materials offers the provider an opportunity to engage the child by having him or her decide on drawing details (e.g., how tall, what facial expression, and what kind of hair).

Additionally, the BHC and primary care provider can use exam room materials to demonstrate important concepts to patients. For example, a BHC might draw a person with their nose on a computer to demonstrate the concept of fusion to an adolescent who is expressing anger in problematic ways. The BHC can ask the patient what the computer screen might say when he's ready to punch another student at school. After teaching a defusion technique, the BHC can draw a picture of the child carrying an open laptop with his or her response to the above question written on the screen. These pictorial teaching aids can be given to patients as reminders of what to practice between clinic visits. Pictorial aids can also be used to brief providers so that they are ready to support the intervention used by the BHC.

Develop Materials Consistent with the Fifteen-Minute Rule

In the initial visit, the BHC has about ten minutes for contextual interviewing and fifteen minutes for conducting a functional analysis and developing an intervention. The purpose of contextual interviewing is to obtain a slice of patients' lives to understand their basic predicament. This involves questions about where they live and with whom, where they attend school and what their experience is there, what they enjoy doing in their free time, their experience with friends, and their repertoire of health protective behaviors. When pushed for time, the BHC may forgo the part of the visit devoted to contextual interviewing and go directly to the functional analysis and intervention. In follow-up sessions, the BHC typically sees the patient for fifteen or twenty minutes rather than thirty. Therefore all ACT materials need to be capable of being used in less than fifteen minutes. It is also wise to develop a five-minute supplementary version, as these are more likely to be implemented by providers.

The Pediatric Bull's-Eye–Primary Care (see figure 3) is an example of an ACT intervention that incorporates the functional analysis and an intervention and for which a five-minute version for the primary care provider is possible (see Lundgren & Robinson, 2007). This is a very versatile approach and can be used with parents as easily as with children and teenagers. In this approach, the BHC draws a bull's-eye (or, alternatively, uses a predrawn form similar to that in figure 3) and explains that the center of the dartboard represents the child's most cherished dream. After making a few notes about what that is, the BHC asks the child or adolescent to indicate what sorts of things make his or her darts fall short of the bull's-eye and notes these, for example, on arrows or darts that curve away from the dartboard. Then the BHC can engage the patient in setting one to three goals that are recorded on the straight arrows directed toward the dartboard. This approach can help the patient monitor progress and provide continuity in care when the patient and family check back with the pediatric primary care provider. The following dialogue demonstrates the use of the Pediatric Bull's-Eye with a seven-year-old girl who was afraid to sleep in her own bed after having watched a horror movie:

BHC: Have you ever seen a dartboard? It looks kind of like this—a group of circles, one larger than the other. The center is called the bull's-eye, and it is the part of the dartboard that brings the most points when you are playing a game of darts. Let's pretend that the center of the dartboard represents your most cherished experiences and dreams in life. What do you really, really care about?

Child: Well, I want to be good at numbers.

BHC: Okay, I'll write that down here. What else matters a lot to you—like maybe something that would fit in the circle just outside of the middle?

Child: Having friends?

BHC: That sounds pretty important to me. I'll write it here.

The BHC can continue in this direction in an effort to identify three or four values. Then, the BHC can ask the child to identify one that he or she wants to pursue at this time. This particular patient chose "being good at numbers."

BHC: Okay, so "being good at numbers" is our direction for now. What do you think makes you curve away from the dartboard?

Child: I don't throw them good? Or maybe there's something wrong with the dart.

BHC: Wonder why?

Child: I'm not very strong, and I get tired.

BHC: How come?

Child: I don't sleep well 'cause I'm scared of monsters.

BHC: Monsters are scary. What do you do when you think of monsters?

Child: I go to Mom's room, but she just puts me back in bed.

BHC: It must be hard to stay in your bed and relax when you're thinking of monsters.

Child: It is. It's awful. I can't do it, so I go sleep on the floor by Mom's door. But then I get scared there too.

The BHC is then in the position to pursue more details about the monsters and the workability of avoidance strategies. Rather quickly, the BHC can ask, "Are you willing to learn how to be afraid of monsters so that you can be better at numbers?" Given the child's willingness, the BHC can help the child develop new skills that will help her change the function of images of monsters at night. For example, the BHC might suggest that monsters sometimes need help settling down and then enlist the child in identifying ways she could help the monsters to be quiet and calm and sleep through the night. Would the child sing to them or offer a blanket? Or perhaps the child would give a simple "Shhh … quiet time …" and then softly hum her favorite nighttime tune. While the BHC may have time to identify three values, three avoidance strategies, and a goal, the busy medical provider might simplify by identifying one value, one avoidance strategy, and one goal. In both circumstances, the provider would teach some type of skill that would help the patient move in the direction of getting more rest and doing well at school.

Figure 5. Pediatric Bull's-Eye–Primary Care

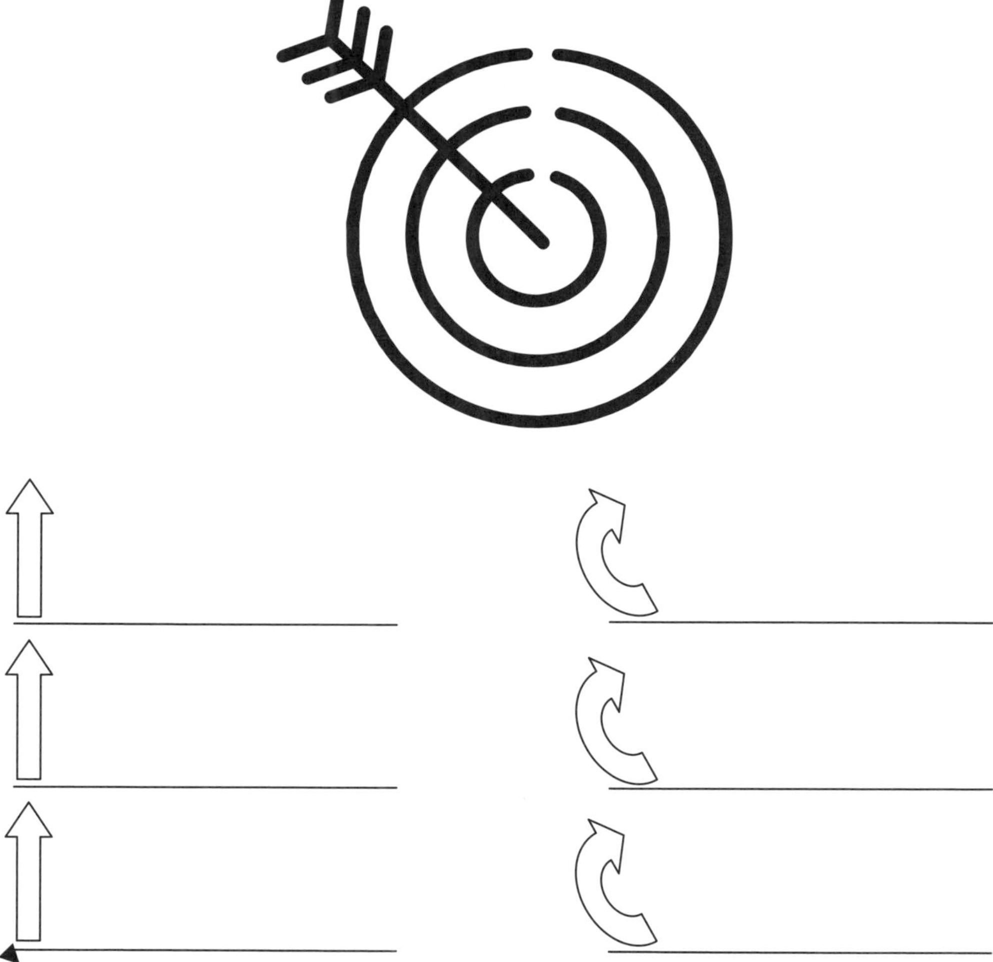

Develop Materials That Are Transparent

Making ACT interventions transparent requires a great deal of mastery over ACT concepts and an understanding of pediatric primary care providers. The idea is to take the core processes and make them user-friendly to providers. A brief list of the core processes with illustrative examples makes the processes comprehensible and encourages the provider toward additional originality. An example of this is a primary care provider who adapted the Human Shell and the Castle for use with adolescents by suggesting that the adolescents pack a travel bag with the tools they need for pursuing the castle. Elegant descriptions and pointed yet brief interventions encourage providers to play with the concepts and extend them further. In response to the provider's innovation, the BHC developed a list of potential dart tools to use in a dart bag with the Bull's-Eye pictorial. This list embodies most of the core concepts in ACT:

- **The Basket of Darts** can serve as a metaphor for teaching the patient and family members about the concept of willingness and the role it plays in living an intentional life. The Willingness Basket holds a variety of darts that help a patient recognize avoidance patterns, develop the observer self, learn to be present, clarify values, and choose valued directions.

- **The Here-and-Now Dart** can serve as an anchor that helps the child discriminate between control strategies and willingness. In using the here-and-now dart, the child learns to breathe in and out with the intention to be present in the here and now.

- **The Jewel Dart** is used to represent values clarification work. When fusion and avoidance patterns emerge during the course of daily living, the patient and family can learn to ask questions such as "What value do I choose to direct me right now?"

- **The I'm-Watching-You Dart** relates to the skills of accepting unpleasant and even painful internal events that are experienced during planned exposure tasks. The idea is to teach the patient and family members to hold these difficult experiences gently, like they might hold a frightened puppy, and maintain the planned direction of behavior.

- **The Banana-Is-a-Dart Dart** can help the BHC teach fusion and defusion. The idea is that thoughts and feelings can tug on a dart so hard that the dart thrower forgets that he or she has a dart. The BHC can also bring up the idea of following unquestioned rules ("step on a crack and break your mother's back") versus tuning into one's experience. Patients learn that a thought is a thought—a group of words. Thoughts don't always help us keep an eye on the road of life, and we need to notice when this happens. Rules we learn accidentally (e.g., "a banana is a dart") may not help us make the throws we could if we believed them less. Sometimes the only way out of the troubling situation is to pay close attention to one's direct experience. It is possible to pick up a dart and make a directed throw, even while thinking "a banana is a dart."

- **The In-a-Driving-Rain Dart** represents committed action. The BHC can explain that sometimes dart throwing is very, very difficult. Then the BHC can help the patient and family identify ways to keep a focus on the dartboard and on throwing even when the rain is pouring down and the water is stinging one's eyes.

Develop Materials That Can Be Used with Individuals and Groups

Given the importance of maintaining a population-based care focus in primary care, groups and classes eventually play an important role in a BHC practice. Initially the BHC focuses on seeing "all comers," but then quickly expands practice to include collaboratively developed pathways that specify a population and actions to be taken with members of that population. These actions may include patient participation in a class or group led by the BHC. For example, a pathway might suggest that providers refer pediatric patients with diabetes and their parents to a monthly support group and education class taught by the BHC. Alternatively, the BHC might colead a monthly class with a primary care provider for the purpose of offering group medical care to patients in that provider's panel. In the class, ACT interventions such as mindfulness could be delivered to improve focus and concentration, along with evaluation of benefits and side effects of medications. Groups or classes offer an excellent opportunity for providers to learn more of the BHC's tools of the trade, and they are most encouraged to learn when there is an overlap between materials and methods used in individual consults and in the context of group visits. The Bull's-Eye approach, for example, works well with individual children or adolescents, parents, family groups, and groups of patients unknown to each other.

Measure ACT Concepts Using Feasible Instruments

Measurement is no less important in primary care than it is in specialty care. The overriding rule in primary care is that measurement needs to be feasible. This translates to no more than five minutes for a nursing assistant to administer and score measures. Brief measures of health-related quality of life may be consistent with the mission of PCBH and sensitive to ACT treatment. Whatever the choice of measures, it is important that they be obtained in all BHC visits so that comparisons are possible. When patients make progress, the BHC needs to return the patient to the primary care provider for ongoing support of gains in functioning.

ACT-PC Population Health Programs

As mentioned previously, population-based health care provides a central focus in the work of the BHC. Following are eight guidelines for developing ACT-PC programs with a population focus:

1. Form a group of colleagues who have a common concern about a population of children, youth, or families.
2. Describe the population of concern and the current health care approach to the population.
3. Describe potential ACT processes that influence health issues for the target population and identify ACT strategies that might improve health outcomes.
4. Design a method for systematically identifying members of the target populations.
5. Select method for tracking identified members of the target population and for assessing outcomes.
6. Use selected measures to assess outcomes of current practices with a sample drawn from the target population.
7. Design an ACT-PC intervention based on current laboratory and clinical evidence that is feasible in the particular clinic setting and that is likely to represent a better use of health care resources.
8. Implement and monitor outcomes while continuing to make changes as needed.

In this section, the issue of prevention of childhood obesity is used to illustrate the use of these steps in creating a program. This problem was selected because it has high impact and is a strong concern for most pediatric providers.

Children and adolescents who exceed the 95th percentile of body mass index (BMI) for their age are considered to be obese (Ogden, Flegal, Carroll, & Johnson, 2002). In 2004, the President's Council on Physical Fitness and Sports reported that over 15 percent of all children and adolescents were obese, which was approximately nine million young people. Further, 10 percent of children two to five years old were overweight. These numbers are almost triple the number of obese children and adolescents identified twenty-five years ago (Ogden et al., 2002).

Obese children are at greater risk of being obese through adolescence and adulthood. Obese children are at risk for numerous health problems including cardiovascular disease, stroke, renal difficulties, limb loss, and blindness (Hannon, Rao, & Arslanian, 2005), and for lowered quality of life and psychosocial functioning (Williams, Wake, Hesketh, Maher, & Waters, 2005). Pediatric diabetes centers in North America have reported an alarming increase in the prevalence of type 2 diabetes, which is related to increases in childhood obesity (Botero & Wolfsdorf, 2005). Attempts to prevent childhood obesity are urgently needed, as they may improve the health of many children and decrease the costs of treating multiple medical problems related to obesity (Wilson, 1994; Yanovski & Yanovski, 2003).

Prevention of Childhood Obesity

In this section, I describe eight steps for delivering and evaluating ACT-consistent care in a primary care setting. The model described below is broadly applicable; however, childhood obesity is used as an example given its high public health relevance.

Step 1: Form a group of colleagues who have a common concern. The above brief literature review on obesity and a reference list was distributed to providers in a clinic in Washington State (Yakima Valley Farm Workers Clinic, a large clinic in a rural area) where I provide BHC services. In addition, a request was made for those with strong interest to sign up for membership in a Clinic Childhood Obesity Prevention (C-COP) committee. Two pediatricians, two nurses, and the BHC indicated an interest in being members of the C-COP committee. One of the nurses, the director of nursing for the clinic, agreed to chair the committee.

Step 2: Describe population of concern and current approach to the population. After forming the C-COP committee, we used clinical experience and empirical research to develop criteria for inclusion in our high-risk group. We considered parent characteristics such as age, gender, race, and health-risk behavior. We also developed a survey to define the services that members of the targeted population typically receive. The resulting decision was to define the high-risk population in the following way:

> *Mothers who bring a child to a twelve-month well-child physical and screen positive on two or more of the following risk factors for being the parent of an obese child: (1) racial or ethnic identification as Hispanic or African American; (2) overweight before pregnancy with twelve-month-old child; (3) smoking cigarettes during pregnancy or currently; (4) working more than ten hours per week on average during the twelve-month-old child's first year of life; and (5) breastfed twelve-month-old baby for less than two months.*

We don't know how well these risks factors predict identification of new child obesity cases prospectively; however, the literature suggests that these factors will help identify mothers who need support and coaching on health issues (Salsberry & Reagan, 2005). Children may benefit from even small improvements in mothers' lifestyle behaviors, such as when mothers provide and model greater health-protection behaviors.

Survey results suggested significant variability in the amount and types of services these mothers had been receiving at our clinic. While some providers indicated asking questions beyond those required on the well-child exam physical, most did not. Few asked risk questions suggested by the literature, and most provided nutritional counseling only when the child was overweight.

Step 3: Describe relevant ACT processes and strategies. From a behavioral analytic perspective, ACT interventions may help mothers identify internal and external factors that have been conditioned to eating, overeating, and sedentary behaviors. Mothers will likely benefit from values clarification exercises concerning the quality of health and type of body they want for themselves and for their babies as they grow into early childhood and adolescence. With a focus on values and with stronger skills for being mindful and accepting of unpleasant internal events (e.g., fear of negative evaluation, shame) and external events (e.g., criticism from others, the baby's crying behavior), the mothers are likely to be more capable of interrupting the chain of overeating and sedentary behaviors (including smoking) that operate in their daily lives and make sustainable changes in the obesigenic home environments. Treatment of overweight from an ACT perspective would include a focus on the context of triggering factors (such as emotions) and the function of unhealthy behaviors (e.g., maternal overeating to self-soothe and alleviate feelings of boredom; overfeeding the child to avoid conflict and ease parent and child distress).

Step 4: Design a method for systematically identifying target population members. It is important to clarify the "how," "when," and "who" aspects of the screening and patient identification process. For our program, the method statement was as follows:

> *Nursing staff will be trained to ask and score obesity risk questions at the start of the twelve-month well-child visit. When a positive screen results, the assistant will page the BHC. The BHC will provide an initial intervention during the context of the well-child exam. The assistant will enter a chart note indicating the results of the risk assessment into the electronic medical chart and relate this finding verbally to the primary care provider.*

Step 5: Select a method for assessing and tracking outcomes. Many primary care clinics have electronic medical records that support creation of registries, which are lists of specific patient populations that support ongoing efforts to improve outcomes for that population. The C-COP committee decided to create a registry for mothers at risk for having babies who become obese during childhood. This registry allows us to track a number of important risk variables, including child and mother BMI, mother smoking, and number of hours per week the mother works. We are also charting child and mother participation in a recommended four-visit ACT-PC intervention and in annual follow-up calls from the BHC, as well as completion of several ACT-specific process measures (i.e., a two-item values clarity measure, a two-item values consistency measure, and a three-item mindfulness measure). These data would be collected as part of the patient's annual well-child exam.

Step 6: Use selected measures to assess outcomes of current practices with a sample from the target population. To obtain more information about the ACT-PC program, the committee randomly selects a small sample of patients from the target population who do not obtain the intervention. Selected measures are then administered to these patients to assess outcomes for people who received standard "treatment as usual" rather than ACT-PC. The C-COP committee decided to select twelve patients who screened positive at the twelve-month well-child exam for receiving usual care. These patients would then be assessed six months later and offered full participation in the ACT-PC intervention after assessment. This approach helped the committee obtain more information about the early impact of the intervention.

Step 7: Design an ACT-PC intervention that is feasible and likely to represent a better use of health care resources. As fusion and experiential avoidance were assumed to be present in behavior patterns related to eating, activity level, and response to stress, the four-visit intervention and the annual follow-up phone calls made by the BHC were designed to: (1) increase the parent's use of mindfulness skills, (2) increase clarity of parenting and health-related values, and (3) increase the parent's rate of engaging in behaviors consistent with her personally chosen values.

Step 8: Implement and monitor outcomes while continuing to make changes as needed. As mentioned in step 6, the C-COP committee planned to obtain measures on an annual basis at the patient's and patient's mother's visit to the clinic for the well-child exam. There was also a decision to look at costs related to care for a group of children who received one-year well-child exams in the period twelve to eighteen months just prior to the start of the new program, and to compare costs with the group who received the program during its first year. The plan was to look at costs of medical services over a five-year period to see if the cost of delivering the new service is offset by a reduction in use of medical services.

Conclusion

Primary care offers ACT therapists many opportunities for improving health outcomes for pediatric patients and their families. Services range from individual consultations to development of programs to improve care for all members of a specific pediatric population. While most children and youth never go to a specialty behavioral health service, nearly 100 percent seek services in primary care. ACT therapists who value making a difference for the many may want to consider a career in primary care. Of course, this is challenging work! The constraints of the setting translate to significant demands on the style of practice, and most new BHCs struggle with making some of the changes. However, there is a community—a growing community—of ACT therapists committed to serving children in primary care, and they are there to support and guide new providers of behavioral services.

References

Botero, D., & Wolfsdorf, J. I. (2005). Diabetes mellitus in children and adolescents. *Archives of Medical Research, 36,* 281–290.

Cummings, N., O'Donohue, W., & Ferguson, K. (Eds.). (2003). *Behavioral health as primary care: Beyond efficacy to effectiveness.* Reno, NV: Context Press.

Donaldson, M. S., Yordy, K. D., Lohr, K. N., & Vanselow, N. A. (Eds.). (1996). *Primary care: America's health in a new era.* Washington, DC: National Academies Press.

Gatchel, R. J., & Oordt, M. S. (2003). *Clinical health psychology and primary care: Practical advice and clinical guidance for successful collaboration.* Washington DC: American Psychological Association.

Hannon, T. S., Rao, G., & Arslanian, S. A. (2005). Childhood obesity and type 2 diabetes mellitus. *Pediatrics, 116,* 473–480.

Hayes, S. C., Strosahl, K. D., & Wilson, K. G. (1999). *Acceptance and commitment therapy: An experiential approach to behavior change.* New York: Guilford.

Katon, W., Robinson, P., Von Korff, M., Lin, E., Bush, T., Ludman, et al. (1996). A multifaceted intervention to improve treatment of depression in primary care. *Archives of General Psychiatry, 53,* 924–932.

Lipkin, M., & Lybrand, W. A. (Eds.). (1982). *Population-based medicine.* New York: Praeger.

Lundgren, T., & Robinson, P. (2007). *The BULLI-PC: Bringing value-driven behavior change to primary care patient education materials.* Manuscript in preparation.

Ogden, C. L., Flegal, K. M., Carroll, M. G., & Johnson, C. L. (2002). Prevalence and trends in overweight among US children and adolescents. *Journal of the American Medical Association, 288,* 1728–1732.

President's Council on Physical Fitness and Sports. (2004). Seeing ourselves through the obesity epidemic. *Research Digest, 5,* 1–8.

Rivo, M. L. (1998). It's time to start practicing population-based health care. *Family Practice Management, 5,* 37–46.

Robinson, P. (1996). *Living life well: New strategies for hard times.* Reno, NV: Context Press.

Robinson, P. (2003). Implementing a primary care depression critical pathway. In N. Cummings, W. O'Donohoe, & K. Ferguson (Eds.), *Behavioral health as primary care: Beyond efficacy to effectiveness* (pp. 69–94). Reno, NV: Context Press.

Robinson, P. (2005). Adapting empirically supported treatments to the primary care setting: A template for success. In W. T. O'Donohue, M. R. Byrd, N. A. Cummings, & D. A. Henderson (Eds.), *Behavioral integrative care: Treatments that work in the primary care setting* (pp. 53–72). New York: Brunner-Routledge.

Robinson, P., & Hayes, S. (1997). Psychological acceptance strategies for the primary care setting. In J. Cummings, N. Cummings, & J. Johnson (Eds.), *Behavioral health in primary care: A guide for clinical integration.* Madison, CT: Psychosocial Press.

Robinson, P., & Reiter, J. T. (2007). *Behavioral consultation in primary care: A guide to integrating services.* New York: Springer.

Robinson, P., Wischman, C., & Del Vento, A. (1996). *Treating depression in primary care: A manual for primary care and mental health providers.* Reno, NV: Context Press.

Salsberry, P. J., & Reagan, P. B. (2005). Dynamics of early childhood overweight. *Pediatrics, 116,* 1329–1338.

Strosahl, K. (1996a). Primary mental health care: A new paradigm for achieving health and behavioral health integration. *Behavioral Healthcare Tomorrow, 5,* 93–96.

Strosahl, K. (1996b). Confessions of a behavior therapist in primary care: The odyssey and the ecstasy. *Cognitive and Behavioral Practice, 3,* 1–28.

Strosahl, K. (1997). Building primary care behavioral health systems that work: A compass and a horizon. In N. A. Cummings, J. L. Cummings, & J. N. Johnson (Eds.), *Behavioral health in primary care: A guide for clinical integration* (pp. 37–68). Madison, CT: Psychosocial Press.

Strosahl, K. (1998). Integrating behavioral health and primary care services: The primary mental health model. In A. Blount (Ed.), *Integrated primary care: The tuture of medical and mental health collaboration* (pp. 139–166). New York: W. W. Norton.

Strosahl, K., & Robinson, P. (2007). The primary care behavioral health model: Applications to prevention, acute care and chronic condition management. In R. Kessler (Ed.), *Case studies in integrated care.* Manuscript in preparation.

Williams, J., Wake, M., Hesketh, K., Maher, E., & Waters, E. (2005). Health-related quality of life for overweight and obese children. *Journal of the American Medical Association, 293,* 70–76.

Wilson, G. T. (1994). Behavioral treatment of childhood obesity: Theoretical and practical implications. *Health Psychology, 13,* 373–383.

Yanovski, J. A., & Yanovski, S. Z. (2003). Treatment of pediatric and adolescent obesity. *Health Psychology, 13,* 373–383.

Chapter 12

The Role of the Behavioral Consultant in Promoting Acceptance in the Schools

Leslie J. Rogers, MA, University of Mississippi;
Amy R. Murrell, Ph.D., University of North Texas;
Catherine Adams, MA, University of Mississippi;
and Kelly G. Wilson, Ph.D., University of Mississippi

We are all whole, complete, and perfect regardless of the circumstances or presenting problem (Murrell, 2006). This is the major assumption that has guided our work in the schools and will organize the work in this chapter. All of our work in educational settings has been guided by a sincere appreciation of the individual and his or her own behavior, with an emphasis on appreciating the function of behavior and being mindful of the context in which people live and work. We care about humans living well and value creating a context in which human beings can live with meaning, integrity, and dignity regardless of the difficulties they face or present to others. We labor to create that context for ourselves, clients, teachers, principals, and parents, and for all the people affected by our work. Before we commence work in schools, we explicitly state this mission or some variant of it and adhere closely to these ideals in all of our interactions with others. In keeping with these values, this chapter is about making a difference for children and the people who support them, and about cultivating this environment and perspective in educational settings. In the following pages we aim to (1) facilitate a rich appreciation for the individual and the context, and (2) broaden awareness and increase clinical skills for implementing more effective acceptance- and mindfulness-based techniques when working with difficult-to-treat clients and when training teachers, school administrators, and parents.

Sensitivity to School Context

At the commencement of our work in schools, others warned us of the difficulties of our task. They told us of the appalling conditions we would witness and the frustrating people we would encounter. They spoke of how difficult it would be for us to remain psychologically present and attend to the client in such deplorable treatment conditions. We soon discovered they were right. It was difficult to remain psychologically present and keep our thoughts, evaluations, emotions, and judgments about these conditions at bay. In the schools where we consulted, there were constant reminders of poverty and deprivation. It was commonplace to see kids learning in classrooms with mold growing on the walls or to consult in classes that had insufficient supplies and were infested with insects and rats. For some children, lunch was the only meal of the day.

As consultants, it was easy to be consumed by the sadness of witnessing these deplorable conditions. In response to this sadness, we would want to look away or change an aspect of the environment without fully examining and appreciating all aspects of the context. Sometimes we did look away. Other times we were tempted to spend all of our free time trying to accumulate more resources for the children and their families. This seemed like a noble task for us as clinicians. In fact, there was an apparent need to address the impoverished conditions. However, it was not our primary duty and when engaging in these practices, we realized that we were not being genuinely mindful. Instead we were attending to and trying to alleviate our own unwanted thoughts and emotions rather than treating the client.

We also soon discovered that the approach of quickly gathering resources and trying to change the system failed to cultivate an appreciation of individuals and their situation. This response also led us to jump to erroneous conclusions about individuals and their environment because our data were incomplete. As a result, our behavior plans were ineffective, and this general approach was inconsistent with our chosen values as clinicians. With continued experience, we began asking ourselves clinically relevant questions that resulted in an appreciation and broader awareness of children and contexts, rather than questions grounded in a need for change. We found that asking the following questions and others like them of ourselves, teachers, administrators, and parents, was useful when entering into contexts or working with clients in scenarios such as the aforementioned:

- What other things or objects are in the room?
- What other parts of the child or the context are we missing?
- What does this child like doing in his free time?

- What is her favorite color?
- What are his dreams?
- What is it like to be in her skin on a good day? What about a bad day?

In asking these questions, we were trying to facilitate a thorough understanding and appreciation of the context as it was, not as what we thought it should have been.

To accomplish the goal of appreciation of individuals in school settings, we assumed that people had everything they needed to move in the direction they wanted to move in their lives. Prior to interacting with each child, teacher, or parent, we reminded ourselves that they were whole, complete, and perfect, and treated them accordingly. Our job as clinicians was to assist our clients in moving in the academic and personal directions that they wanted. We found that when we committed to and worked to create a context where all individuals were appreciated and treated as whole, complete, and perfect, amazing things occurred. Noncompliant children excelled in their studies. Teachers or principals who were previously resistant to assisting a child began actively participating in treatment planning. We witnessed a decrease in teacher write-ups for particular students after mindfulness strategies were introduced to teachers. Parents who were overly punitive or uninvolved with children and their academic success became more supportive. Children who had ceased communication about their concerns or values began vocalizing them. Conversely, we found that when individuals were treated as broken, inefficient, angry, judgmental, or insignificant, they typically went away either physically or psychologically, retaliated in some way, or behaved in accordance with our expectations.

The Whole, Complete, Perfect Stance

Creating a context in which individuals are both recognized and treated as whole, complete, and perfect greatly increases the odds that they will do something extraordinary. We found that when we bet on people, they defied the odds. To increase the probability of this happening in schools, we continuously had to put aside our judgments and evaluations of what we thought others needed or should be doing. We also repeatedly asked others to teach us what it was like to live in their world. In accordance with Brown and Ryan's (2003) definition of mindfulness, we continually strove to attune ourselves to the present experience, all the while being sensitive to specific aspects of that experience and not attempting to change it. Being ever mindful and attending to all aspects of an experience was quite challenging at times.

We found that training and operating out of this assumption in an ever-evolving school context was often difficult. Behavior plans fell by the wayside. Some teachers were overly critical and even afraid of the children they were trying to educate. Our child clients did not uphold their treatment contracts. Juggling all the varying demands of both teachers and clients can be frustrating, if not exhausting, for the consultant.

At times, we found ourselves wishing that overly harsh teachers would retire or that our child clients would have some level of spiritual or behavioral awakening that would leave them difficulty free. Instead we were left with the reality that being a clinician in a school system is difficult or nearly impossible. We have thought that if only teachers, parents, children, or school systems would cooperate and comply with our treatment plans, then our jobs would be stress free.

In 1948, B. F. Skinner foreshadowed our experience in the school system or any context when treating humans. In the quote below, he accurately delineates our struggle in the schools:

> To put it bluntly as possible—the idea of having my own way. "Control" expresses it, I think. The control of human behavior ... In my early experimental days it was a frenzied, selfish desire to dominate. I remember the rage I used to feel when predictions went awry. I could have shouted at the subjects of my experimenters, "Behave, damn you! Behave as you ought!" Eventually I realized that the subjects were always right. They always behaved as they should have behaved. It was I who was wrong. I had made a bad prediction. (Skinner, 1976, p. 271)

Here Skinner expresses a rich appreciation for the organism and the organism's behavior within the context in which he or she lives, learns, and teaches. Our interpretation of Skinner's quote is that all behavior of any organism is whole, complete, and perfect in any given context. Part of our job is to ensure that the student, teacher, and clinician are coming from this perspective. Behavior is functional in nature and is done in a context to meet the specific needs of the organism. In turn, this behavior may be frustrating and upsetting at times. It also may be ineffective at attaining desired outcomes.

When consulting, we try to keep in mind Skinner's quote, especially the words "Behave as you ought!" We recognize that it is tempting to try to change another person's behavior. Whether you are the clinician, consultant, or teacher, we can all relate to trying to force change in the behavior of another. Thoughts such as "If that teacher would just follow my behavior plan," "That teacher is wrong about this child," "The teacher or principal simply don't understand," "My poor client," "Please let my client follow his behavior plan," "This is too hard," "Please don't let my client get in trouble again," "That kid is uneducable," and "I quit!" are all genuine thoughts that we have experienced or that have occurred to us when providing educational and psychological services in school settings. At times, we worked to silence a teacher or to prove him or her wrong. Other times, we tried to change the teacher's psychological experience of our child clients. We tried to "educate" teachers with the hopes that if they saw psychopathology through the lens of a qualified mental health professional, they would never write up or expel another child again for trivial behaviors. Like Skinner, through our repeated trial learning with teachers, we found that we in fact were the ones making the bad predictions. Our behavior plans and consultations were aimed at trying to persuade the teachers and administrators to change their minds about the context in which they lived and worked. We tried to make them think differently about the child client, about us, about psychology. When teachers failed to change their minds about their experience, we tried harder to force our perspective on them; we "villianized" them, or we simply gave up. In an educational system ripe with injustices, distress, and shortages of resources, any and all of these options failed. Learning from our early mistakes, we recognized the need to treat teacher verbal reports of their experience as data to be incorporated into our behavior and treatment planning. We began to treat people as if they have everything they need to help us be useful; we began treating them as whole, complete, and perfect.

Treating people as whole, complete, and perfect was incredibly difficult, especially when they had horrendous histories or when they behaved in ways that made us think they were broken, deficient, or lacking. In response to these "broken" human behaviors, we noticed that we and others (e.g., teachers, parents, administrators, school counselors) oftentimes responded accordingly. We did things to avoid getting hurt. We defended ourselves. We attempted to alleviate the pain of others by trying to make their bad thoughts or memories go away. We sometimes quit listening. These mechanisms of escape ultimately served little good and caused us to miss important aspects of the environment that would have been useful for handling the situation.

Instead of focusing on our clients, we spent time trying to present ourselves as competent and worthy. According to the "just world" hypothesis, people (including clinical consultants) erroneously tend to hold the belief that good things happen to good people and bad things happen to bad people (Fiske & Taylor, 1991). Consistent with this hypothesis, much of our effort was spent trying to "be good." We falsely believed that only competent, worthy, and good people were respected and treated well by others. And when we felt insufficient or hurt by another, we spent much time trying to change the situation, thereby distancing ourselves from the offending person. We believed that by improving or changing ourselves, being treated poorly would not happen again.

This constant repairing and attending to our self-concept and presentation came at a cost. It interfered with our social interactions and our ability to do the job in schools. Constantly trying to project competency and worthiness took away from our ability to attend to the context and our interactions with others' suffering. Rather than effectively responding to the contingencies in the immediate context, we responded behaviorally to our negative thoughts of either our own or others' unworthiness, inadequacies, or scripts about how we, teachers, students, parents, or administrators should have been living or behaving.

We found that responding in this manner hindered the cultivation of whole, complete, and perfect. People responded to our attempts at projecting competency with their own competency behaviors. We noticed that when we as consultants showed a teacher how smart we were by utilizing fancy technical speech, the teacher was likely to respond in the same fashion. She would assert her authority or attempt to prove to us why she was doing her job correctly. This interaction was not only ineffective but also a deviation from the clinician's primary job in schools.

As consultants, we were there to assist the teacher, child, parent, or administrator. Our job was not to display our intelligence or to convince others of our aptitude. Our experience suggests that teachers and clients are less likely to retaliate, go away, or behave poorly if we as the "experts" are willing to put aside the need to protect ourselves. In taking an accepting and mindful posture to the individual, we have found it easier to build alliances and model desired clinical and educational behaviors in aversive situations. When we have modeled open and accepting postures in response to client behaviors, teacher distress, or administrator complaints, our treatment plans have been received more openly. To be of most benefit to teachers, clients, administrators, and parents in a context that elicited aversive cognitions and emotions, as clinicians we had to be willing to employ a great amount of acceptance of ourselves and others. Modeling this type of accepting posture has taught those in the schools we work with to be more accepting of children with severe difficulties as well.

Engagement in Safety Behaviors

Hayes (2004) suggests that acceptance is the active, nonjudgmental embracing of present-moment experience where the individual is willing to experience thoughts, feelings, and bodily sensations directly, without the use of safety behaviors that often emerge during suppression. In our efforts to suppress unwanted experiences, we often engaged in safety behavior and witnessed teachers, clients, administrators, and other clinicians doing the same—projecting smartness, staying busy, acting apathetic, trying to change people by fixing their issues, staying quiet, denying our own and others' abilities, treating us and others as if we were lacking something, and choosing less difficult tasks, to name a few. All of these behaviors served to insulate either us or the people we care about from experiencing painful thoughts, emotions, or aversive social interactions. Most often, we noticed they were tactics employed by the individual to avoid feeling broken or deficient. At times, in some contexts, engagement in these safety behaviors was adaptive and necessary to achieve goals. Take the following example, for instance:

> *Imagine that you are in an elementary school gymnasium helping a child improve his social skills. Across the gym, you notice a kindergarten teacher unknown to you walking across the gym with her class in tow. Twenty children are behind her, walking steadily in a single-file line, doing their best to keep it straight. At the rear of the line is a little boy who is intently concentrating on keeping up with the group until he spots a Christmas tree glowing with colored lights in the corner of the gym. Mouth agape, the little boy stops to gaze at the tree in pure wonder and excitement. You look at him in awe, thinking how it is that little ones can admire things with such innocent fascination. What a perfect moment … He is a nice reminder of why you work with children—until his teacher intervenes. She has noticed that he has fallen behind and hindered her progress. Stopping the line, she walks up to the little boy and begins to reprimand him. You can hear her*

yelling at the little boy from across the gym. She is rapidly firing questions and commands at him: "Why did you get out of line? Why? Answer me. You have kept us waiting! Why won't you answer me?" The little boy appears dumbstruck. He never answers. As the teacher is yelling at the child, she looks up at you.

You are seething with anger, and yet you say nothing. Instead you silently pray that your face is expressionless and neutral. You are engaged in safety behaviors, as you should be in this situation. As the consultant in a school context, you have learned from repeated interactions with teachers and school administrators that you cannot always say what you feel freely and uninhibitedly to others. Any outward expression of anger needs to be suppressed as you have a job to do here. You have a social skills contract with the client, not a working contract with the teacher. Here suppression and the engagement of safety behaviors are adaptive. You did not take away from your session with your client or have an altercation with the teacher. If you had voiced your anger, it would have made the situation worse and been frowned upon by the school administration.

It is when safety behaviors occur as "musts" that there can be difficulties. We call this the "have-to disease." People with alcoholism have to drink to avoid unwanted psychological or physiological pain. People with obsessive-compulsive disorder have to count, clean, or do similar behaviors to avoid unwanted thoughts or sensations. People who are therapists "have to" be experts; they have to be smart; they have to save their clients from pain; they have to make things better to avoid feeling the psychological pain of being unable to assist a client. All of these cases are characterized by high levels of behavioral inflexibility.

Imagine now that you are a therapist in a middle school. A teacher and a new child client walk into your office. Your new referral is a twelve-year-old African American girl. As she walks into the room with her teacher, you sense she is afraid to be there with you. Your thoughts are confirmed as she tries to leave, but the teacher holds her shoulders and reassures her that you are there to help her. When the two of you are left alone, the girl sits down in front of you and promptly stares at the floor. She is visibly trembling, and you see a tear fall. You don't move for fear you will startle her. Instead you begin to tell her who you are and why you are here. She says nothing and continues to tremble, and another tear falls. You can feel the pain that this little girl is in.

Then, without looking up, she says, "I feel really bad, really, really, really bad. My teacher says this will do me good, but nothing is going to make me feel better." She then tells you she was molested. She says that she has been sold to men by her mother in exchange for drugs ever since she can remember. Last month the Department of Human Services found out and finally took her and her sister away. Tears stream down her face as she tells you that she has not seen her sister since and that she misses her terribly. She does not understand why they won't let her talk to her sister. Her sister was all she had. She tells of being prodded by a man at the age of two with a hot curling iron and of being

> *beaten and raped by unknown men, sometimes with her mom in the room.*
>
> *While the young girl is telling her story, you experience thoughts such as "No child should experience this"; "How do I fix this?"; and "What do I do?" You don't want to hear any more details. This story is making you feel nauseated, and you can't make this child better if you feel awful. You start reassuring the child after each detail "all is going to be okay." The child then begins to cry more. She ceases speaking. You hesitantly ask what is wrong, since it is your job to do so. You are afraid of what she is going to say next. The girl starts to cry more and says, "But I am not okay. Everyone is telling me that I am. But I don't feel okay. You are just like everyone else. You don't understand me." You think, ouch.*

Here engagement in safety behaviors such as reassuring and not listening to aversive content kept you from doing the job and making the difference you wanted to make for your client. After session, your mind is racing, and you ask yourself, "If I don't hear her and if I don't know what it is like to be in her skin, then who will?" In your assessment, you realized that no one in this child's world wants to listen because what she is saying is so painful and difficult to hear. However, as the clinician, do you want to be one more person who fails to hear what it is like to be in your client's skin? If you don't hear her, not only does she feel even more isolated, but you will be missing important aspects of the context in which she lives. How accurate will your treatment or behavior plans be? What kind of difference can you make for her if you are stuck on your evaluation of her case and missing the content?

In the previous two scenarios, the use of safety behaviors served differing functions. In the first scenario, safety behaviors assisted the clinician in meeting the goals of the session and work in the schools. Avoiding an altercation allowed the clinician to continue working with the client and also limited potential damage to a future alliance with the teacher. In the latter scenario, the safety behaviors allowed the clinician to feel somewhat insulated from the client's report of aversive verbal content. Insulation from aversive verbal content is not always necessarily a bad or ineffective strategy. However, in this context the clinician compromised the commitment to the client, which was to hear her. To properly determine whether or not safety behaviors will facilitate goal attainment, clinicians must first determine if their behavior is consistent with the commitment or contract they have made for themselves and their clients. Second, the clinician must be willing to discard ineffective safety behaviors.

Discarding Safety Behaviors in Difficult Situations: Setting the Context

In our opinion, one of the first safety behaviors to discard is "acting big." This behavior includes the use of intellectual banter and usually stems from the need to hide out from feelings of incompetence or fear (what we refer to as "feeling small").

Using big words and sophisticated technological jargon oftentimes creates a context in which people respond similarly. When teachers are spoken to with technical psychological jargon, they typically respond by either asserting their own claims of intelligence ("getting big") or by nodding in agreement while staring blankly off into space ("playing small"). Instead of attending to what the clinician/consultant is saying, the teachers are responding behaviorally with their own safety behaviors. These safety behaviors often consist of not listening, playing small, or getting busy when the consultant makes them feel mad, upset, stupid, afraid, or uncertain. After these types of interactions, we have found that teachers are often unable to repeat the content of what has been said, including general content about a particular client and the specifics of a behavior plan we are trying to implement. This is of concern given that teachers provide services to our clients and are integral in implementing our treatment plans. In our work, we therefore model a different stance.

Creating a context in which teachers are willing to have open and honest conversations about their experience of both the consultant and the client is important for several reasons: First, clinicians take jobs to make a difference for people. In making teachers' lives difficult, we are going against our commitment to the profession. Second, clinicians are asking teachers to assist in treatment planning and behavior management, which are often difficult tasks. Communication needs to be open and honest. Teachers need to feel that they can candidly give critical feedback on behavior plans. Third, the extent to which the clinician or the situation around the clinician is negative will likely carry over into the classroom or into the teacher-student relationship. Thus, if the teacher is implementing your behavior plan and thinking about how much he or she dislikes you, it will likely impact the child being served.

Given that we have witnessed this negative impact several times, and that we now know that we are more effective in transmitting information when we reduce impression management strategies, technical jargon is not used in the present chapter. While it is tempting to sound overly intelligent and sophisticated in a book that will be read by many, doing so would deviate from the manner in which this technology has been trained to lay populations and other mental health professionals. In keeping with this convention, we will speak frankly of our frustrations, shortcomings, and successes. It is the first step in showing you, teachers, and parents that these experiences can coexist with one another instead of being mutually exclusive. Taking this stance is the first step in teaching those in schools how to communicate effectively and think about psychopathology as well as how to expect the extraordinary in the bleakest of situations.

Identifying and Reconnecting with Purpose

From a theoretical perspective, by modeling and explicitly stating our mission, we are attempting to shape your expectations of us and your behaviors when interacting with this material. We would like you to consider the context from which we are coming and to consider the possible functions of not only our own behavior but also the behavior of those being served in schools. First, prior to any contact with a school administrator, child, or teacher, it is necessary to become mindful about the purpose of consultation. Often before interacting with a teacher, we have experienced a variety of emotions or thoughts. Such emotions have ranged from anger over a child being suspended or punished one more time to sadness over a familial or social situation the child is currently experiencing. We have often had negative thoughts about teachers and child clients who are not successfully meeting the objectives of the behavior plan. When we have tried to suppress these thoughts and emotions, our ability to notice contingencies in the educational context was impaired.

Hence, when negative experiences come up, rather than trying to make ourselves feel better, we center ourselves. We remind ourselves of why we are working in the schools in the first place. Our negative emotions and aversive cognitions are treated by us as important data that indicate a value. Prior to entering a school, we ask ourselves questions that cover why we are entering that school, why we are serving a particular client, or even why we are working in the field. These questions serve as a reminder that we are in the schools for purposes other than engaging in safety behaviors or proving our competency. After all, most behavioral consultants would not answer the aforementioned questions with "to look good" or "to be right about everything." We treat the negative content of others in the same way, and we ask similar questions. Most clinicians and teachers alike would respond with "to assist others." After centering ourselves, we commence with the work. In our initial interactions with school staff, we delineate why we are in the schools. We also describe what it is like to work with us, both the good and bad aspects of this process. By laying our cards out on the table, we not only teach others how to interact with us but also take the first step in our teaching them to interact with difficult content and individuals (e.g., consultants, administrators, parents, students).

A Brief Return to Safety Behaviors of Teachers and Consultants

Behaving as if what you do matters increases the likelihood that teachers will be candid with the consultant regarding treatment planning. Oftentimes, as mentioned in our discussion of safety behaviors, teachers will agree to implement a behavior plan but then fail to follow through. As a result, the student fails to receive the prescribed services. Modeling this type of communicative behavior sets a context in which the teacher may honestly communicate with the consultant, which leads to more effective treatment planning. On the first day of meeting a new teacher, administrator, or parent, we may say something like the following:

> *Hi, I am Bess. I am a therapist who [describe role in the school district]. I was referred by the county office [or alternate referral source]. I heard that there is a child in your class who is having difficulties.*

We have found it useful to pause and wait for either a verbal or physical response such as a nod from the teacher. If the consultant does not wait for a response or does not receive an agreement from the teacher, there is not a working contract. A working contract is essential for success. If there is no contract, we have found that teachers will not effectively execute treatment plans or will work to undermine them. If the teacher assents and begins immediately to explain the difficulty, the clinician might gently stop her after she has expressed her concern or at a pause in her response. If the teacher is urgently pressing on in speech, we try to avoid responding with pressed speech. We have found that responding in this manner only perpetuates the use of pressed speech in both parties. Instead we suggest responding in a slow and respectful manner. The clinician might notice any unpleasant emotions or cognitions about the teacher or situation. If there is a pressing need to stop the teacher from speaking or a desire to change her mind, we suggest taking a deep breath and asking, "Is my response to the teacher designed to alleviate my own distress?" We then remind ourselves that we are here to collect data about the child. The teacher is giving us data about both the child and herself. She is another part of the child's context that is to be appreciated. If possible, it is wise to stay silent and keep this posture until the teacher slows down verbally. If the teacher does not slow down, we allow her to finish and then validate her concern. Also, if the teacher's report is abrasive or overly harsh of the child, we avoid trying to talk her out of her experience. Her reports are data for treating and assisting the child. If she is repeatedly reporting the same frustration, we might respond with something like, "I get that he is incredibly frustrating. I will do whatever I can to assist you." If the teacher responds with more complaints, we might repeat the concern until she feels that we have heard her. Afterward we might say something like the following:

> *Before I do anything, I just want to let you know in advance that I am here to help. Oftentimes in working with children, things get worse before they get better. However, I can assure you that I will work really, really hard for you. I will also work really, really hard for the child. That being said, sometimes I get ahead of myself in behavior or treatment planning. I may accidentally step on your toes. I do not mean to. At any time, if you do not like what I am doing or if you disagree, I urge you to tell me. This classroom is your domain, and I will respect that. If I am making a plan that does not fit with your class [or school] or that makes you mad, then please tell me because it increases the likelihood that I am creating something that will not work. I promise you I can take the hits. [The next sentence might be filled in with a vulnerability of yours or a common complaint that is given about you when you have worked with someone.] I sometimes have a tendency to not fully explain myself or speak four sentences ahead without filling in the blanks. So if you are having difficulty following me, it's probably me, not you. I will do whatever I need to do to make a difference here. Do you think we can work together? What can I do for you? What do you think I need to do for this child?*

Another common way people present themselves is to hold a differing opinion or to behave in a manner counter to their beliefs, at least until the expert leaves the room. Teachers sometimes do this. For teachers, experts come in the form of authority figures such as principals, school board members, and mental health consultants. In other words, experts are people who evaluate them or have some type of influence over their jobs. Teachers may hold negative expectations about the pending interaction, get mad about behavior or treatment plans, or disagree with the consultant but say nothing for fear of being negatively evaluated. After all, no one likes to be evaluated. Take a moment here to think about the last time you were evaluated by someone. Ask yourself these questions:

- Who was it?
- What were they evaluating you on?
- What was it like walking into the room to receive the feedback?
- What thoughts and/or concerns showed up while you were receiving the feedback?

As a clinician or mental health consultant, you may be asking yourself, "Why would teachers worry about what I think of them? They know I am not their boss." You are correct in that assumption. However, teachers frequently report to us that by the time they have referred a child for outside assistance, they feel as if they as teachers have failed and are now publicly admitting failure to the child, their fellow teachers, and administrators. Prior to referring the child, most teachers will have tried multiple interventions to assist the child in learning or to decrease problematic classroom behavior. They have given the child their best efforts and have made little or no progress. As a result of this "failure," a behavioral or psychological expert has come in to provide feedback and may potentially even take control of the classroom at the risk of making the teacher's job more difficult.

The Consultant's Role in Cultivating Safety

It is important to consider how the other person asking for help may perceive you. How many of us have had a social or work interaction in which we thought we did well, only to find out later that others had a different opinion? You thought someone wanted your help but later found out they were upset that you offered it in the first place. Or perhaps even worse, your efforts were unhelpful. Afterward you may have found yourself thinking, "How could I have missed that? How could I have not seen that my assistance was unhelpful, ineffective, or unwelcome?" As humans, we make attributional errors about our efforts and the perceptions of others' behaviors quite frequently. For example, when a teacher is making comments about a child being uneducable, crazy, psychotic, and stupid, we as clinicians may be tempted to make a dispositional inference about the teacher—for example, she is mean, evil, and unhelpful. Behaving inflexibly, we may respond to our judgments about the teacher by actually treating her as a mean, evil, and unhelpful person.

Social psychology provides many examples in which people misjudge another's behavioral intentions or character. As humans, we oftentimes overlook valuable aspects of the context or the social interaction. As clinicians, it is essential to be aware of the variables that influence what we see in the schools and how others see us. Once individuals have a certain expectation or opinion, they treat us accordingly. To make matters worse, once people have made up their mind about a person, situation, or phenomena, it is quite difficult to change it while they are engaged in their day-to-day behaviors and routines (Kenrick, Neuberg, & Cialdini, 2005). Rather than spending unnecessary time considering and deeply thinking about each task or person we interact with, we fill in the blanks about a person's character with information from our learning histories, social scripts, and expectations. These expectations of people, situations, and things direct our behavior daily. As a result, we miss valuable data about other people, places, or things, and we treat people accordingly.

It is important to recognize how our expectations and the expectations of others can influence our interactions. When people are treated in accordance with another person's negative or positive expectations of them, they are likely to respond in a manner confirming the expectation (Rosenthal, 2002). These expectancy effects have been demonstrated in more than four hundred studies across a variety of settings, both educational and noneducational, with adults, children, and animals (Gurland & Grolnick, 2003; Rosenthal, 2002). Studies in educational environments have demonstrated that teacher expectancies have an effect on the performance of children in classroom settings (e.g., Rosenthal, 2002; Madon et al., 2001; Weinstein, Marshall, Sharp, & Botkin, 1987; Raudenbush, 1984).

The context in which individuals hold positive or negative expectations is influenced by differing factors (Harris & Rosenthal, 1985). One variable raised within this study was that of educational climate. The meta-analysis revealed that students educated in more positive climates exhibited better outcomes. Task orientation and criticism were shown to contribute little, if any, to student outcomes (Harris & Rosenthal, 1985). Nonverbal behaviors such as smiles, closer physical proximity, longer interactions, interacting more often, frequent eye contact, verbal praise, and creating a less negative climate have all been found to be necessary for positive outcomes sufficient to override the detrimental impact of negative expectations on individuals and their social interactions (Harris & Rosenthal, 1985). In schools, when a teacher expects a child to be successful, he or she will smile more frequently, interact more closely, and praise the child's performance. This in turn positively impacts the student's performance. Given the impact that teacher expectancies have on student outcomes, it is necessary to cultivate the whole, complete, and perfect in them. The situation described below is an example of negative expectancies affecting the interaction:

> *You are working with a teacher, Mr. Johnson, who is experiencing difficulty interacting with a child, David. David has a history of being a defiant student whose primary presenting problem is aggression and work refusal. In class, David frequently makes antagonistic comments toward Mr. Johnson and his peers. Mr. Johnson has tried various interventions including multiple behavior plans and counseling. These interventions have not served to curb David's behavior or Mr. Johnson's frustration. Upon arrival, Mr. Johnson reports to you that David is uneducable and does not care about getting an education. Mr. Johnson tells you that he is doing his best to ignore David and that it is only a matter of time before he is expelled. Reducing behaviors decrease the frequency of interactions between himself and David. David's off-task behavior in class has increased, and his academic performance has decreased. Mr. Johnson is no longer assisting in the shaping of relevant academic success behaviors. After speaking with Mr. Johnson and observing David, you decide that the function of David's behavior is attention. You suggest to Mr. Johnson that the root of David's problem is nondispositional in nature and can be accommodated with natural environmental supports, a behavior plan that will provide attention in both academic and nonacademic tasks.*

Related to the aforementioned findings on expectancy, the quality of the working alliance between therapist and client has been shown to impact treatment outcomes (Martin, Garske, & Davis, 2000). Having a good working alliance with one's therapist has been found to be a consistent, albeit modest, predictor of outcome in psychotherapy (Horvath & Symonds, 1991; Martin, Garske, & Davis, 2000). In a mixed clinical sample, an early client alliance with a therapist was related to improved psychotherapy outcomes (Barber, Connolly, Crits-Christoph, Gladis, & Siqueland, 2000). Working alliances also impact teacher job satisfaction and the teacher's choice to continue working with children who suffer from emotional and behavioral disorders (George, George, Gersten, & Groesnick, 1995). Administrative support in educational settings has been found to attenuate both job attrition rates and occupational distress (Billingsley, 2004; George et al., 1995). George et al. (1995) also found that teachers who left their jobs perceived far less support from parents and community agencies. In a more recent study conducted by Ingersoll (2001) investigating the organizational characteristics and conditions of schools, results suggested that the general teacher attrition rate was influenced by their personal experience of the following variables: administrative support, student discipline problems, limited input into decision making, and, to a lesser extent, lower salaries. Given the robust impact that expectations, the working alliance, and administrative support have on varying populations and their performance, it is of critical importance that mental health practitioners are mindful of these variables when interacting with others in educational settings.

Hence, it is imperative to develop a total understanding of the context in which teachers, administrators, and children are operating. In keeping with our quest to be mindful of the context, the first set of questions we ask ourselves when consulting is this:

- What is it like to be this teacher, right now?
- If we felt the same way about a student, would we respond similarly?
- If we were frustrated, what would we do?
- Would we yell at the child?
- What would our behavioral response be?
- What is it like to be this administrator, right now?
- Would we be responding the same way in the same situation?
- What is it like to be this child, right now?
- Would we look at the teacher this way?
- What would we do if we thought a teacher was bossy?

We also ask the same questions in regard to any others with whom we come into contact in the schools.

Appreciating the Current Educational Context

Traditionally the sole purpose of schools has been to educate children. As children's primary educational providers, teachers are trained to teach a general education curriculum while making minor adjustments for developmentally disabled children who are in need of special education services. As a result of the No Child Left Behind Act of 2002 (NCLB) and the current trends in mental health prevalence, teachers are often asked to go beyond the scope of their training while working in overcrowded and understaffed schools and classrooms. This has led to numerous problems in the classrooms and has contributed to the stressors faced by both children and teachers.

The report of the Surgeon General's conference on children's mental health found that schools are the nation's primary mental health care provider for children (U.S. Public Health Service, 1999). Approximately 70 percent of children who receive mental health services receive them through the educational system (Burns et al., 1995). Given that one in five children, or 21 percent of youth in the United States (U.S. Public Health Service, 1999; Lahey et al., 1996), meets diagnostic criteria for a diagnosable mental or addictive disorder, there is a high demand placed on educators and school administration. A classroom of twenty-five children potentially has five children who meet criteria for some type of *DSM-IV* disorder. There are a number of psychiatric disorders that are very unfamiliar to teachers; although some disorders (e.g., attention-deficit/hyperactivity disorder, emotional disorders, and specific phobias) are fairly common in childhood, presentations may vary greatly between children. Thus teachers may have the daunting responsibility of tailoring their lessons and classroom management in a wide variety of ways for which they have received little or no training.

Until the NCLB Act, the provisioning of mental health services through the school system had minimal impact in the immediate classroom context and few implications for teachers. With its passing, NCLB provided for increased teacher and school accountability for the academic success of all children regardless of their disability. Teachers and administrators are now required to demonstrate that all children are learning at an academically sufficient level. Schools and teachers must also now provide sufficient and necessary academic supports at whatever cost. Supports offered by schools vary from those targeting behavioral difficulties to achievement-oriented psychological difficulties. Accommodations for these problematic areas range from extended time on a test for a child diagnosed with attention-deficit/hyperactivity disorder (ADHD), to the use of one-on-one assistance in curbing behavioral and emotional outbursts.

The classroom has also been impacted by NCLB. Many classrooms have now shifted to an inclusion-based model, in which children in special education are educated alongside those enrolled in regular education. Additionally, children enrolled in special education now take the same examinations and are typically given the same amount of work relative to their peers in regular education. Determining who needs these services now largely depends upon the teachers and school's ability to recognize and identify what a child needs psychologically or behaviorally to succeed in the classroom. Although teachers are experts in educating children, they oftentimes have little to no training in or knowledge of psychological disabilities. Thus schools and teachers are often at a loss when it comes to devising adequate behavior or treatment plans to ensure academic success.

In the schools, we have found that teachers are often reluctant to treat the child similarly to non-special-education peers. Instead they may engage in behaviors that are too lenient, believing the child with the disability is deficient or lacking and does not belong in the regular education classrooms. At times, we have wished teachers would treat these children more humanely and have thought, "If they only could see what I see, all would be well." Yet, from our perspective, it makes sense why the teacher would be afraid of the child or diagnosis.

> *Think about the first client you ever had. What was it like walking in to see him or her? What were your thoughts or concerns? What did it feel like sitting in the room? Were you worried? Imagine that tomorrow a client with borderline personality disorder walks into your office, and you are assigned to teach her math for an hour, then test and correct her. How would you feel? What if you had to do this one hour every day for five days? What are your present thoughts and feelings? What if you had to teach her four to six topics (e.g., English, math, spelling) for six hours a day, five days a week? What about six hours a day, five days a week, nine months of the year? How do you feel about the situation now? We would now like to remind you that this client must also be at or above grade level at the end of the nine months and, because of*

NCLB, she cannot fail the six classes you are assigned to teach her. If she does fail, your boss and her parents will have to speak with you. What thoughts show up now? Any concerns?

Now we would like you to imagine that you are a teacher. What is it like to be in his or her skin? What are the demands in the present context? How would you respond to these demands? Typically we imagine ourselves standing in front of the classroom that is frustrating the teacher. We ask ourselves what shows up when looking at the class, watching them behave as they do. Do we as clinicians become frustrated or feel similarly to the teacher? If so, we draw up a plan or a set of recommendations that would alleviate these concerns. If we have difficulty relating to the teacher, we may ask him what would best alleviate his distress. We may ask the teacher questions such as "How do you do stay on track when you get angry, frustrated, or agitated with your class?" and "What keeps you coming back day after day?" In response to these questions, we draw up a plan that is based on the teacher's self-report and that puts him in contact with the reinforcement for coming to class daily. For instance, if the teacher responds, "I wanted to make a difference," we may ask the teacher to look around his class and point out instances in which he made a difference when things were not possible for a specific child. If the teacher cannot think of an instance in which he has made a difference for a child, we typically ask questions such as "How can we make a difference in this class? What would we need to do this?"

Imagine that you are a fourth-grade teacher in a regular education class. You have twenty-five children in your class. You get your roster on the first day of class. Of your twenty-five students, four need accommodations because of differing psychological and learning disabilities. Of these four children, three of the diagnoses you know nothing about. By the end of the school year, these children have to be at or above grade level. The following thoughts run through your mind: "I hope she is on medication" and "How am I going to juggle all of these children for the next year?" You stand there and look out at the faces in your classroom and wonder, "Which ones are they? How will I help them?"

For the teacher, meeting the demands of all students, special education and non–special education, may seem like an overwhelming task. Some teachers worry about the lack of environmental supports, experience doubts about their behavioral repertoire, and feel overwhelmed. However, we have also worked with teachers who wished they had more students with disabilities because they reportedly "love going above and beyond the call of duty" to make a difference. This example highlights the need to ask teachers about their experience in a particular context (e.g., classroom). As consultants, we similarly do this with the children, administrators, and parents that we serve. It is essential to inquire, as individuals respond differently to different contexts.

Now we would like you to imagine the aforementioned teacher standing in front of her class still looking at the roster. On the same day, a consultant walks in and gives her a behavior plan for the child with ADHD that addresses his difficulties with engaging in attention-seeking behaviors with both peers and other adults. The behavioral consultant thinks the plan is quite simple as it has worked for most kids with ADHD. He briefly explains it to the teacher, then leaves. How do you think the teacher feels? We will consider this next.

Working Effectively with Teachers

To assist the teacher in this scenario, the consultant might work with the child while providing support to the teacher. We have found that in meeting the needs of the teachers, whether directly or indirectly related to the child, the behavior plans often write themselves. When time is invested in teaching the teachers acceptance and mindfulness of undesirable behavior, experiences, or thoughts, they often end up writing the plans for us. Teachers mimic our responses to child psychopathology. As a benefit, teachers end up thinking similarly to us about psychological and behavioral difficulties. They will more likely cease doing classroom behaviors that either contribute to or increase the acting-out behaviors of child clients. They will learn how to assess the environment for natural supports and how to conduct adequate functional analyses, of both their own behavior and their students' behavior. We have found that providing services in this manner leads to long-term behavior change in the teacher and is also the most effective way to provide psychological services to children in schools. When working with a teacher, we spend ample time determining the function of his or her behavior and also do a reinforcement assessment of the teacher. Questions that are particularly effective to ask ourselves are these:

- What is the teacher's primary method of disciplining students?
- Why use this particular method?
- What types of interventions can we do that will best fit the teacher's disciplinary style?

We do still see children individually. However, we would first work with teachers and other school staff to increase the likelihood that a child would be present for service delivery. Disciplinary practices often interfered with our plans. If a teacher is writing up a child or punishing him or her frequently, the child is significantly less likely to be in school because it is an aversive place. In one particular school, attending class was so aversive that many students cut class. As a result of the large amount of truant students, the school had a "no calling for a student over the intercom" policy. If an administrator or teacher was looking for a student, the office would refuse to page the student as it would disrupt classes significantly. Expulsion and corporal punishment have also interfered with treating our child clients. On days on which they have been paddled, our child clients do not wish to speak with us, as we are one more adult in their life asking, "What happened?" Understanding the functions of aversive teacher or administrator behavior is essential if the behavior or treatment plan is going to work for the child in school.

Imagine that you are consulting at a middle school in a small rural southern town. You are called in by a teacher, Ms. Smith, who reports that she has a twelve-year-old Caucasian boy, Noah, who she swears is going to be a serial killer someday. According to Ms. Smith, Noah wears all black, listens to "angry" music, and does not comply with teacher requests. As evidence of her unpleasant experiences with Noah, Ms. Smith further reports that he has been written up eight times in the past month alone. As the teacher is talking about Noah, you can tell she is visibly angry with him and with his family. She is highly upset about Noah's poor classroom behaviors and performance. The teacher, for the next fifteen minutes, then proceeds to give you specific examples of Noah's incorrigible behavior. After visiting with the teacher, you review Noah's records. The record review reveals that six of the eight write-ups have been from Ms. Smith for dress code infractions. The dress code infractions have ranged from shoelaces being untied to Noah's shirt not being properly tucked in. On three of the seven write-ups, you notice that Noah has been corporally punished (i.e., paddled) for these dress code violations. After reviewing the records, you interview Noah's other teachers. In interviewing Noah's other teachers, you learn that they all view him as a bright, likable, exceptional student who does well in all his classes except for Ms. Smith's class. Noah's teachers report that Ms. Smith is too hard on him and just simply "does not like him and looks for reasons to write him up." After the records review and teacher interviews, you go speak with Ms. Smith again. You gently tell her that the other teachers are not having difficulty with Noah and that the write-ups mainly suggest he has difficulty with attire, not necessarily behavior. You ask her what you can do to help her, and she curtly responds, "Nothing," and walks away.

In situations such as this, we have been tempted to respond to the immediate content of what Ms. Smith is saying, attempting to do one or any combination of the following: (1) convince Ms. Smith that she needs our help; (2) respond tersely and curtly back to her, perhaps even adding a backhanded comment to let Ms. Smith know we think she is being unreasonable in her treatment of Noah; (3) walk away and work closely with Noah on exhibiting perfect behavior in the presence of Ms. Smith; or (4) leave and then complain to the administration. As an alternative, we might analyze the context that Ms. Smith works in and determine the functions of her behavior. We consider the possible functions of escape, attention seeking, or obtaining sensory stimulation or tangibles. We attempt to reduce her write-up behavior by devising a behavior or treatment plan that would address these functions.

Our experience tells us that, by addressing these functions, Ms. Smith's complaints will likely lessen more than if we immediately entered the class and devised a behavior plan for Noah. Later we may devise a behavior plan for Noah if there is a need.

However, when first entering a classroom, we always ask what the teacher needs or what is most frustrating and why. It is apparent that Ms. Smith will write Noah up regardless of what he does. As evidenced by both verbal and written reports, Ms. Smith is more upset that he is "dressed inappropriately and looks different than the other kids," which may be threatening to her. In response to feeling threatened, Ms. Smith's write-up behavior functions to help her escape from unwanted stimuli (discomfort surrounding Noah's clothing). Thus, as consultants, we might spend time with Ms. Smith, noting antecedents (e.g., judgments, feelings of discomfort) to escape behavior (e.g., writing students up or sending them away). We tentatively hypothesize that Ms. Smith probably has a history with respect to the escape-maintained behavior of writing students up for behaviors both large and small. We review her write-up record and ask her what types of behaviors or students bother her the most. In addition, we ask what she finds reinforcing in a student and about her job.

In other words, our job is to find out what Ms. Smith is working for and then devise a plan that is reinforcing for her as well. At the same time, we also work on getting her to interact with Noah differently to reduce Ms. Smith's problematic escape behavior (e.g., sending him to the office). We do this by teaching Ms. Smith to be mindful of contextual variables and their influence on a child's behavior as well as hypothesizing about the function of Noah's behavior with Ms. Smith present. In this particular case, the only aspect of the context Ms. Smith is paying attention to when Noah enters the room is his attire. Here we would ask Ms. Smith other questions, both related and unrelated to Noah's attire, to commence developing an appreciation for Noah in a broader context. Questions might include "What do you think his favorite color is?" and "Do you think he ever gets picked on for wearing that type of clothing?"

Working with Ms. Smith in this manner has several benefits. First, it addresses her concerns directly. You do not have to wait and hope the student follows through with his behavior plan. Second, through the process of conducting a functional analysis with Ms. Smith, we are both modeling and teaching her the desired behaviors that we would like her to exhibit when looking at other students. Ultimately we want our teachers and those we work with in schools to be able to appreciate the child as whole, complete, and perfect in that all behaviors are functional.

Conclusion

Appreciating individuals and their behavior in any given context with an open and accepting posture is an oftentimes difficult position to take and train as a clinician. However, this position is not impossible. By being mindful of one's own behavior and the context in which behaviors are operating, a clinician may develop more accurate treatment and behavioral plans and model how to approach and treat psychological difficulties. We have found that when this posture has been taken, teachers, parents, and administrators are significantly more likely to appreciate psychological dysfunction and to respond in a manner that better assists the child. Teaching this appreciation is important given that it is widely contended in school settings that undesirable behavior or undesirable students are not whole, complete, and perfect, but should be changed or dismissed. As clinicians, when we engage in symptomatic behavior or symptom removal strategies, we are actually perpetuating broken behaviors and deficient outlooks. Students, teachers, clinicians, clients, parents, and administrators realize when they are being treated in this manner, whether it is verbally acknowledged or not. Our behavior, whether explicit or implicit, conveys our true intentions. In schools, children are expelled, suspended, ineffectively punished, and ignored every day. Teachers are lectured, ignored, or brushed off. As a result, they may respond accordingly to people who treat them this way.

We are asking readers to attend to the functions of child, teacher, parent, and administrator behavior when working in schools. In keeping with Skinner and the assumptions underlying our clinical stance, all behavior in schools, whether it be aversive or appetitive, is as it should be. Teaching teachers, administrators, clinicians, and parents to appreciate and treat behavior and psychological difficulties from this perspective is essential if acceptance and mindfulness techniques are to be employed.

References

Barber, J. P., Connolly, M. B., Crits-Christoph, P., Gladis, L., & Siqueland, L. (2000). Alliance predicts patient's outcome beyond in-treatment change in symptoms. *Journal of Consulting and Clinical Psychology, 68*, 1027–1032.

Billingsley, B. (2004). Special education teacher retention and attrition: A critical analysis of the research literature. *Journal of Special Education, 38*, 39–55.

Brown, K., & Ryan, R. (2003). The benefits of being present: Mindfulness and its role in psychological well-being. *Journal of Personality and Social Psychology, 84*, 822–848.

Burns, B. J., Costello, E. J., Angold, A., Tweed, D., Stangl, D., Farmer, E. M., et al. (1995). Children's mental health service use across service sectors. *Health Affairs, 14*, 147–160.

Fiske, S. T., & Taylor, S. E. (1991). *Social cognition* (2nd ed.). New York: McGraw-Hill.

George, N. L., George, M. R., Gersten, R., & Groesnick, J. K. (1995). An exploratory study of teachers with students with emotional and behavioral disorders. *Remedial and Special Education, 16*, 227–236.

Gurland, S. T., & Grolnick, W. S. (2003). Children's expectances and perceptions of adults: Effects on rapport. *Child Development, 74*, 1212–1224.

Harris, M. J., & Rosenthal, R. (1985). Mediation of interpersonal expectancy effects: 31 meta-analyses. *Psychological Bulletin, 97*,, 363–386.

Hayes, S. C. (2004). Acceptance and commitment therapy and the new behavior therapies: Mindfulness, acceptance, and relationship. In S. C. Hayes, V. M. Follette, & M. M. Linehan, (Eds.), *Mindfulness and acceptance: Expanding the cognitive-behavioral tradition* (pp. 1–29). New York: Guilford.

Horvath, A. O., & Symonds, B. D. (1991). Relation between working alliance and outcome in psychotherapy: A meta-analysis. *Journal of Counseling Psychology, 38,* 139–149.

Ingersoll, R. M. (2001). Teacher turnover and teacher shortages: An organizational analysis. *American Educational Research Journal, 38,* 499–534.

Kenrick, D. T., Neuberg, S. L., & Cialdini, R. B. (2005). *Social psychology: Unraveling the mystery* (3rd ed.). Boston: Pearson Education Group.

Lahey B. B., Flagg, E. W., Bird, H. R., Schwab-Stone, M. E., Canino, G., Dulcan, M. K., et al. (1996). The NIMH methods for the epidemiology of child and adolescent mental disorders (MECA) study: Background and methodology. *Journal of the American Academy of Child and Adolescent Psychiatry, 35,* 855–864.

Madon, S., Smith, A., Jussim, L., Russell, D. W., Eccles, J., Palumbo, P., et al. (2001). Am I as you see me or do you see me as I am? Self-fulfilling prophecies and self-verification. *Personality and Social Psychology Bulletin, 27,* 1214.

Martin, D. J., Garske, J. P., & Davis, M. K. (2000). Relation of the therapeutic alliance with outcome and other variables: A meta-analytic review. *Journal of Consulting and Clinical Psychology,* 68, 438–450.

Murrell, A. R. (2006, July). *It is what it is: Appreciating whole, complete, and perfect in ourselves, our clients, our work, and each other.* Address presented at the Second World Conference on Acceptance and Commitment Therapy, Relational Frame Theory, and Contextual Behavioral Science, London, England.

Raudenbush, S. W. (1984). Magnitude of teacher expectancy effects on pupil IQ as a function of the credibility of expectancy induction: A synthesis of findings from 18 experiments. *Journal of Educational Psychology, 76,* 85–97.

Rosenthal, R. (2002). Covert communications in classrooms, clinics, courtrooms, and cubicles. *American Psychologist, 57,* 839–849.

Skinner, B. F. (1976). *Walden two.* New York: MacMillian.

U.S. Public Health Service. (1999). *Report of the surgeon general's conference on children's mental health: A national section agenda.* Washington, DC: U.S. Department of Health and Human Services. Retrieved February 13, 2007, from www.surgeongeneral.gov/library/mentalhealth/toc.html.

Weinstein, R. S., Marshall, H. H., Sharp, L., & Botkin, M. (1987). Pygmalion and the student: Age and classroom differences in children's awareness of teacher expectations. *Child Development, 58,* 1079–1093.

Laurie A. Greco, Ph.D., is assistant professor of psychology at the University of Missouri, St. Louis. She is a clinical psychologist and psychotherapist with more than ten years of clinical experience with children, adolescents, and families. Greco has published more than twenty articles and book chapters and has given more than eighty conference presentations. In the past five years, she has conducted some forty workshops and professional trainings at the national and international level on topics germane to acceptance and commitment therapy and behavioral parent training. She lives in St. Louis, MO.

Steven C. Hayes, Ph.D., is University of Nevada Foundation Professor of Psychology at the University of Nevada, Reno, and the founder of acceptance and commitment therapy (ACT). He has authored thirty-two books, including *Get Out of Your Mind and into Your Life*, and more than four hundred scientific articles. Hayes has focused his career on understanding language and cognition functionally and applying this perspective to prevention and intervention. He lives in Reno, NV.

Index

A

C

D

E

F

G

H

I

J

K

L

M

N

O

P

Q

R

S

T

V

W

Y